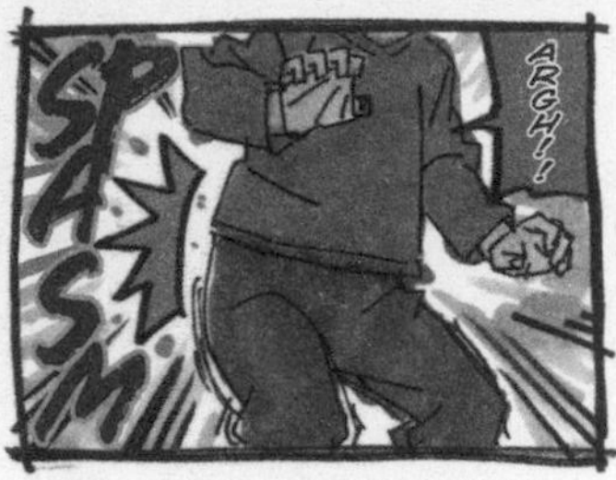
SPASM
ARGH!!

It was fixed for the graphic novel, but when Number 334 ("The Black Metamorphoses...!!") was printed in *Jump* it was still in penciled format. I had herniated a disk for the first time in my life and just couldn't sit at my desk... Please forgive me for the hard-on-the-eyes manuscript.

岸本斉史

—Masashi Kishimoto, 2007

Author/artist Masashi Kishimoto was born in 1974 in rural Okayama Prefecture, Japan. After spending time in art college, he won the Hop Step Award for new manga artists with his manga **Karakuri** (Mechanism). Kishimoto decided to base his next story on traditional Japanese culture. His first version of **Naruto**, drawn in 1997, was a one-shot story about fox spirits; his final version, which debuted in **Weekly Shonen Jump** in 1999, quickly became the most popular ninja manga in Japan.

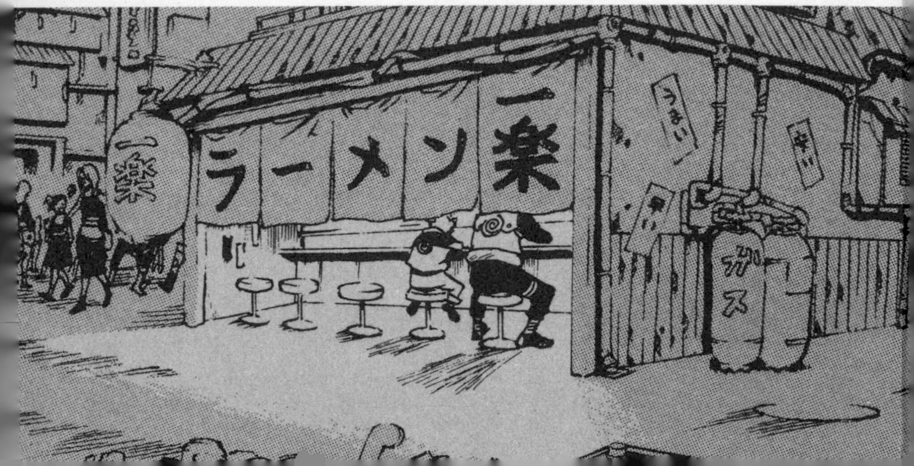
一楽
ラーメン一楽

NARUTO VOL. 37
SHONEN JUMP Manga Edition

STORY AND ART BY MASASHI KISHIMOTO

Translation/Mari Morimoto
English Adaptation/Deric A. Hughes, Benjamin Raab
Touch-up Art & Lettering/Inori Fukuda Trant
Design/Sean Lee
Editor/Joel Enos

Printed in the U.S.A.

Published by VIZ Media, LLC
P.O. Box 77010
San Francisco, CA 94107

10 9 8 7 6 5 4 3
First printing, February 2009
Third printing, December 2015

www.viz.com

THE WORLD'S
MOST POPULAR MANGA

www.shonenjump.com

SHONEN JUMP MANGA EDITION

NARUTO

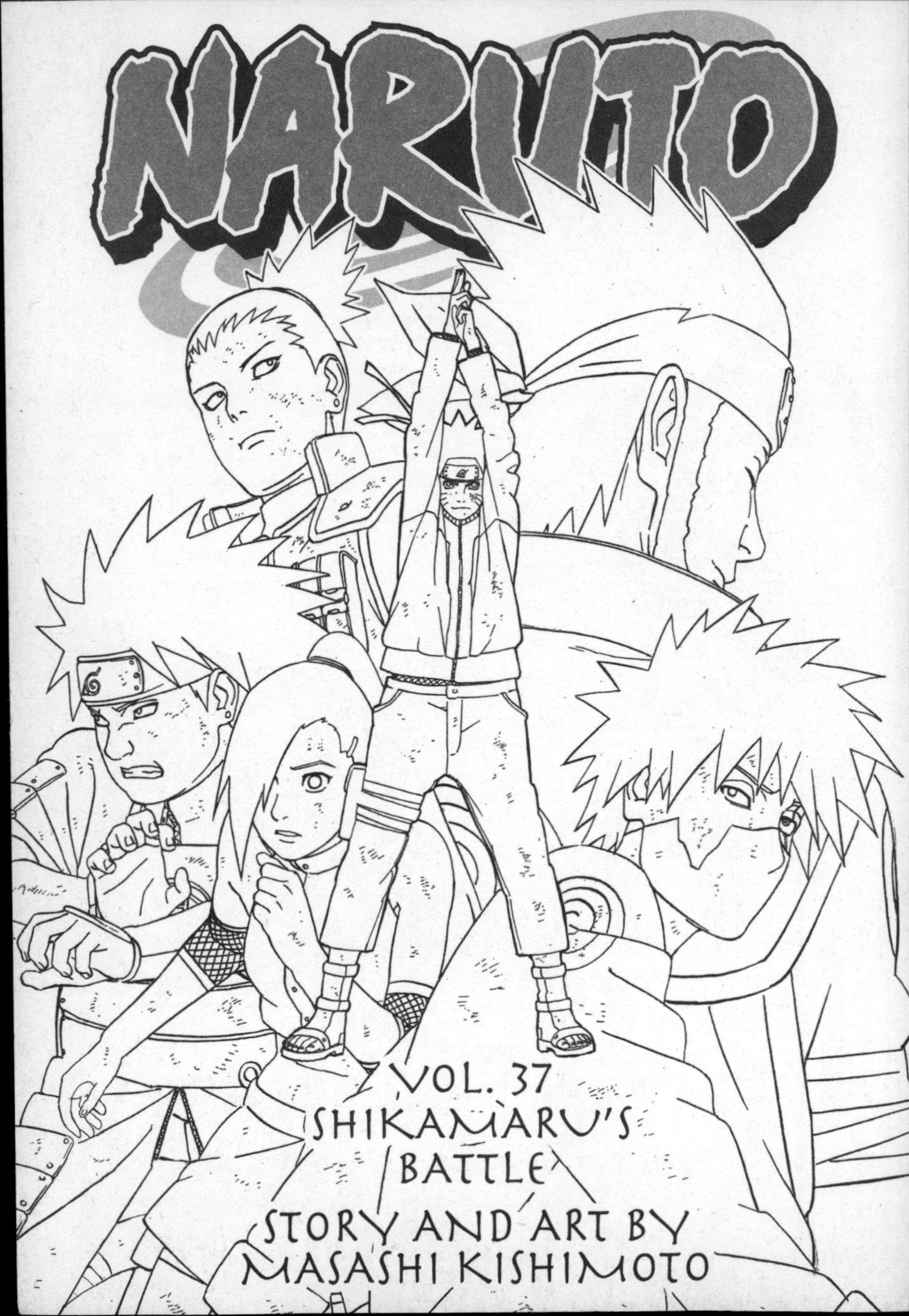

VOL. 37

SHIKAMARU'S BATTLE

STORY AND ART BY

MASASHI KISHIMOTO

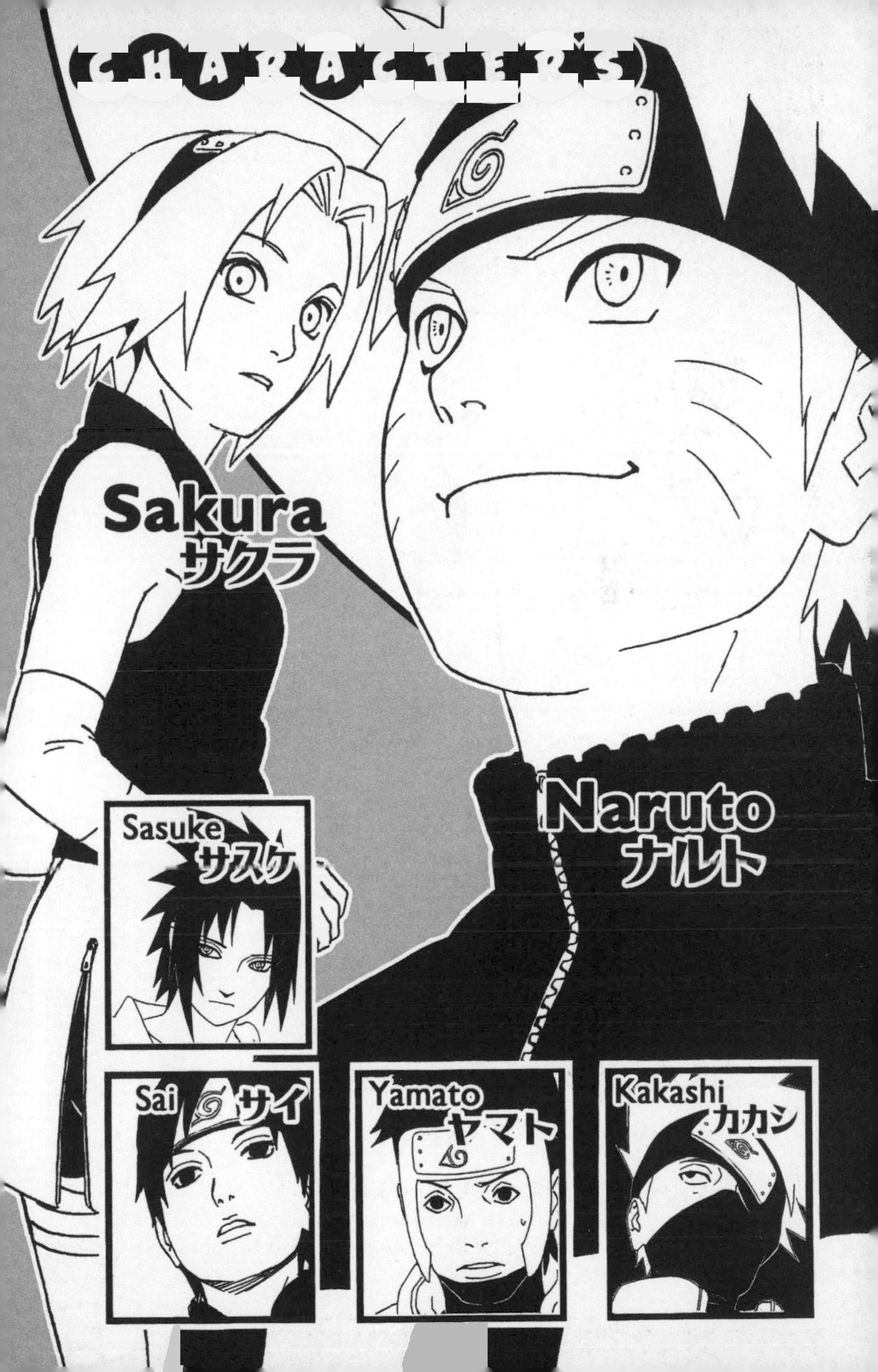
CHARACTERS
Naruto
ナルト
Sakura
サクラ
Sasuke
サスケ
Kakashi
カカシ
Yamato
ヤマト
Sai
サイ

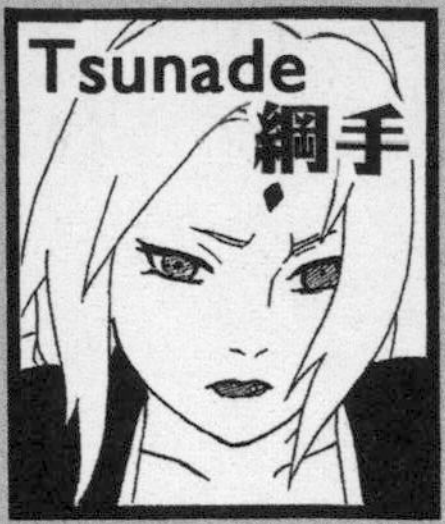
Tsunade
綱手

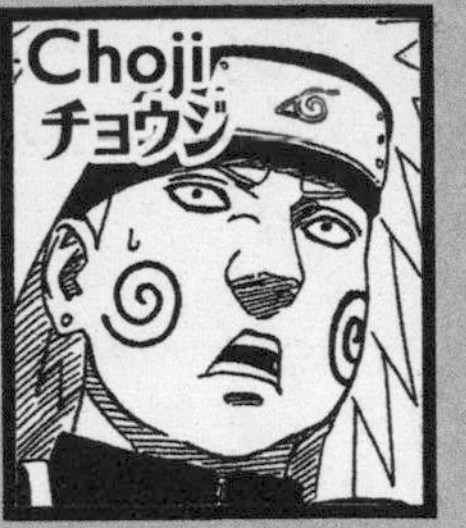
Choji
チョウジ

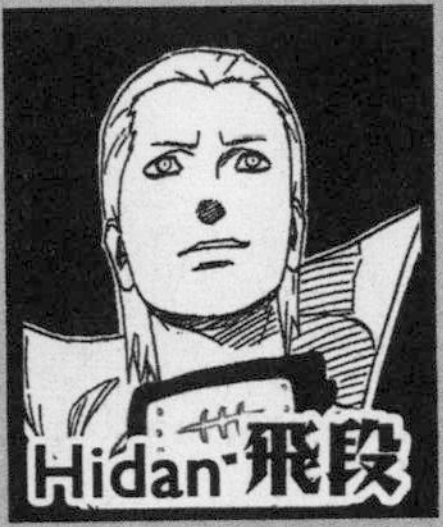
Hidan 飛段

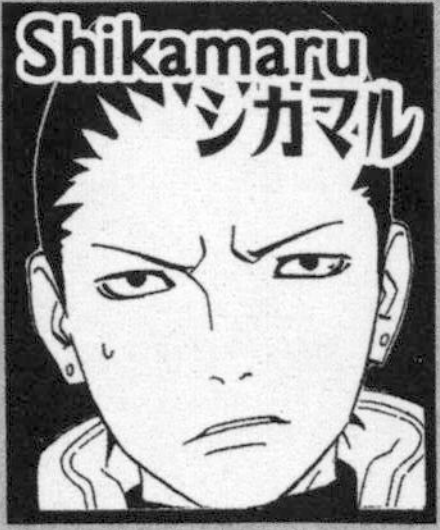
Shikamaru
シカマル

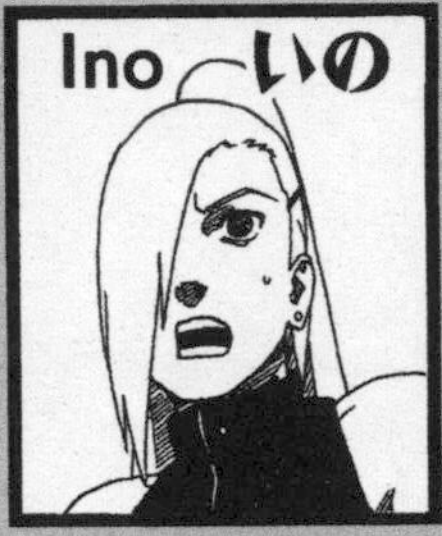
Ino いの

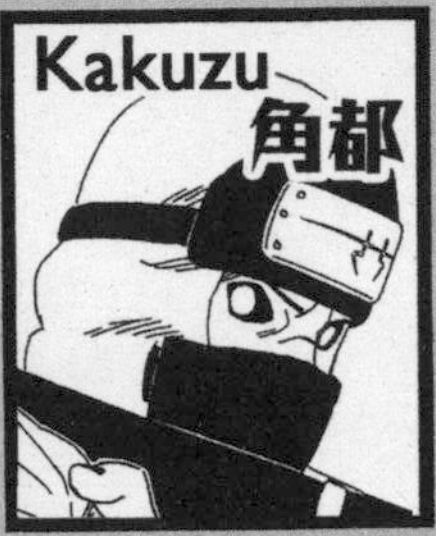
Kakuzu
角都

The Story So Far…

Against all odds, Uzumaki Naruto, the student least likely to graduate from the Ninja Academy in Konohagakure, becomes a ninja along with his classmates—and closest friends—Sasuke and Sakura. During the Chûnin Selection Exams, however, the turncoat ninja Orochimaru launches *Operation Destroy Konoha*, forcing Naruto's mentor, the Third Hokage, to sacrifice his own life to stop the attack and save the village.

Further tragedy follows when Sasuke—now one of Konoha's best and brightest shinobi—falls prey to Orochimaru's schemes and becomes his hapless thrall. Though Naruto fights valiantly to stop Sasuke from becoming slave to one of their worst enemies, he ultimately fails. Sasuke flees to Orochimaru, and Naruto vows to rescue his friend someday…

Two years pass. Naruto and his comrades grow up and track down Sasuke. However, they are left in the dust again by Sasuke's immense power and he gets away once more.

In order to gain strength himself, Naruto trains with Kakashi again. Elsewhere, Asuma dies during a battle against an Akatsuki two-man team. What will the surviving Cell Number 10 do now?!

CONTENTS

NUMBER 330: THE HEARTBREAKING NOTICE…!!   7

NUMBER 331: CELL NUMBER 10 SETS OUT…!!   25

NUMBER 332: SHIKAMARU'S BATTLE!!   42

NUMBER 333: AFFINITIES…!!   63

NUMBER 334: THE BLACK METAMORPHOSES…!!   81

NUMBER 335: THE FEARSOME SECRET!!   99

NUMBER 336: TURNABOUT DILEMMA…!!   117

NUMBER 337: SHIKAMARU'S GENIUS!!   134

NUMBER 338: PAYBACK…   155

NUMBER 339: THE NEW JUTSU…!!   173

Number 330: The Heartbreaking Notice...!!

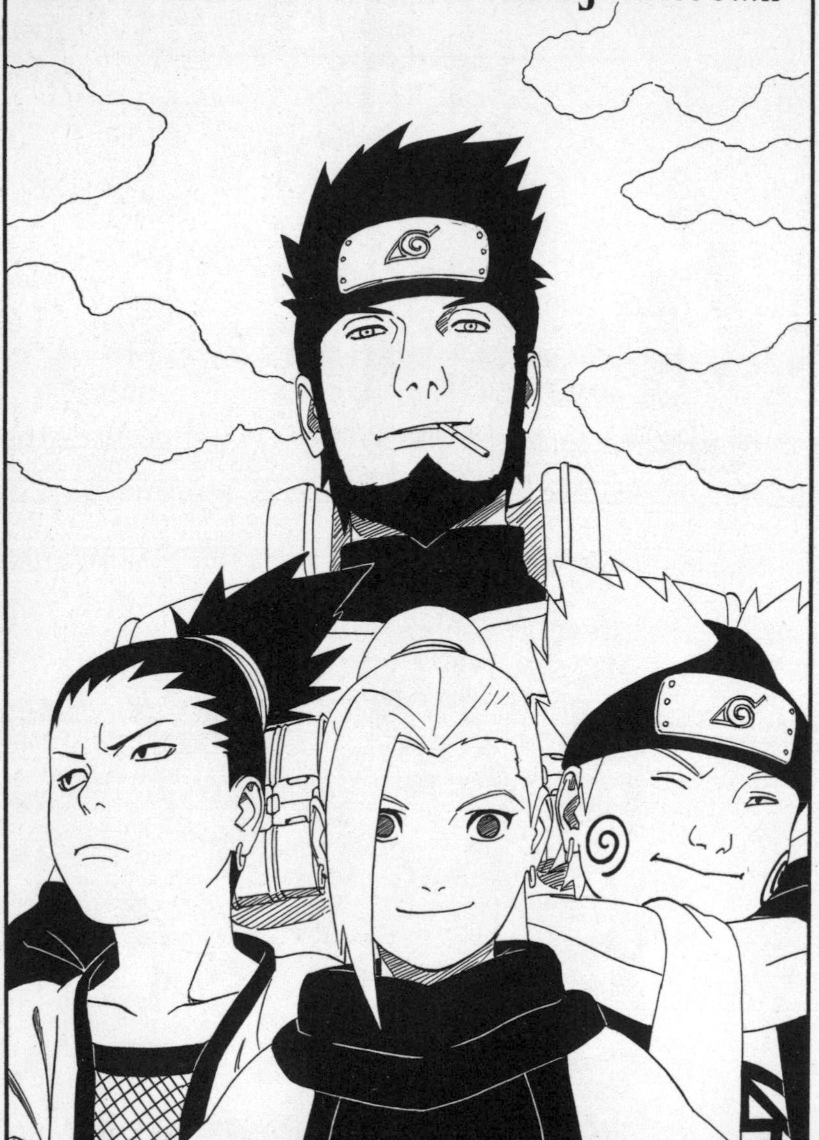

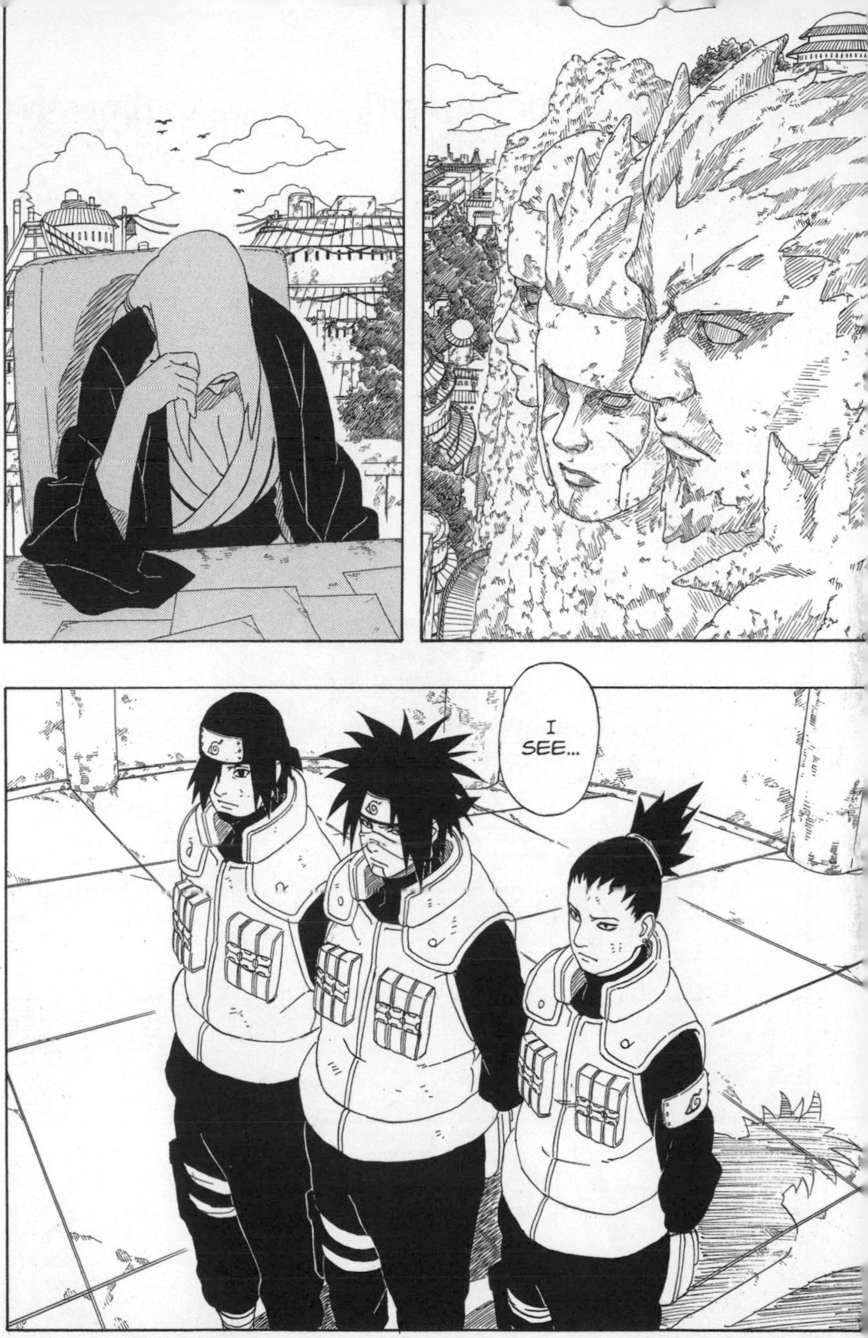
I SEE...

READ THIS WAY

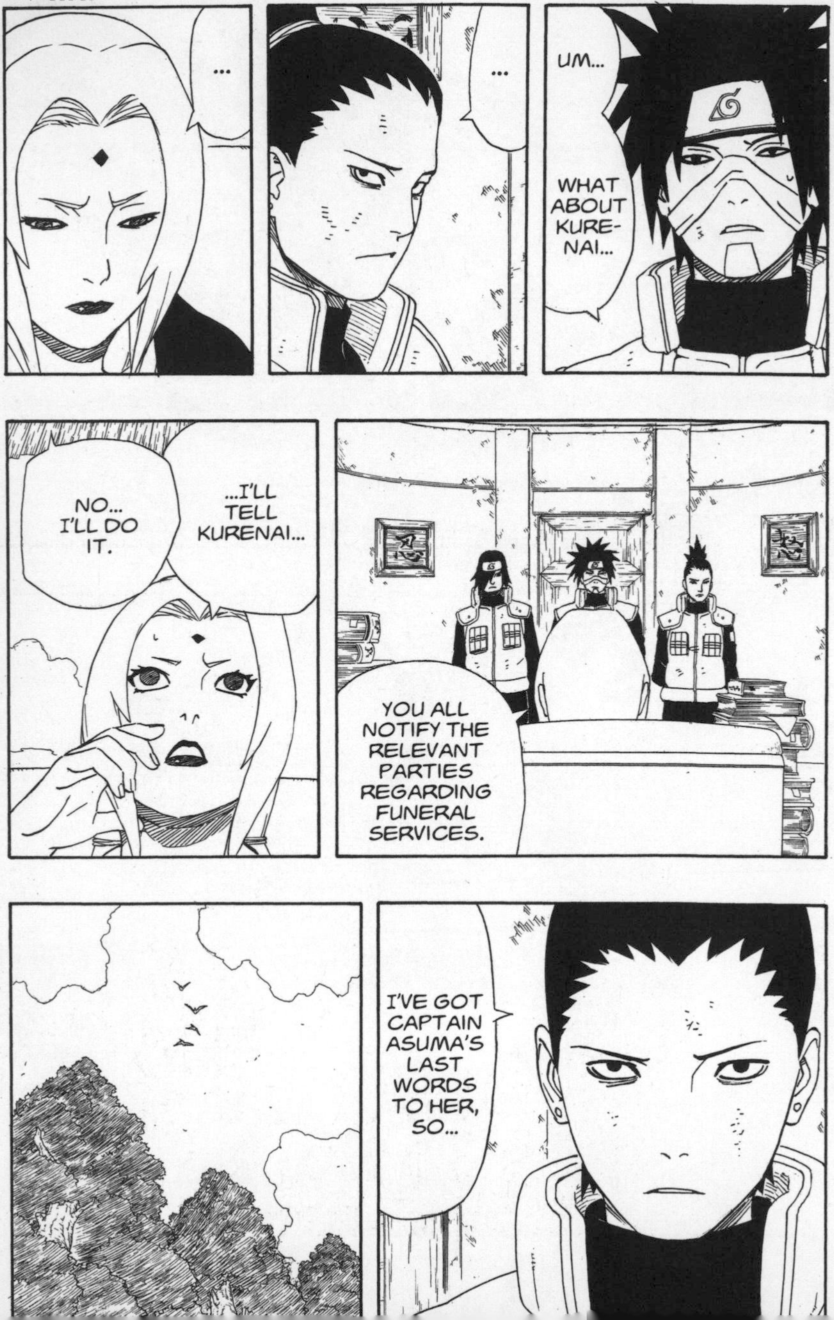
UM...
WHAT ABOUT KURE-NAI...
...
...
YOU ALL NOTIFY THE RELEVANT PARTIES REGARDING FUNERAL SERVICES.
...I'LL TELL KURENAI...
NO... I'LL DO IT.
I'VE GOT CAPTAIN ASUMA'S LAST WORDS TO HER, SO...

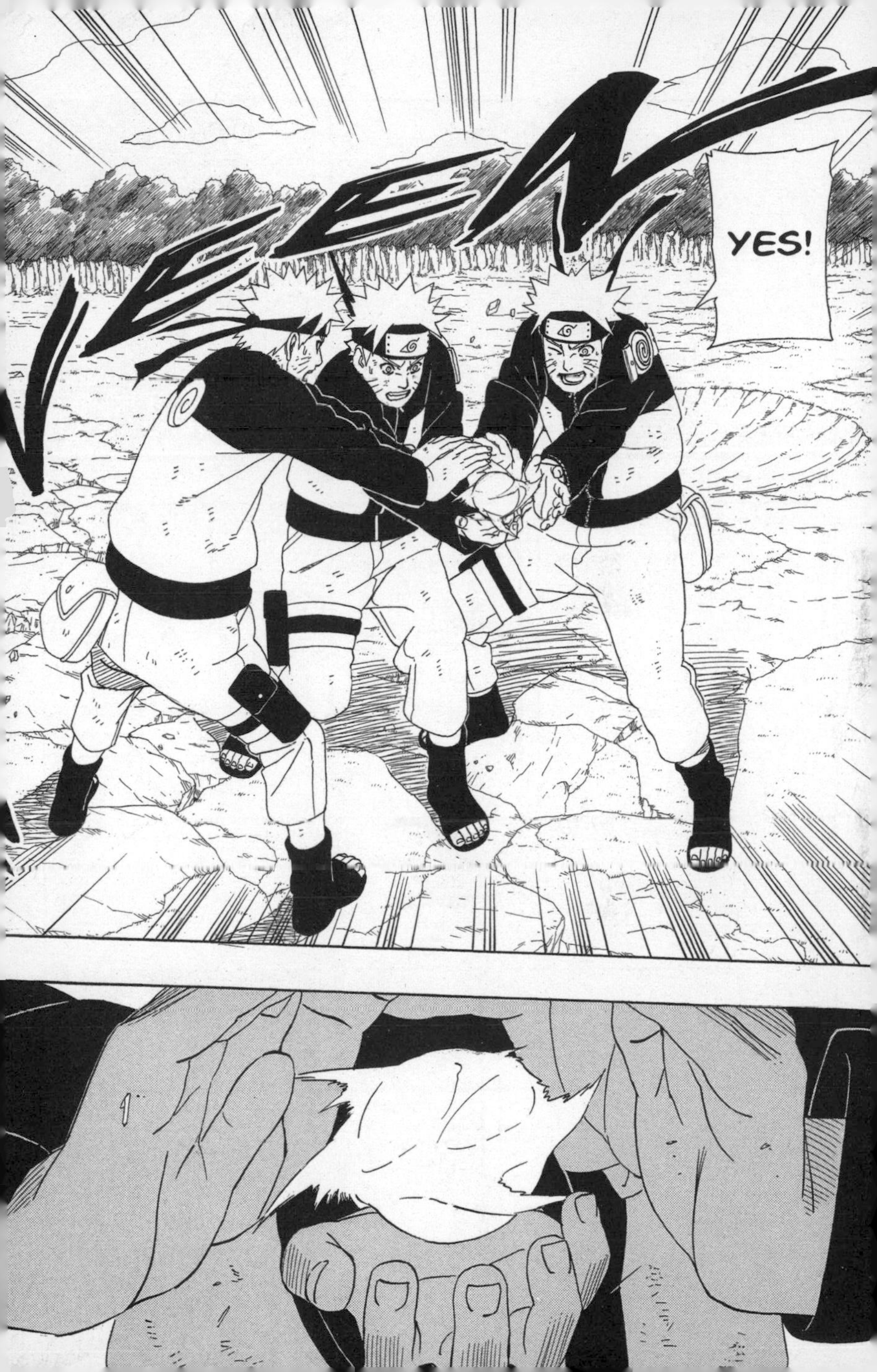
YES!

READ THIS WAY

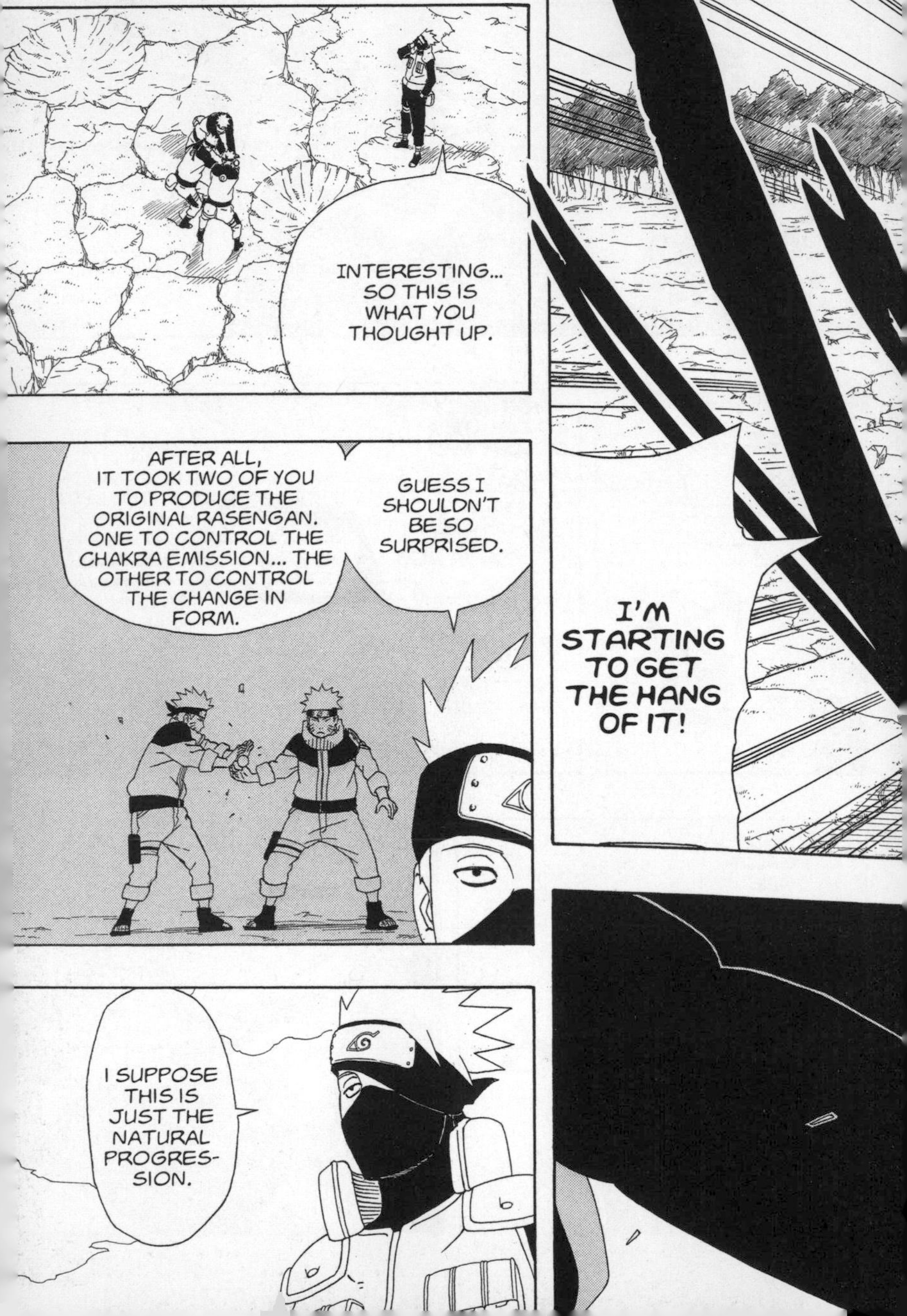
I'M STARTING TO GET THE HANG OF IT!
INTERESTING... SO THIS IS WHAT YOU THOUGHT UP.
GUESS I SHOULDN'T BE SO SURPRISED.
AFTER ALL, IT TOOK TWO OF YOU TO PRODUCE THE ORIGINAL RASENGAN. ONE TO CONTROL THE CHAKRA EMISSION... THE OTHER TO CONTROL THE CHANGE IN FORM.
I SUPPOSE THIS IS JUST THE NATURAL PROGRES-SION.

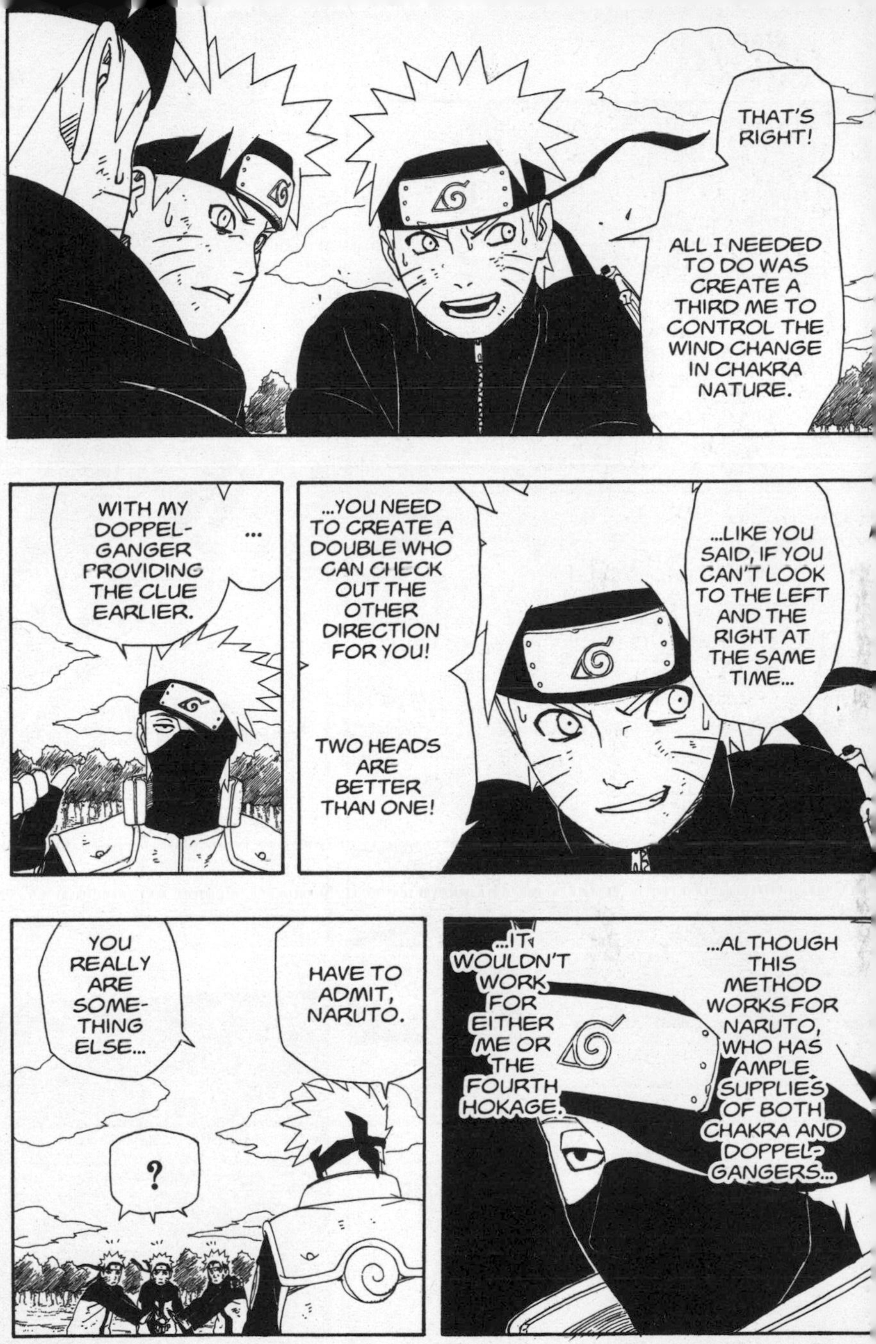
THAT'S RIGHT!
ALL I NEEDED TO DO WAS CREATE A THIRD ME TO CONTROL THE WIND CHANGE IN CHAKRA NATURE.
...LIKE YOU SAID, IF YOU CAN'T LOOK TO THE LEFT AND THE RIGHT AT THE SAME TIME...
...YOU NEED TO CREATE A DOUBLE WHO CAN CHECK OUT THE OTHER DIRECTION FOR YOU!
TWO HEADS ARE BETTER THAN ONE!
...
WITH MY DOPPEL-GANGER PROVIDING THE CLUE EARLIER.
...ALTHOUGH THIS METHOD WORKS FOR NARUTO, WHO HAS AMPLE SUPPLIES OF BOTH CHAKRA AND DOPPEL-GANGERS...
...IT WOULDN'T WORK FOR EITHER ME OR THE FOURTH HOKAGE.
HAVE TO ADMIT, NARUTO.
YOU REALLY ARE SOME-THING ELSE...
?

READ THIS WAY

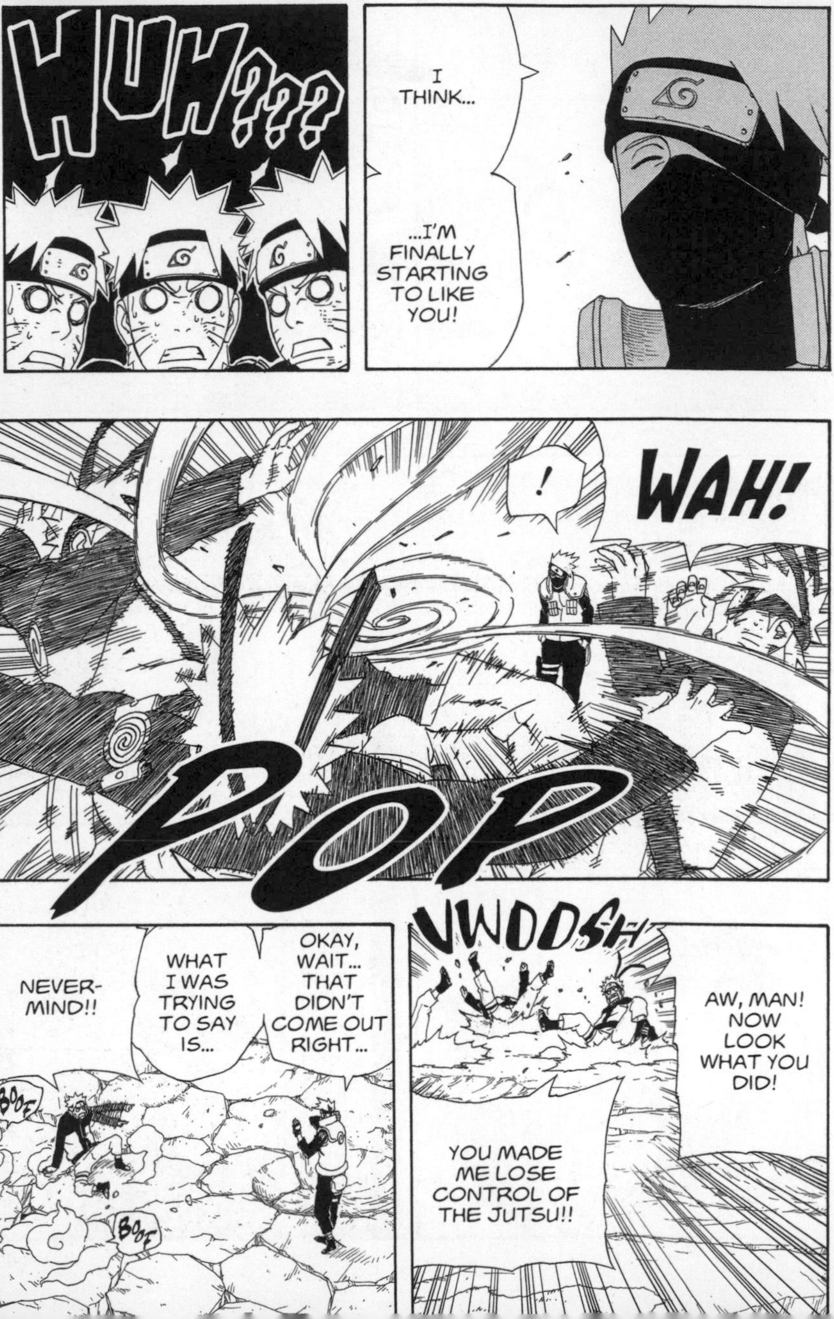

I THINK...
...I'M FINALLY STARTING TO LIKE YOU!
HUH???
WAH!
!
POP
VWOOSH
AW, MAN! NOW LOOK WHAT YOU DID!
YOU MADE ME LOSE CONTROL OF THE JUTSU!!
OKAY, WAIT... THAT DIDN'T COME OUT RIGHT...
WHAT I WAS TRYING TO SAY IS...
NEVER-MIND!!
BOOF
BOOF

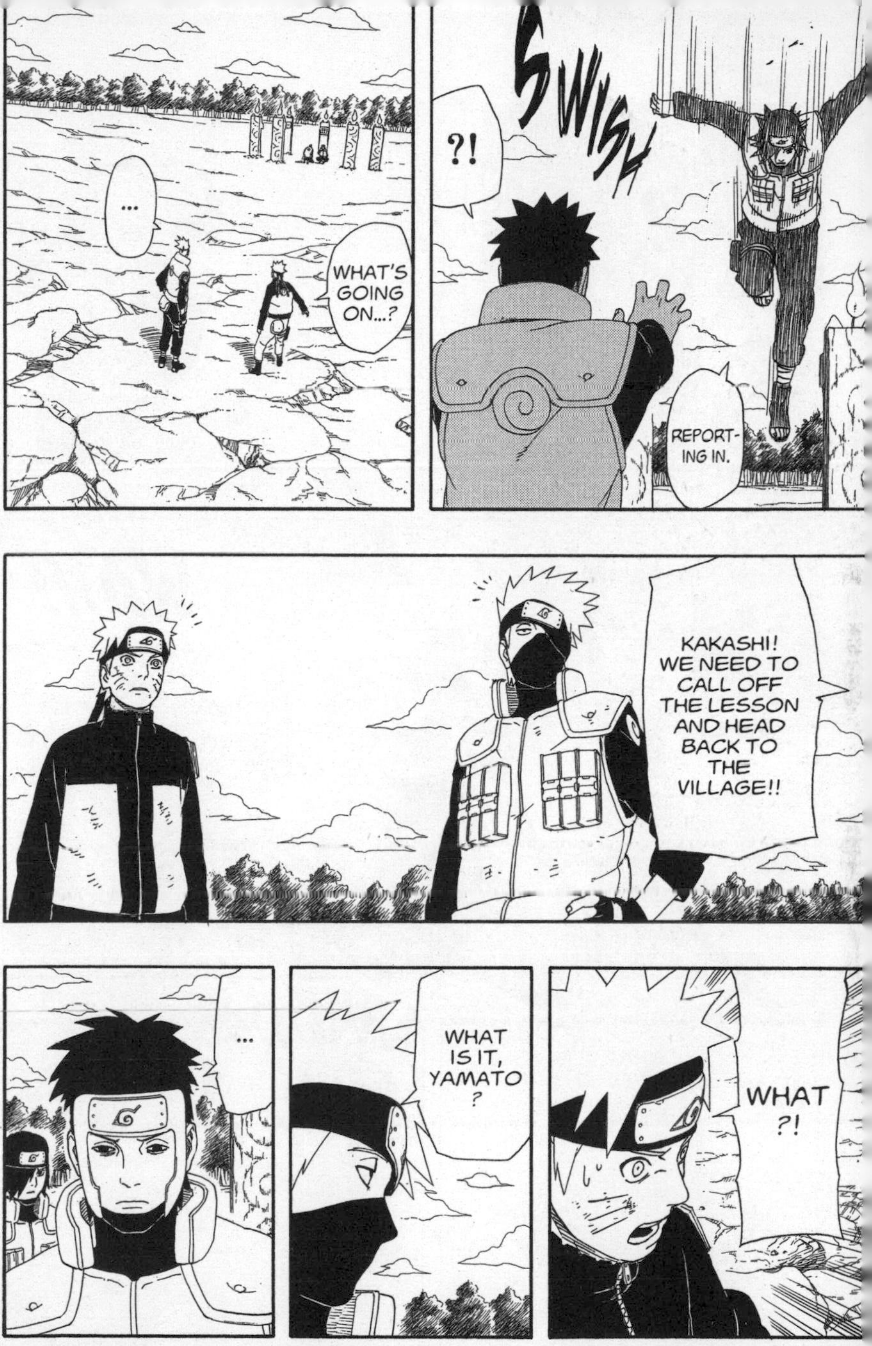
SWISH
?!
REPORTING IN.
...
WHAT'S GOING ON...?
KAKASHI! WE NEED TO CALL OFF THE LESSON AND HEAD BACK TO THE VILLAGE!!
WHAT ?!
WHAT IS IT, YAMATO ?
...

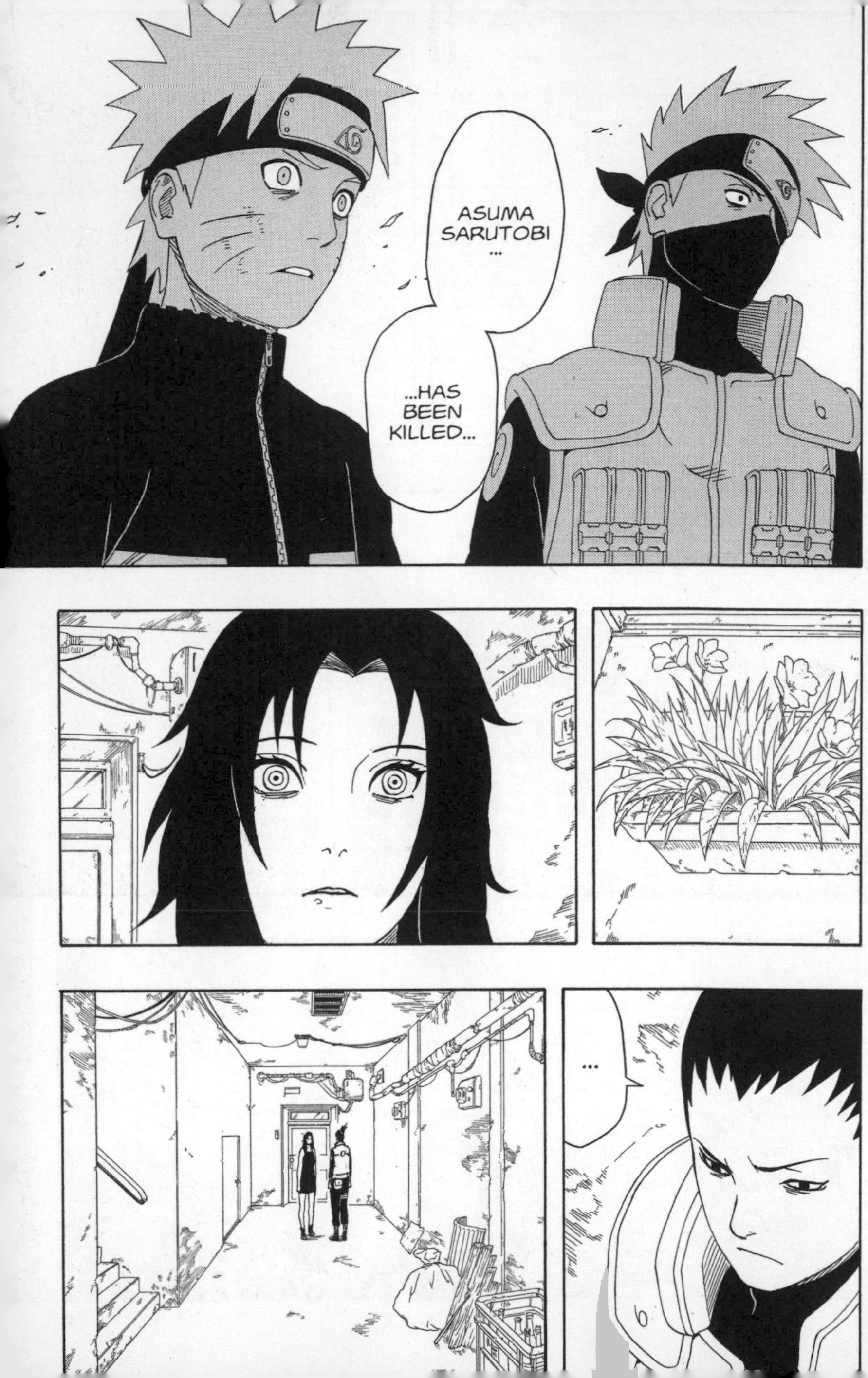
ASUMA SARUTOBI ...
...HAS BEEN KILLED...
...

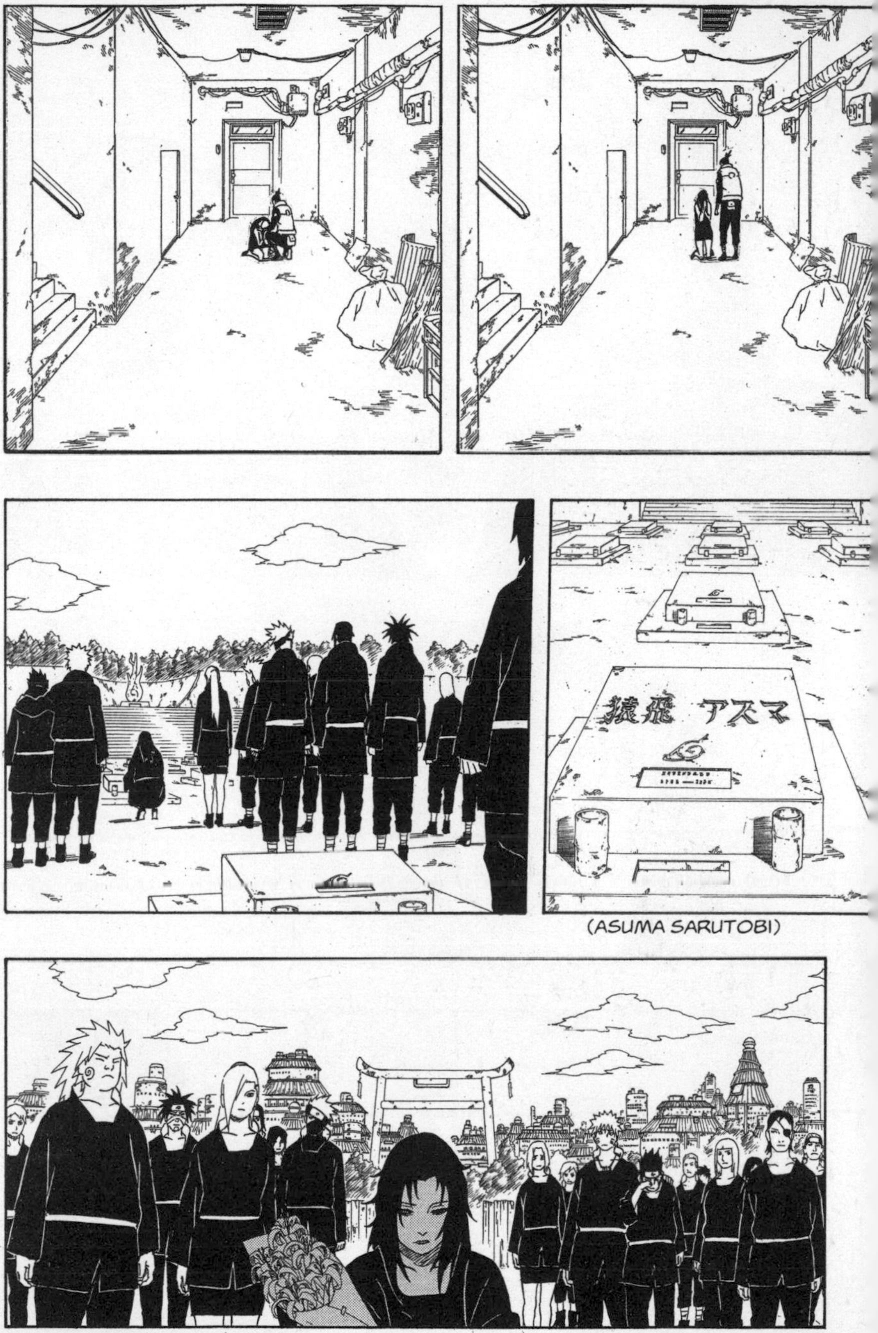
猿飛 アスマ
(ASUMA SARUTOBI)

READ THIS WAY

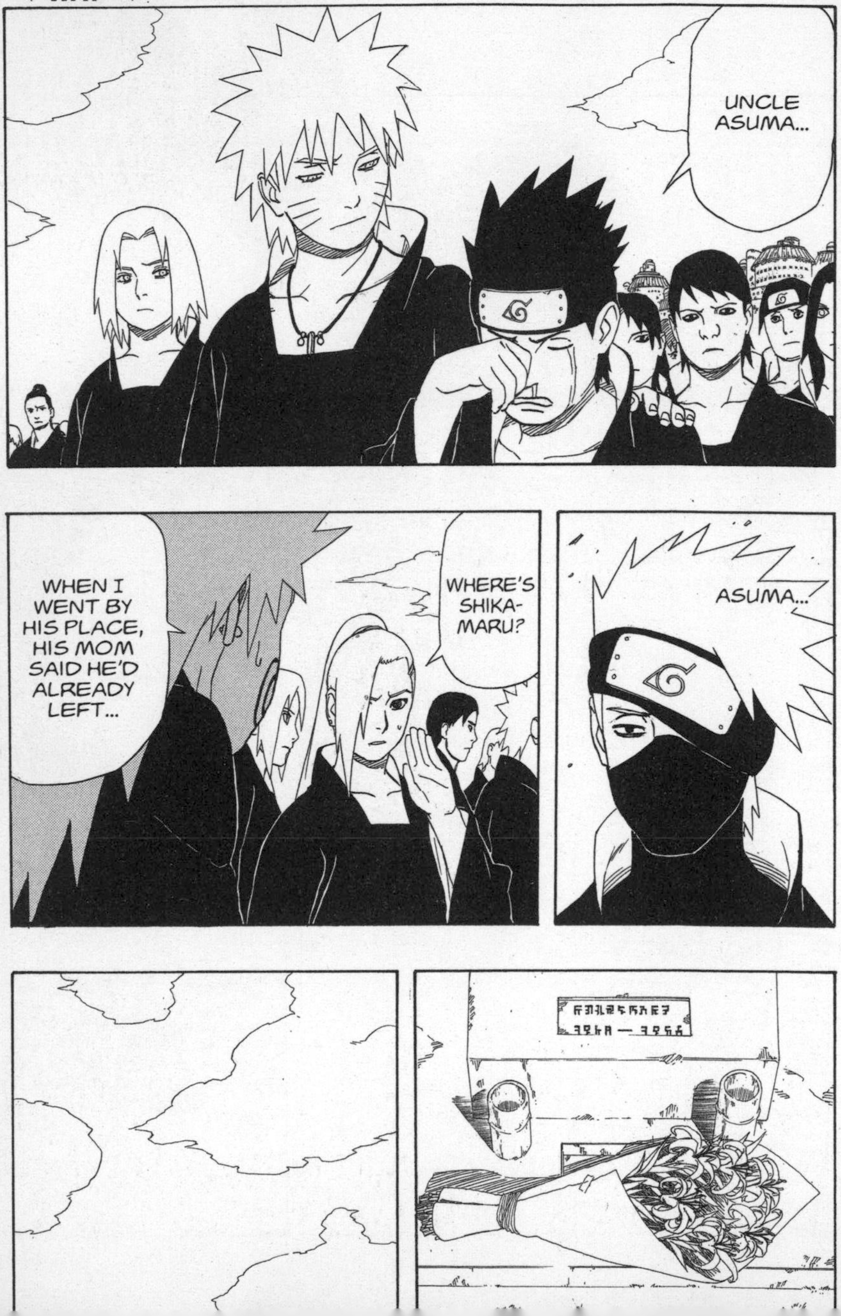
UNCLE ASUMA...
ASUMA...
WHERE'S SHIKA-MARU?
WHEN I WENT BY HIS PLACE, HIS MOM SAID HE'D ALREADY LEFT...

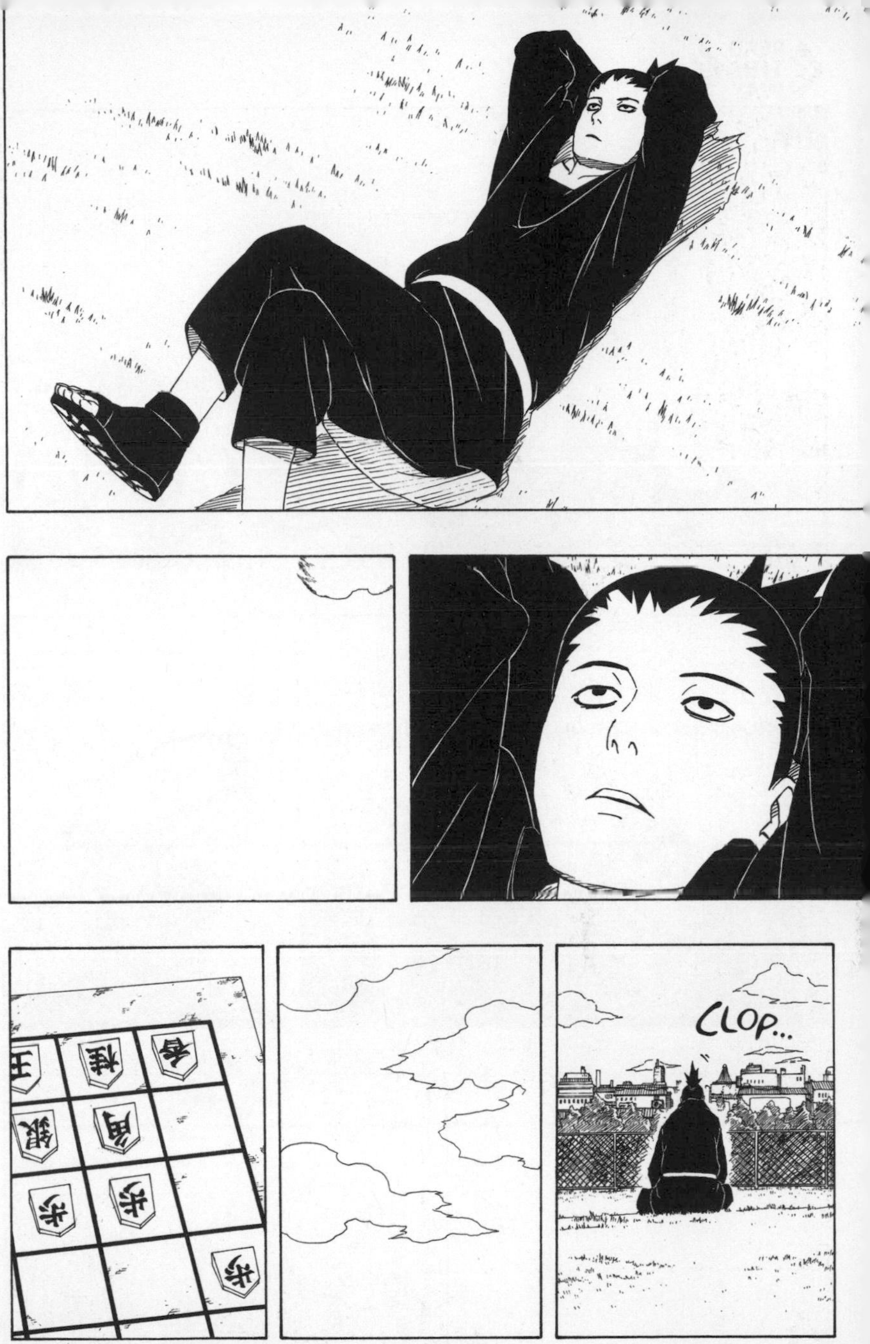
CLOP...

READ THIS WAY

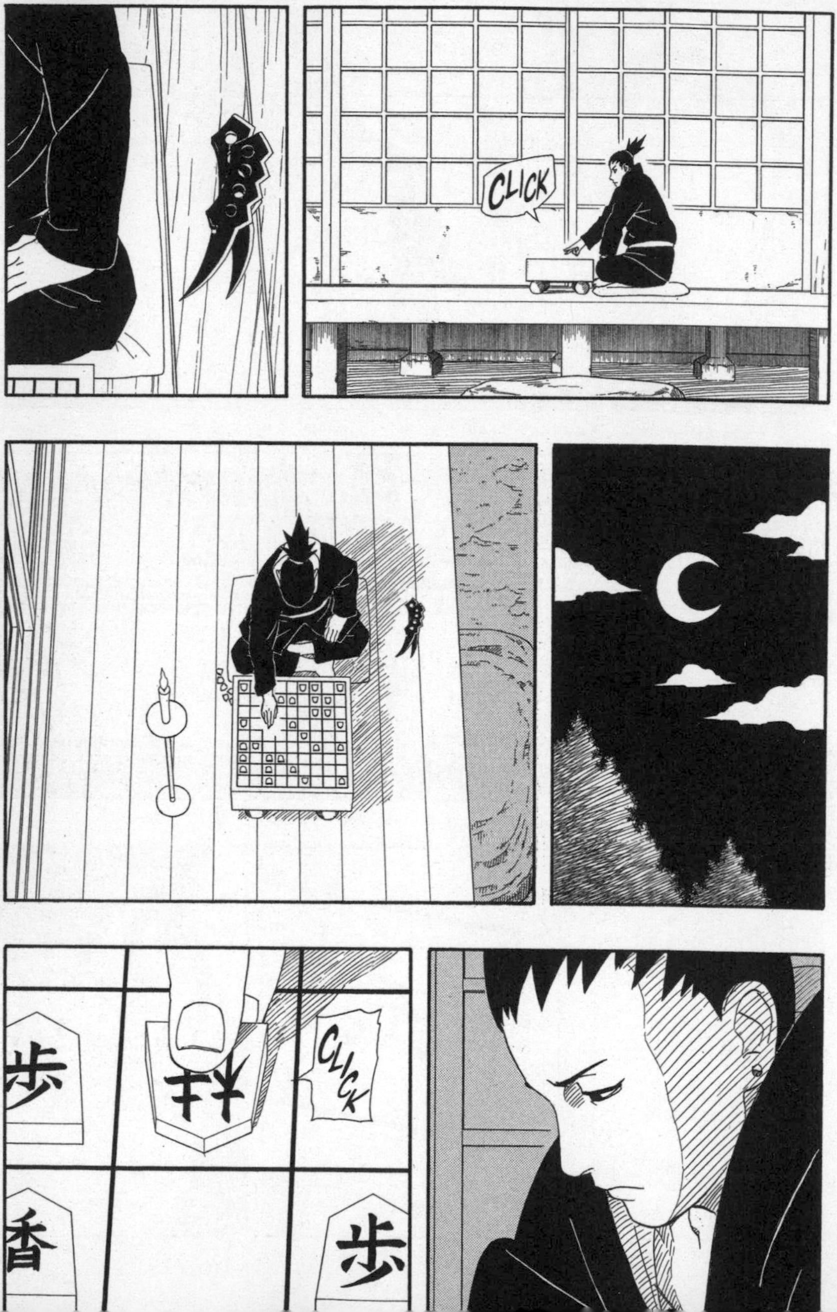
CLICK
CLICK

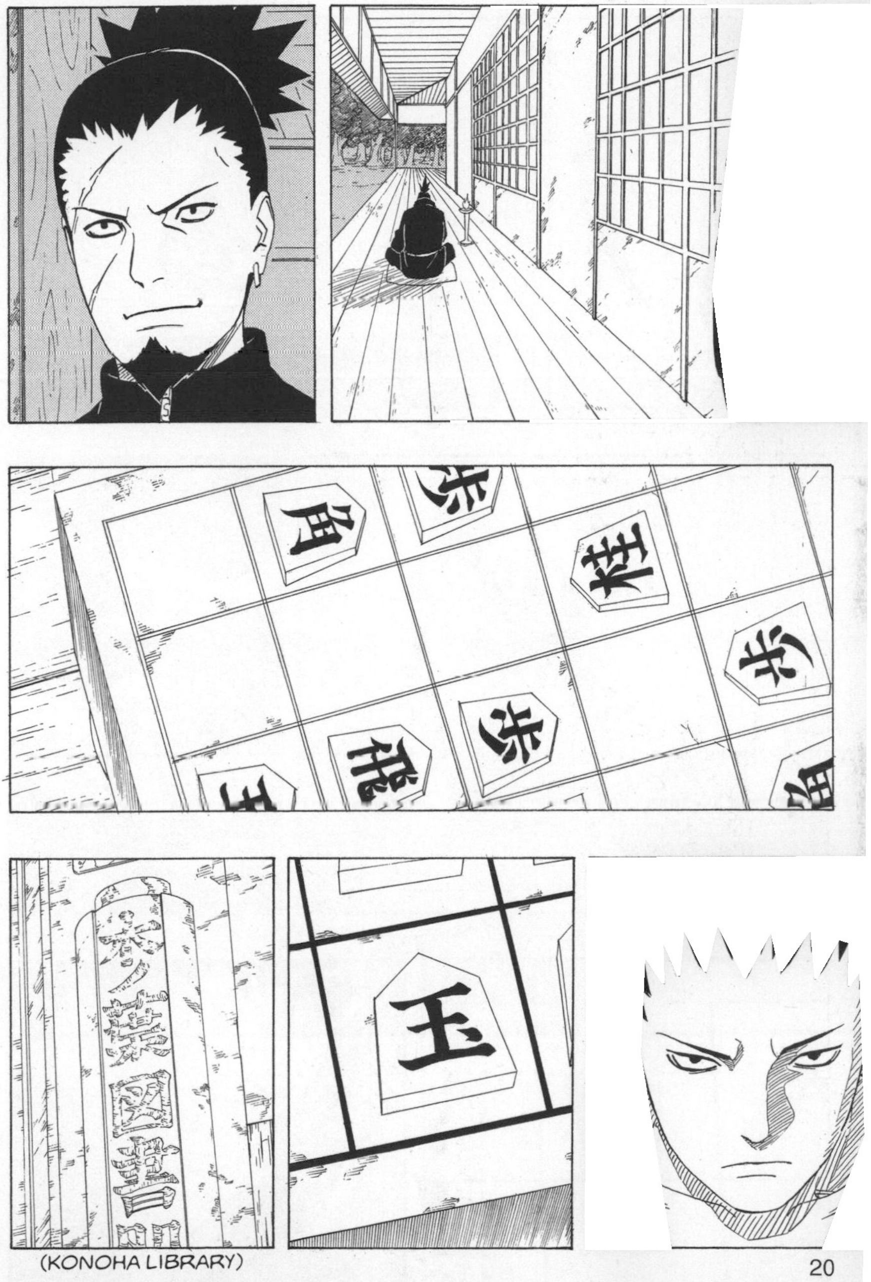
(KONOHA LIBRARY)

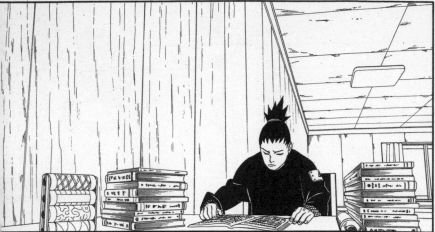

HAH!

CHAK

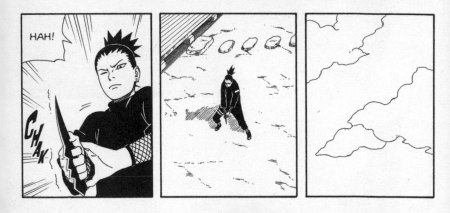

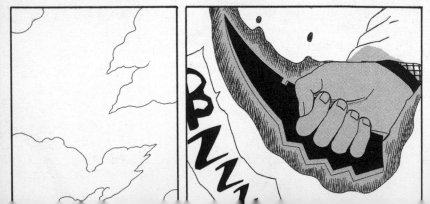

BZZZ

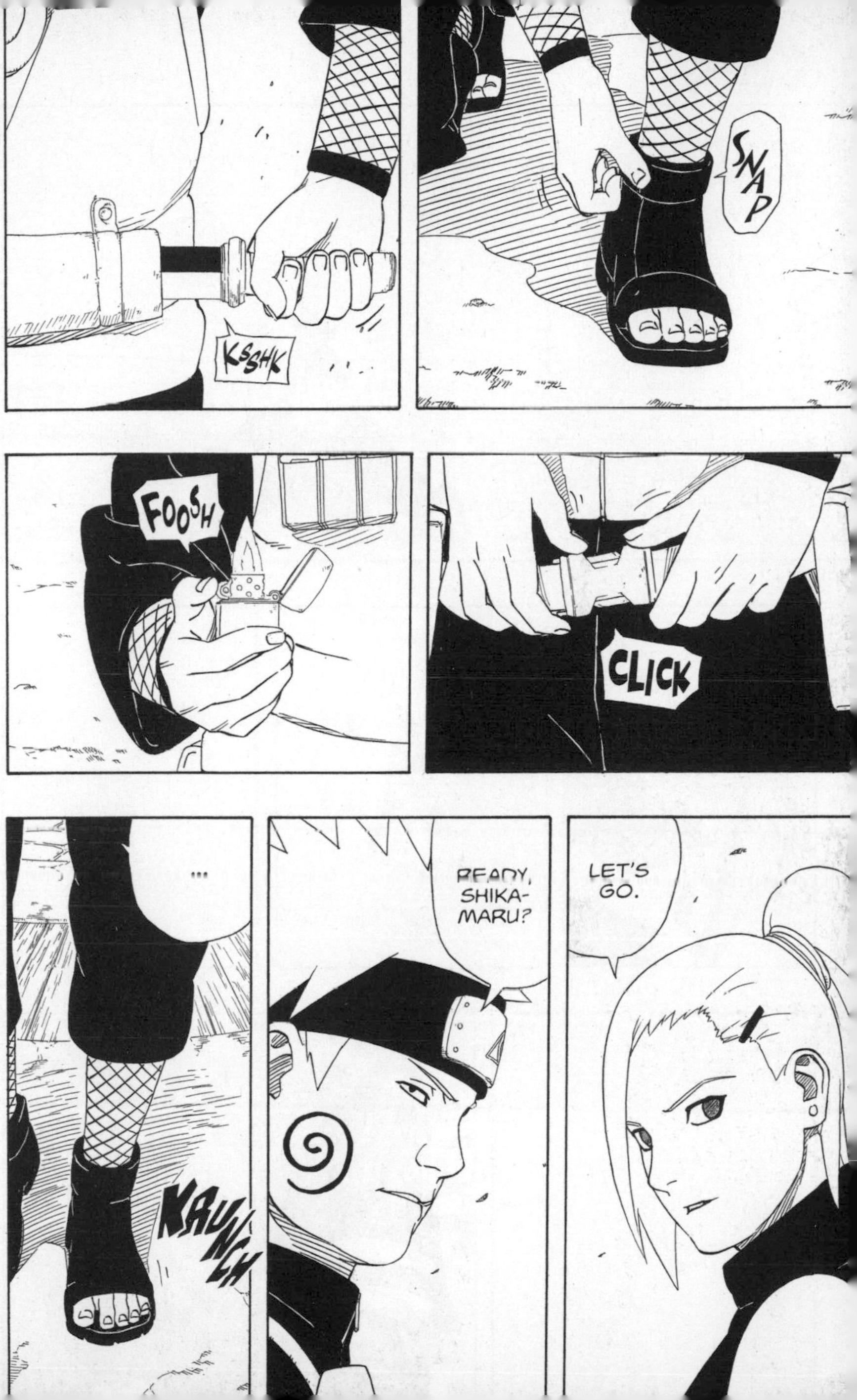
SNAP
KSSHK
CLICK
FOOSH
LET'S GO.
READY, SHIKAMARU?
...
KRUNCH

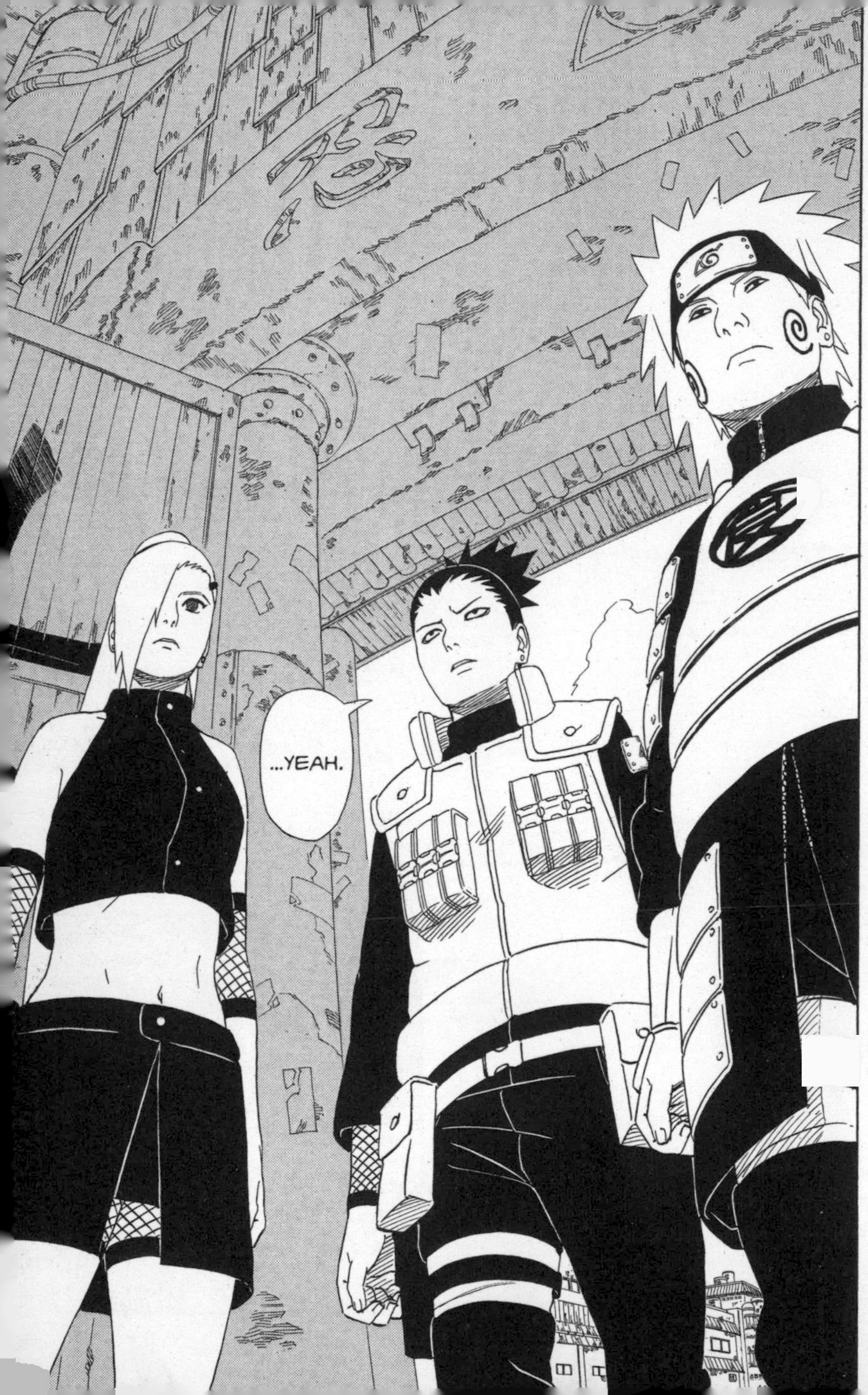
...YEAH.

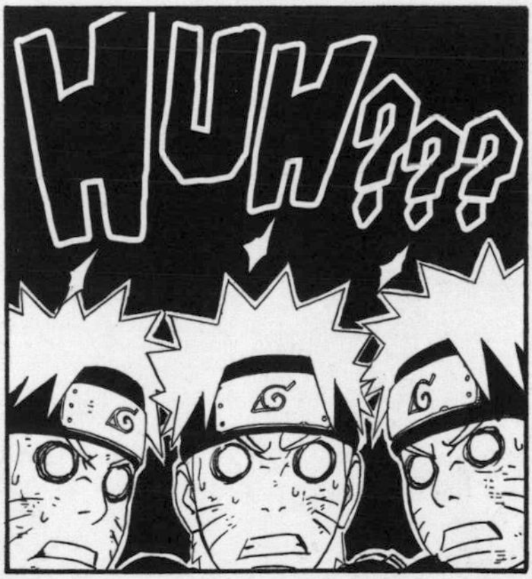
HUH???

Number 331: Cell Number 10 Sets Out...!!

SHP
SHP
HOLD IT!
!
...?! ...

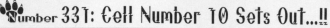

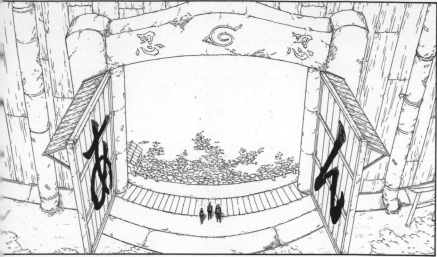

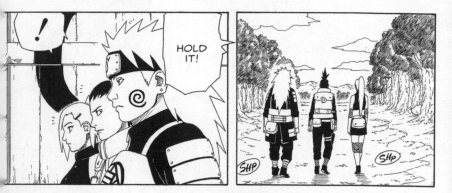

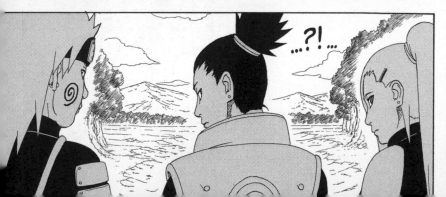

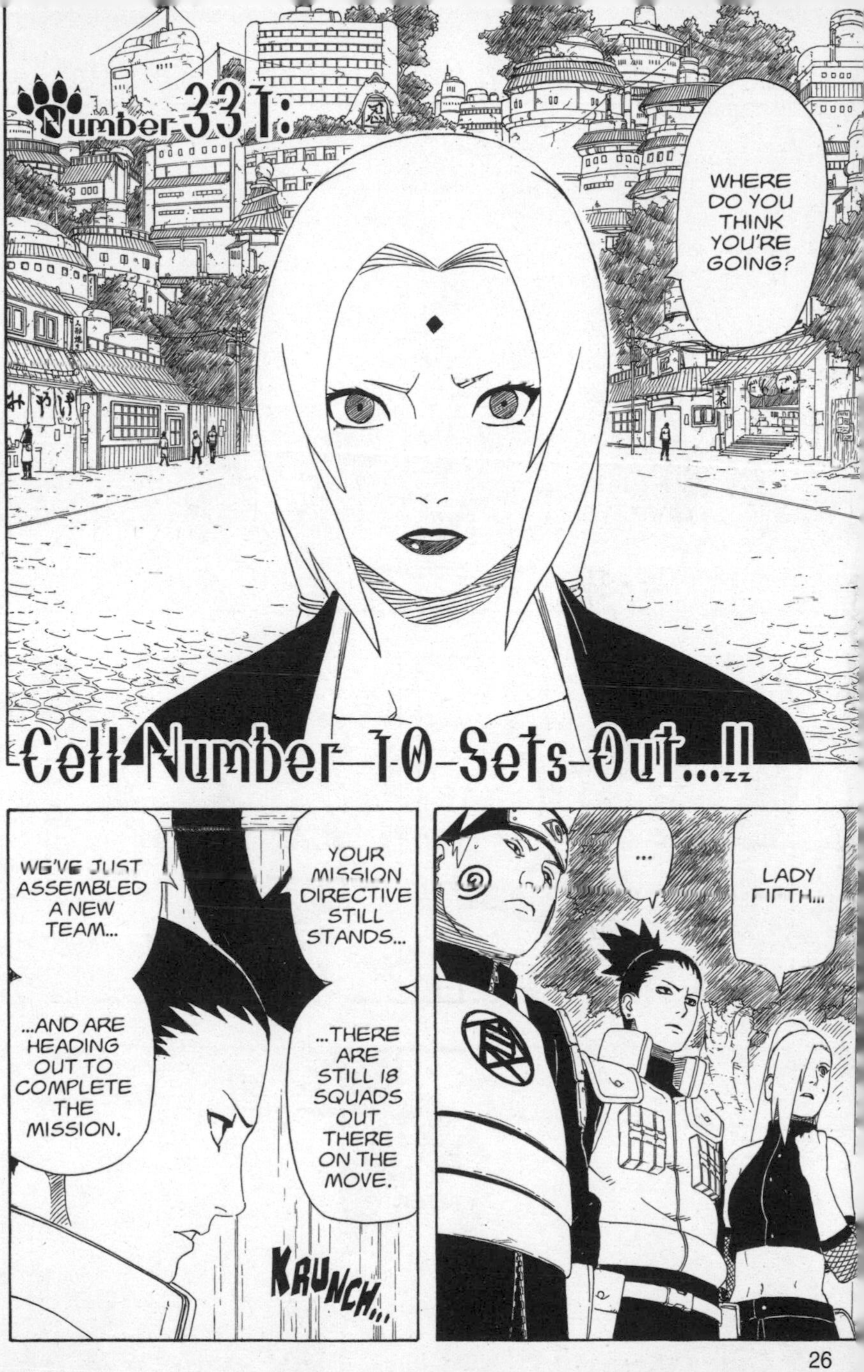
Number 331:
WHERE DO YOU THINK YOU'RE GOING?
Cell Number 10 Sets Out...!!
LADY FIFTH...
...
YOUR MISSION DIRECTIVE STILL STANDS...
...THERE ARE STILL 18 SQUADS OUT THERE ON THE MOVE.
WE'VE JUST ASSEMBLED A NEW TEAM...
...AND ARE HEADING OUT TO COMPLETE THE MISSION.
KRUNCH...

READ THIS WAY

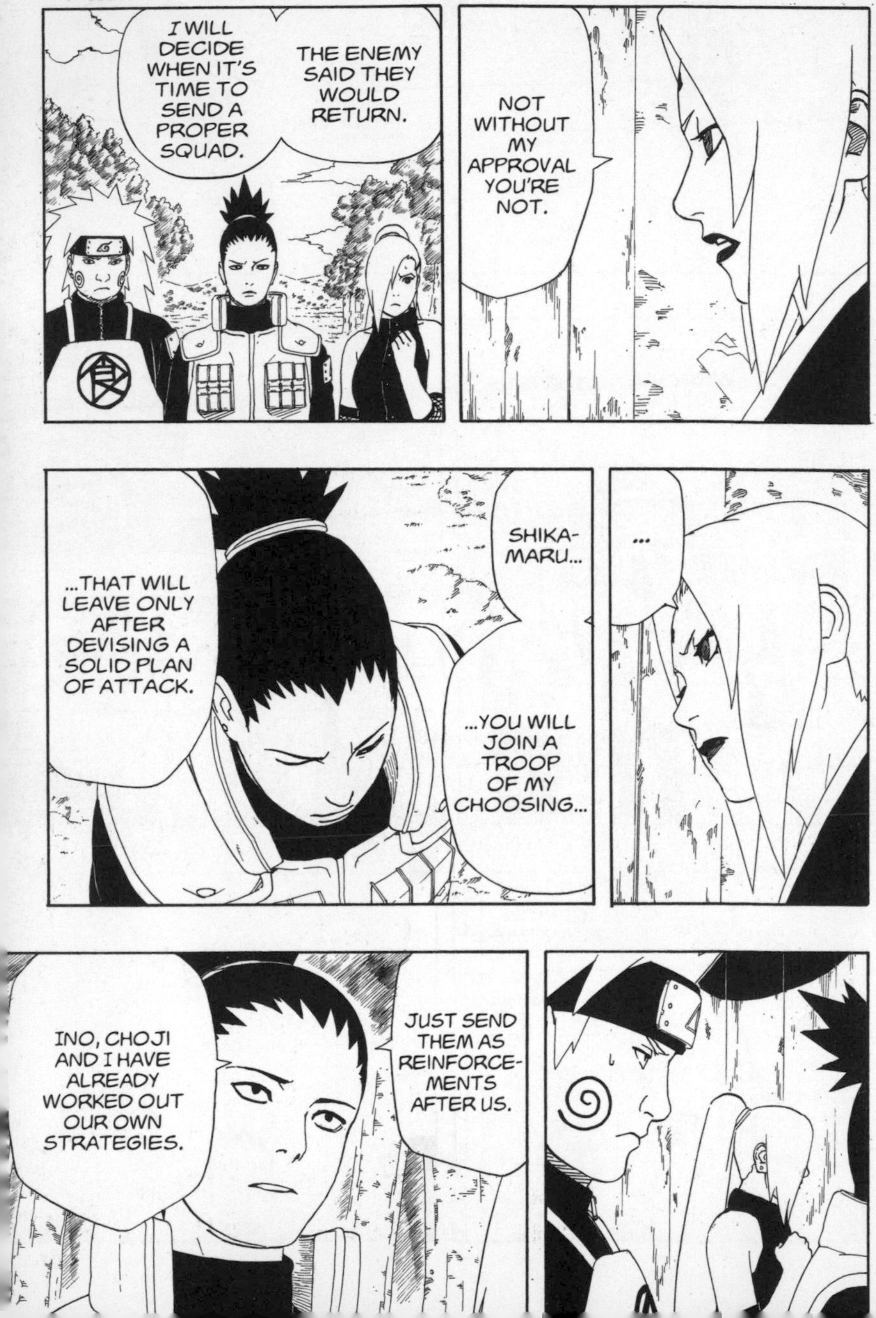
NOT WITHOUT MY APPROVAL YOU'RE NOT.
THE ENEMY SAID THEY WOULD RETURN.
I WILL DECIDE WHEN IT'S TIME TO SEND A PROPER SQUAD.
...
SHIKAMARU...
...YOU WILL JOIN A TROOP OF MY CHOOSING...
...THAT WILL LEAVE ONLY AFTER DEVISING A SOLID PLAN OF ATTACK.
JUST SEND THEM AS REINFORCEMENTS AFTER US.
INO, CHOJI AND I HAVE ALREADY WORKED OUT OUR OWN STRATEGIES.

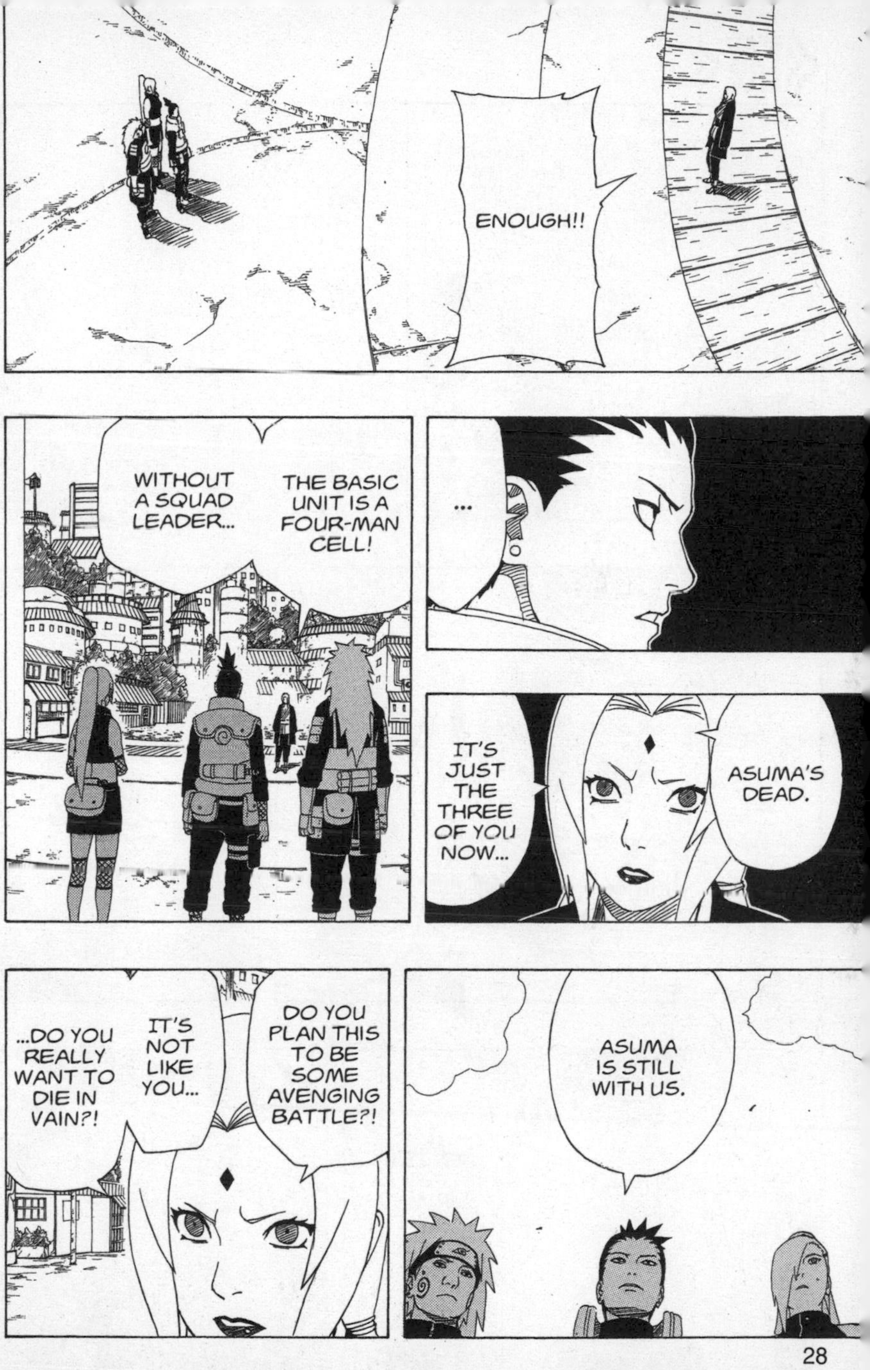
ENOUGH!!
...
ASUMA'S DEAD.
IT'S JUST THE THREE OF YOU NOW...
THE BASIC UNIT IS A FOUR-MAN CELL!
WITHOUT A SQUAD LEADER...
ASUMA IS STILL WITH US.
DO YOU PLAN THIS TO BE SOME AVENGING BATTLE?!
IT'S NOT LIKE YOU...
...DO YOU REALLY WANT TO DIE IN VAIN?!

READ THIS WAY

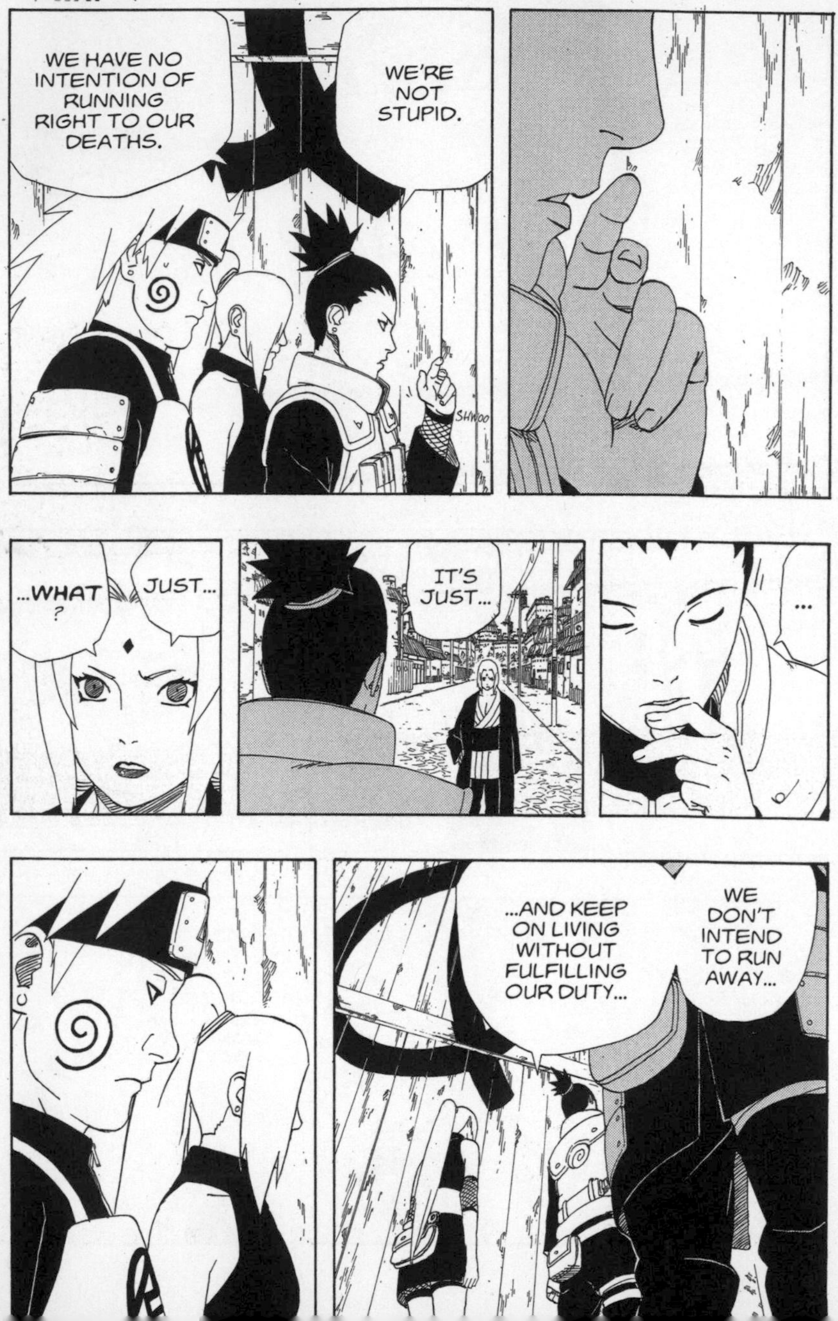
WE'RE NOT STUPID.
WE HAVE NO INTENTION OF RUNNING RIGHT TO OUR DEATHS.
SHWOO
...
IT'S JUST...
JUST...
...WHAT?
WE DON'T INTEND TO RUN AWAY...
...AND KEEP ON LIVING WITHOUT FULFILLING OUR DUTY...

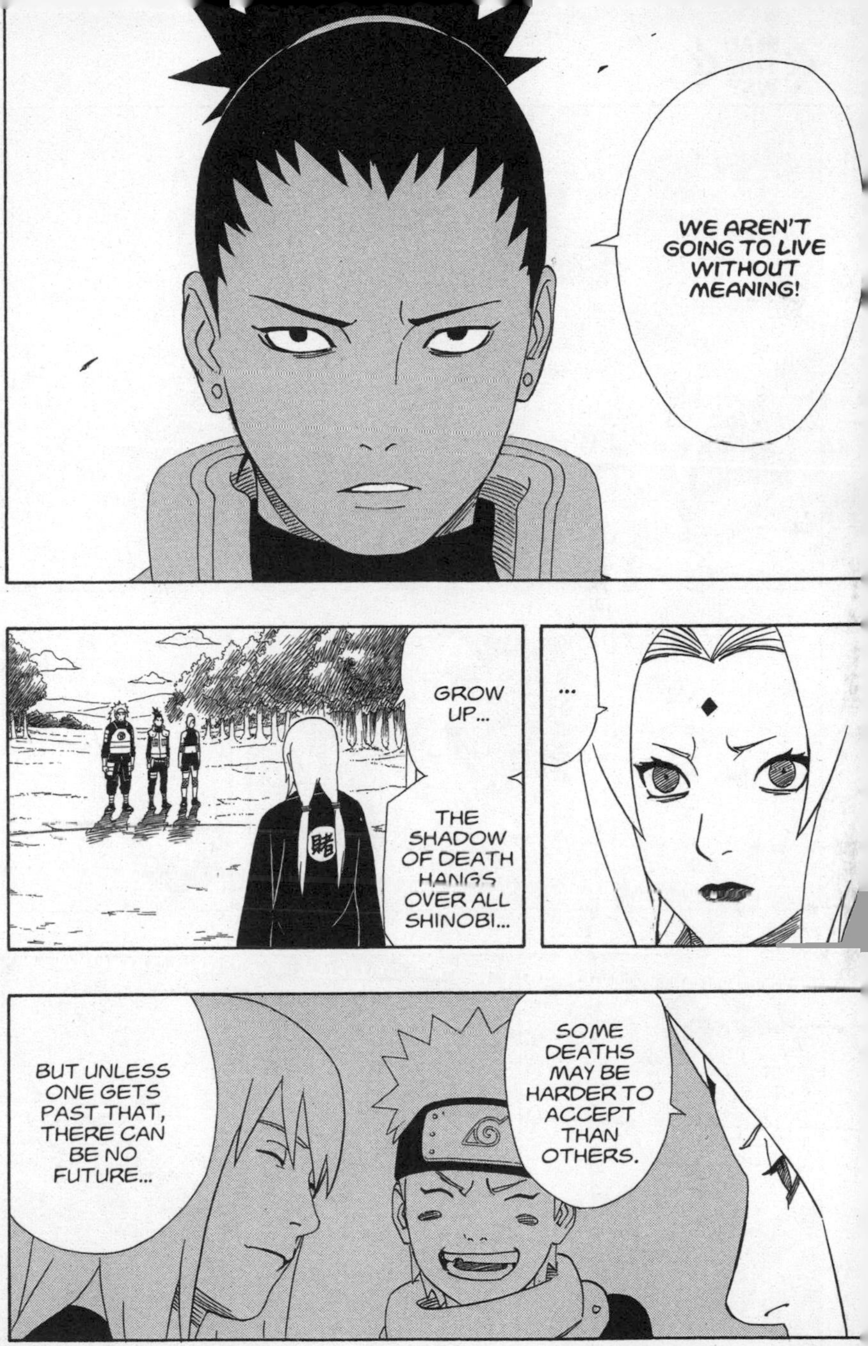
WE AREN'T GOING TO LIVE WITHOUT MEANING!
...
GROW UP...
THE SHADOW OF DEATH HANGS OVER ALL SHINOBI...
SOME DEATHS MAY BE HARDER TO ACCEPT THAN OTHERS.
BUT UNLESS ONE GETS PAST THAT, THERE CAN BE NO FUTURE...

READ THIS WAY

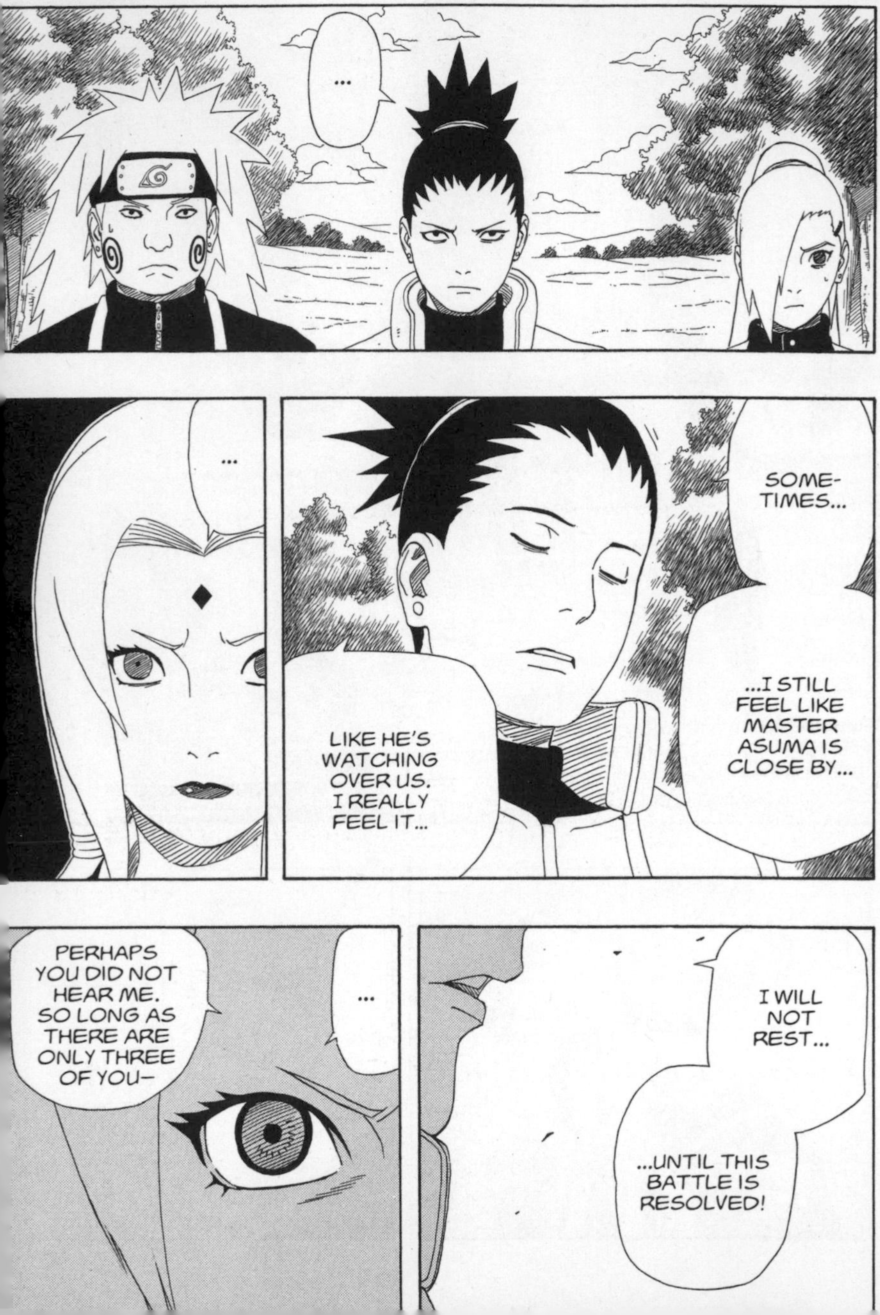
...
SOME-TIMES...
...I STILL FEEL LIKE MASTER ASUMA IS CLOSE BY...
LIKE HE'S WATCHING OVER US. I REALLY FEEL IT...
...
I WILL NOT REST...
...UNTIL THIS BATTLE IS RESOLVED!
...
PERHAPS YOU DID NOT HEAR ME. SO LONG AS THERE ARE ONLY THREE OF YOU–

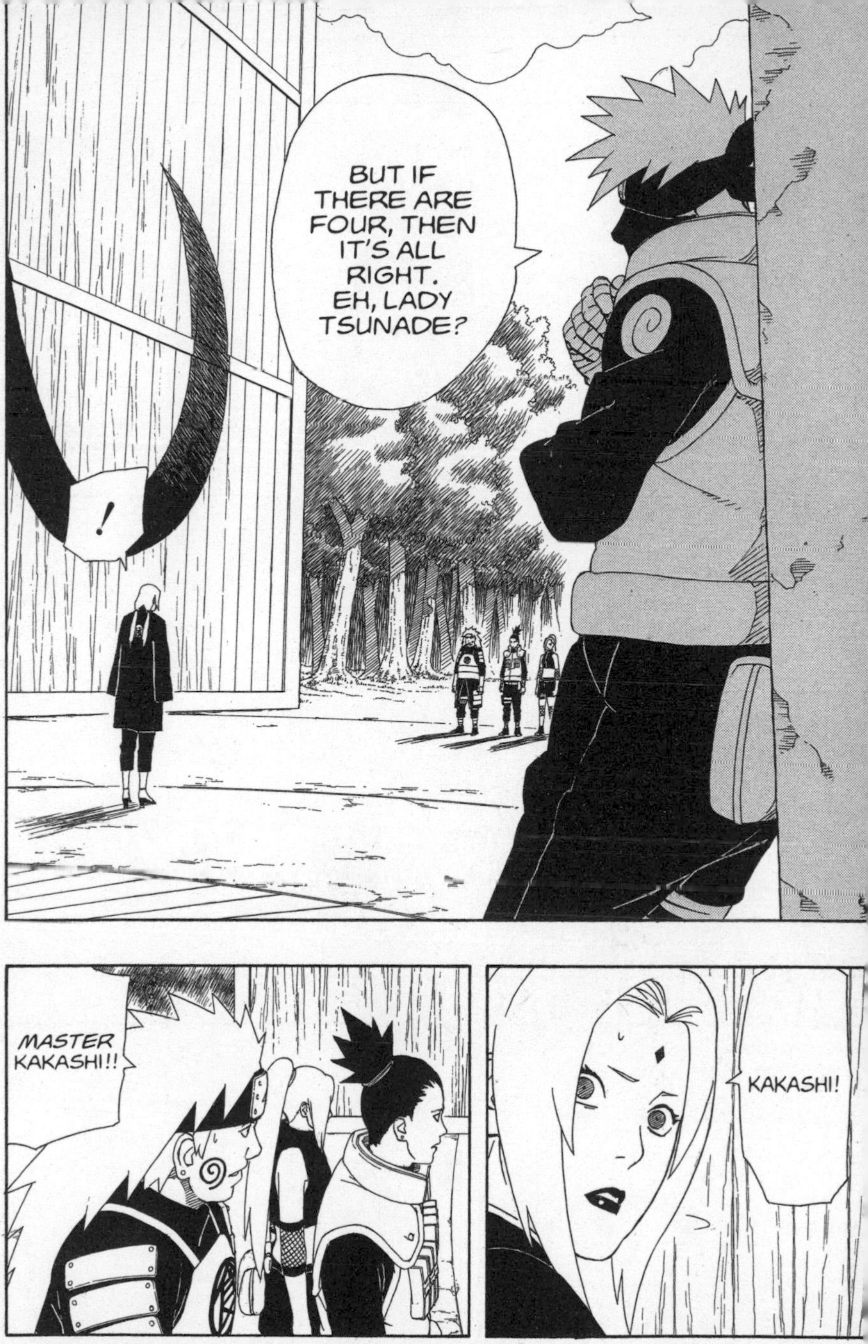
BUT IF THERE ARE FOUR, THEN IT'S ALL RIGHT. EH, LADY TSUNADE?
!
KAKASHI!
MASTER KAKASHI!!

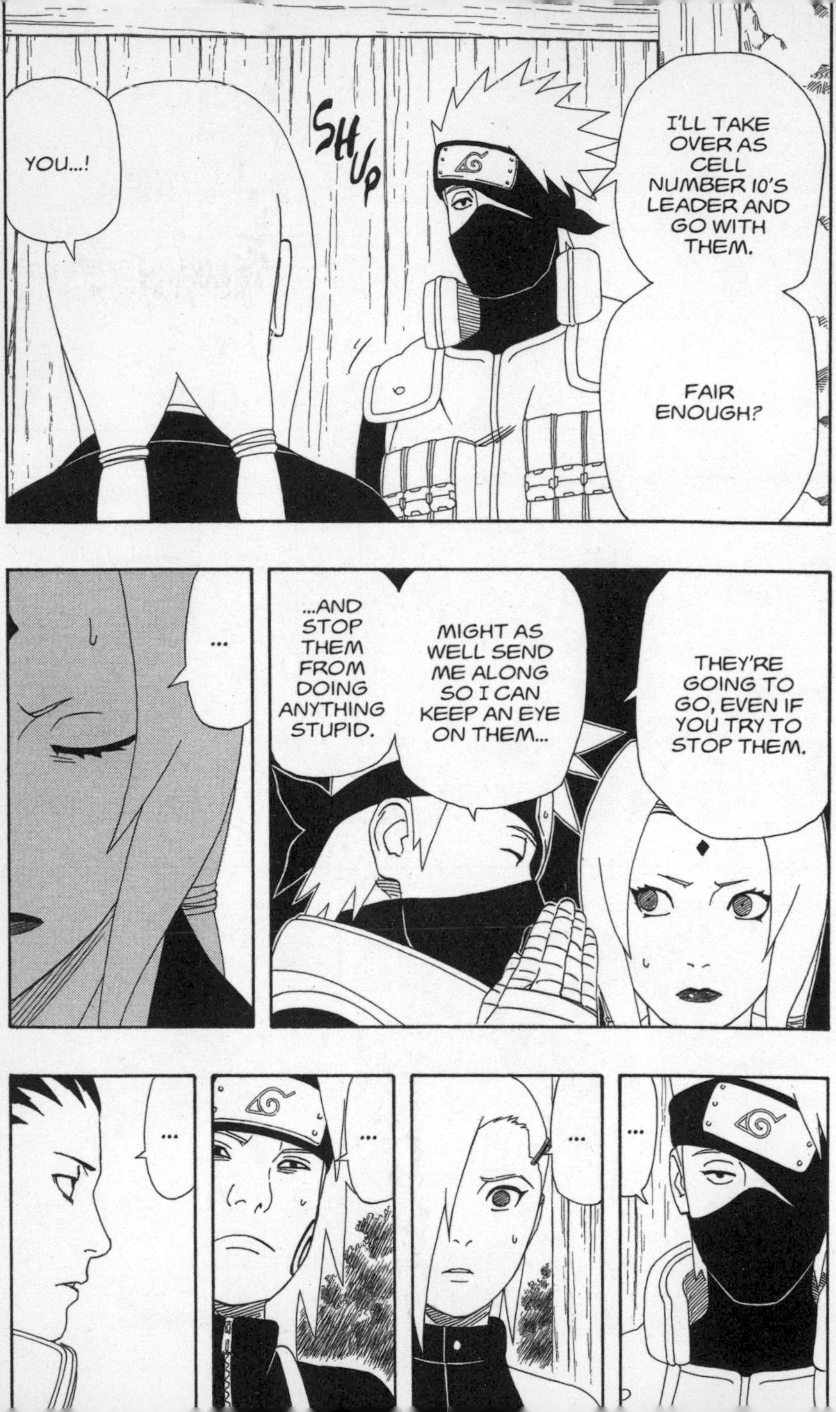
I'LL TAKE OVER AS CELL NUMBER 10'S LEADER AND GO WITH THEM.
FAIR ENOUGH?
SHUP
YOU...!
THEY'RE GOING TO GO, EVEN IF YOU TRY TO STOP THEM.
MIGHT AS WELL SEND ME ALONG SO I CAN KEEP AN EYE ON THEM...
...AND STOP THEM FROM DOING ANYTHING STUPID.
...
...
...
...
...

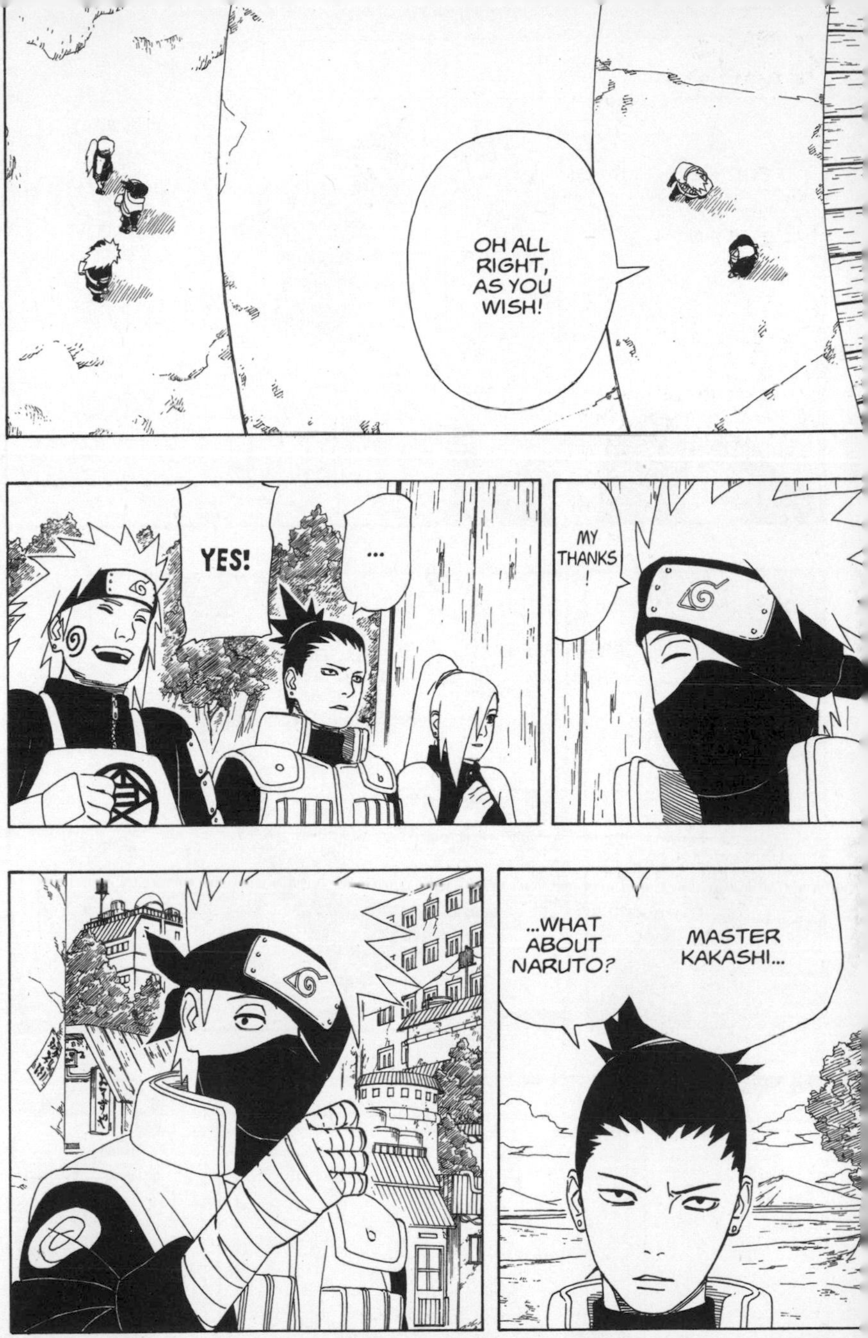
OH ALL RIGHT, AS YOU WISH!
MY THANKS!
...
YES!
MASTER KAKASHI...
...WHAT ABOUT NARUTO?

READ THIS WAY

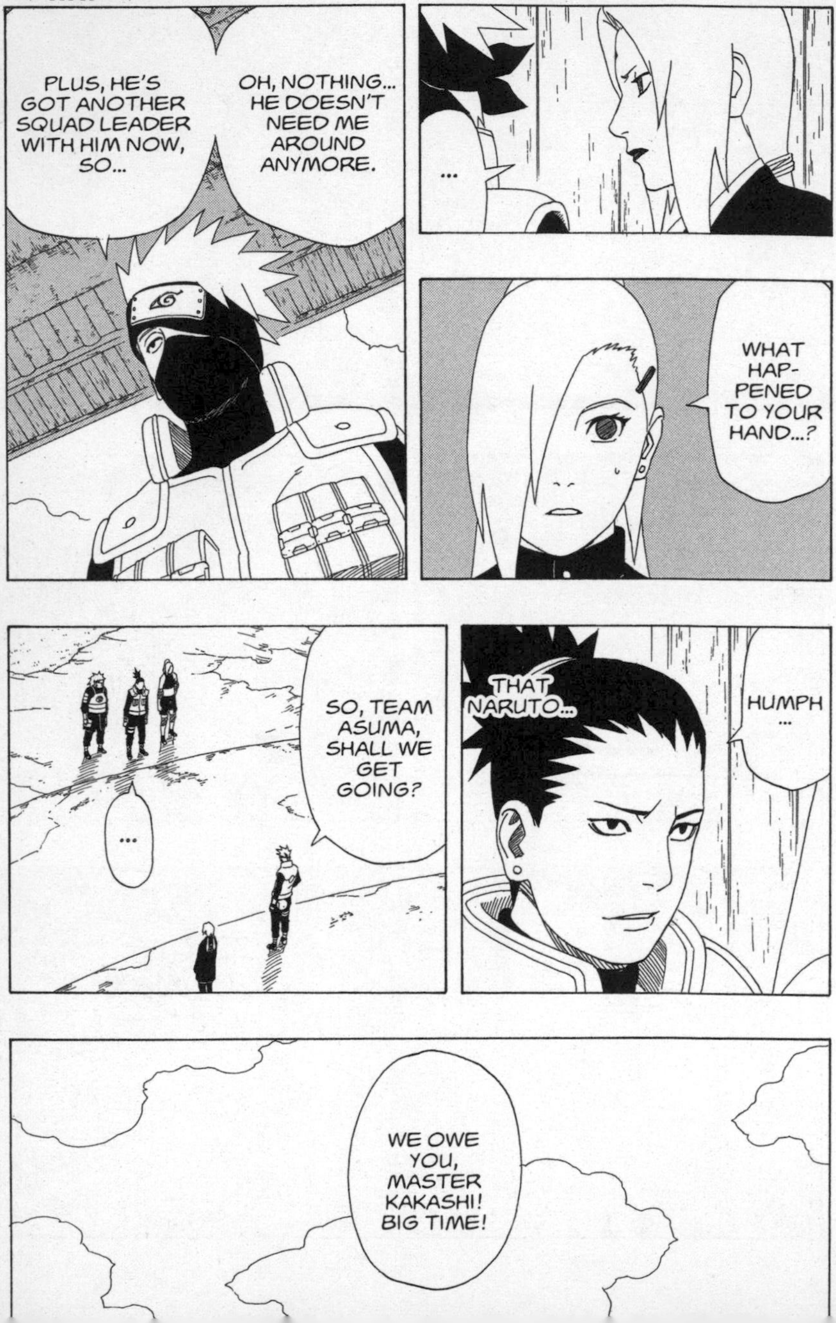
...
WHAT HAPPENED TO YOUR HAND...?
OH, NOTHING... HE DOESN'T NEED ME AROUND ANYMORE.
PLUS, HE'S GOT ANOTHER SQUAD LEADER WITH HIM NOW, SO...
HUMPH ...
THAT NARUTO...
SO, TEAM ASUMA, SHALL WE GET GOING?
...
WE OWE YOU, MASTER KAKASHI! BIG TIME!

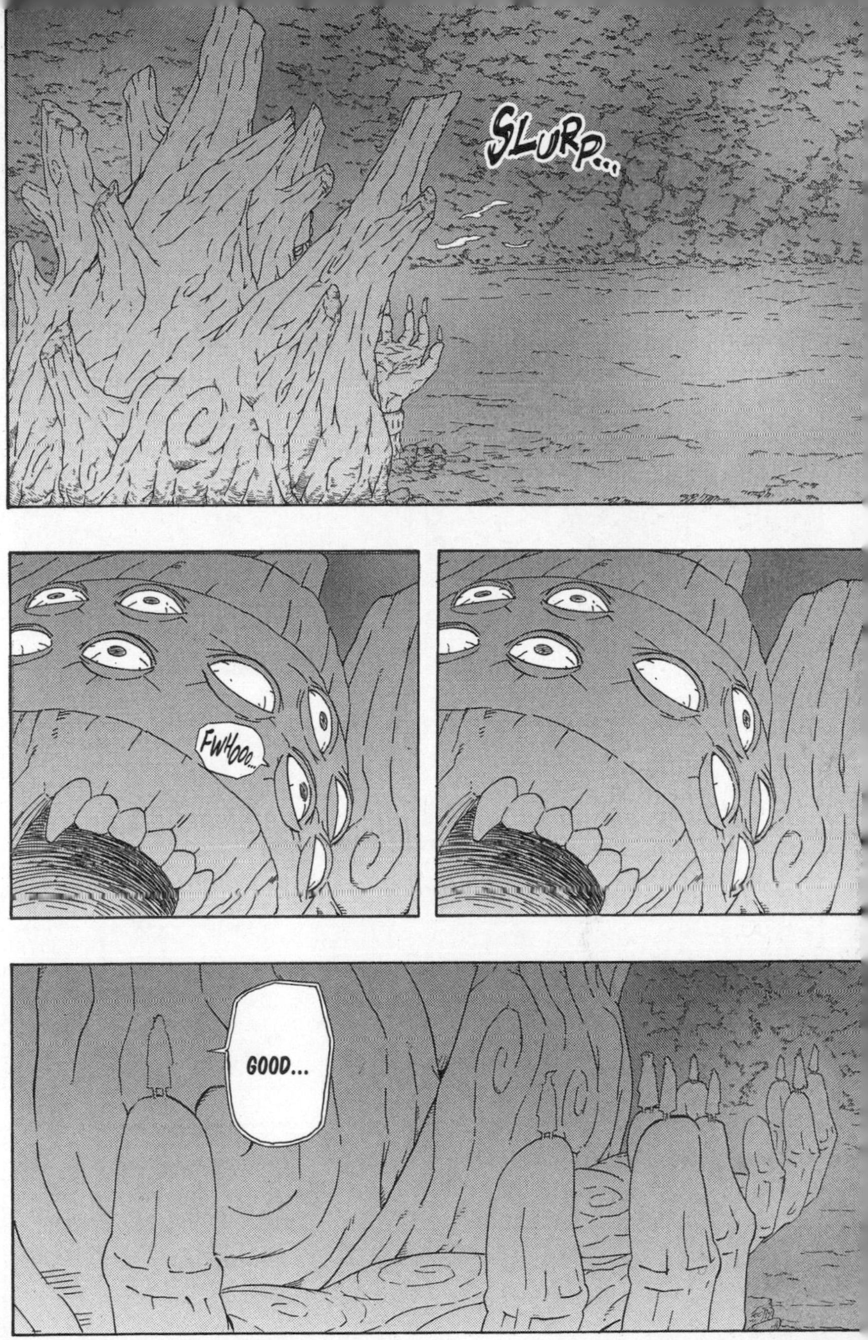
SLURP...
FWHOOO...
GOOD...

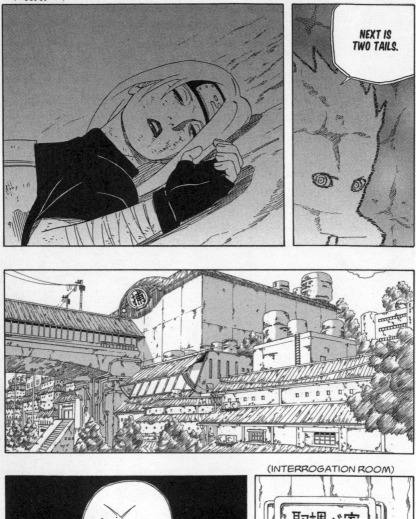

NEXT IS TWO TAILS.

(INTERROGATION ROOM)

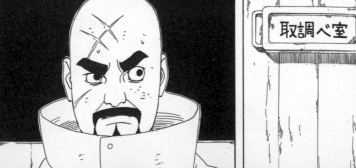

取調べ室

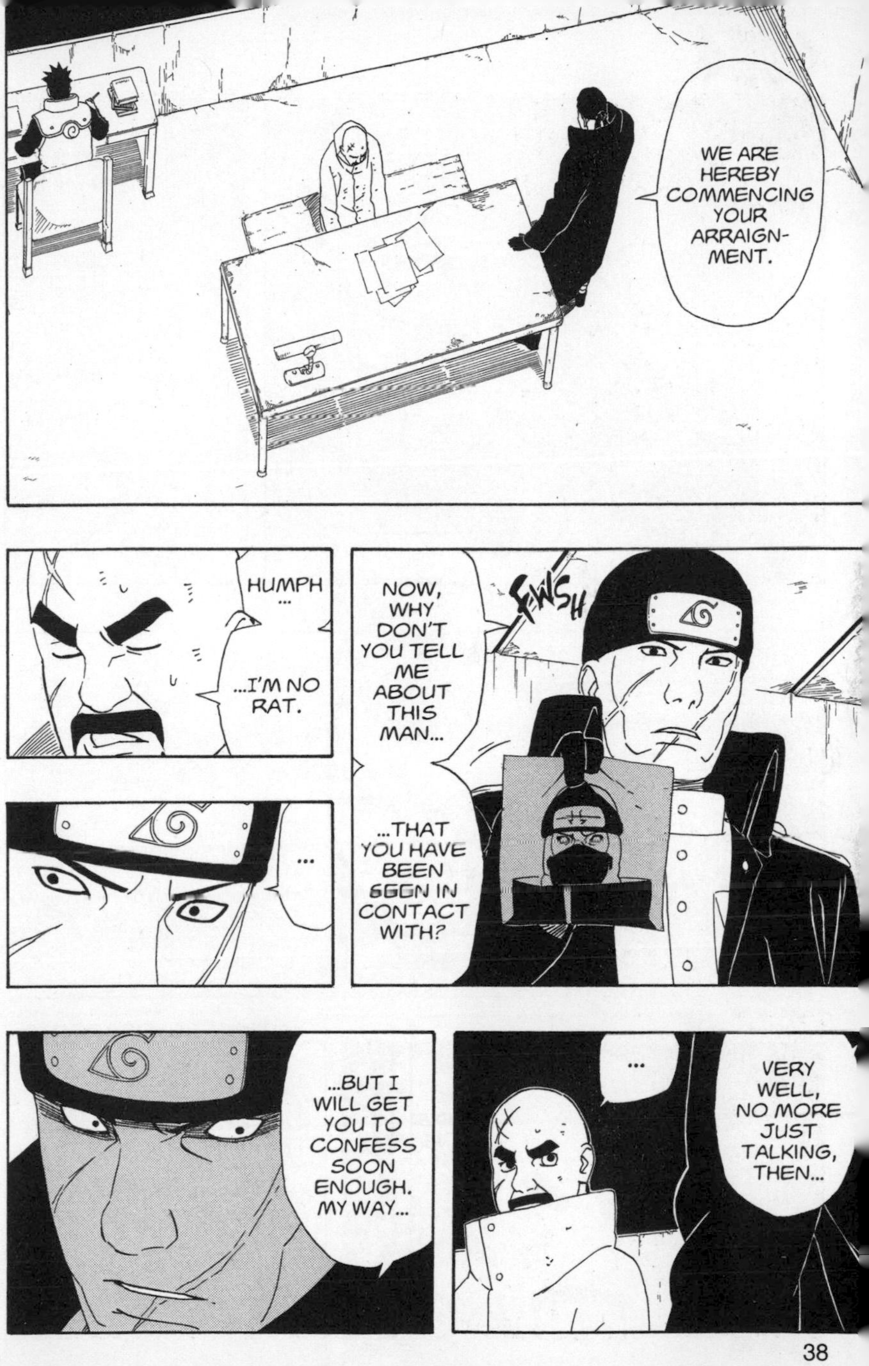
WE ARE HEREBY COMMENCING YOUR ARRAIGNMENT.
FWSH
NOW, WHY DON'T YOU TELL ME ABOUT THIS MAN...
...THAT YOU HAVE BEEN SEEN IN CONTACT WITH?
HUMPH ...
...I'M NO RAT.
...
VERY WELL, NO MORE JUST TALKING, THEN...
...
...BUT I WILL GET YOU TO CONFESS SOON ENOUGH. MY WAY...

READ THIS WAY

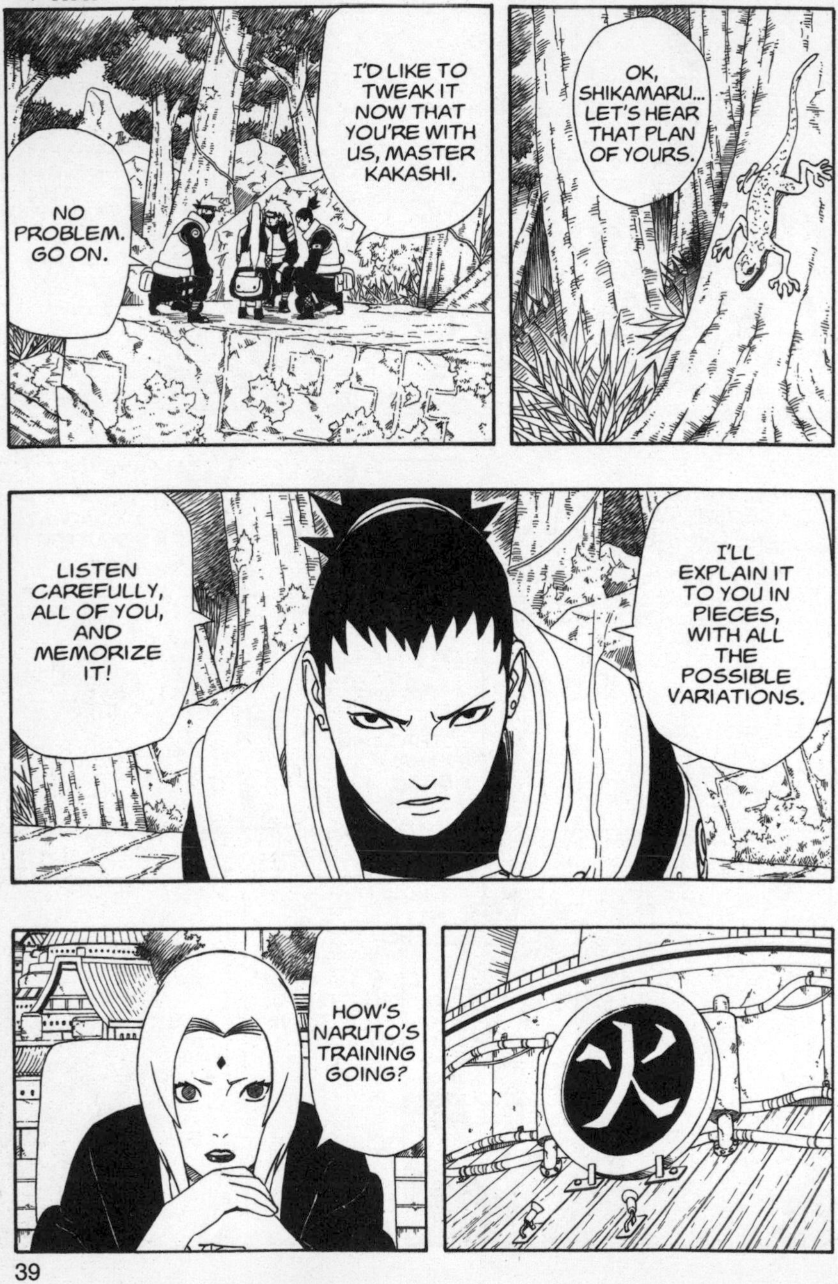
OK, SHIKAMARU... LET'S HEAR THAT PLAN OF YOURS.
I'D LIKE TO TWEAK IT NOW THAT YOU'RE WITH US, MASTER KAKASHI.
NO PROBLEM. GO ON.
I'LL EXPLAIN IT TO YOU IN PIECES, WITH ALL THE POSSIBLE VARIATIONS.
LISTEN CAREFULLY, ALL OF YOU, AND MEMORIZE IT!
HOW'S NARUTO'S TRAINING GOING?

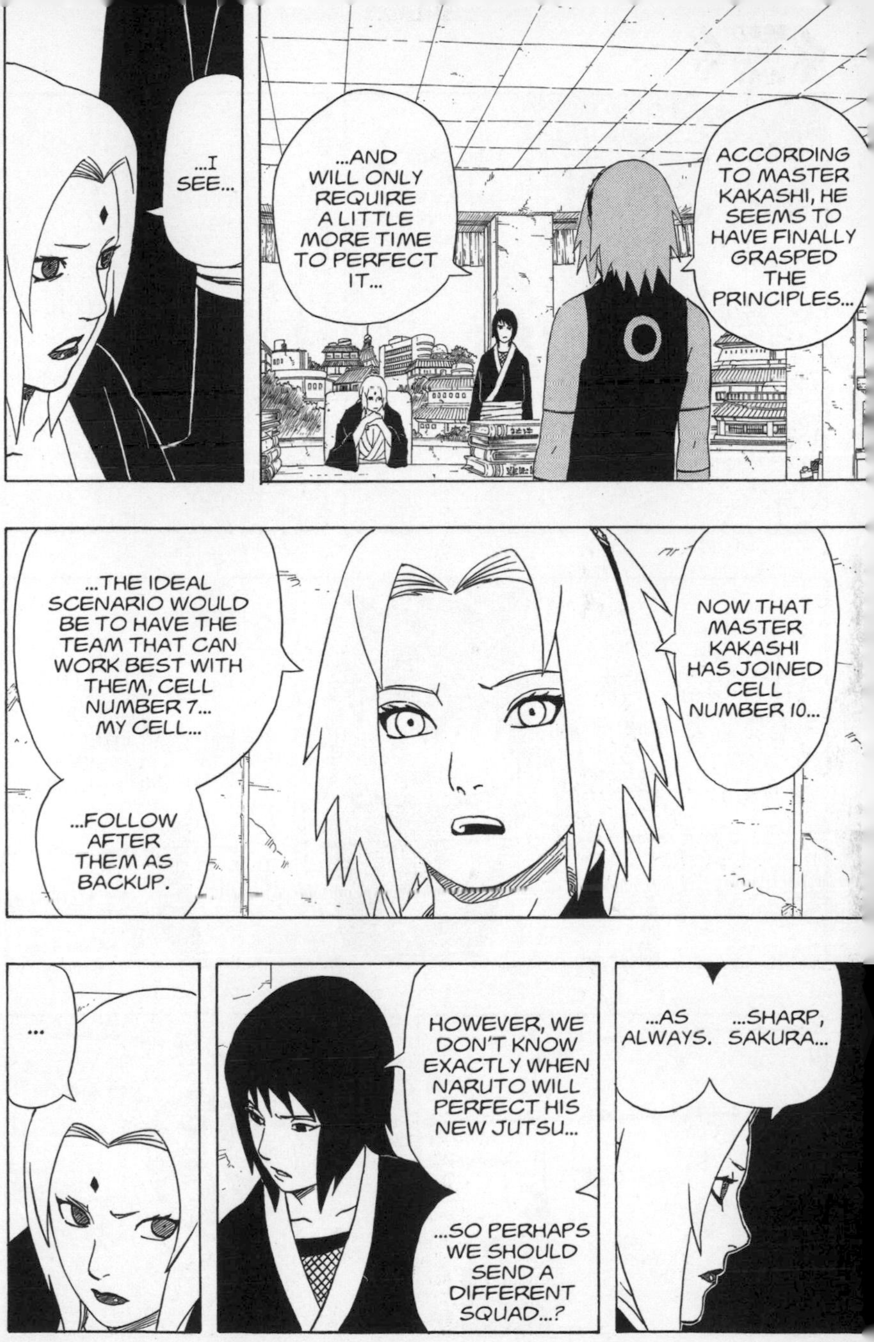
ACCORDING TO MASTER KAKASHI, HE SEEMS TO HAVE FINALLY GRASPED THE PRINCIPLES...
...AND WILL ONLY REQUIRE A LITTLE MORE TIME TO PERFECT IT...
...I SEE...
NOW THAT MASTER KAKASHI HAS JOINED CELL NUMBER 10...
...THE IDEAL SCENARIO WOULD BE TO HAVE THE TEAM THAT CAN WORK BEST WITH THEM, CELL NUMBER 7... MY CELL...
...FOLLOW AFTER THEM AS BACKUP.
...SHARP, SAKURA...
...AS ALWAYS.
HOWEVER, WE DON'T KNOW EXACTLY WHEN NARUTO WILL PERFECT HIS NEW JUTSU...
...SO PERHAPS WE SHOULD SEND A DIFFERENT SQUAD...?
...

READ THIS WAY

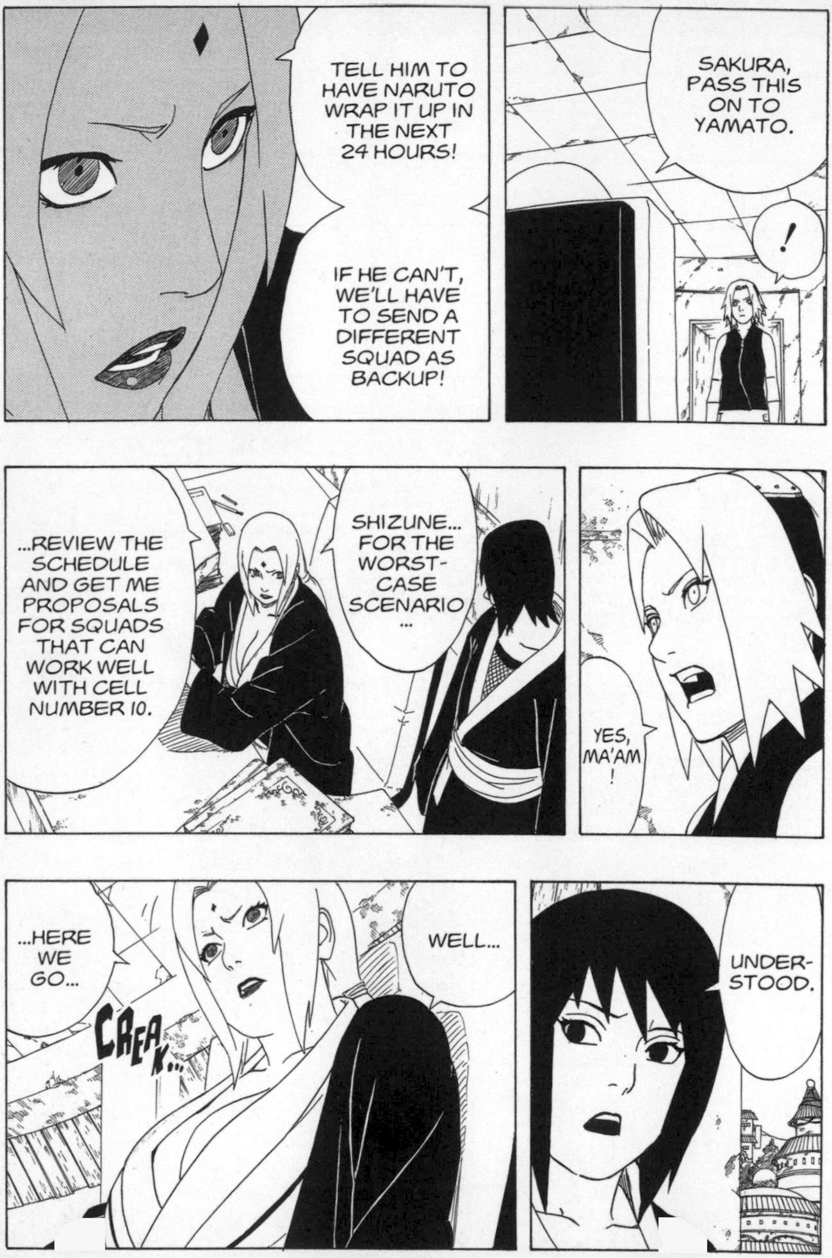
SAKURA, PASS THIS ON TO YAMATO.
!
TELL HIM TO HAVE NARUTO WRAP IT UP IN THE NEXT 24 HOURS!
IF HE CAN'T, WE'LL HAVE TO SEND A DIFFERENT SQUAD AS BACKUP!
YES, MA'AM!
SHIZUNE... FOR THE WORST-CASE SCENARIO...
...REVIEW THE SCHEDULE AND GET ME PROPOSALS FOR SQUADS THAT CAN WORK WELL WITH CELL NUMBER 10.
UNDER-STOOD.
WELL...
...HERE WE GO...
CREAK...

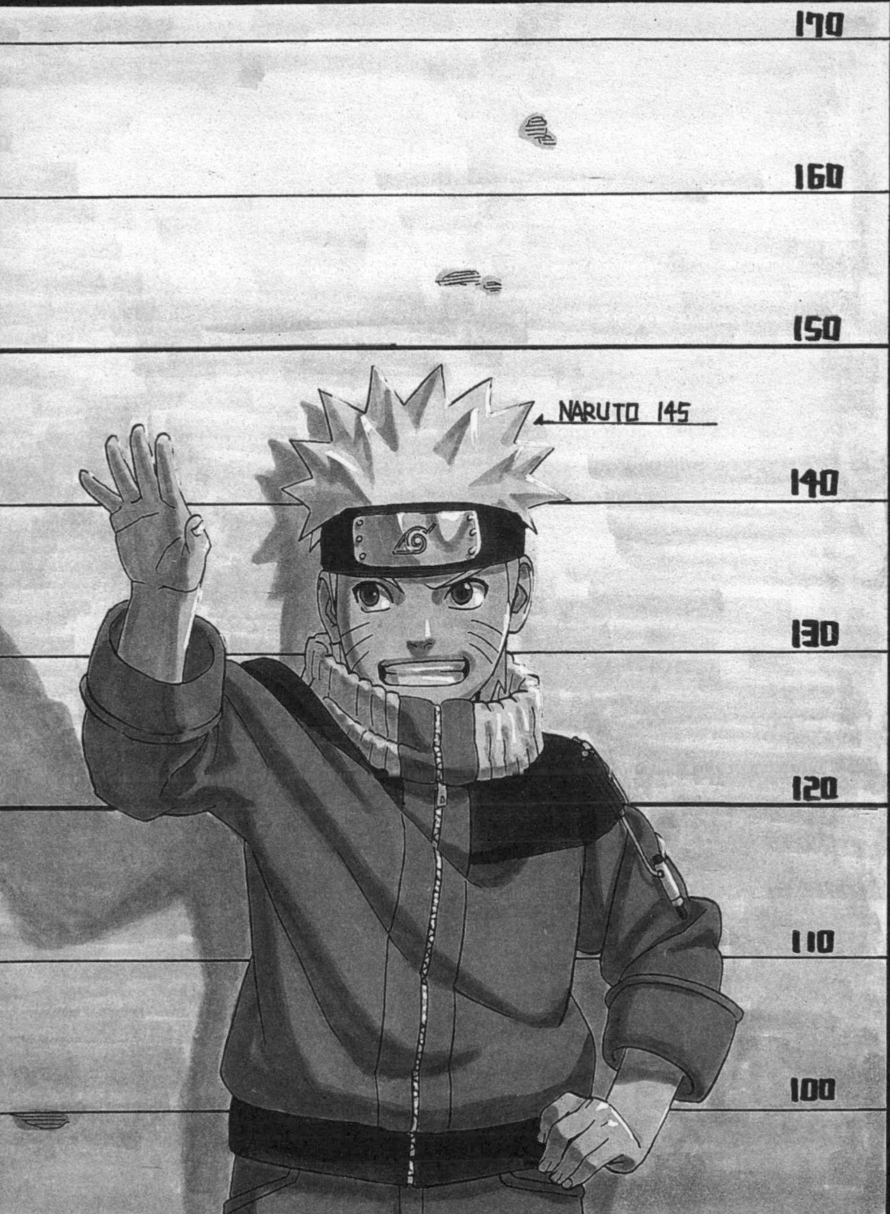
170
160
150
NARUTO 145
140
130
120
110
100

Number 332: Shikamaru's Battle!!

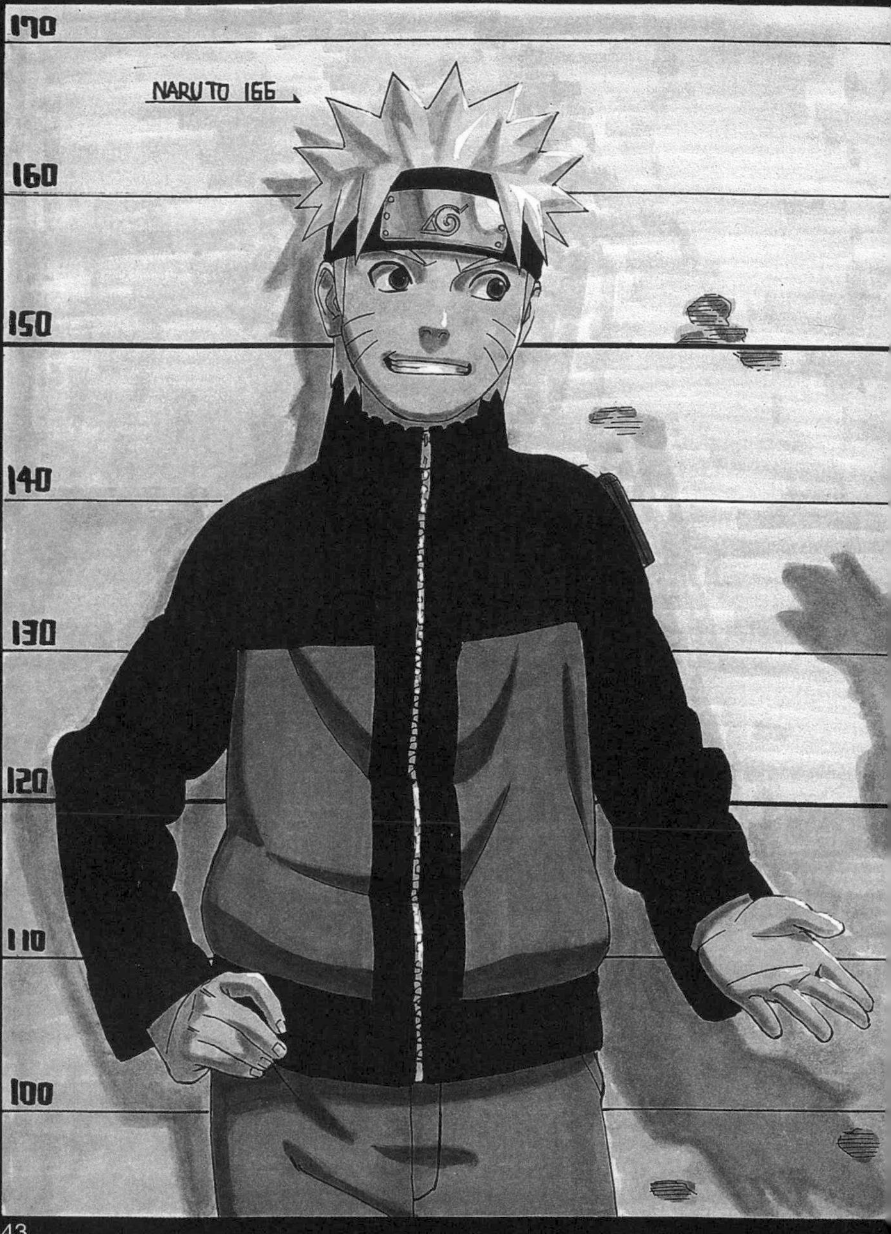
170
NARUTO 166
160
150
140
130
120
110
100

NARUTO

火

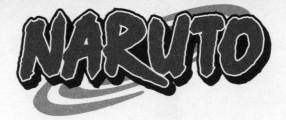

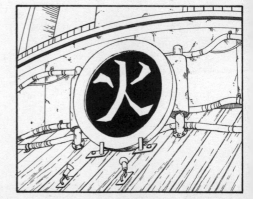

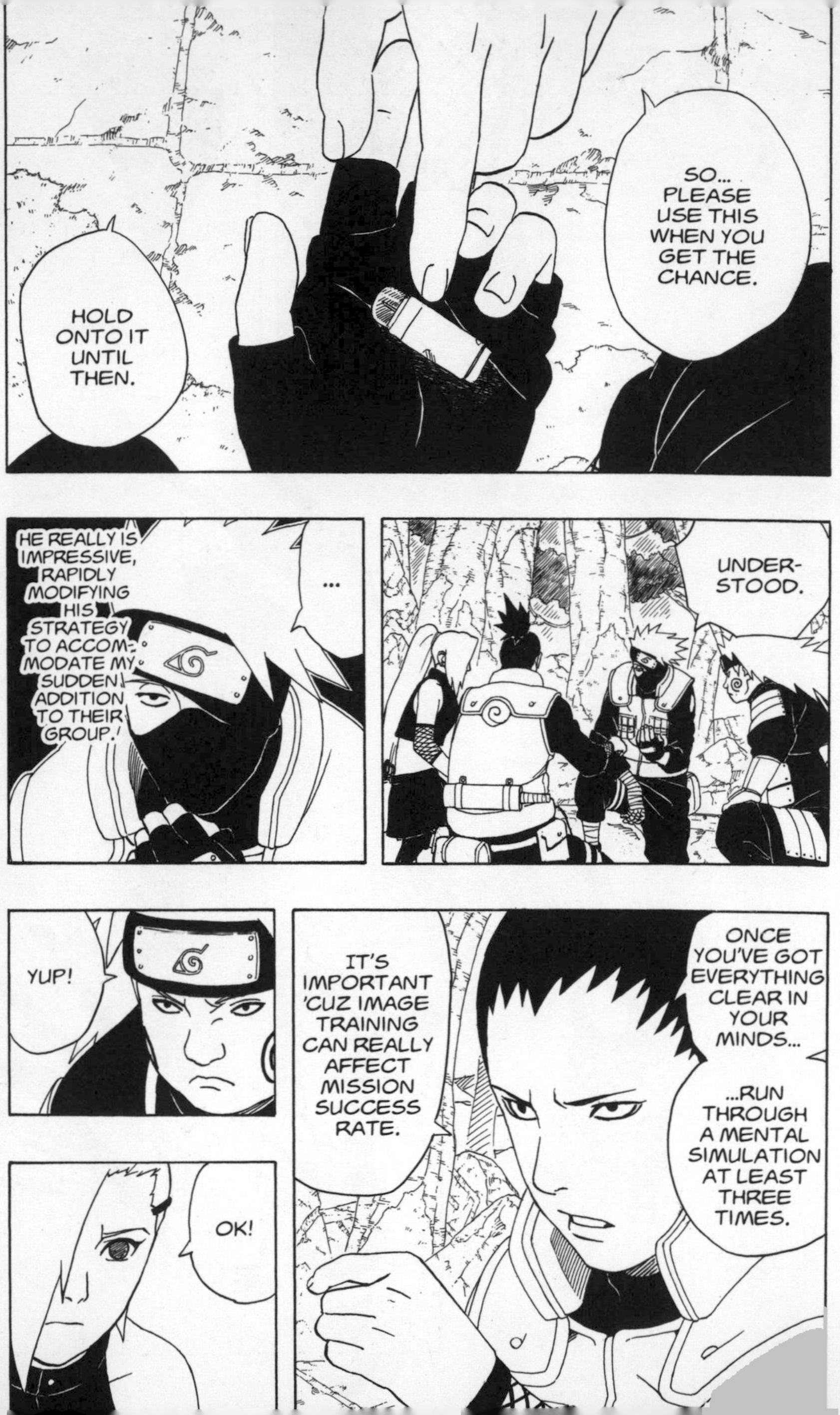
SO... PLEASE USE THIS WHEN YOU GET THE CHANCE.
HOLD ONTO IT UNTIL THEN.
UNDER-STOOD.
...
HE REALLY IS IMPRESSIVE, RAPIDLY MODIFYING HIS STRATEGY TO ACCOM-MODATE MY SUDDEN ADDITION TO THEIR GROUP.
ONCE YOU'VE GOT EVERYTHING CLEAR IN YOUR MINDS...
...RUN THROUGH A MENTAL SIMULATION AT LEAST THREE TIMES.
IT'S IMPORTANT 'CUZ IMAGE TRAINING CAN REALLY AFFECT MISSION SUCCESS RATE.
YUP!
OK!

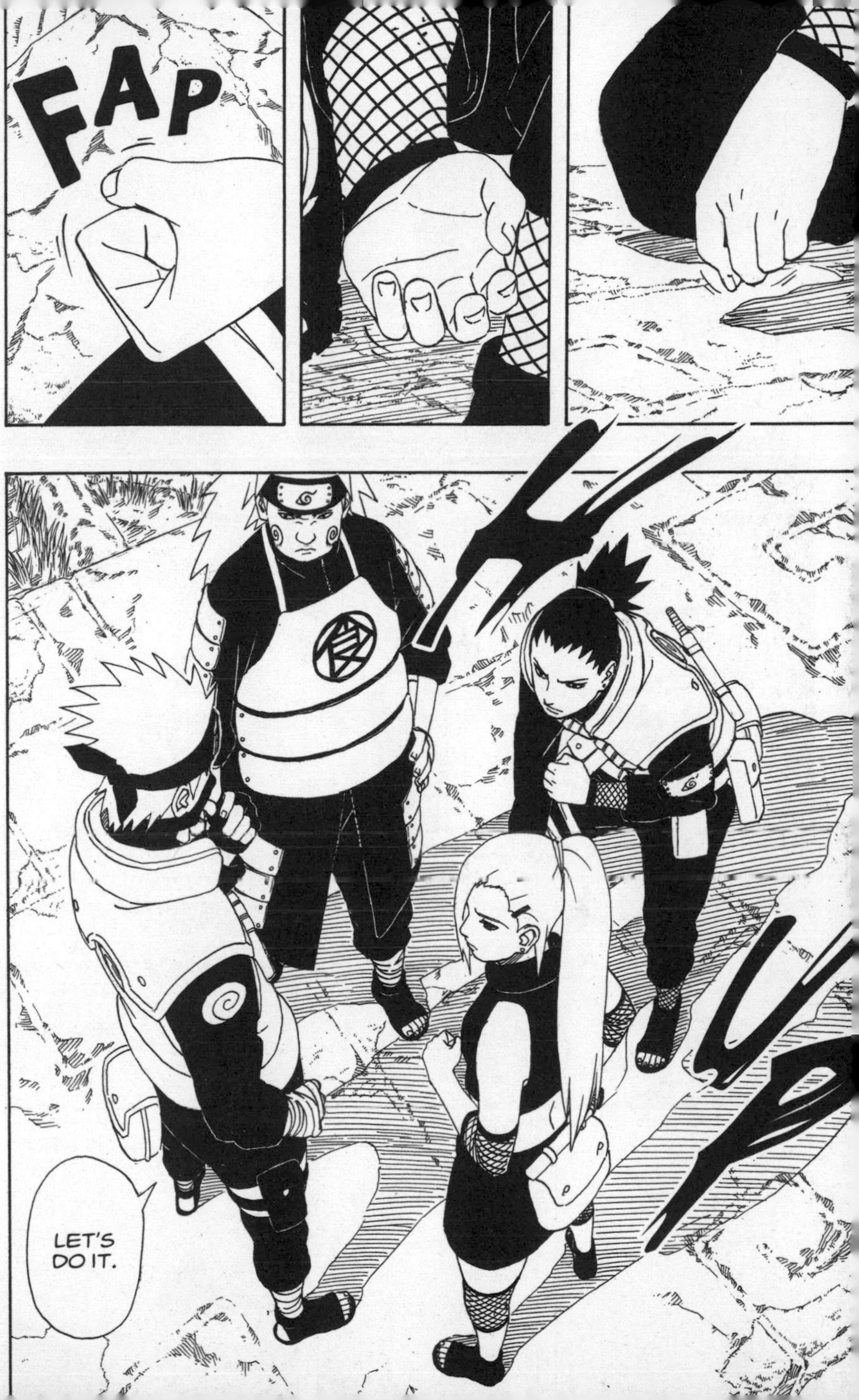
FAP
LET'S DO IT.

READ THIS WAY

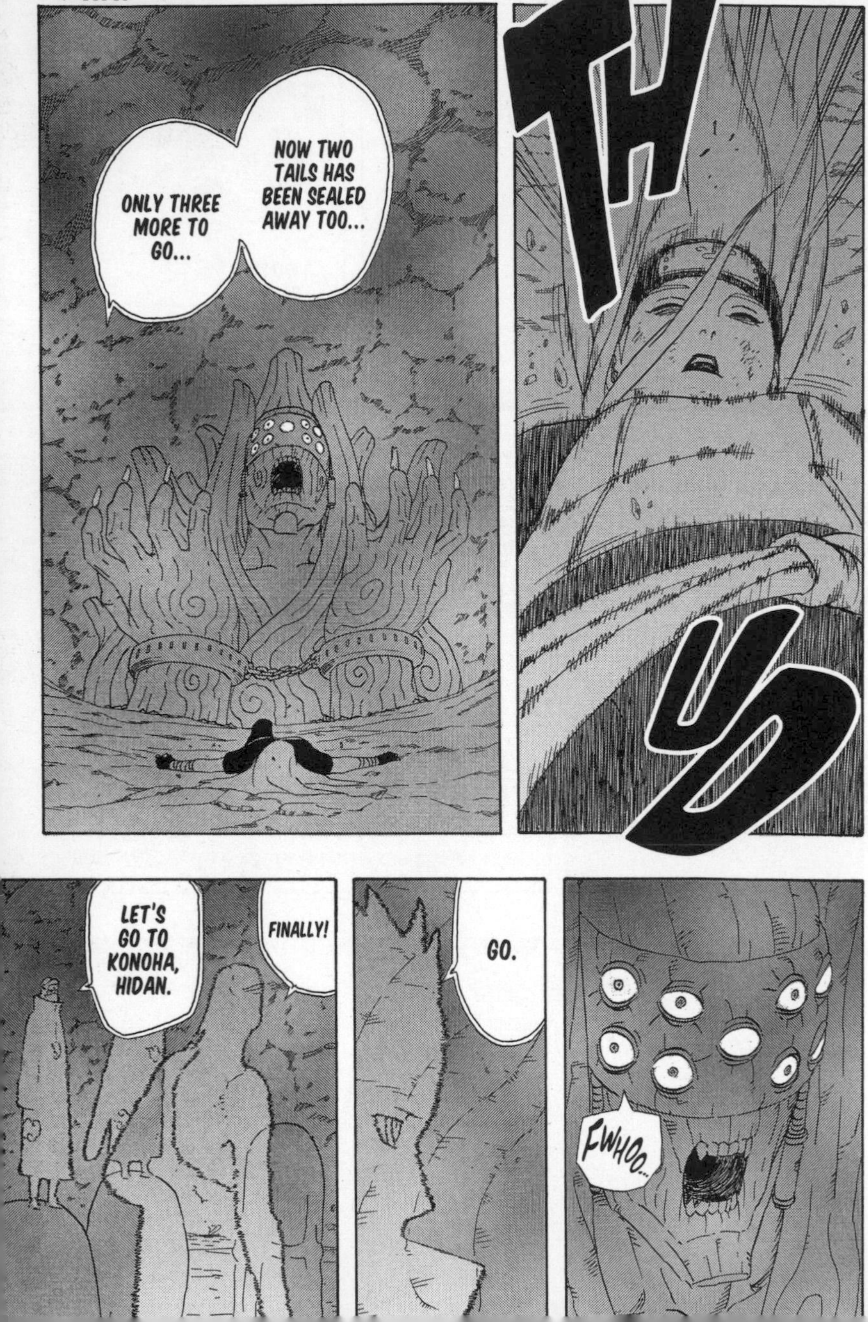
THUD
NOW TWO TAILS HAS BEEN SEALED AWAY TOO...
ONLY THREE MORE TO GO...
FWHOO...
GO.
FINALLY!
LET'S GO TO KONOHA, HIDAN.

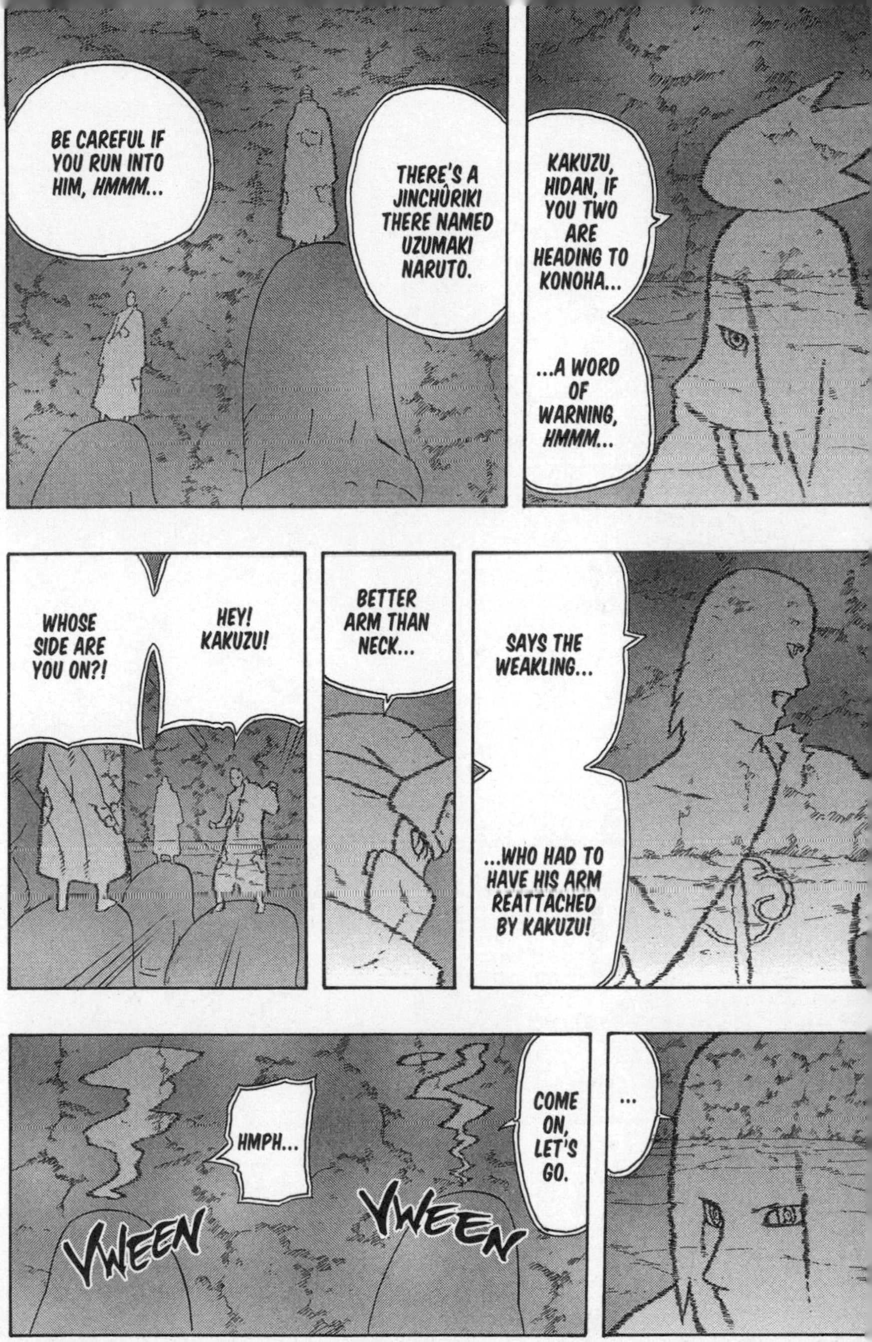
KAKUZU, HIDAN, IF YOU TWO ARE HEADING TO KONOHA...
...A WORD OF WARNING, HMMM...
THERE'S A JINCHÛRIKI THERE NAMED UZUMAKI NARUTO.
BE CAREFUL IF YOU RUN INTO HIM, *HMMM*...
SAYS THE WEAKLING...
...WHO HAD TO HAVE HIS ARM REATTACHED BY KAKUZU!
BETTER ARM THAN NECK...
HEY! KAKUZU!
WHOSE SIDE ARE YOU ON?!
...
COME ON, LET'S GO.
VWEEN
HMPH...
VWEEN

READ THIS WAY

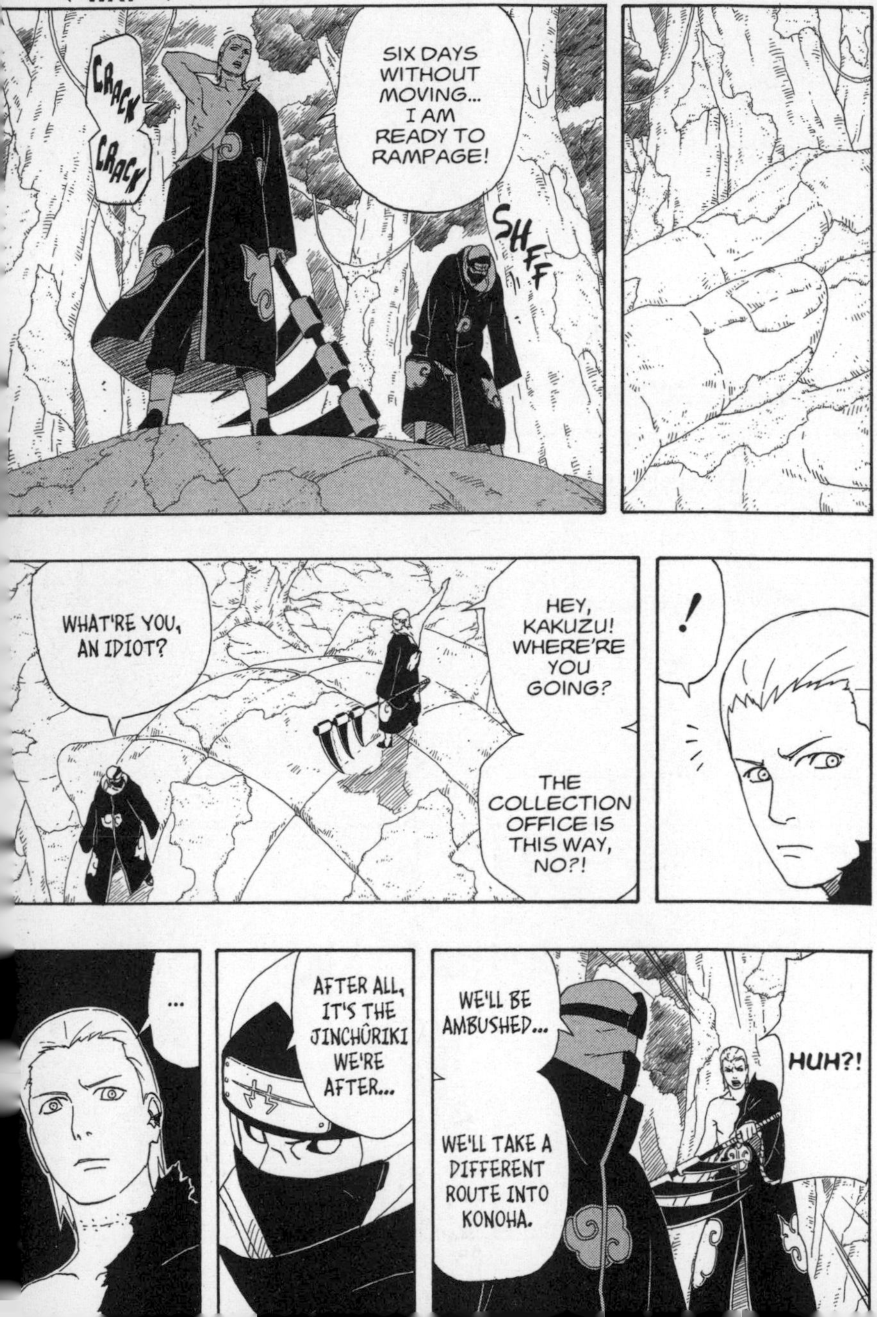
SIX DAYS WITHOUT MOVING... I AM READY TO RAMPAGE!
CRACK
CRACK
SHFF
!
HEY, KAKUZU! WHERE'RE YOU GOING?
THE COLLECTION OFFICE IS THIS WAY, NO?!
WHAT'RE YOU, AN IDIOT?
HUH?!
WE'LL BE AMBUSHED...
WE'LL TAKE A DIFFERENT ROUTE INTO KONOHA.
AFTER ALL, IT'S THE JINCHÛRIKI WE'RE AFTER...
...

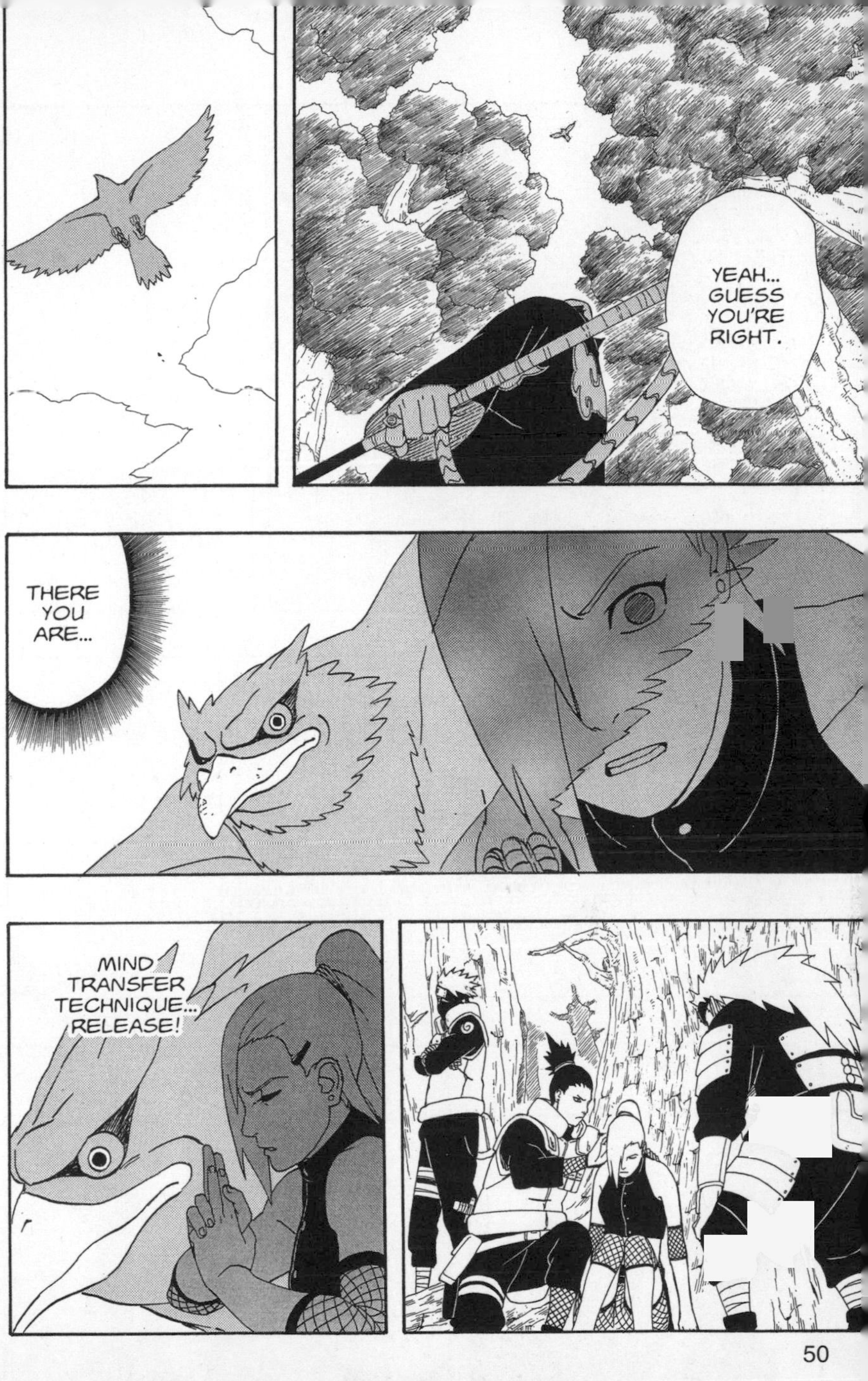
YEAH... GUESS YOU'RE RIGHT.
THERE YOU ARE...
MIND TRANSFER TECHNIQUE... RELEASE!

READ THIS WAY

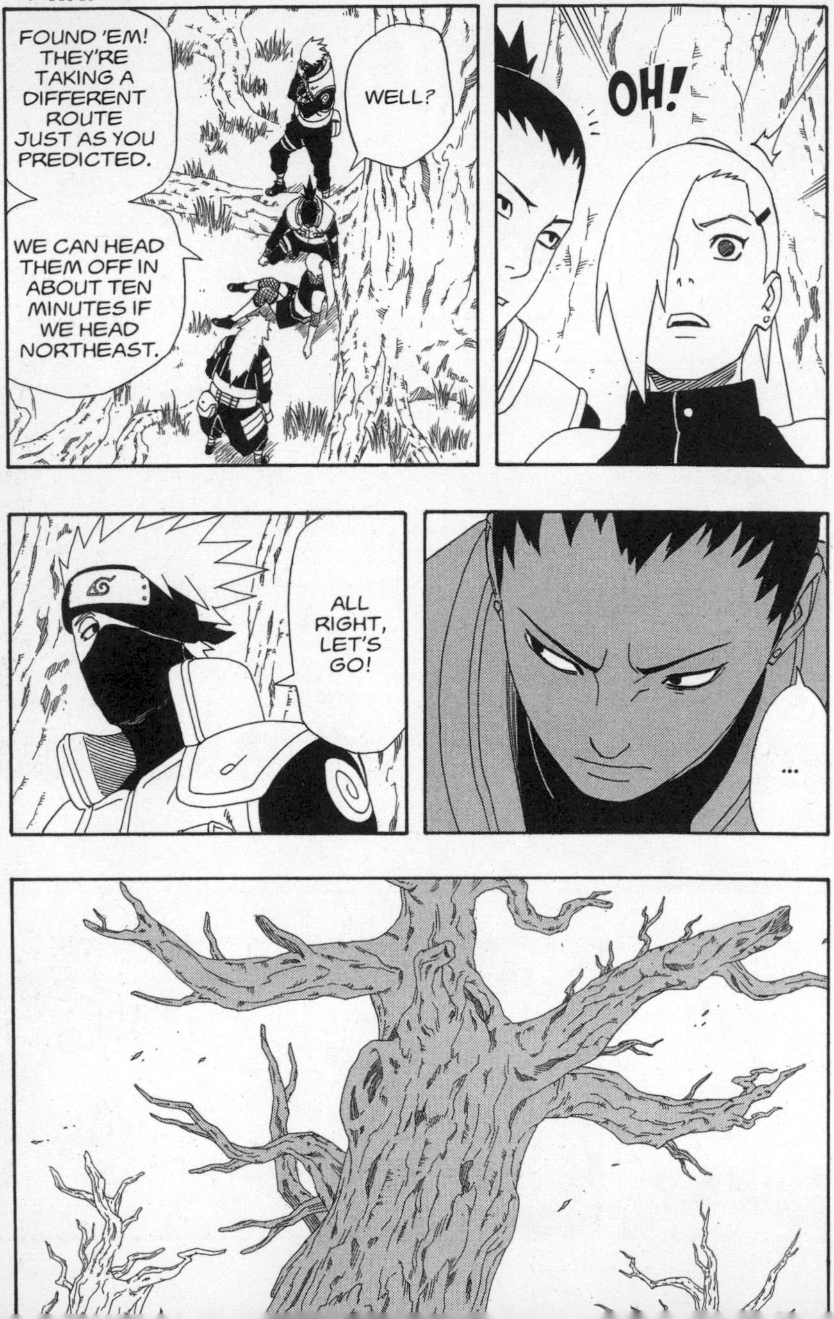
OH!
WELL?
FOUND 'EM! THEY'RE TAKING A DIFFERENT ROUTE JUST AS YOU PREDICTED.
WE CAN HEAD THEM OFF IN ABOUT TEN MINUTES IF WE HEAD NORTHEAST.
...
ALL RIGHT, LET'S GO!

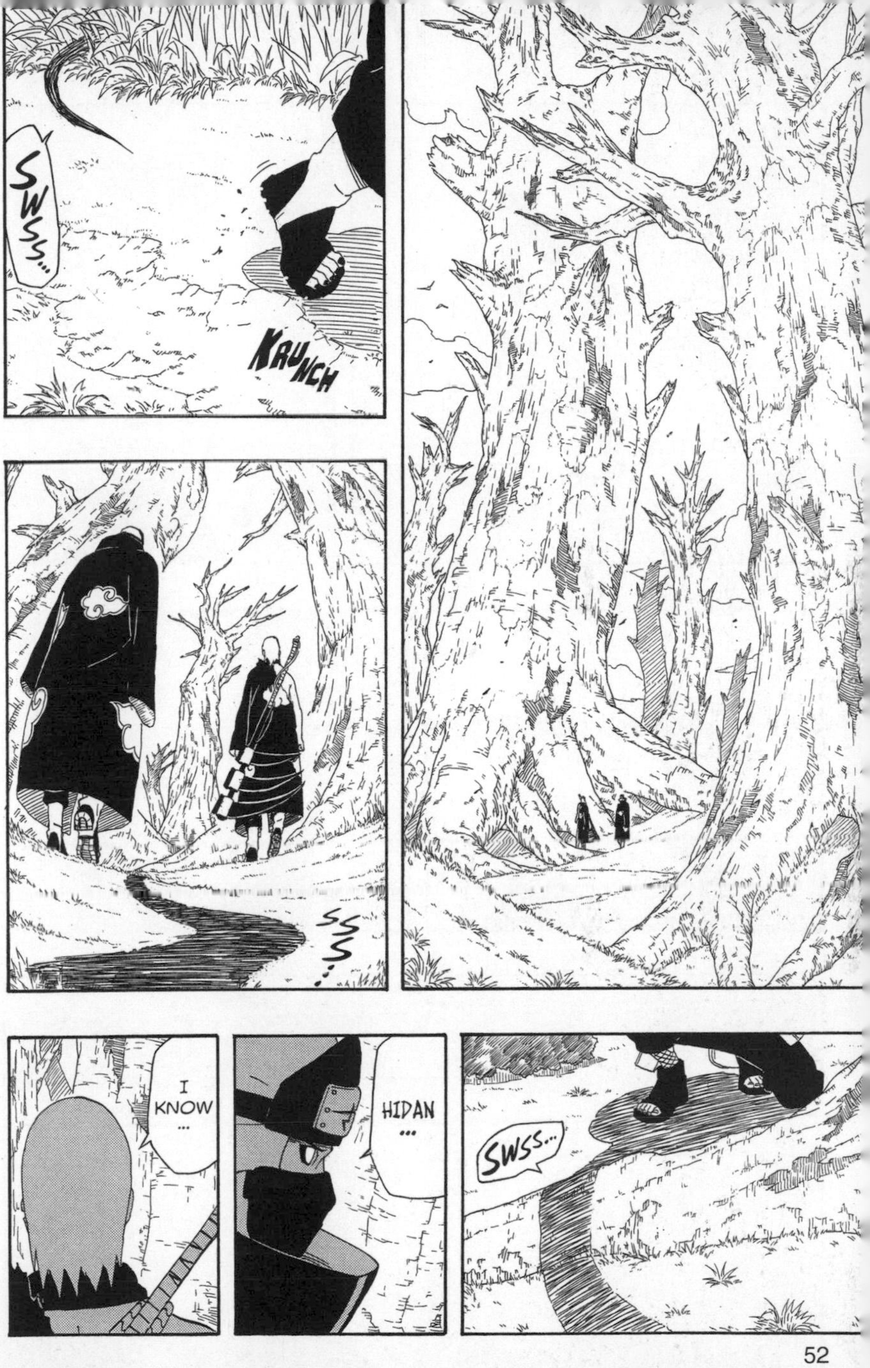
SWSS...
KRUNCH
SSS...
SWSS...
HIDAN ...
I KNOW ...

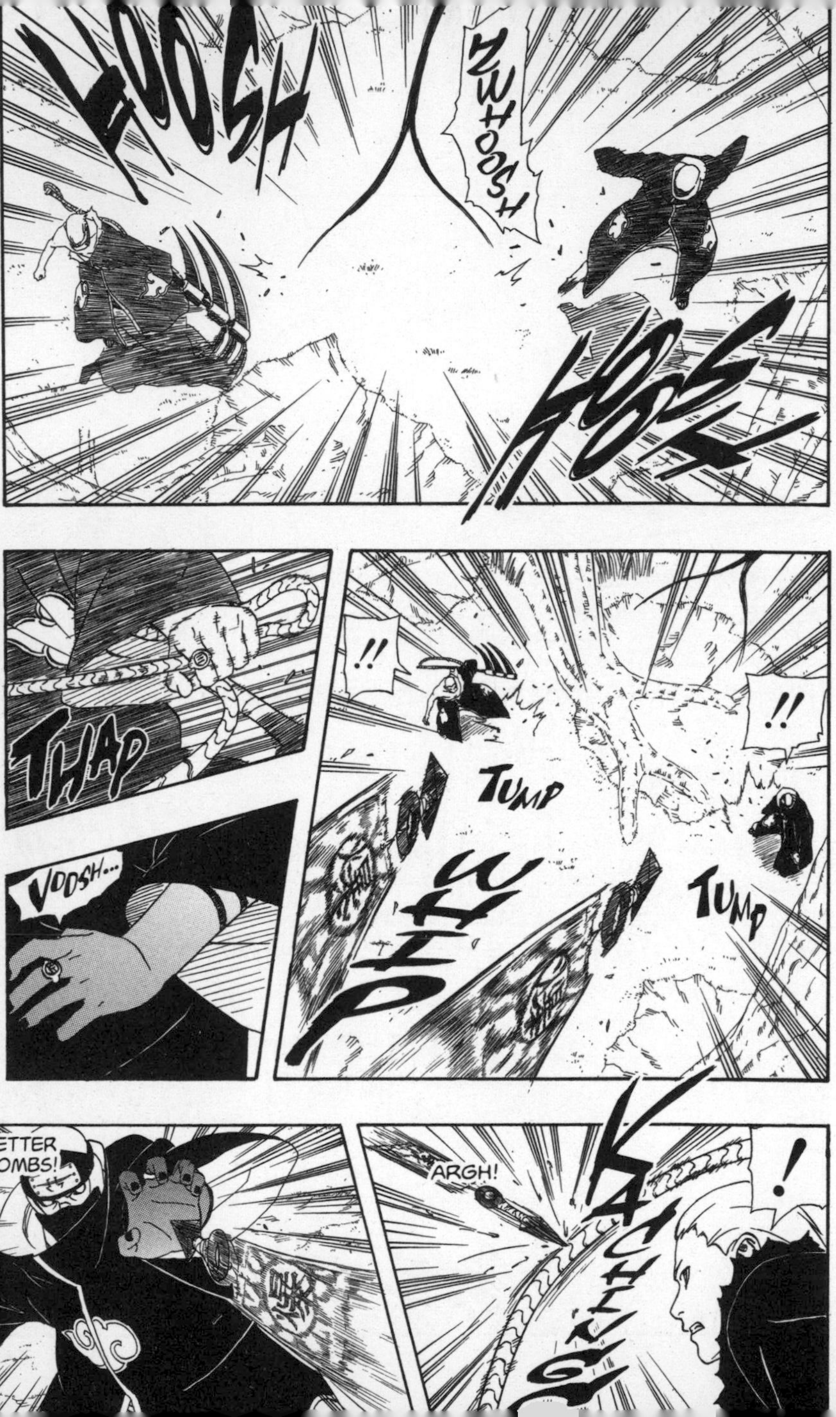
ZWHOOSH
HOOSH
HOOSH
!!
!!
TUMP
TUMP
WHIP
THAP
VOOSH...
!
KACHING
ARGH!
LETTER BOMBS!

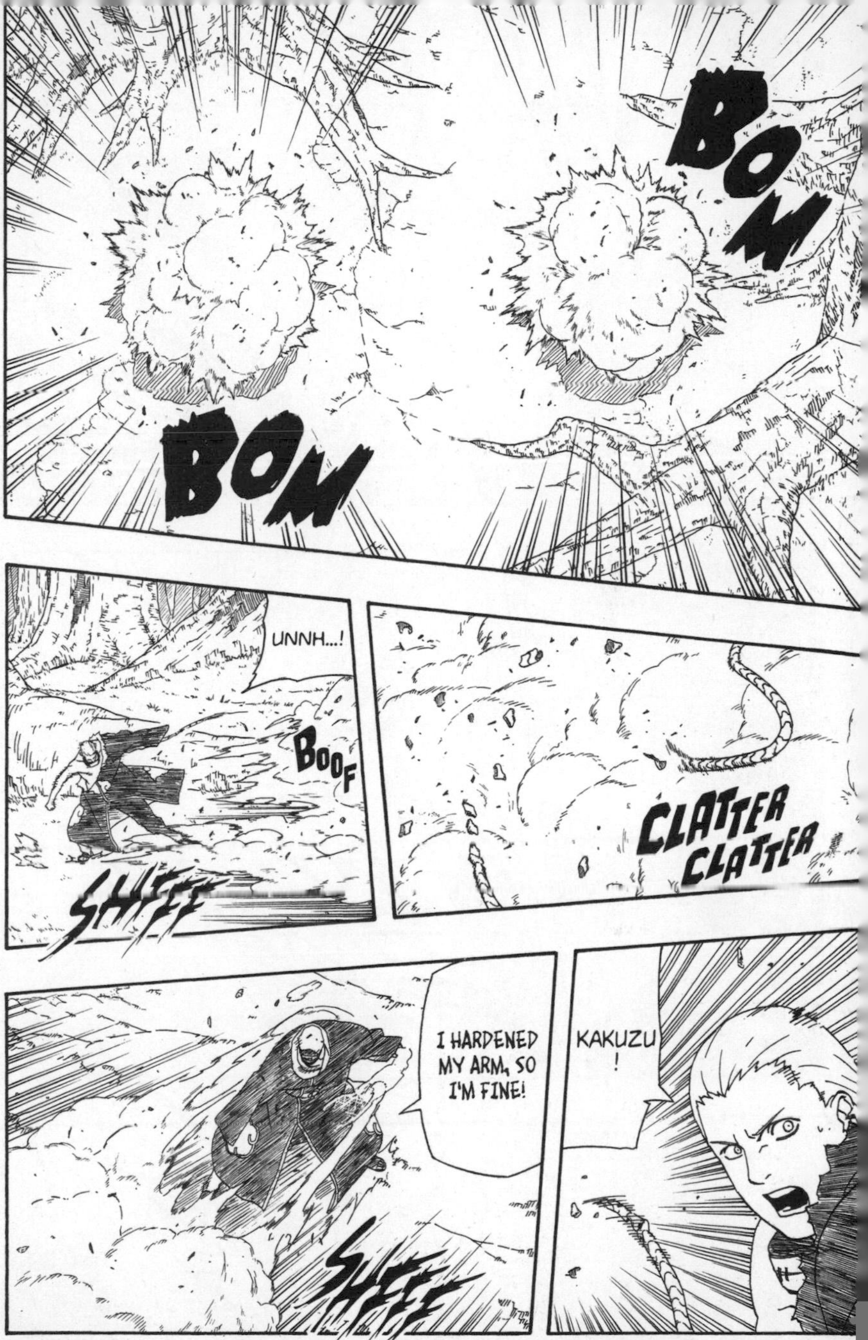
BOM
BOM
CLATTER CLATTER
UNNH...!
BOOF
SHFF
KAKUZU!
I HARDENED MY ARM, SO I'M FINE!
SHFF

READ THIS WAY

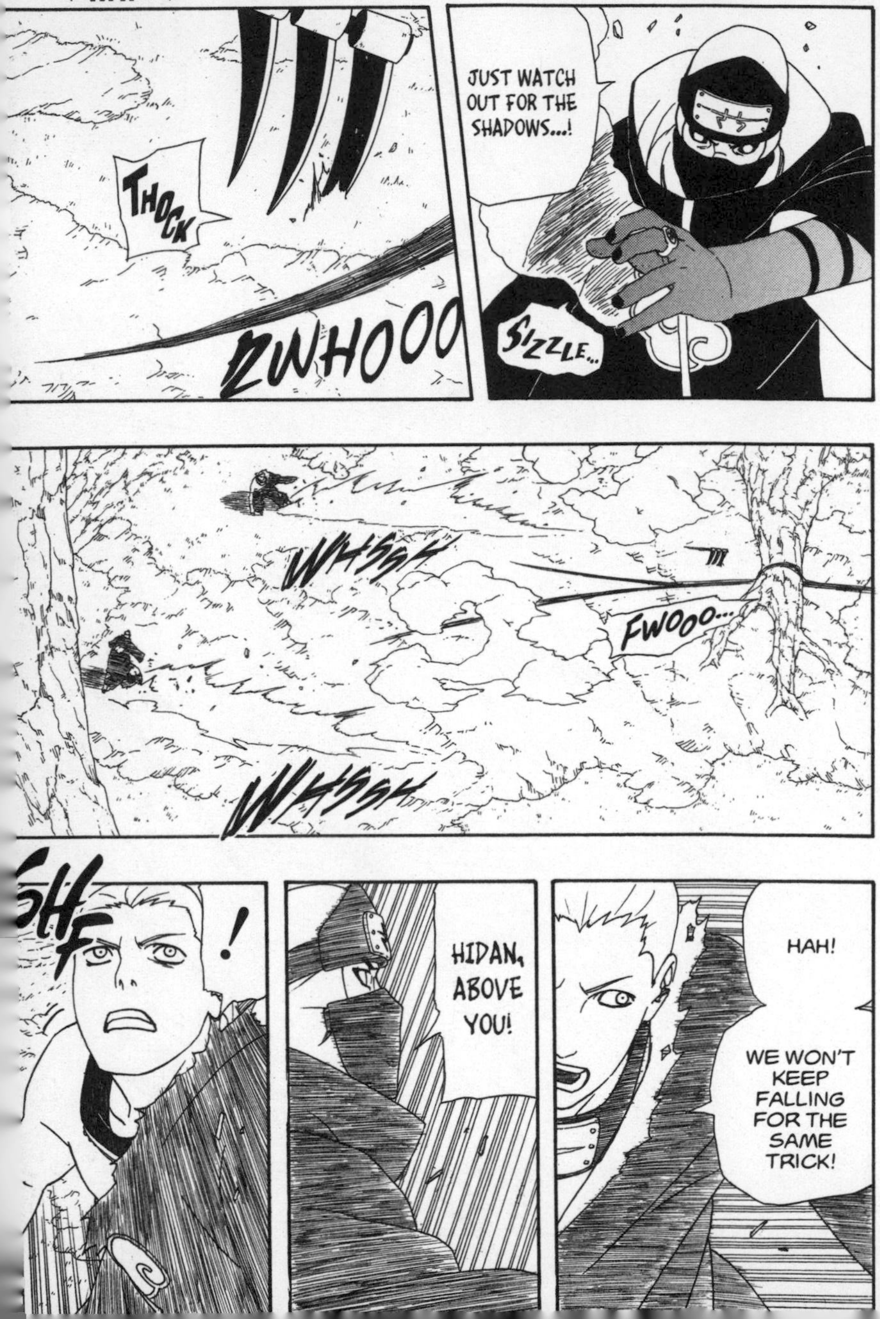
JUST WATCH OUT FOR THE SHADOWS...!
SIZZLE...
THOCK
ZWHOOO
WHSSH
FWOOO...
WHSSH
HAH!
WE WON'T KEEP FALLING FOR THE SAME TRICK!
HIDAN, ABOVE YOU!
SHF
!

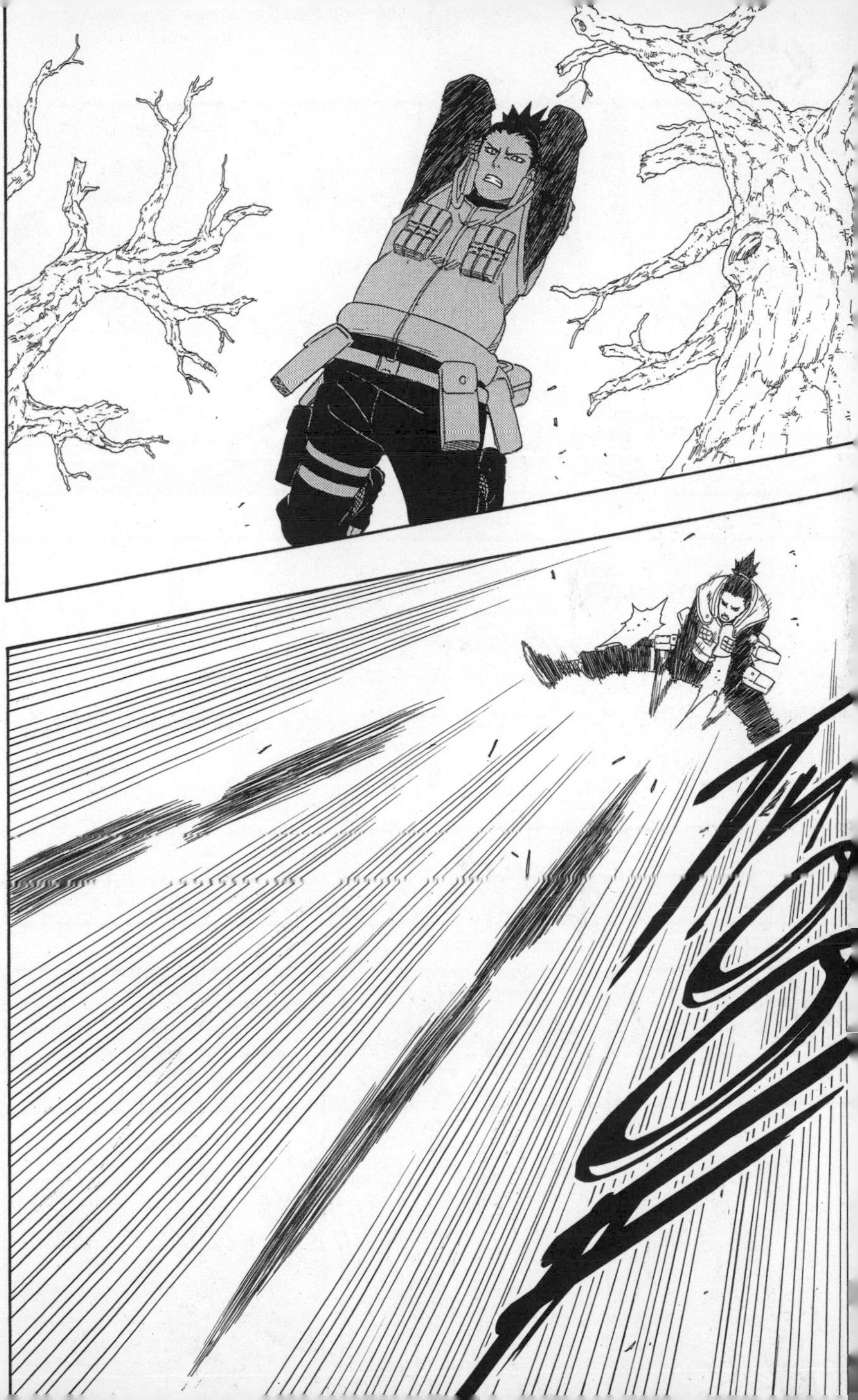

READ THIS WAY

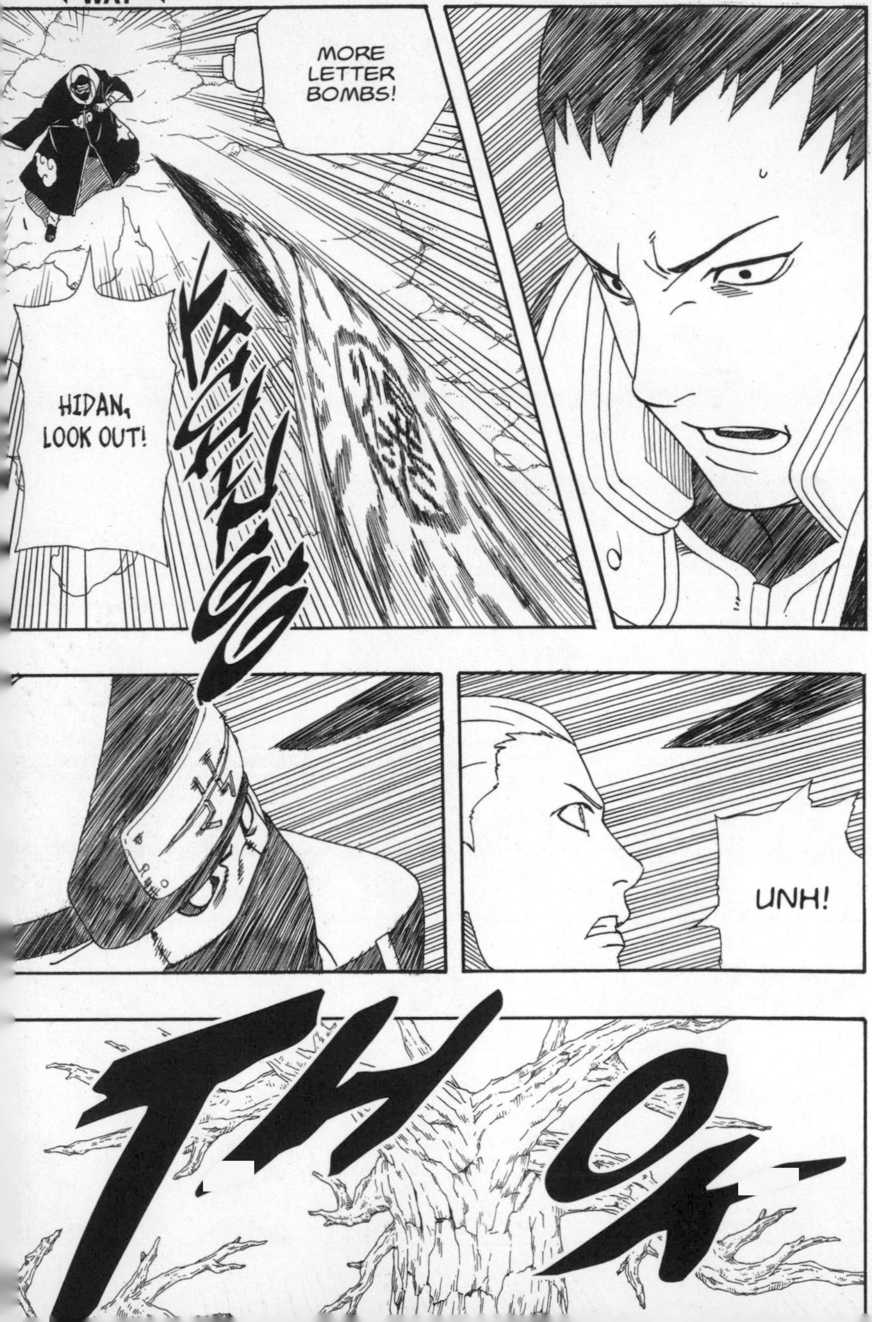
MORE LETTER BOMBS!
HIDAN, LOOK OUT!
UNH!

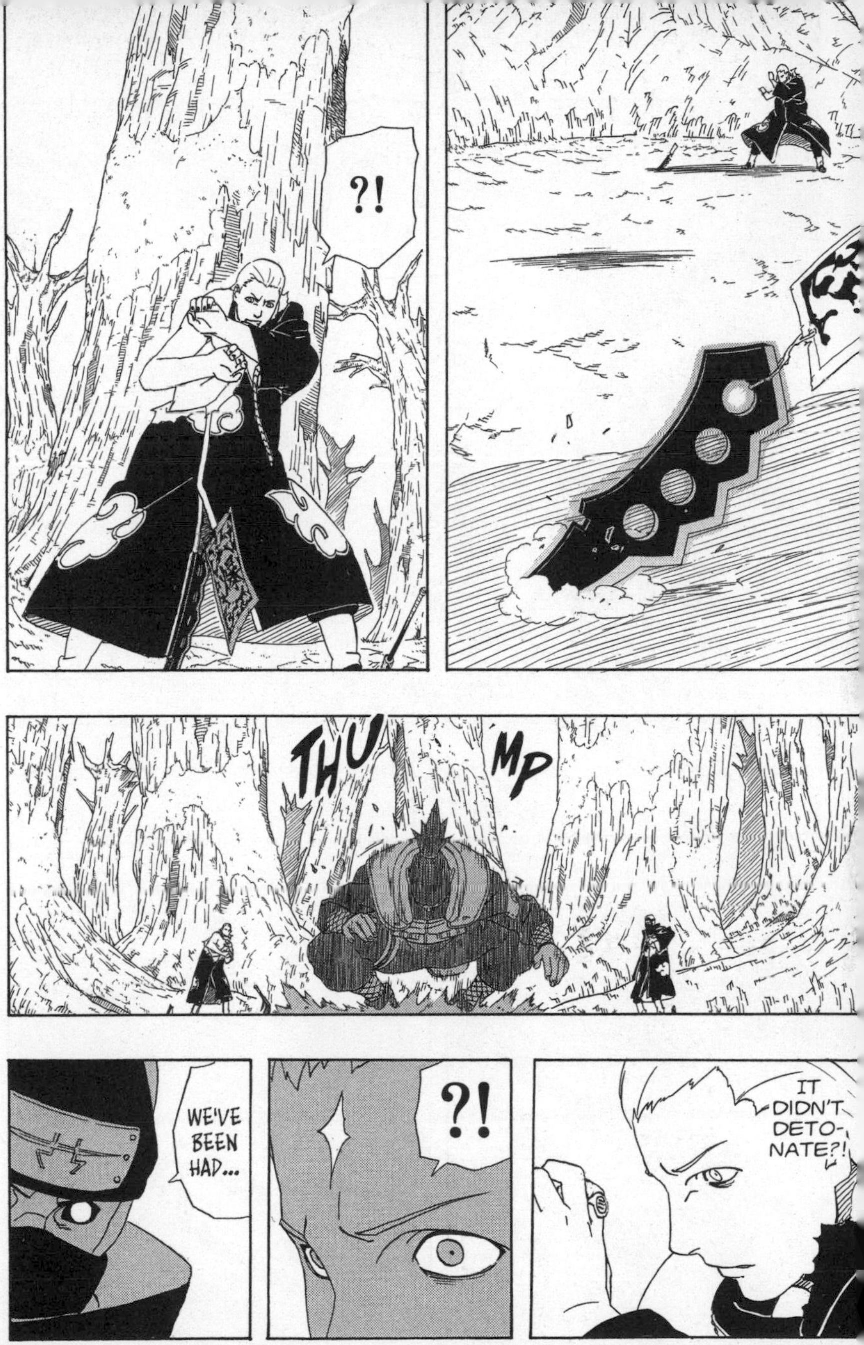
?!
THUMP
IT DIDN'T DETO-NATE?!
?!
WE'VE BEEN HAD...

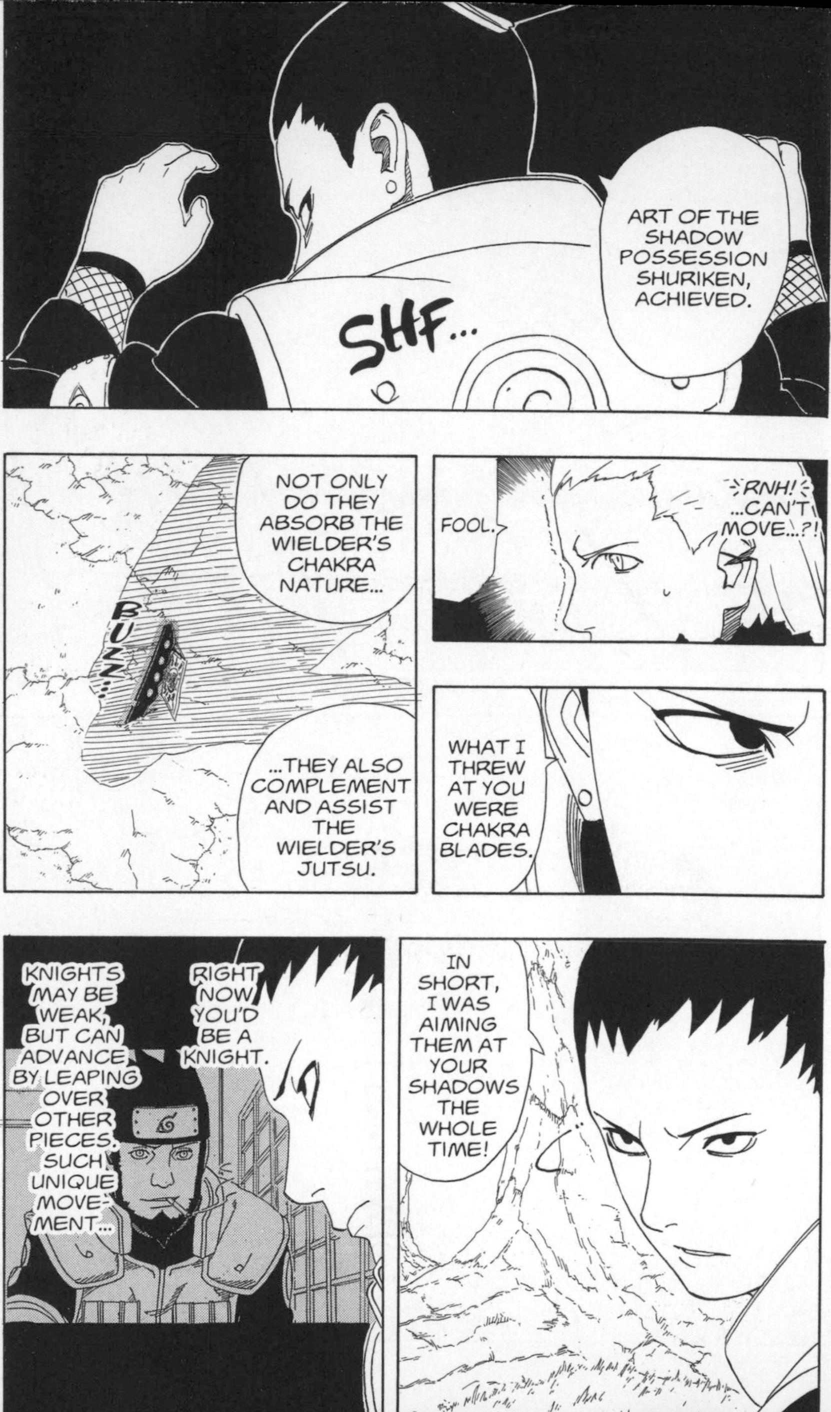
ART OF THE SHADOW POSSESSION SHURIKEN, ACHIEVED.
SHF...
RNH! ...CAN'T MOVE...?!
FOOL.
WHAT I THREW AT YOU WERE CHAKRA BLADES.
NOT ONLY DO THEY ABSORB THE WIELDER'S CHAKRA NATURE...
BUZZ...
...THEY ALSO COMPLEMENT AND ASSIST THE WIELDER'S JUTSU.
IN SHORT, I WAS AIMING THEM AT YOUR SHADOWS THE WHOLE TIME!
RIGHT NOW YOU'D BE A KNIGHT.
KNIGHTS MAY BE WEAK, BUT CAN ADVANCE BY LEAPING OVER OTHER PIECES. SUCH UNIQUE MOVEMENT...

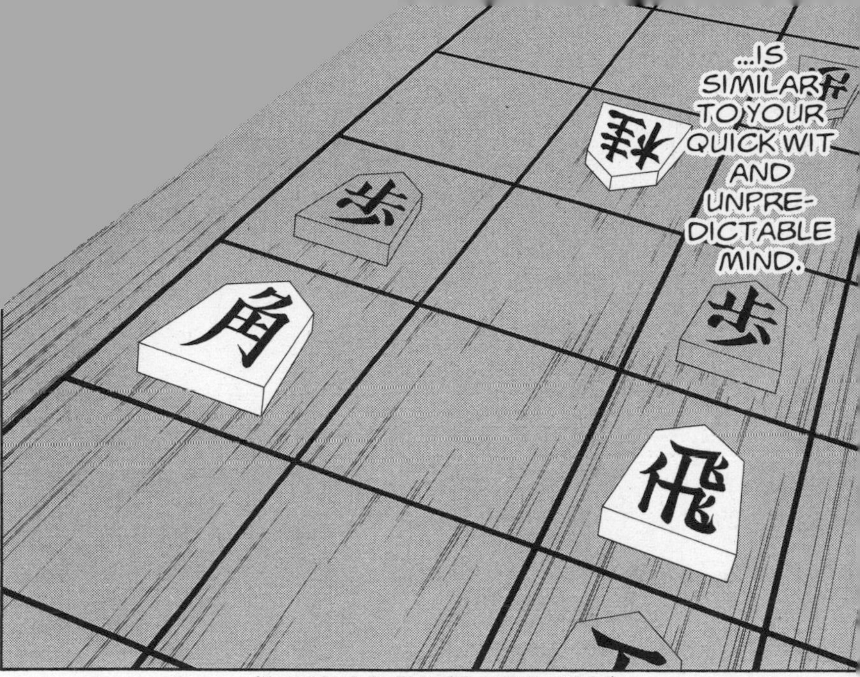
...IS SIMILAR TO YOUR QUICK WIT AND UNPRE-DICTABLE MIND.

(桂: KNIGHT, 角: BISHOP, AND 飛: ROOK)

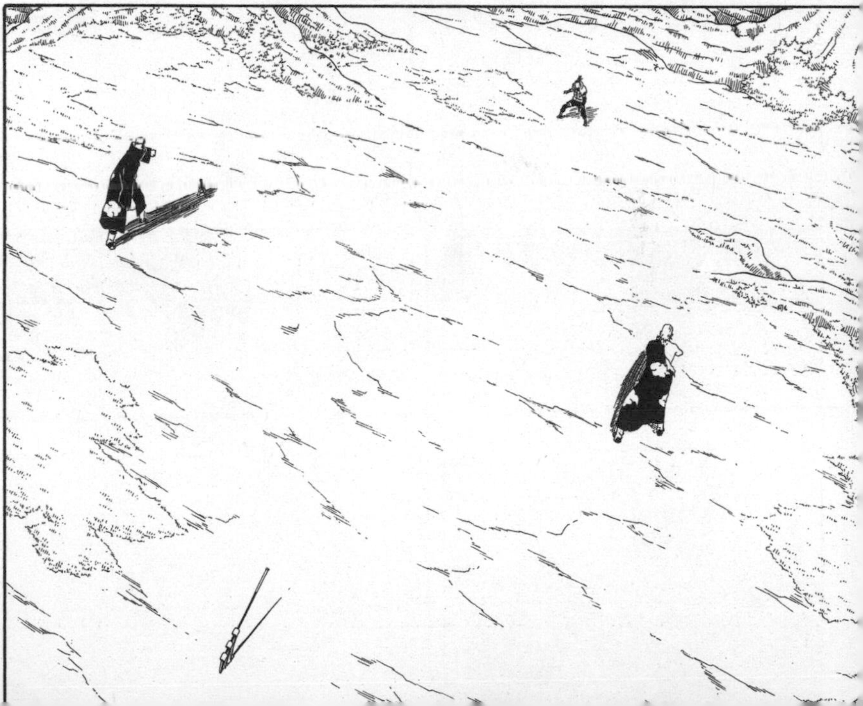

READ THIS WAY

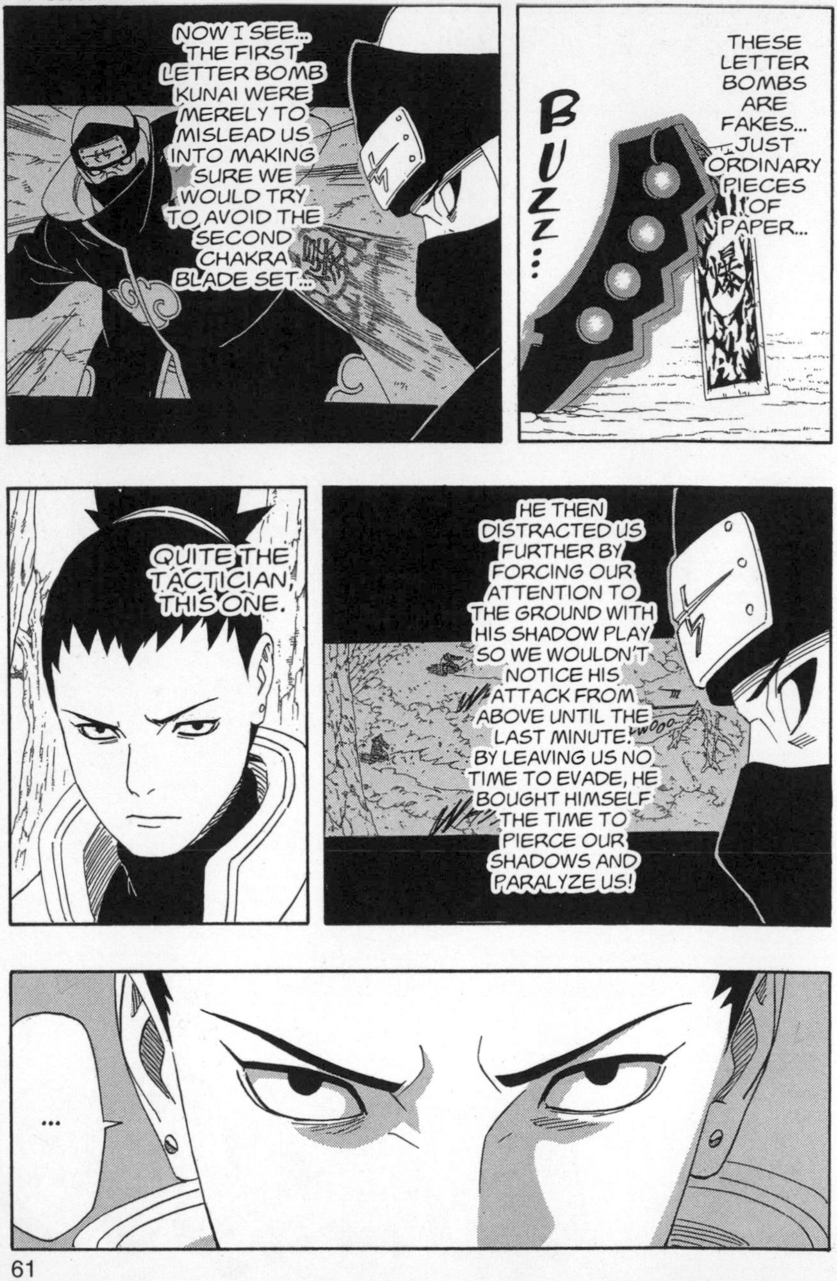
THESE LETTER BOMBS ARE FAKES... JUST ORDINARY PIECES OF PAPER...
BUZZ...
NOW I SEE... THE FIRST LETTER BOMB KUNAI WERE MERELY TO MISLEAD US INTO MAKING SURE WE WOULD TRY TO AVOID THE SECOND CHAKRA BLADE SET...
HE THEN DISTRACTED US FURTHER BY FORCING OUR ATTENTION TO THE GROUND WITH HIS SHADOW PLAY SO WE WOULDN'T NOTICE HIS ATTACK FROM ABOVE UNTIL THE LAST MINUTE.
BY LEAVING US NO TIME TO EVADE, HE BOUGHT HIMSELF THE TIME TO PIERCE OUR SHADOWS AND PARALYZE US!
QUITE THE TACTICIAN, THIS ONE.
...

NARUTO

Number 333: Affinities...!!

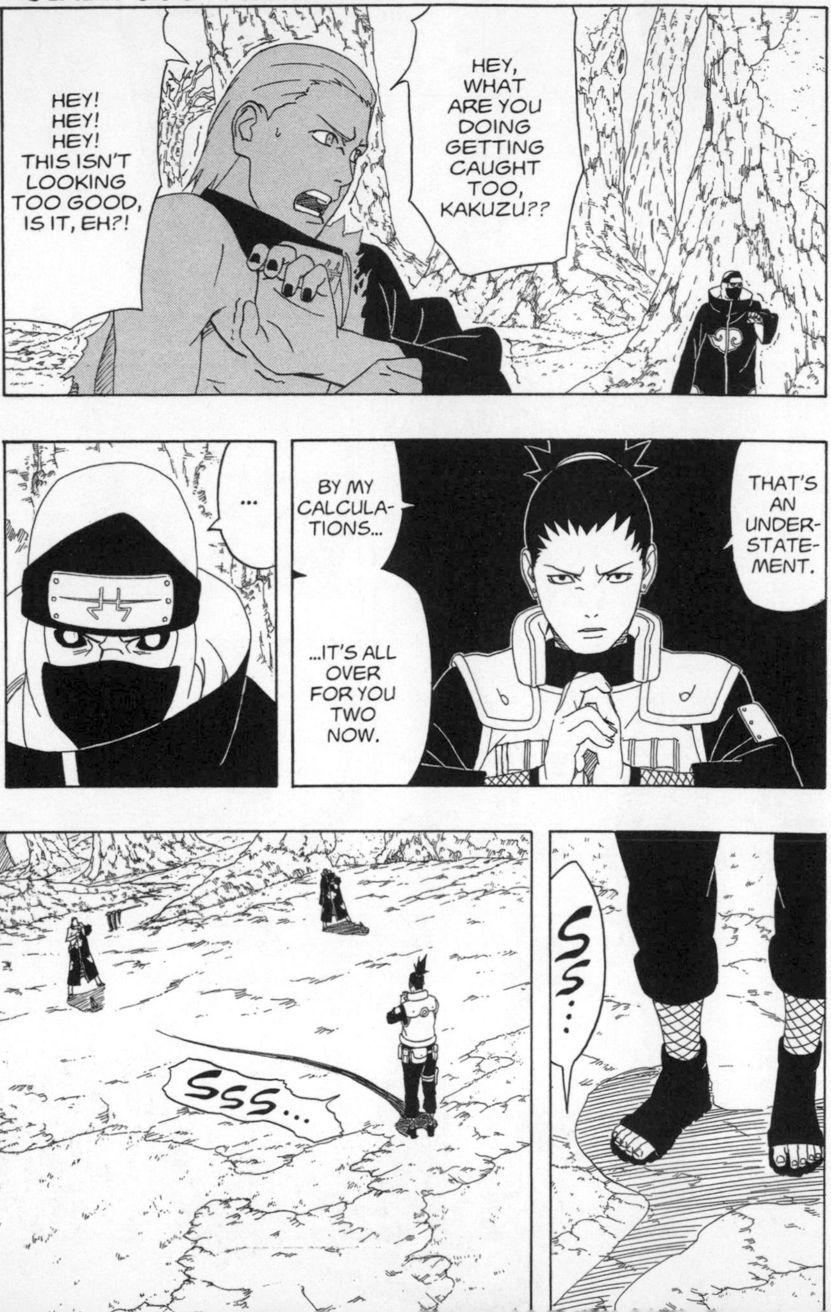
HEY, WHAT ARE YOU DOING GETTING CAUGHT TOO, KAKUZU??
HEY! HEY! HEY! THIS ISN'T LOOKING TOO GOOD, IS IT, EH?!
THAT'S AN UNDER-STATE-MENT.
BY MY CALCULA-TIONS...
...IT'S ALL OVER FOR YOU TWO NOW.
...
SS...
SSS...

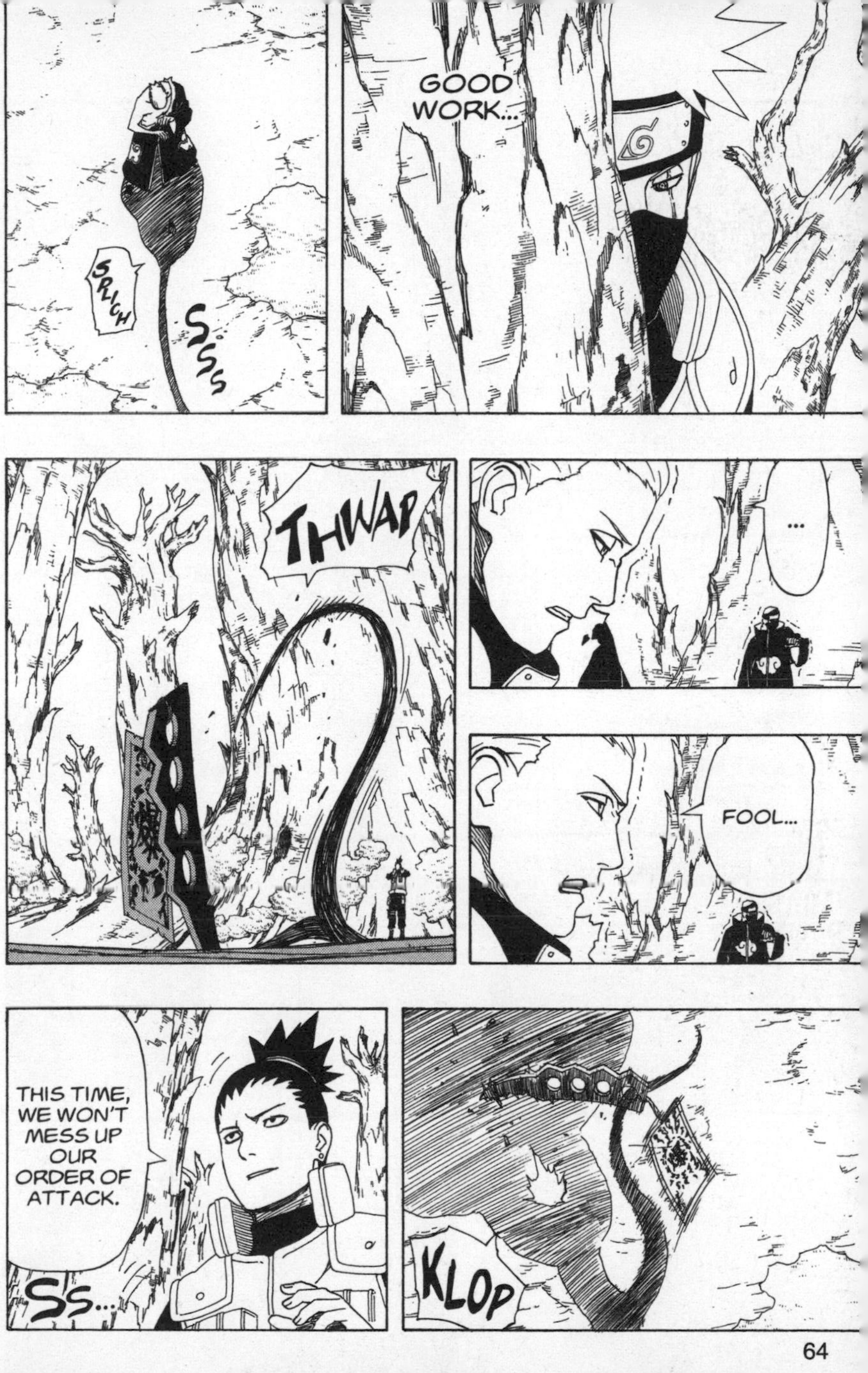
GOOD WORK...
SPLICH
SSSS
...
FOOL...
THWAP
KLOP
THIS TIME, WE WON'T MESS UP OUR ORDER OF ATTACK.
S'S...

READ THIS WAY

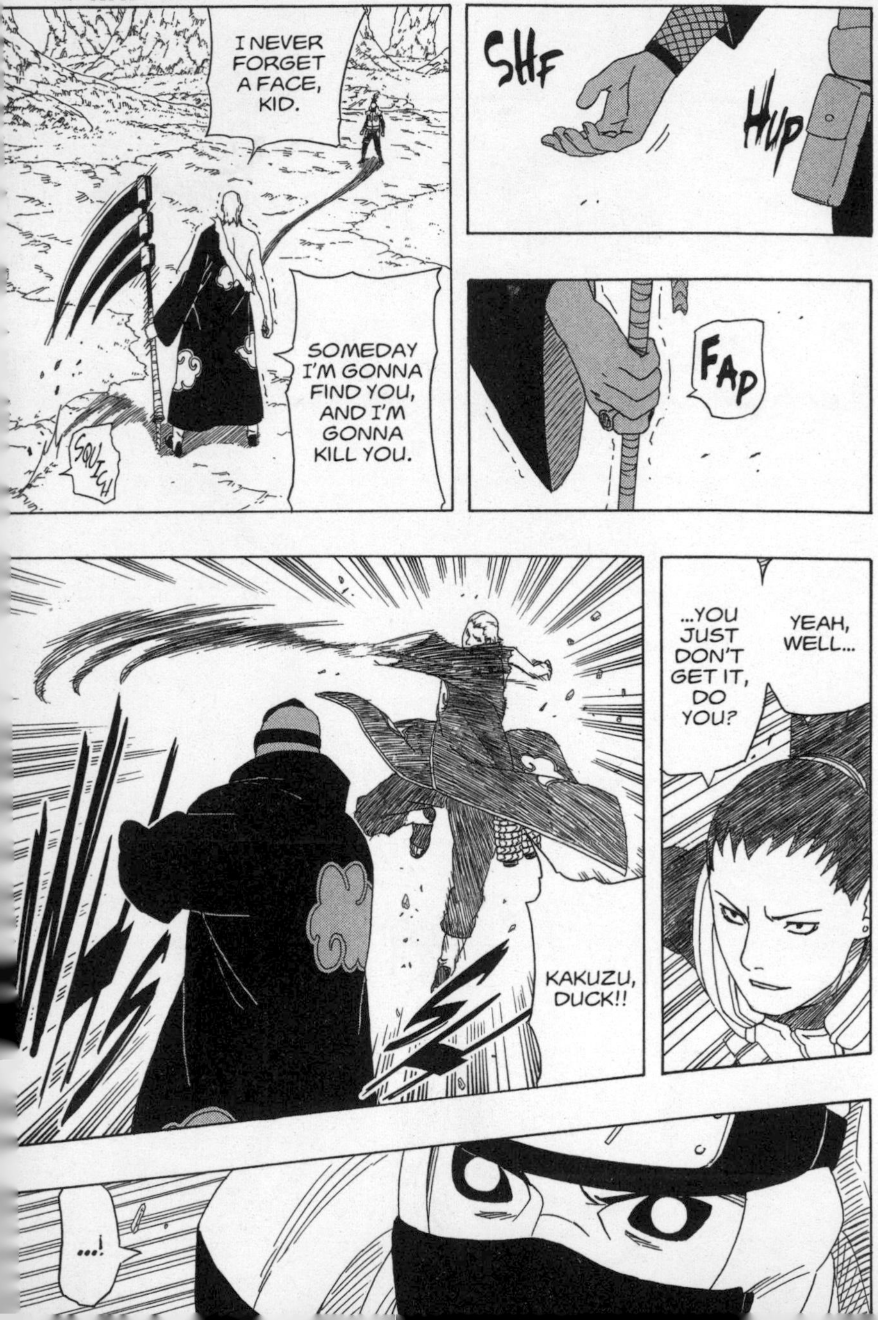
SHF
HUP
FAP
I NEVER FORGET A FACE, KID.
SOMEDAY I'M GONNA FIND YOU, AND I'M GONNA KILL YOU.
SQUICH
YEAH, WELL...
...YOU JUST DON'T GET IT, DO YOU?
KAKUZU, DUCK!!
...!

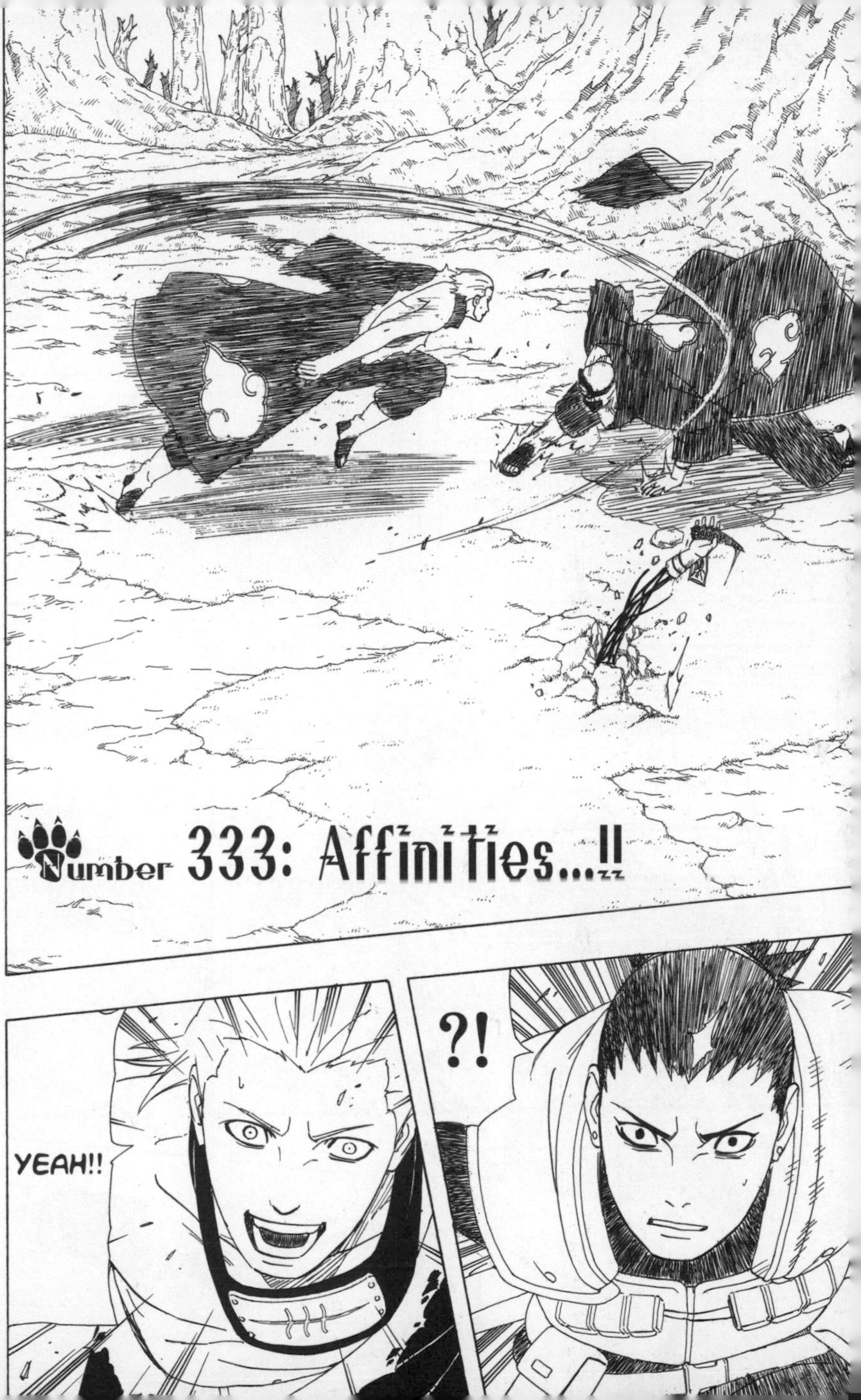
Number 333: Affinities...!!
?!
YEAH!!

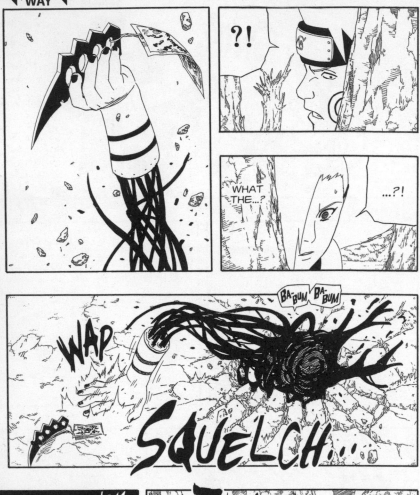

?!

WHAT THE...?

...?!

BA-BUM BA-BUM

WAP

SQUELCH...

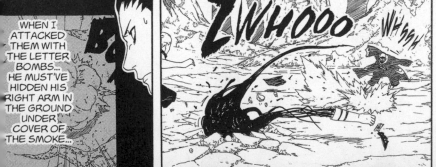

WHEN I ATTACKED THEM WITH THE LETTER BOMBS... HE MUST'VE HIDDEN HIS RIGHT ARM IN THE GROUND UNDER COVER OF THE SMOKE...

ZWHOOO

WHSSH

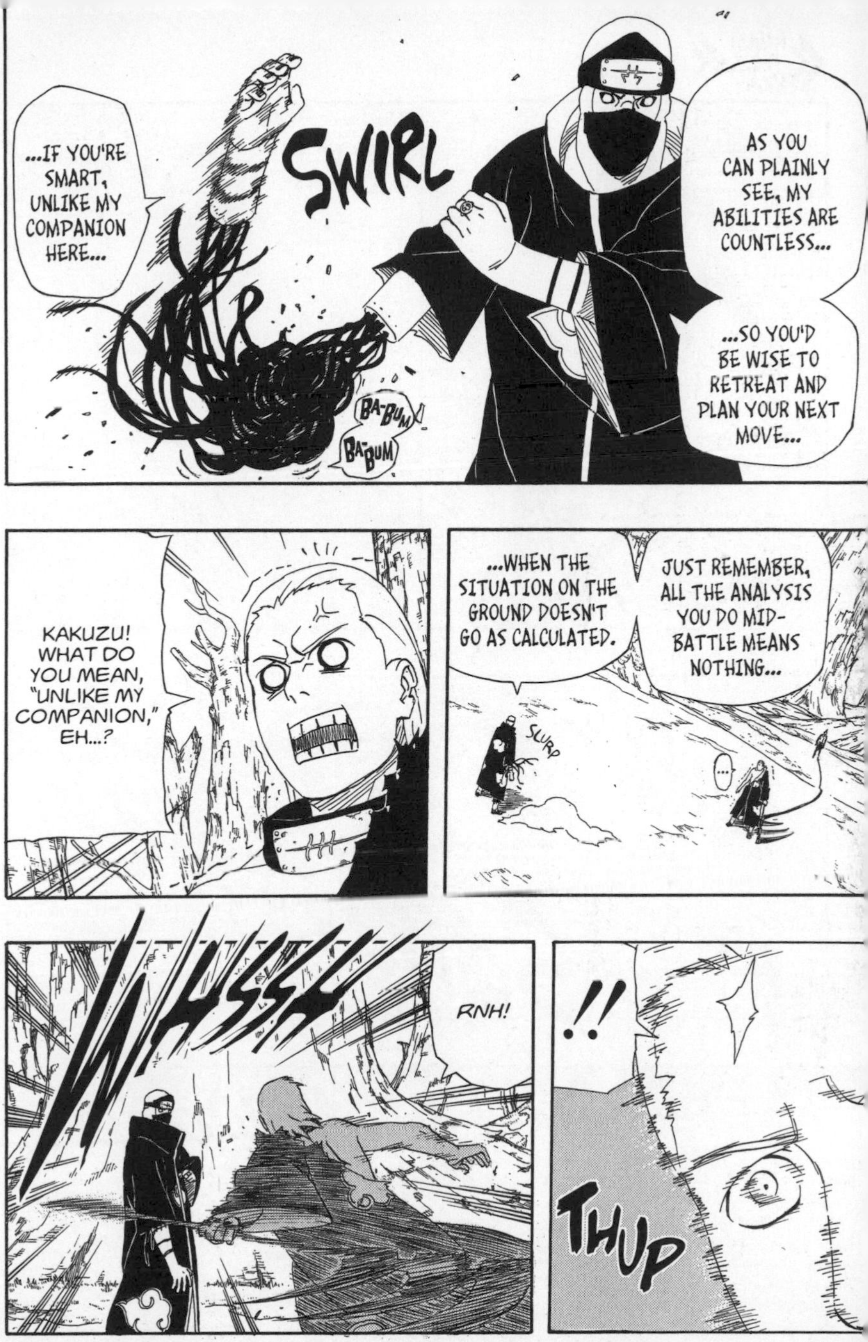
AS YOU CAN PLAINLY SEE, MY ABILITIES ARE COUNTLESS...
...IF YOU'RE SMART, UNLIKE MY COMPANION HERE...
SWIRL
...SO YOU'D BE WISE TO RETREAT AND PLAN YOUR NEXT MOVE...
BA-BUM
BA-BUM
JUST REMEMBER, ALL THE ANALYSIS YOU DO MID-BATTLE MEANS NOTHING...
...WHEN THE SITUATION ON THE GROUND DOESN'T GO AS CALCULATED.
SLURP
...
KAKUZU! WHAT DO YOU MEAN, "UNLIKE MY COMPANION," EH...?
!!
THUP
RNH!
WHSSH

READ THIS WAY

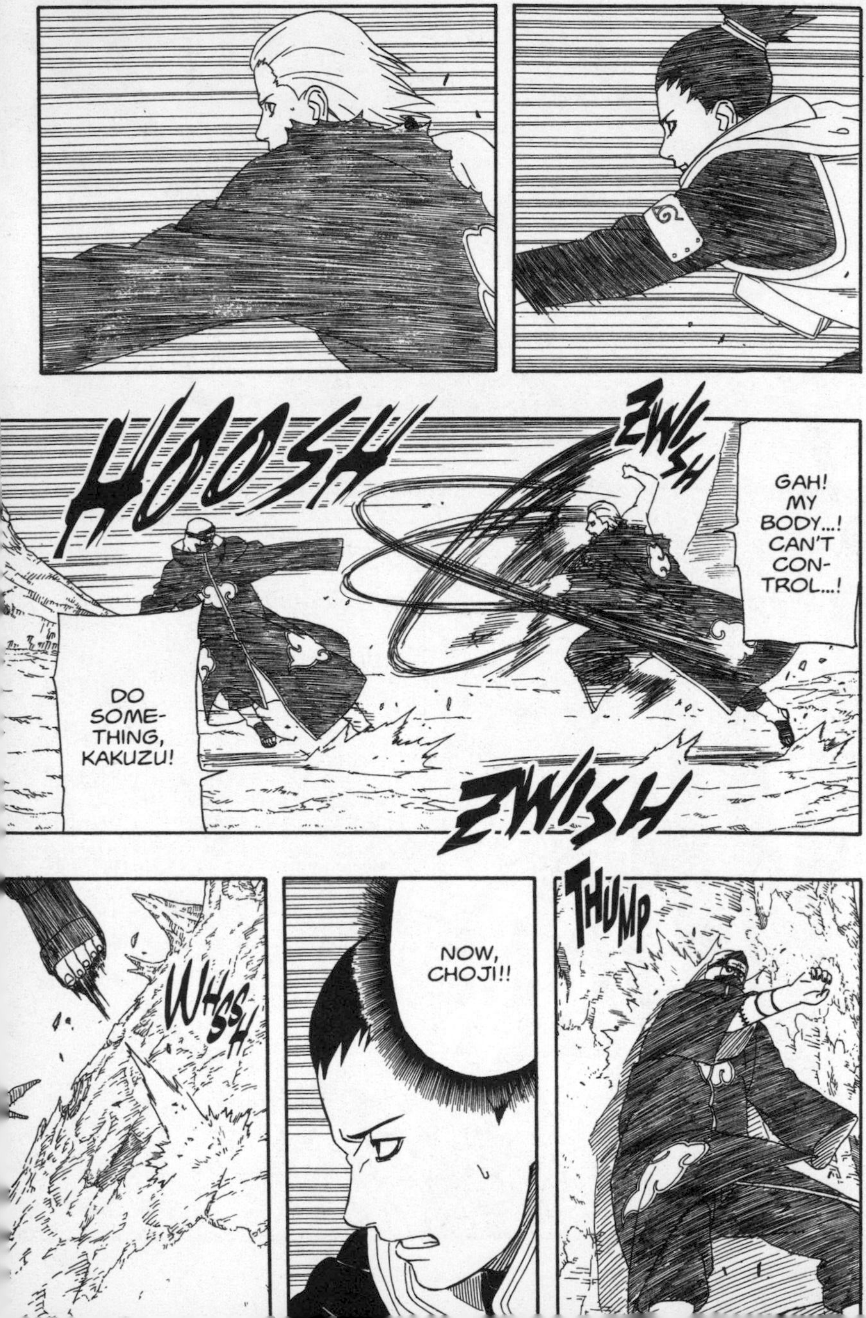
ZWISH
GAH! MY BODY...! CAN'T CON-TROL...!
HOOSH
DO SOME-THING, KAKUZU!
ZWISH
THUMP
NOW, CHOJI!!
WHSSH

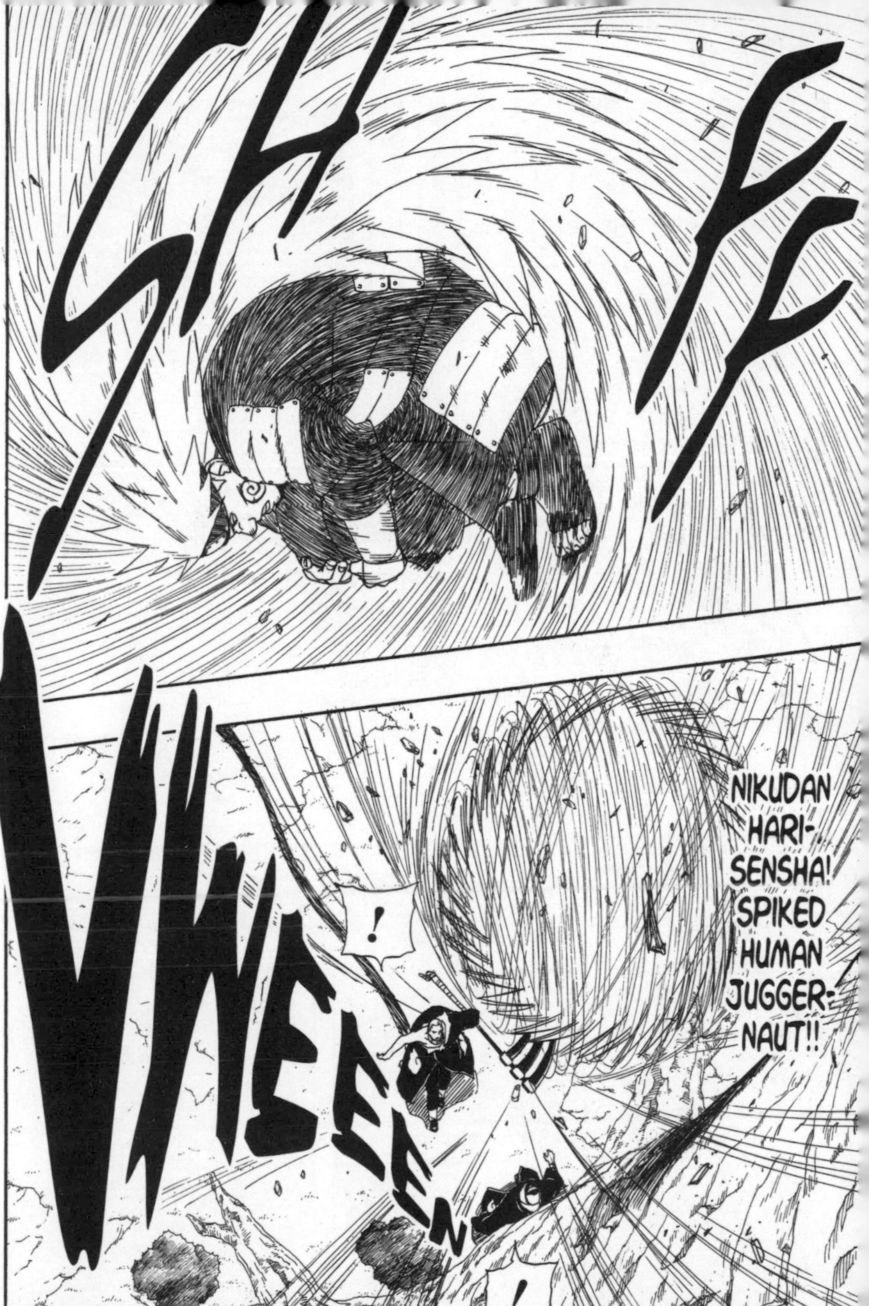
SHFF
NIKUDAN HARI-SENSHA! SPIKED HUMAN JUGGER-NAUT!!
!
!

READ THIS WAY

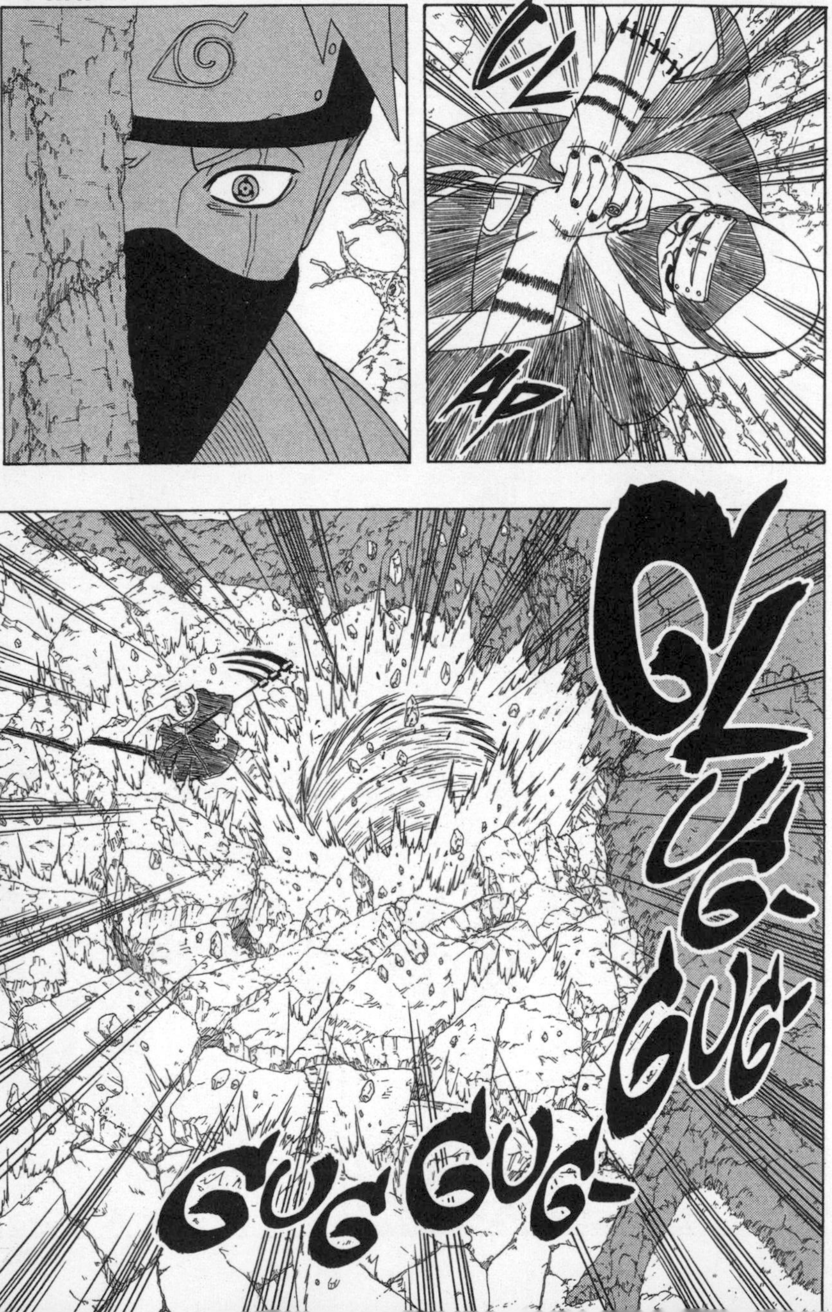
CL
AP
GUG-GUG-
GUG GUG-

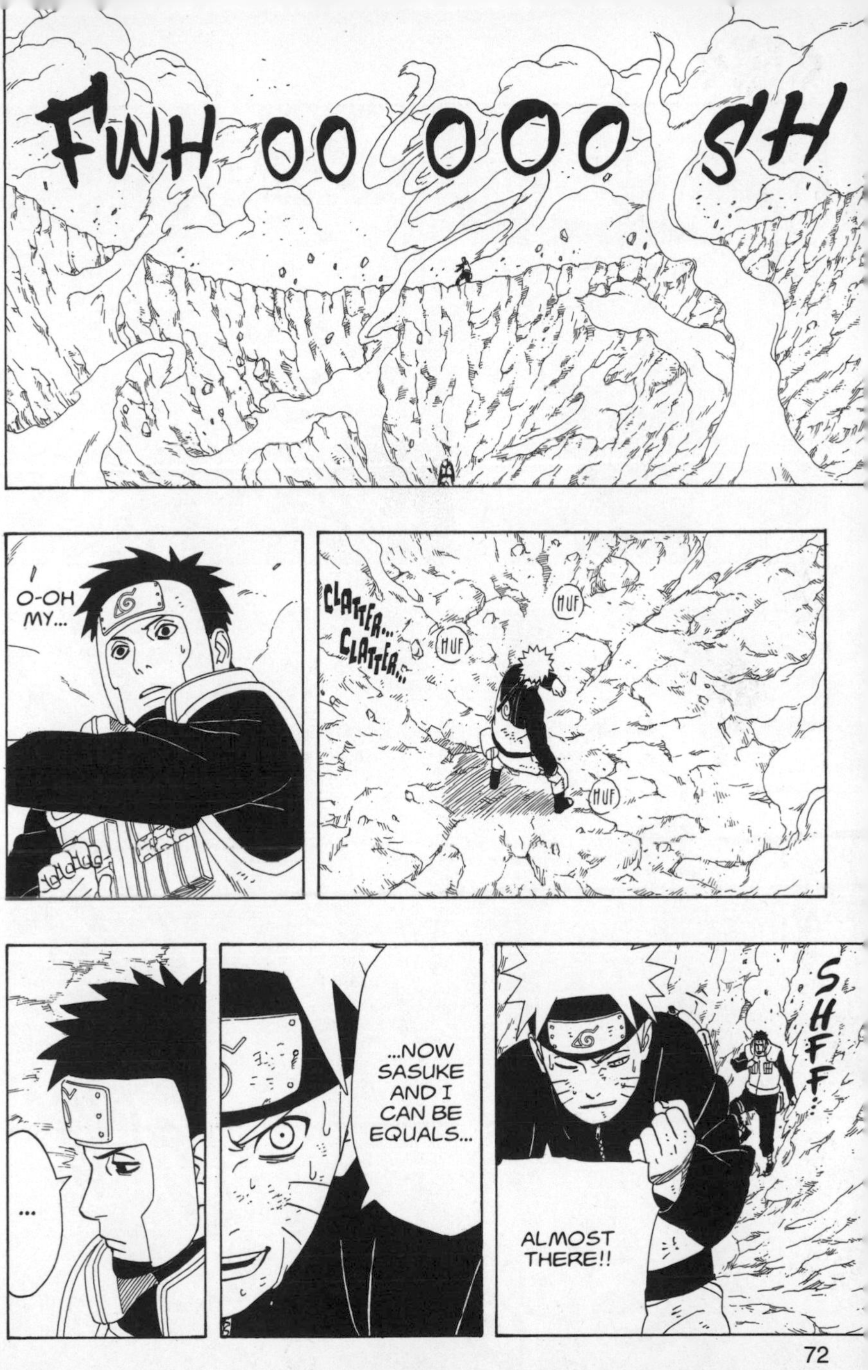
FWHOOOOOOSH
CLATTER... CLATTER...
HUF
HUF
HUF
I O-OH MY...
SHFF...
ALMOST THERE!!
...NOW SASUKE AND I CAN BE EQUALS...
...

READ THIS WAY

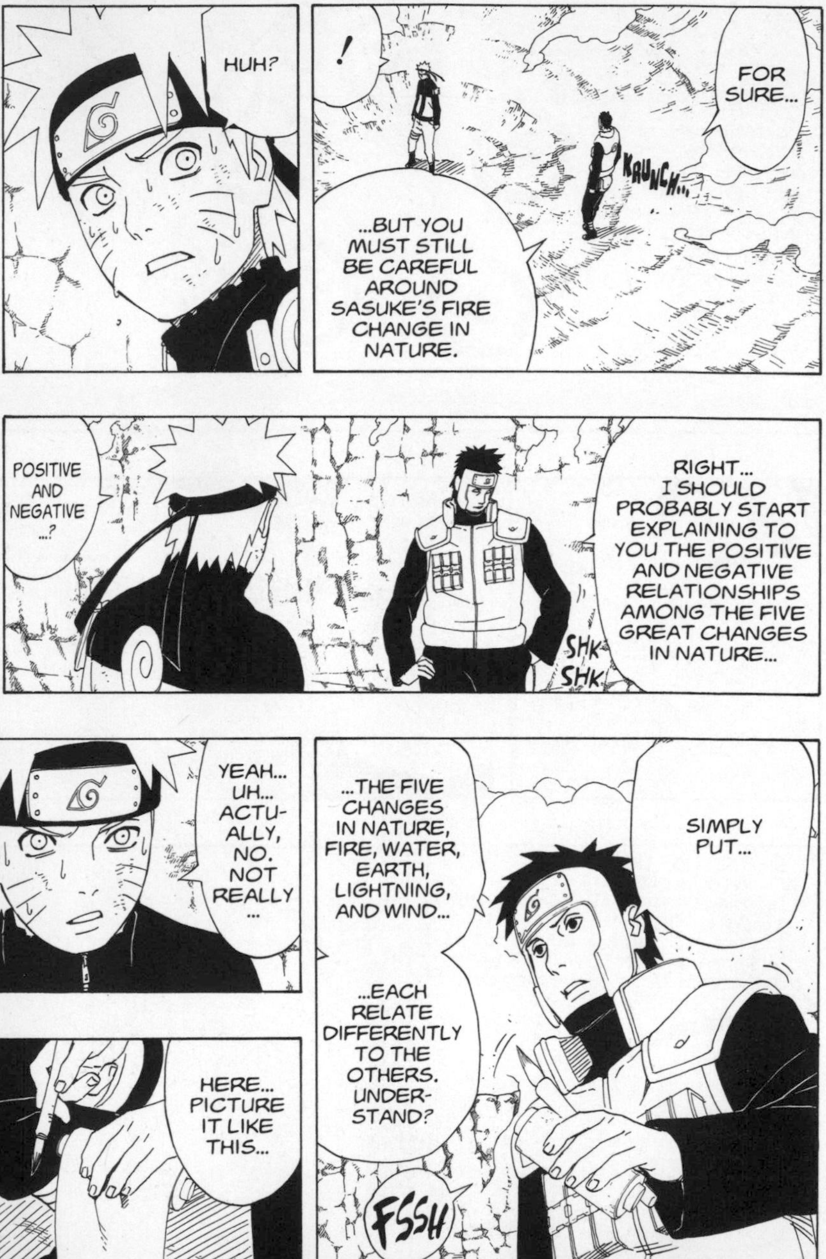
FOR SURE...
!
KRUNCH...
...BUT YOU MUST STILL BE CAREFUL AROUND SASUKE'S FIRE CHANGE IN NATURE.
HUH?
RIGHT... I SHOULD PROBABLY START EXPLAINING TO YOU THE POSITIVE AND NEGATIVE RELATIONSHIPS AMONG THE FIVE GREAT CHANGES IN NATURE...
SHK SHK
POSITIVE AND NEGATIVE ...?
SIMPLY PUT...
...THE FIVE CHANGES IN NATURE, FIRE, WATER, EARTH, LIGHTNING, AND WIND...
...EACH RELATE DIFFERENTLY TO THE OTHERS. UNDER-STAND?
FSSH
YEAH... UH... ACTU-ALLY, NO. NOT REALLY ...
HERE... PICTURE IT LIKE THIS...

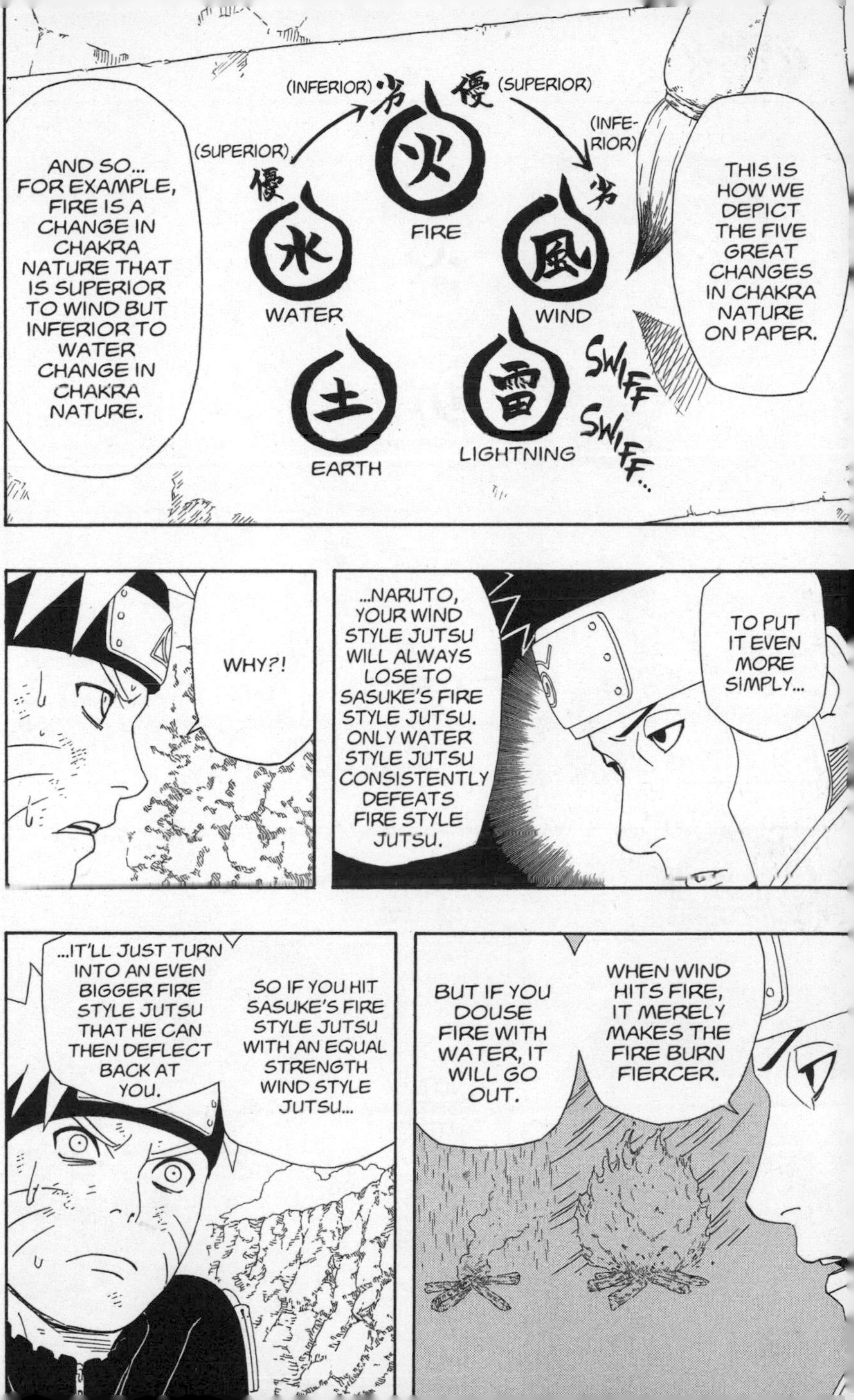
THIS IS HOW WE DEPICT THE FIVE GREAT CHANGES IN CHAKRA NATURE ON PAPER.
(INFERIOR) 劣
優 (SUPERIOR)
(INFE-RIOR) 劣
(SUPERIOR) 優
火
FIRE
水
WATER
風
WIND
土
EARTH
雷
LIGHTNING
SWIFF
SWIFF...
AND SO... FOR EXAMPLE, FIRE IS A CHANGE IN CHAKRA NATURE THAT IS SUPERIOR TO WIND BUT INFERIOR TO WATER CHANGE IN CHAKRA NATURE.
TO PUT IT EVEN MORE SIMPLY...
...NARUTO, YOUR WIND STYLE JUTSU WILL ALWAYS LOSE TO SASUKE'S FIRE STYLE JUTSU. ONLY WATER STYLE JUTSU CONSISTENTLY DEFEATS FIRE STYLE JUTSU.
WHY?!
WHEN WIND HITS FIRE, IT MERELY MAKES THE FIRE BURN FIERCER.
BUT IF YOU DOUSE FIRE WITH WATER, IT WILL GO OUT.
SO IF YOU HIT SASUKE'S FIRE STYLE JUTSU WITH AN EQUAL STRENGTH WIND STYLE JUTSU...
...IT'LL JUST TURN INTO AN EVEN BIGGER FIRE STYLE JUTSU THAT HE CAN THEN DEFLECT BACK AT YOU.

READ THIS WAY

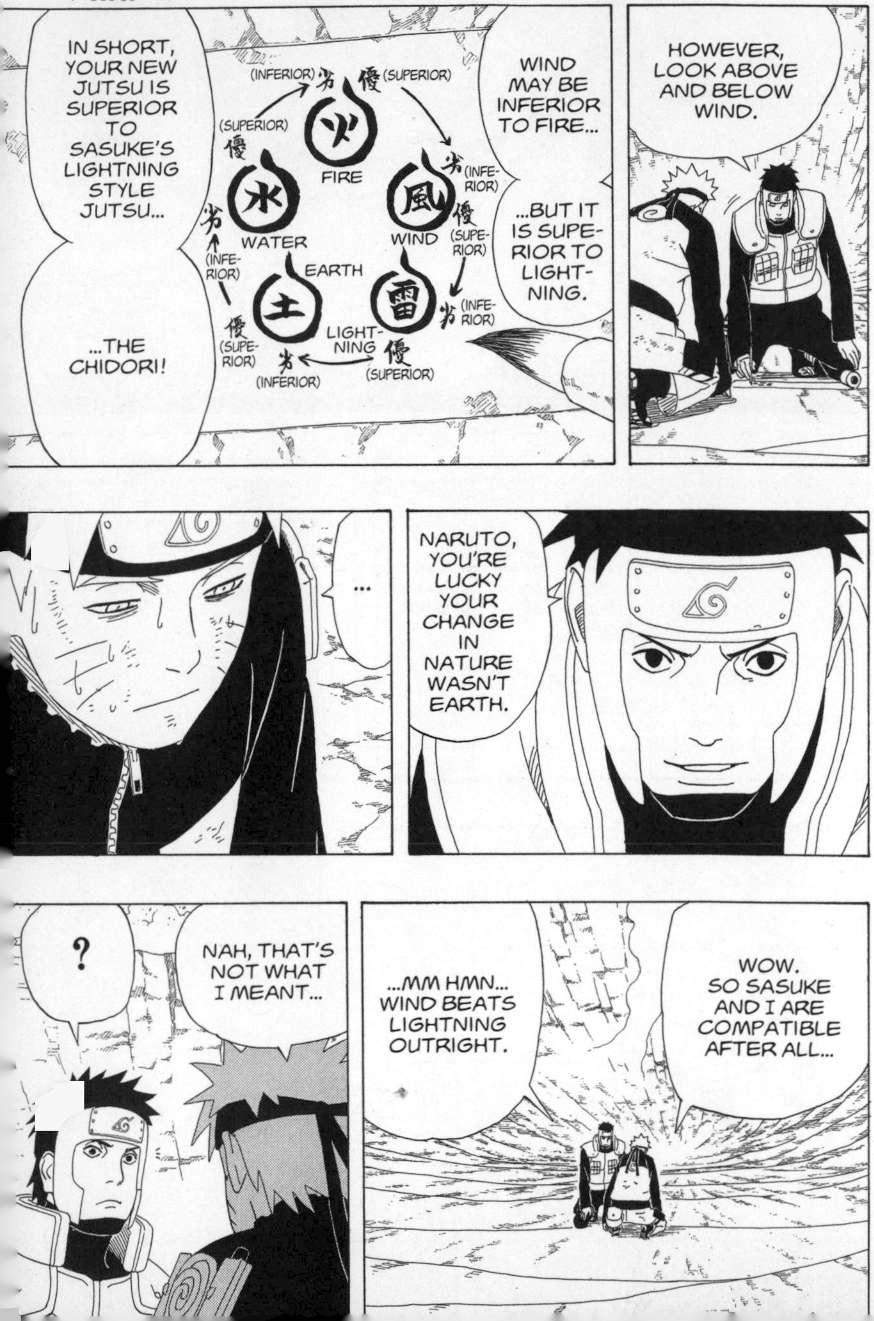
HOWEVER, LOOK ABOVE AND BELOW WIND.
WIND MAY BE INFERIOR TO FIRE...
...BUT IT IS SUPERIOR TO LIGHTNING.
火 FIRE
風 WIND
雷 LIGHTNING
土 EARTH
水 WATER
優 (SUPERIOR)
劣 (INFERIOR)
IN SHORT, YOUR NEW JUTSU IS SUPERIOR TO SASUKE'S LIGHTNING STYLE JUTSU...
...THE CHIDORI!
NARUTO, YOU'RE LUCKY YOUR CHANGE IN NATURE WASN'T EARTH.
...
WOW. SO SASUKE AND I ARE COMPATIBLE AFTER ALL...
...MM HMN... WIND BEATS LIGHTNING OUTRIGHT.
NAH, THAT'S NOT WHAT I MEANT...
?

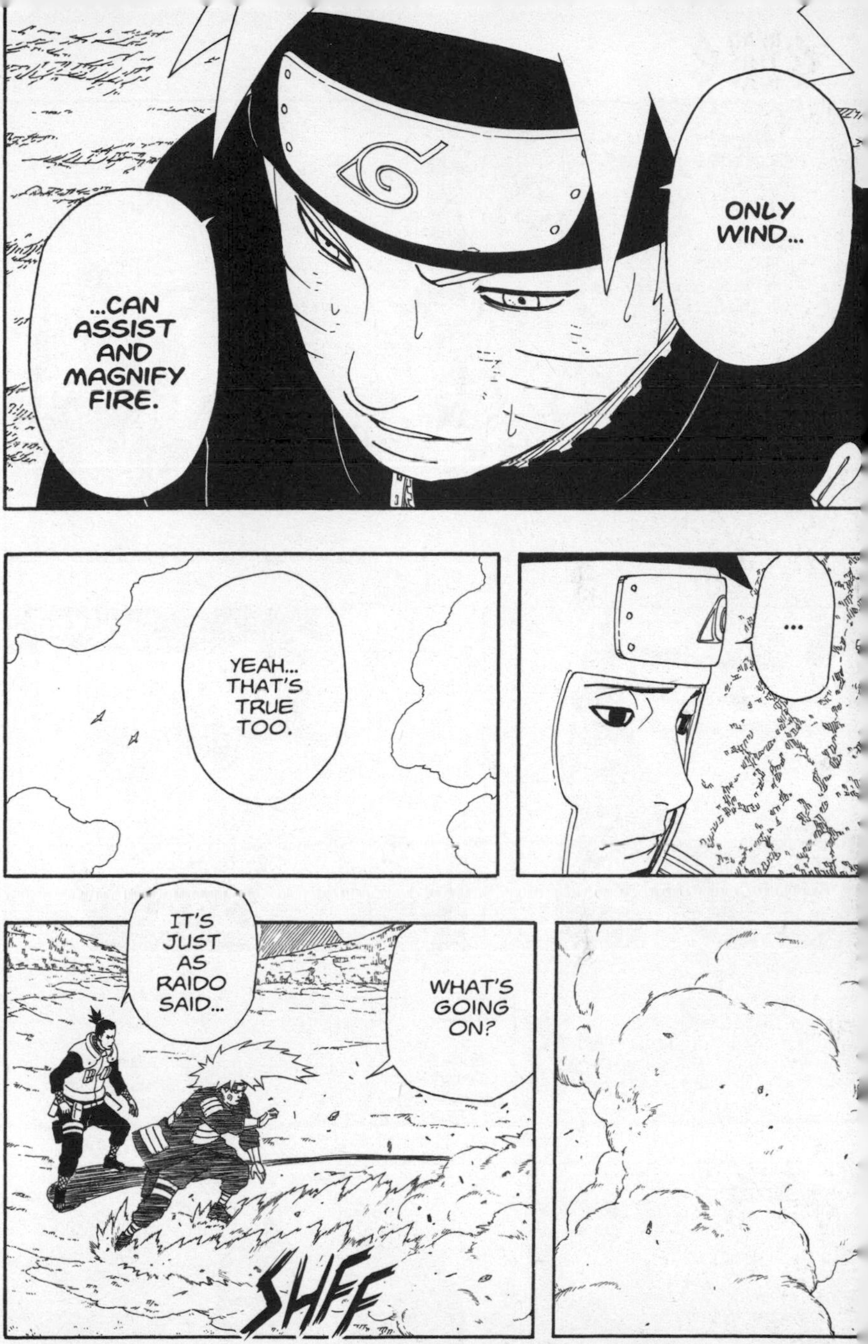
ONLY WIND...
...CAN ASSIST AND MAGNIFY FIRE.
...
YEAH... THAT'S TRUE TOO.
WHAT'S GOING ON?
IT'S JUST AS RAIDO SAID...
SHFF

READ THIS WAY

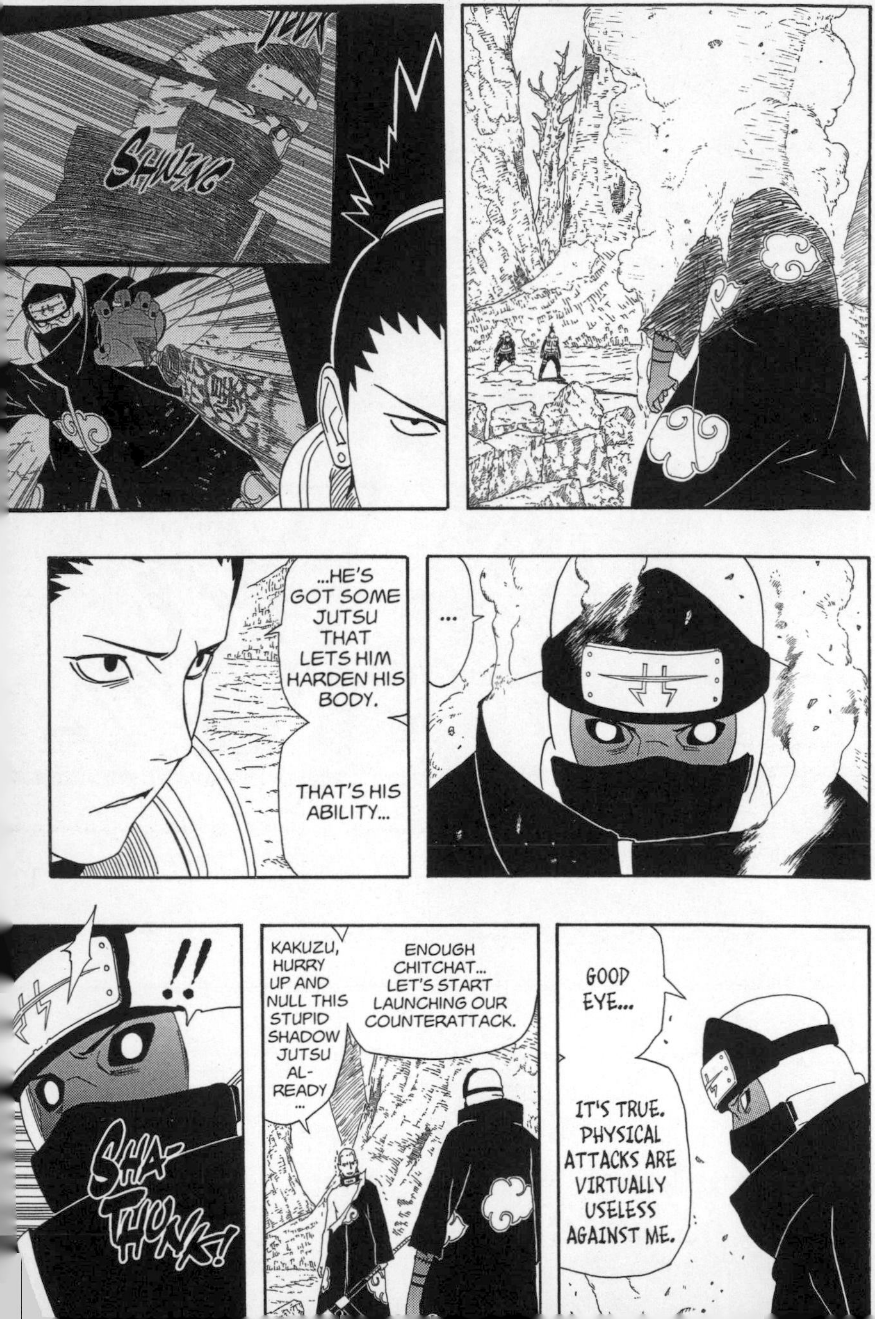
...
...HE'S GOT SOME JUTSU THAT LETS HIM HARDEN HIS BODY.
THAT'S HIS ABILITY...
GOOD EYE...
IT'S TRUE. PHYSICAL ATTACKS ARE VIRTUALLY USELESS AGAINST ME.
ENOUGH CHITCHAT... LET'S START LAUNCHING OUR COUNTERATTACK.
KAKUZU, HURRY UP AND NULL THIS STUPID SHADOW JUTSU AL-READY...
!!
SHA-THUNK!

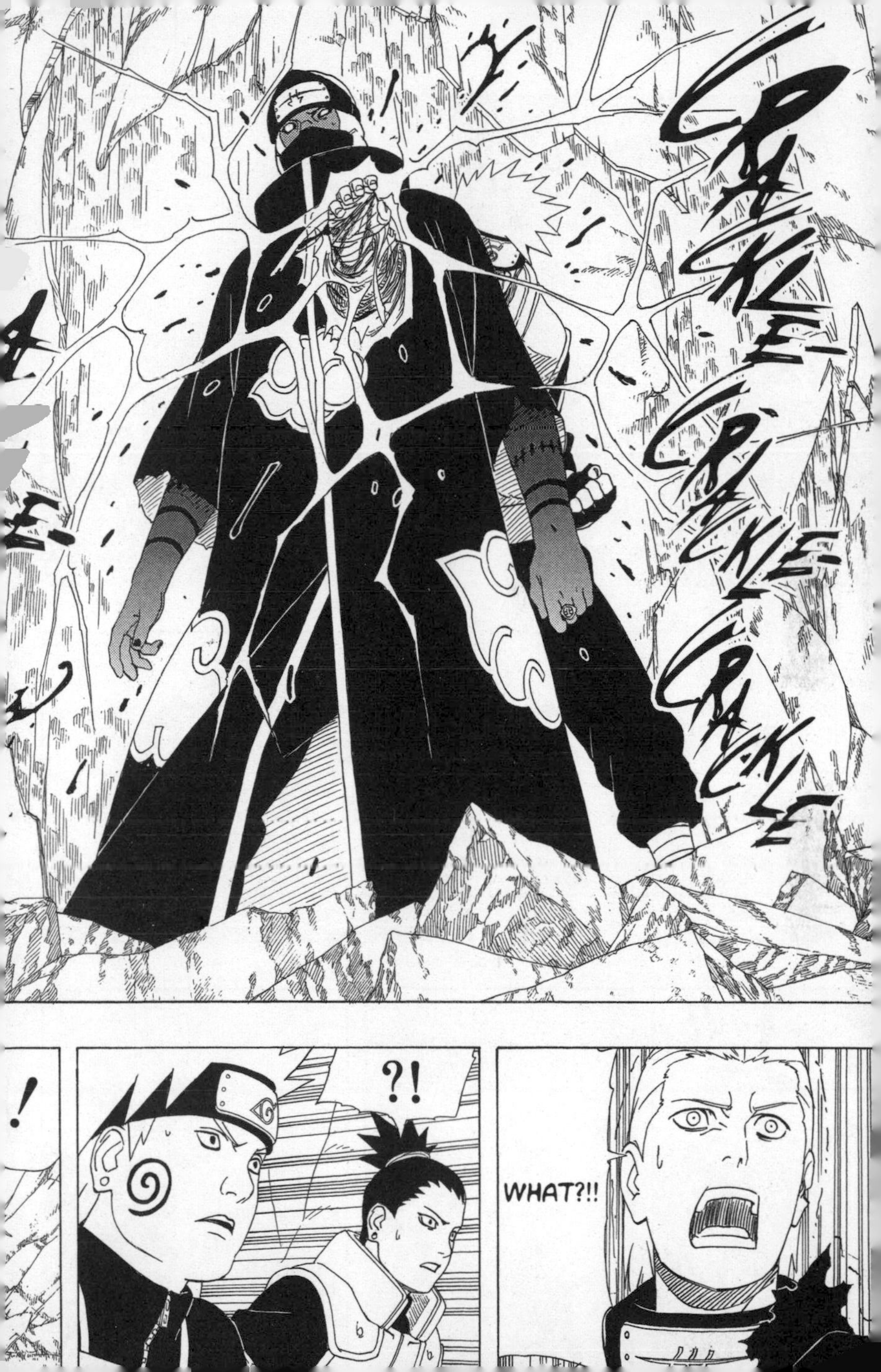
CRACKLE-
CRACKLE-
CRACKLE
WHAT?!!
?!
!

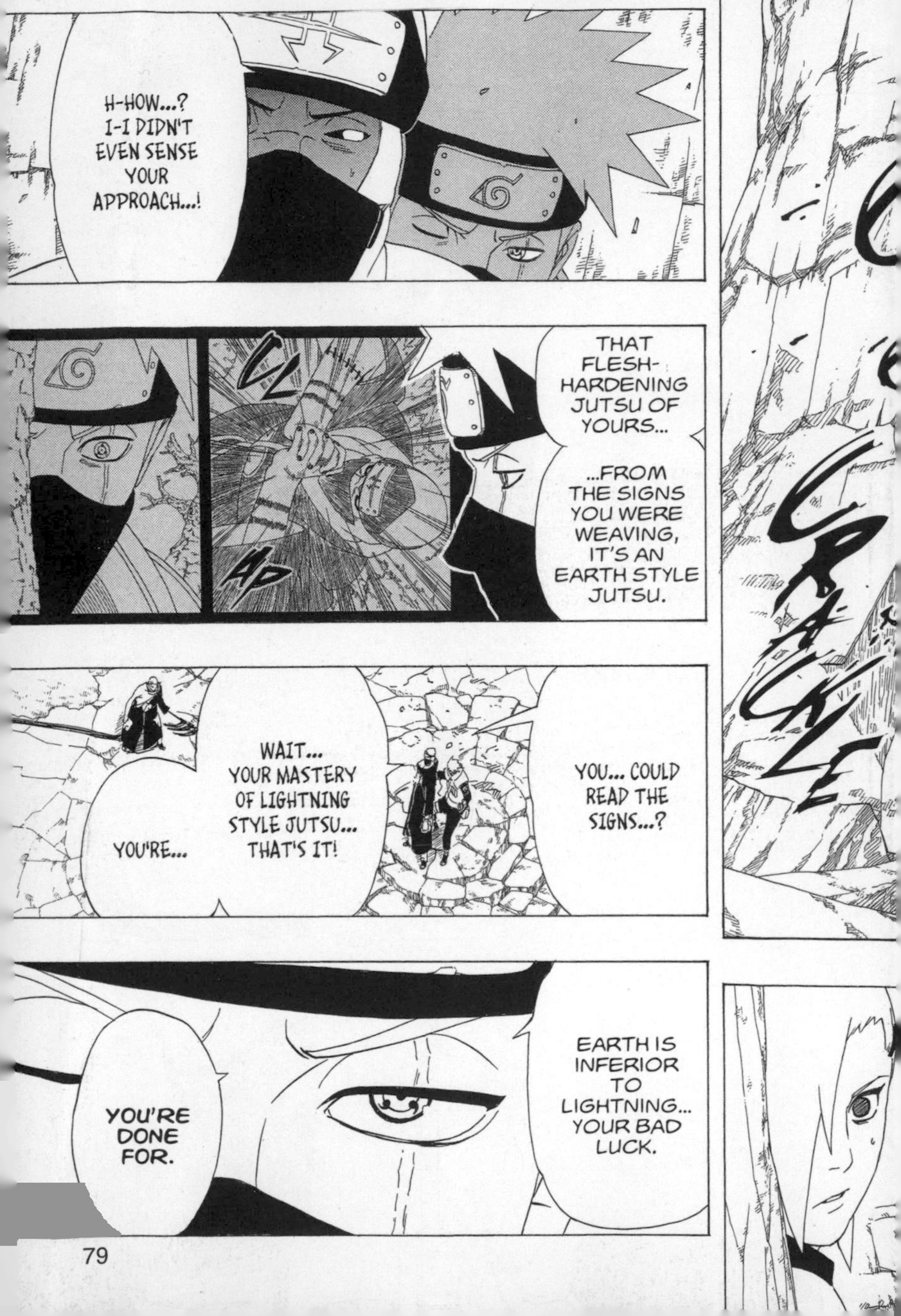
CRACKLE
H-HOW...? I-I DIDN'T EVEN SENSE YOUR APPROACH...!
THAT FLESH-HARDENING JUTSU OF YOURS...
...FROM THE SIGNS YOU WERE WEAVING, IT'S AN EARTH STYLE JUTSU.
YOU... COULD READ THE SIGNS...?
WAIT... YOUR MASTERY OF LIGHTNING STYLE JUTSU... THAT'S IT!
YOU'RE...
EARTH IS INFERIOR TO LIGHTNING... YOUR BAD LUCK.
YOU'RE DONE FOR.

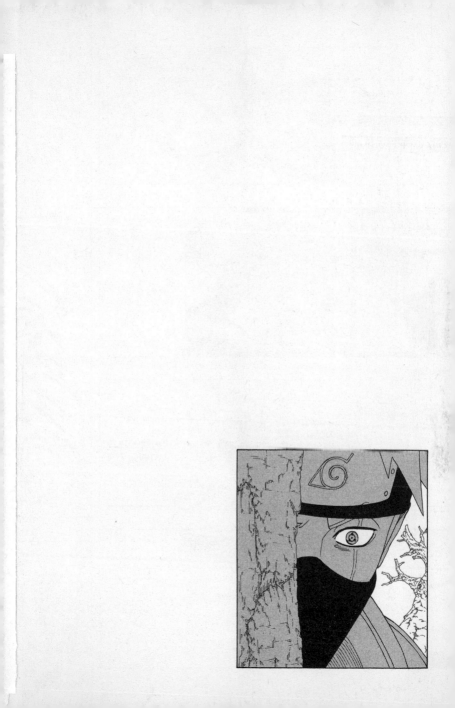

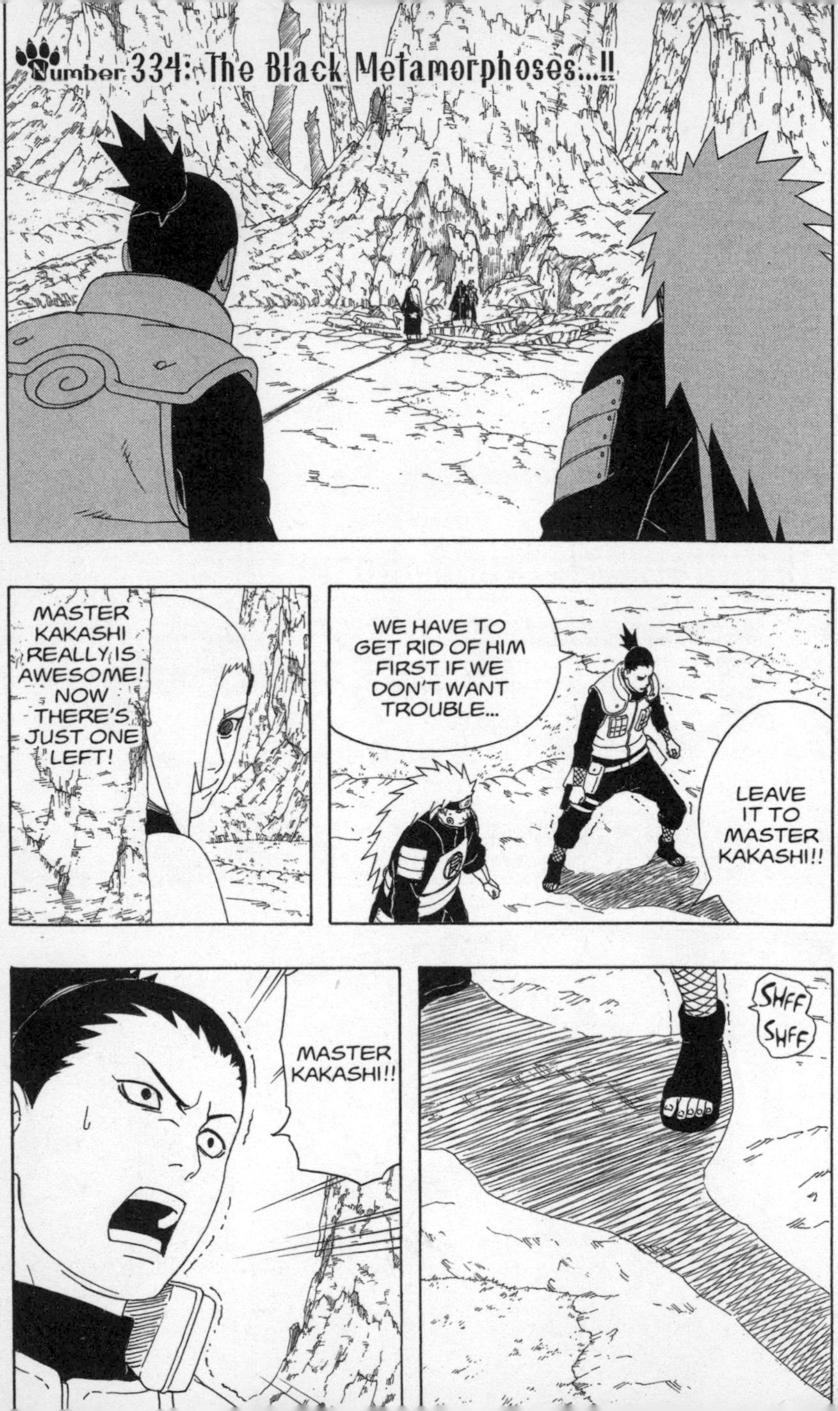
Number 334: The Black Metamorphoses...!!
MASTER KAKASHI REALLY IS AWESOME! NOW THERE'S JUST ONE LEFT!
WE HAVE TO GET RID OF HIM FIRST IF WE DON'T WANT TROUBLE...
LEAVE IT TO MASTER KAKASHI!!
MASTER KAKASHI!!
SHFF
SHFF

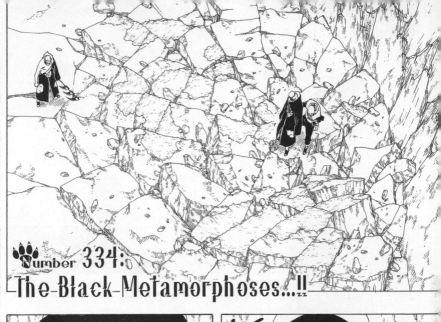

Number 334:
The Black Metamorphoses...!!

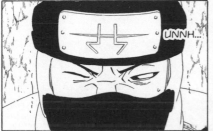

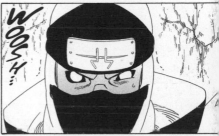

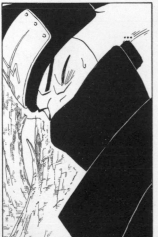

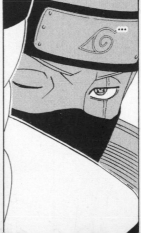

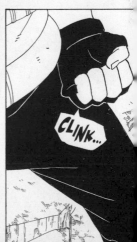

READ THIS WAY

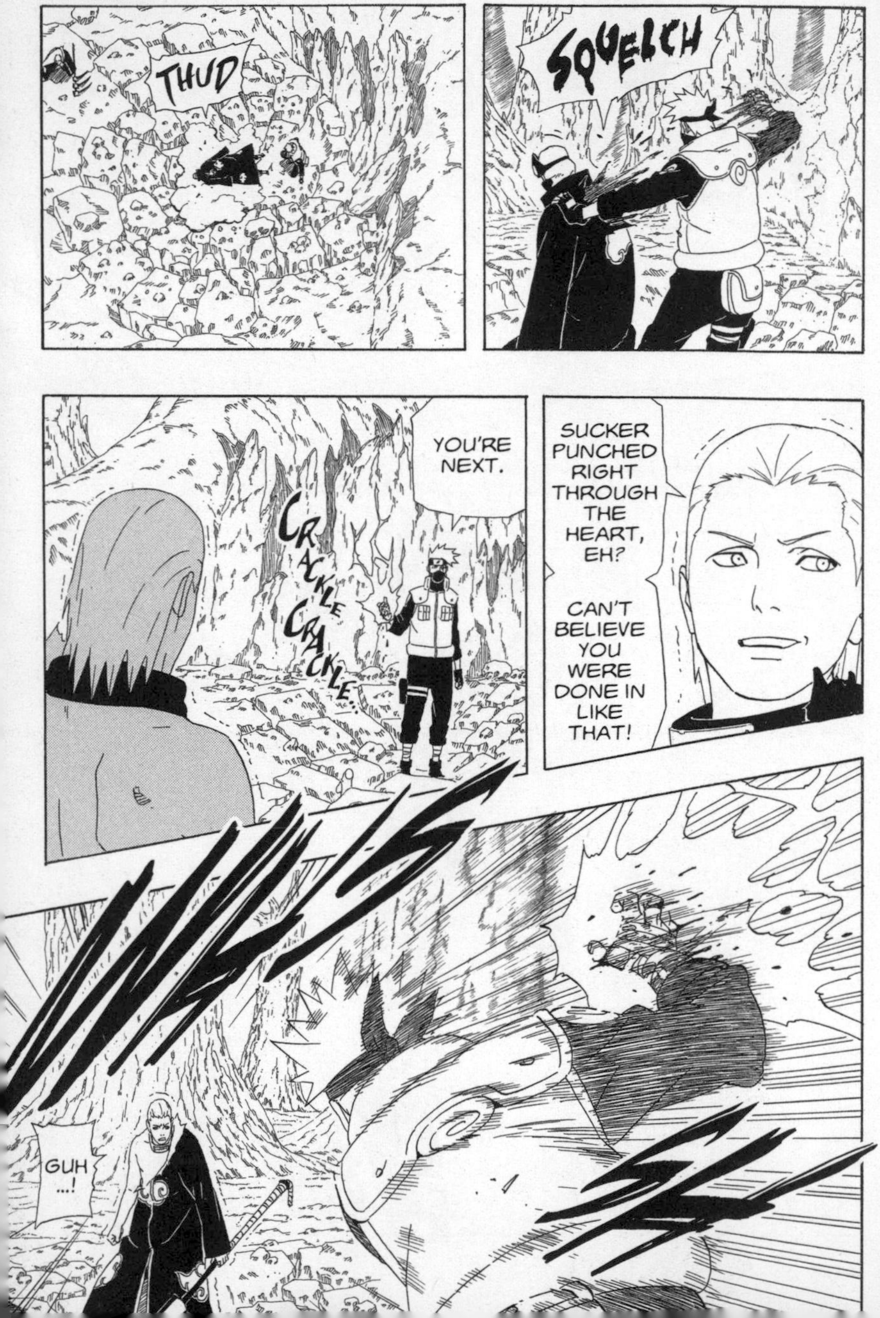
SQUELCH
THUD
SUCKER PUNCHED RIGHT THROUGH THE HEART, EH?
CAN'T BELIEVE YOU WERE DONE IN LIKE THAT!
YOU'RE NEXT.
CRACKLE CRACKLE...
GUH ...!

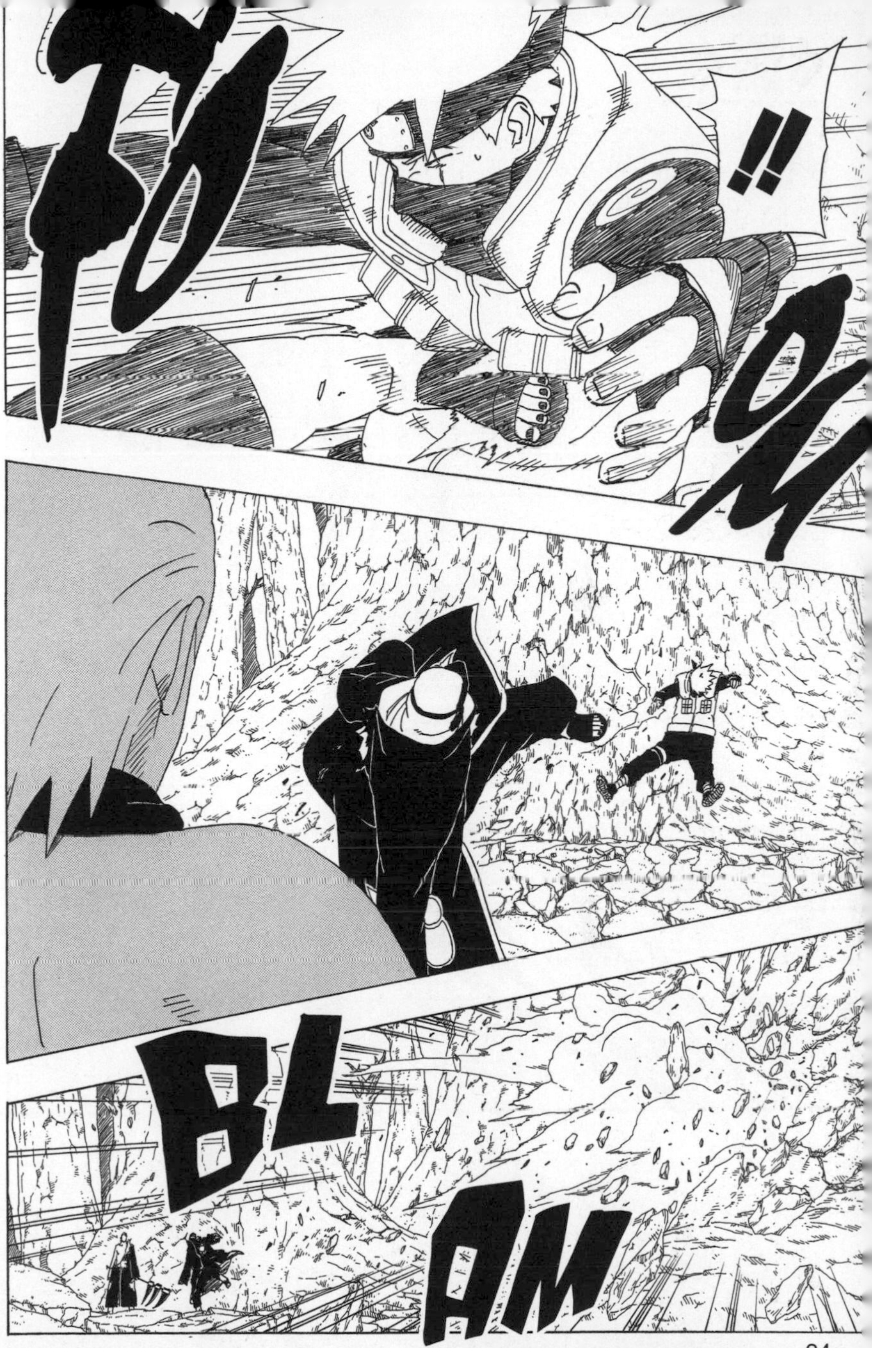
FOOM
!!
BLAM

READ THIS WAY

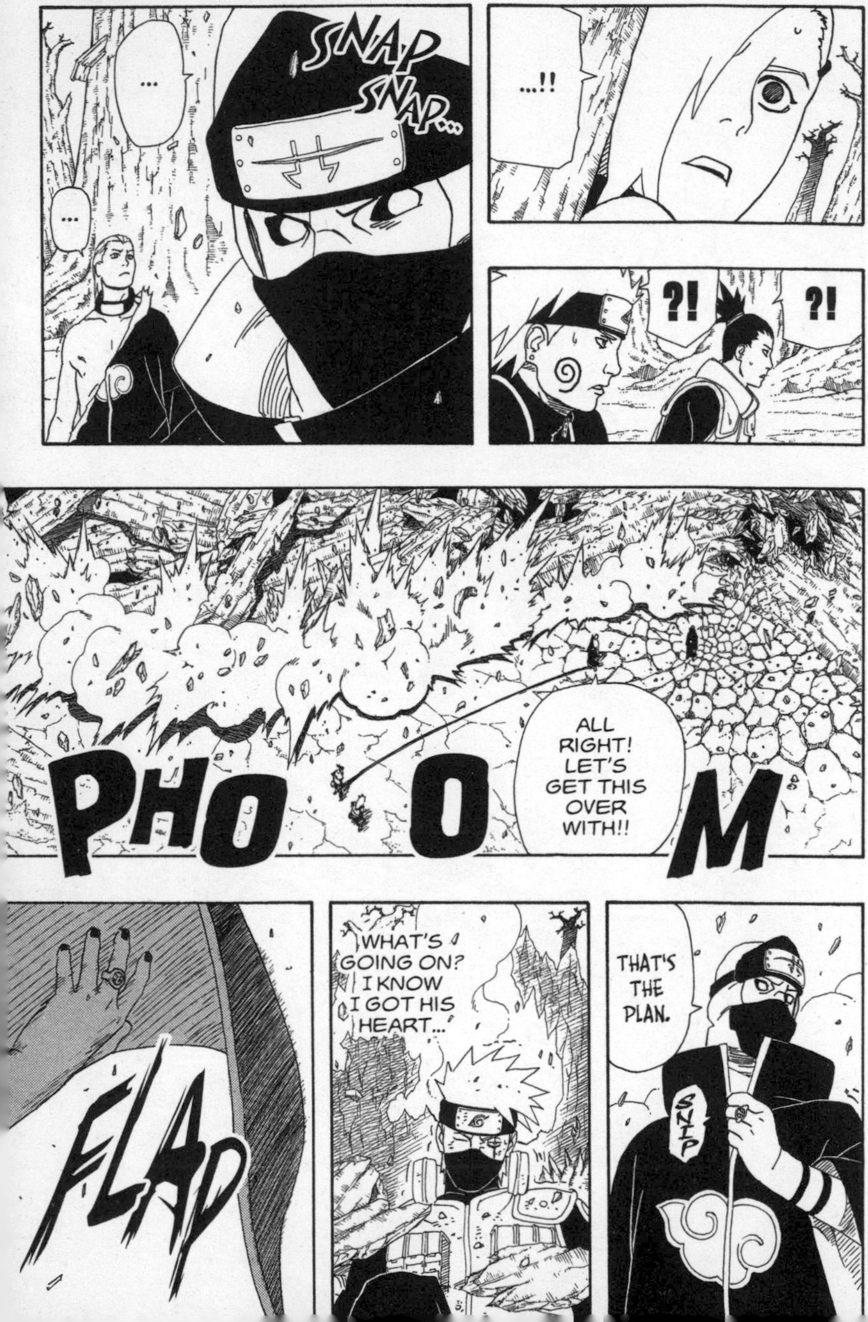

...!!
?!
?!
SNAP
SNAP...
...
...
PHOOM
ALL RIGHT! LET'S GET THIS OVER WITH!!
THAT'S THE PLAN.
SNIP
WHAT'S GOING ON? I KNOW I GOT HIS HEART...
FLAP

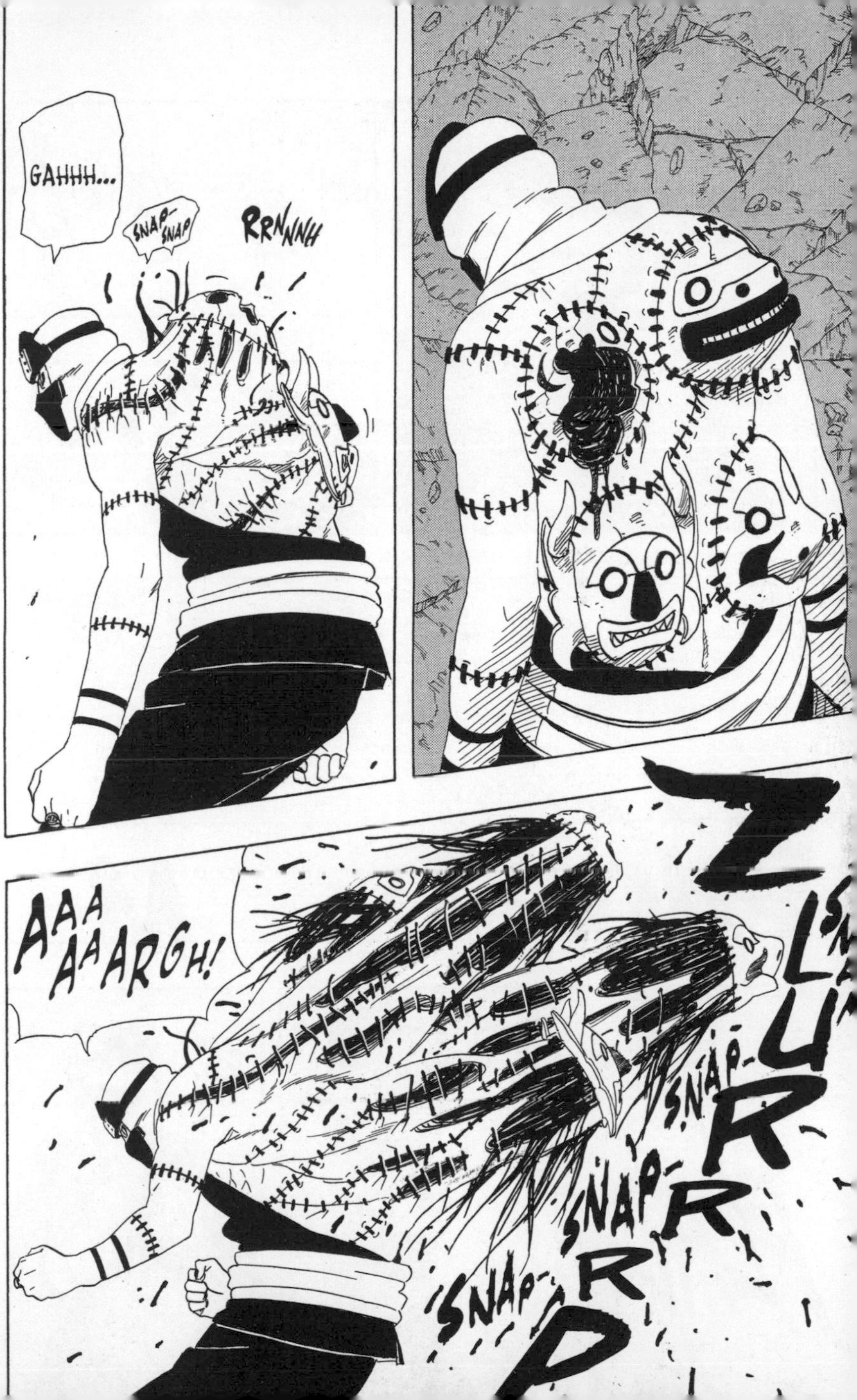
GAHHH...
SNAP-SNAP
RRNNNH
ZLURRRP
SNAP-
SNAP-
SNAP-
AAAAAARGH!

READ THIS WAY

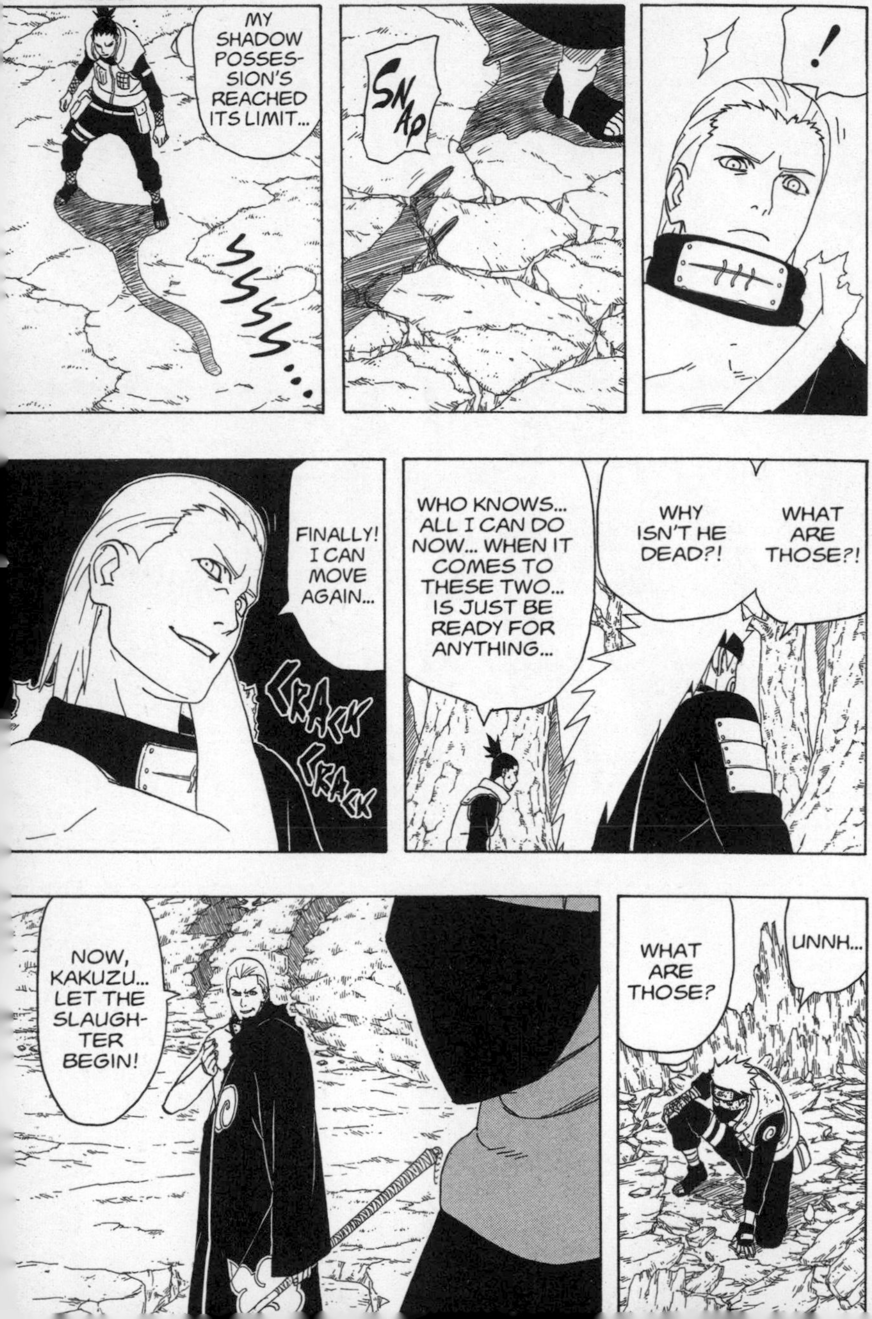
!
SNAP
MY SHADOW POSSES-SION'S REACHED ITS LIMIT...
SSSS...
WHAT ARE THOSE?!
WHY ISN'T HE DEAD?!
WHO KNOWS... ALL I CAN DO NOW... WHEN IT COMES TO THESE TWO... IS JUST BE READY FOR ANYTHING...
FINALLY! I CAN MOVE AGAIN...
CRACK
CRACK
UNNH...
WHAT ARE THOSE?
NOW, KAKUZU... LET THE SLAUGH-TER BEGIN!

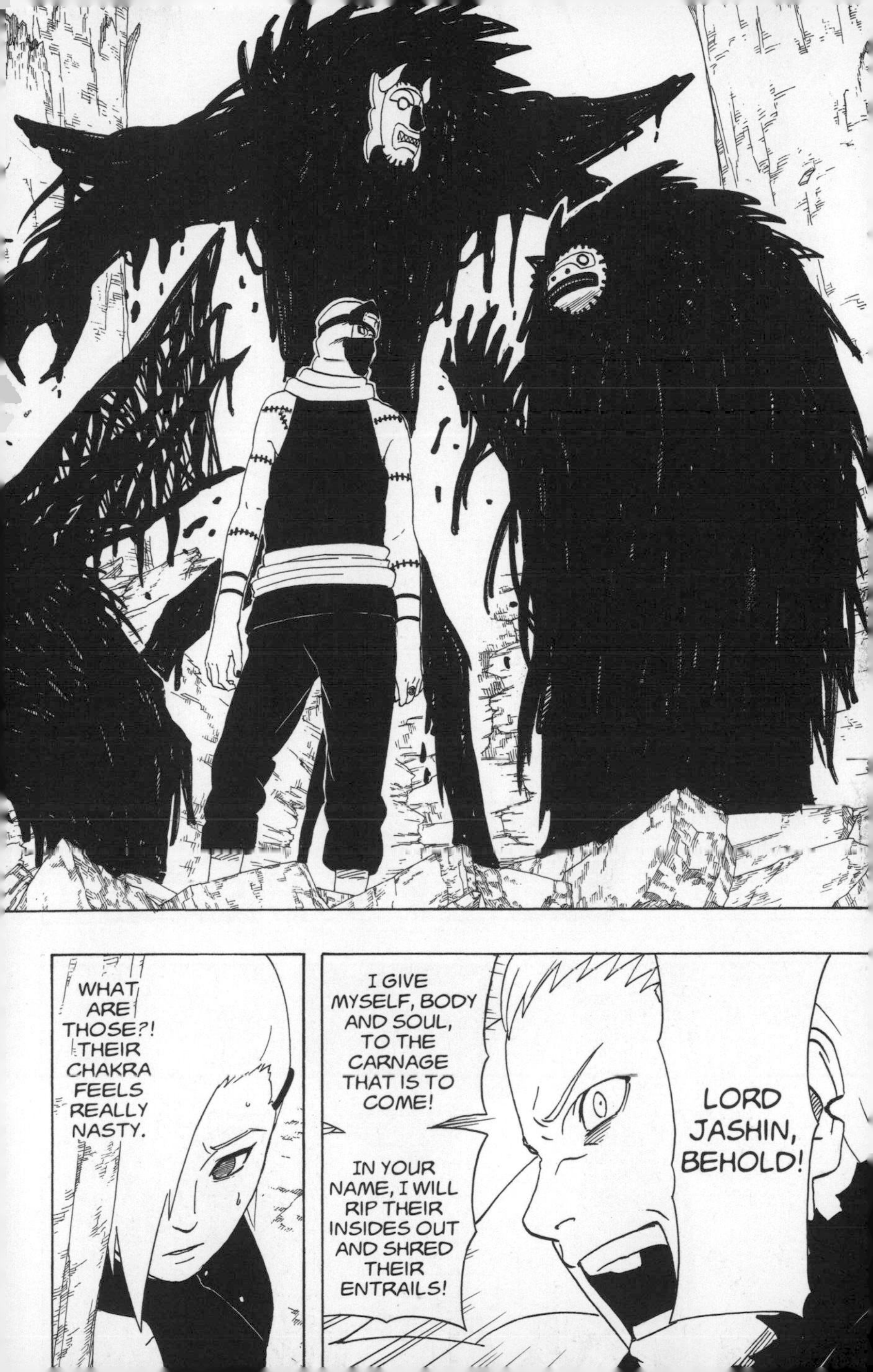
LORD JASHIN, BEHOLD!
I GIVE MYSELF, BODY AND SOUL, TO THE CARNAGE THAT IS TO COME!
IN YOUR NAME, I WILL RIP THEIR INSIDES OUT AND SHRED THEIR ENTRAILS!
WHAT ARE THOSE?! THEIR CHAKRA FEELS REALLY NASTY.

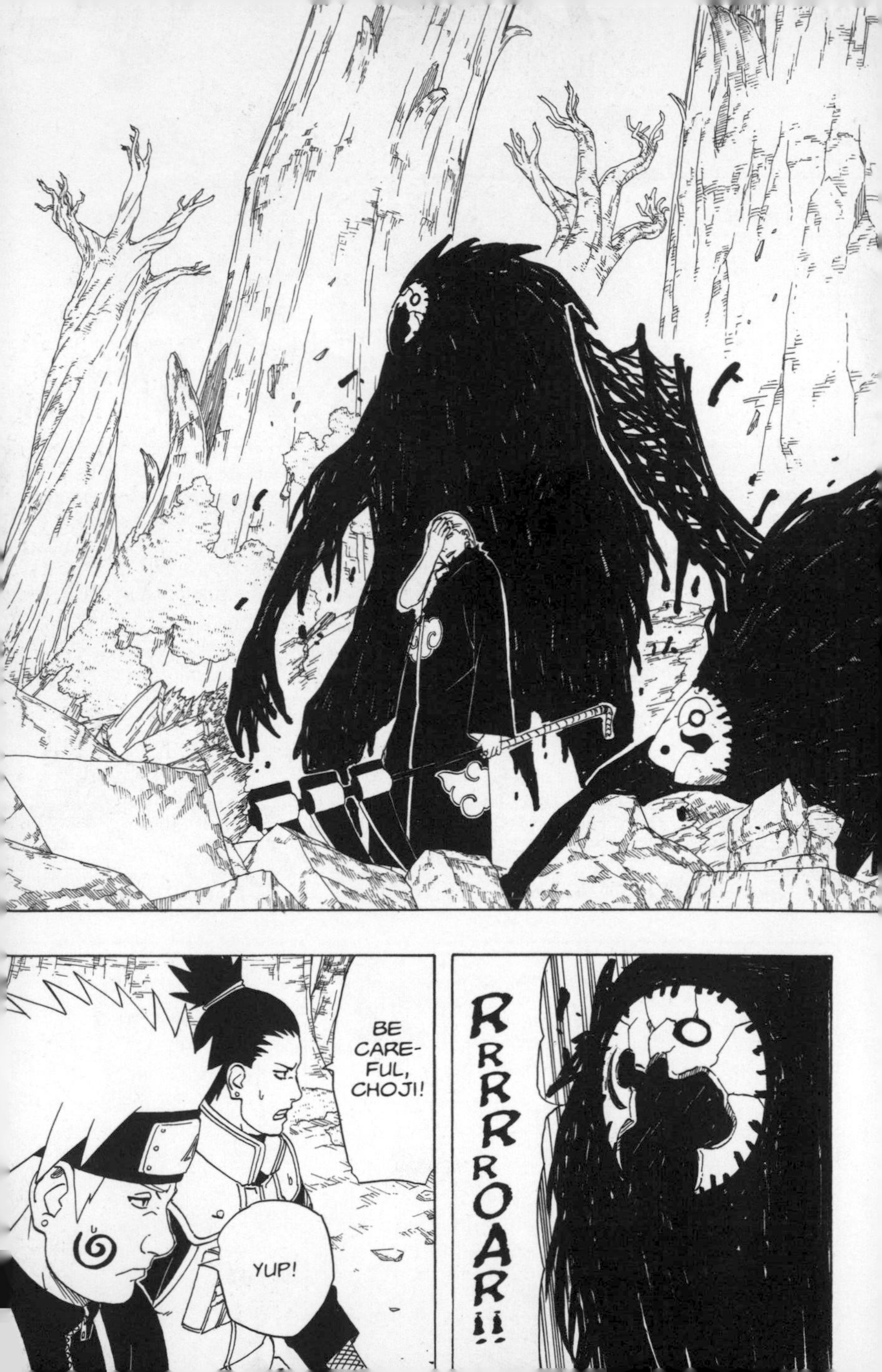
RRRROAR!!
BE CAREFUL, CHOJI!
YUP!

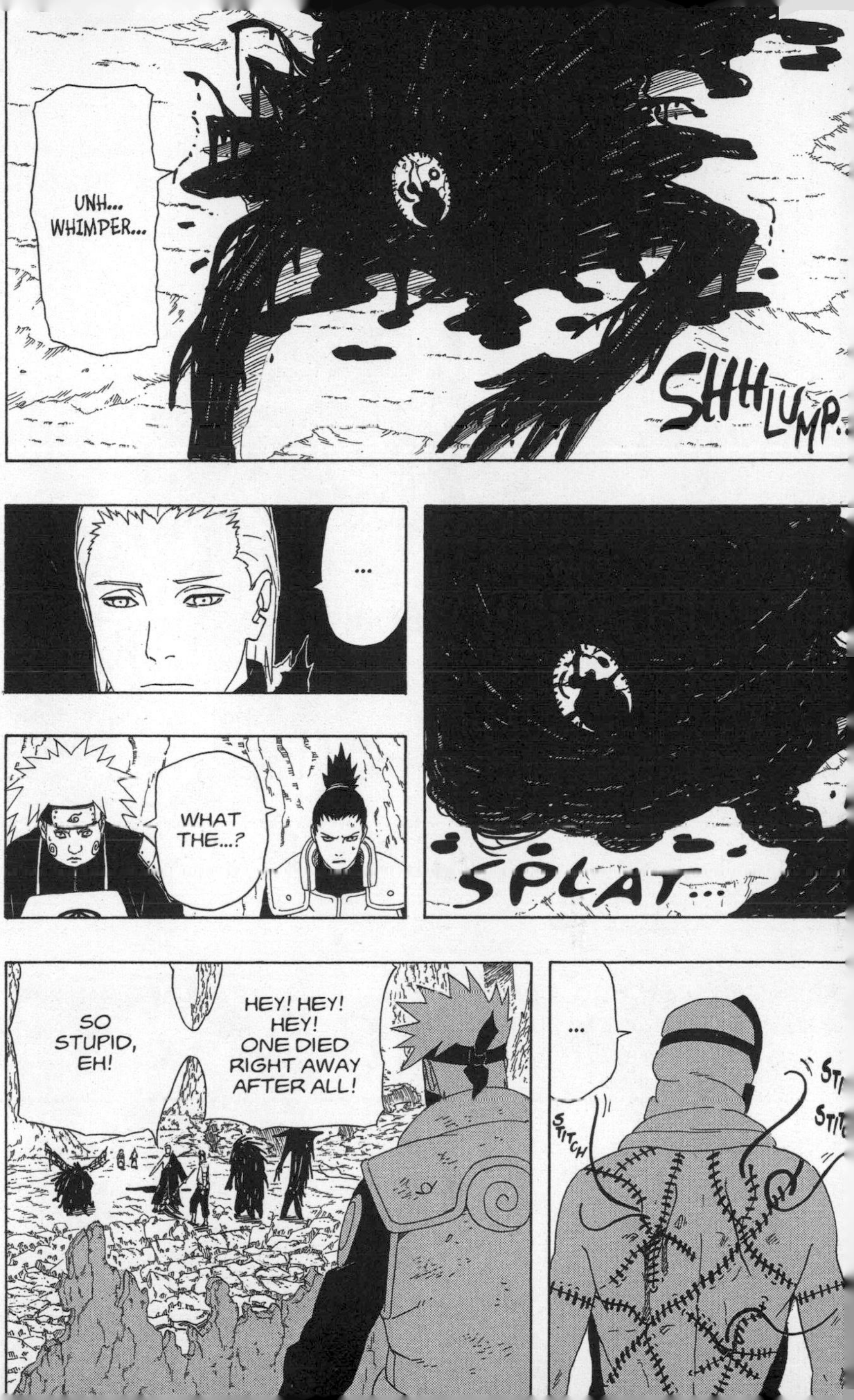
UNH... WHIMPER...
SHHLUMP...
SPLAT...
...
WHAT THE...?
...
STITCH
HEY! HEY! HEY! ONE DIED RIGHT AWAY AFTER ALL!
SO STUPID, EH!

READ THIS WAY

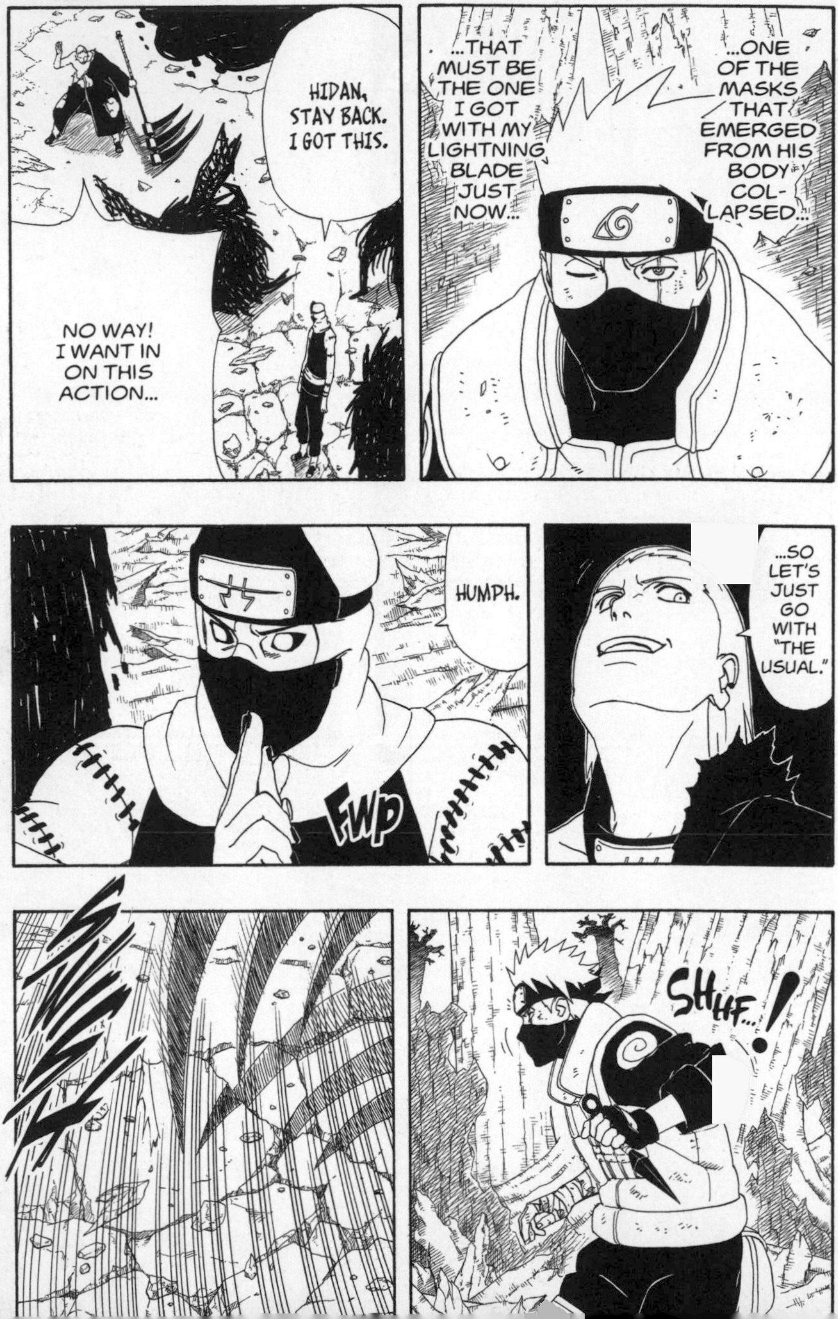
...ONE OF THE MASKS THAT EMERGED FROM HIS BODY COL-LAPSED...
...THAT MUST BE THE ONE I GOT WITH MY LIGHTNING BLADE JUST NOW...
HIDAN, STAY BACK. I GOT THIS.
NO WAY! I WANT IN ON THIS ACTION...
...SO LET'S JUST GO WITH "THE USUAL."
HUMPH.
FWP
SHHF...!

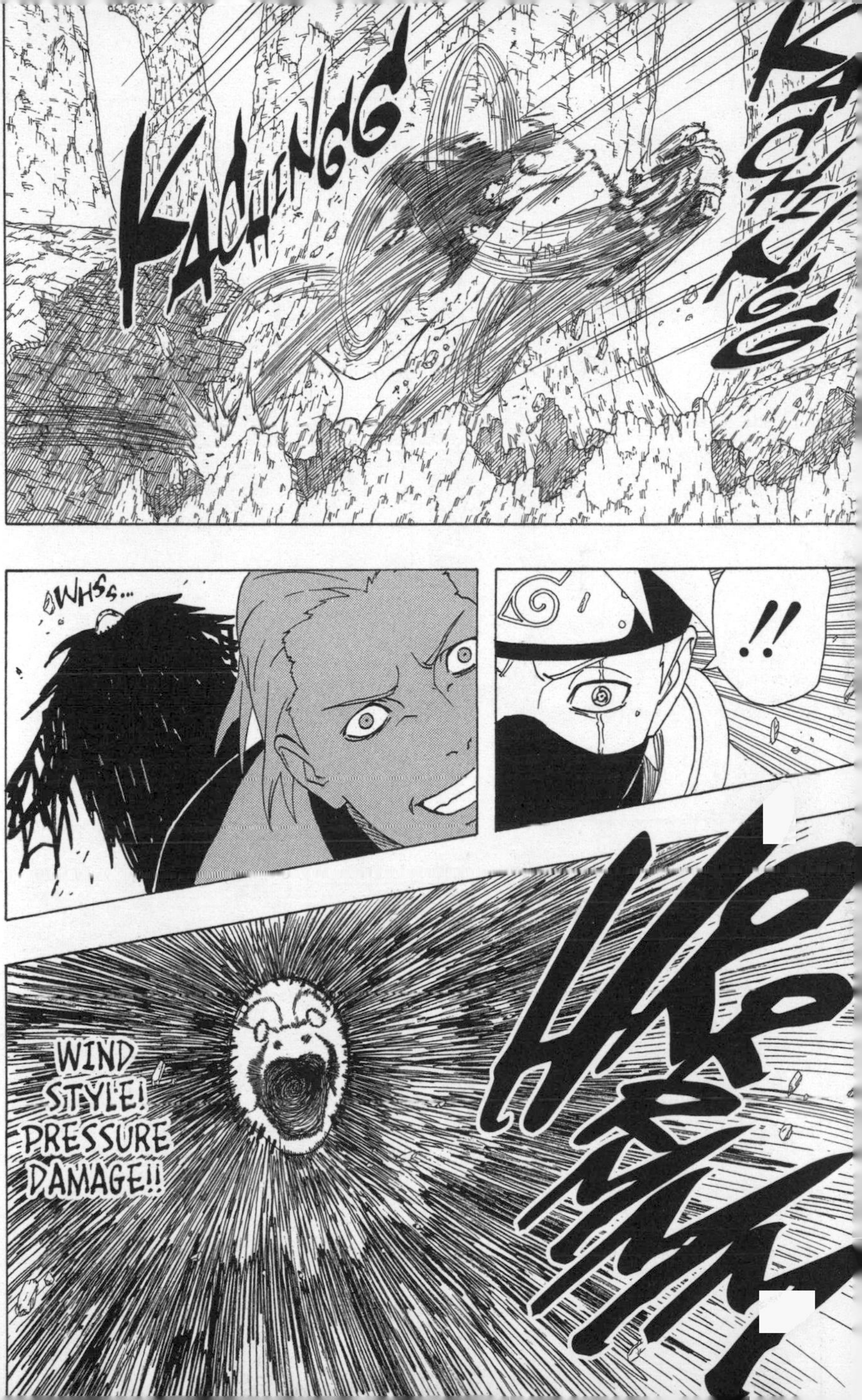
KACHINGG
KACHINGG
!!
WHSS...
WIND STYLE! PRESSURE DAMAGE!!

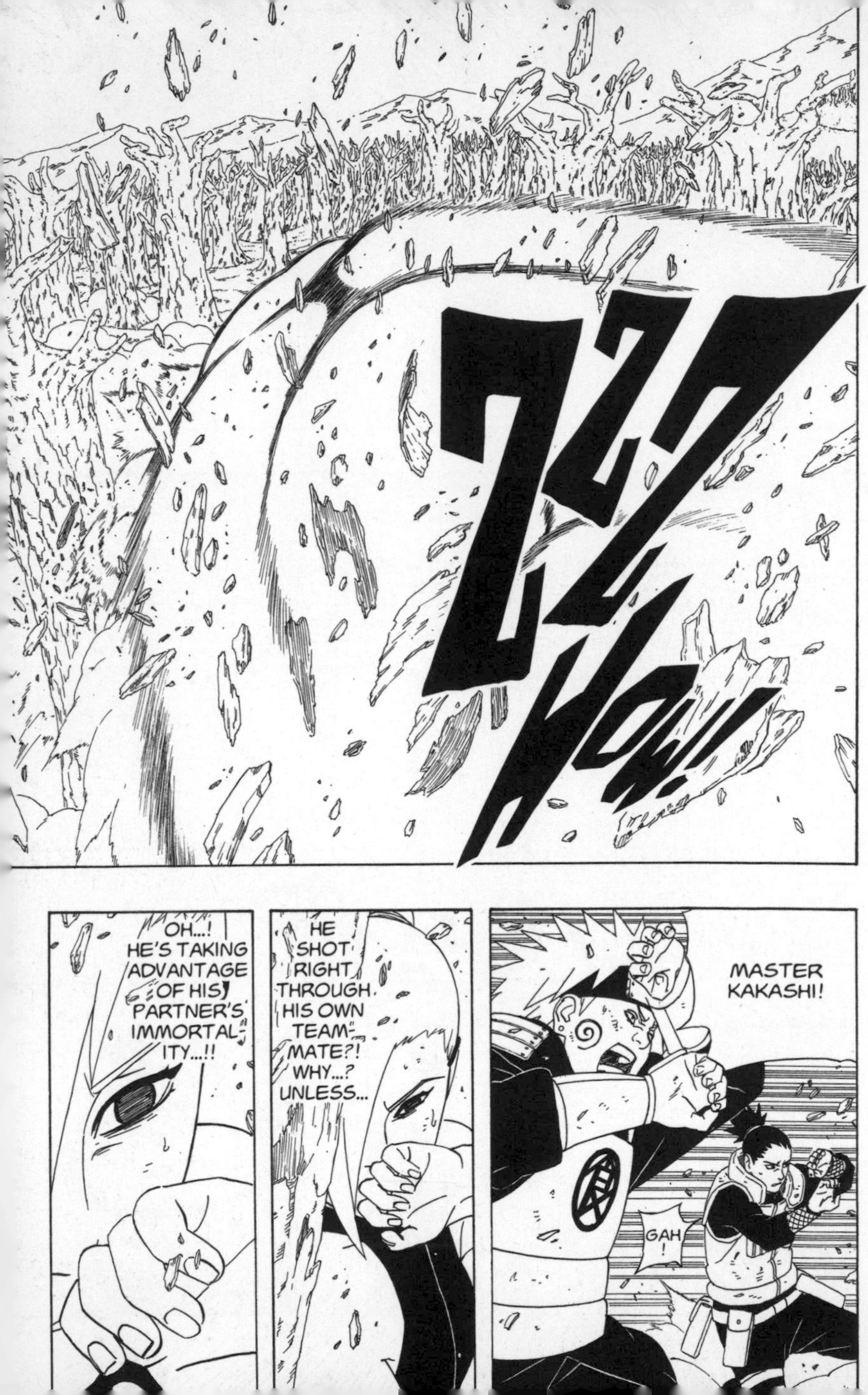
MASTER KAKASHI!
GAH!
HE SHOT RIGHT THROUGH HIS OWN TEAM-MATE?! WHY...? UNLESS...
OH...! HE'S TAKING ADVANTAGE OF HIS PARTNER'S IMMORTAL-ITY...!!

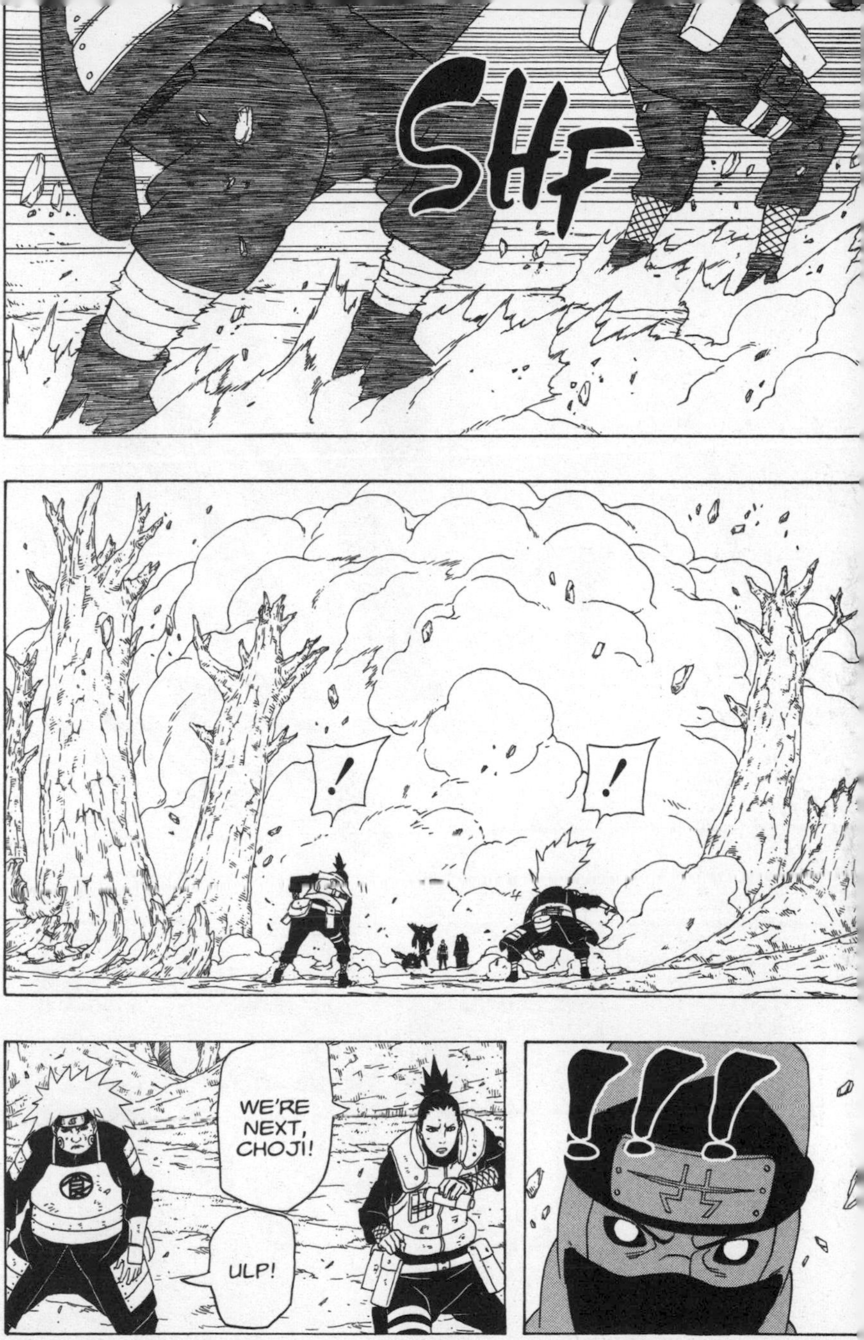
SHF
!
!
!!!
WE'RE NEXT, CHOJI!
ULP!

READ THIS WAY

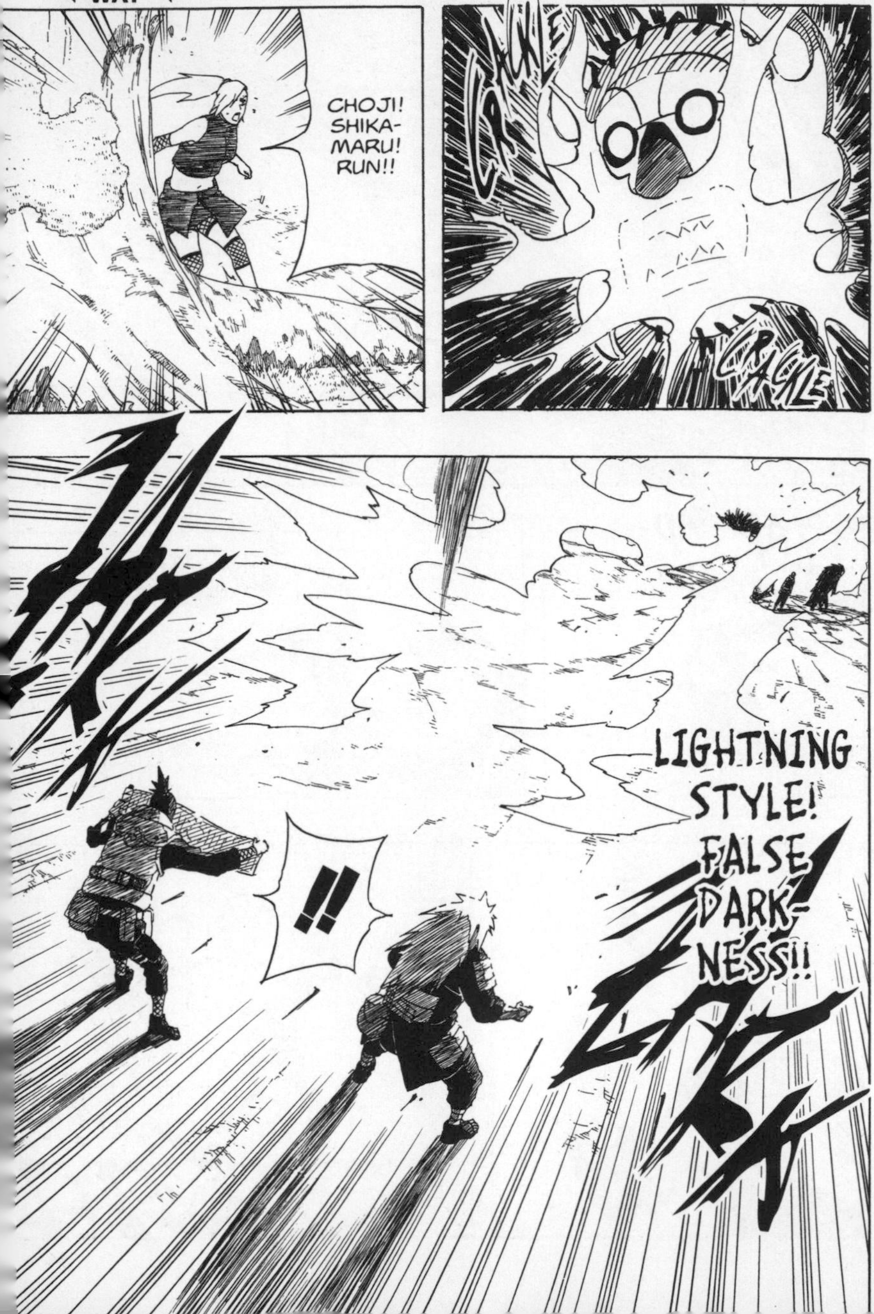
CRACKLE
CRACKLE
CHOJI! SHIKA-MARU! RUN!!
LIGHTNING STYLE! FALSE DARK-NESS!!
!!

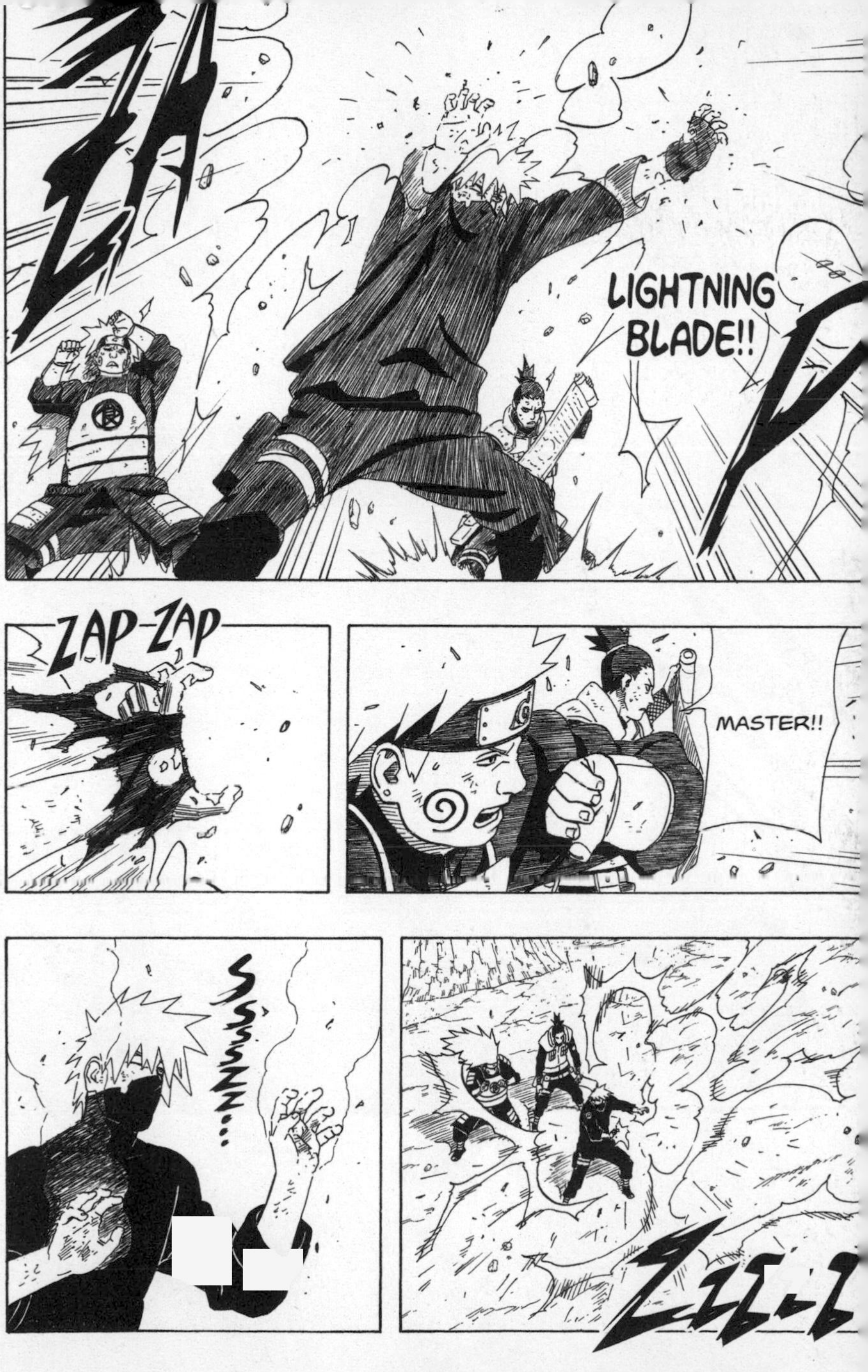
LIGHTNING BLADE!!
MASTER!!
ZAP-ZAP
SSSSZZZ...

READ THIS WAY

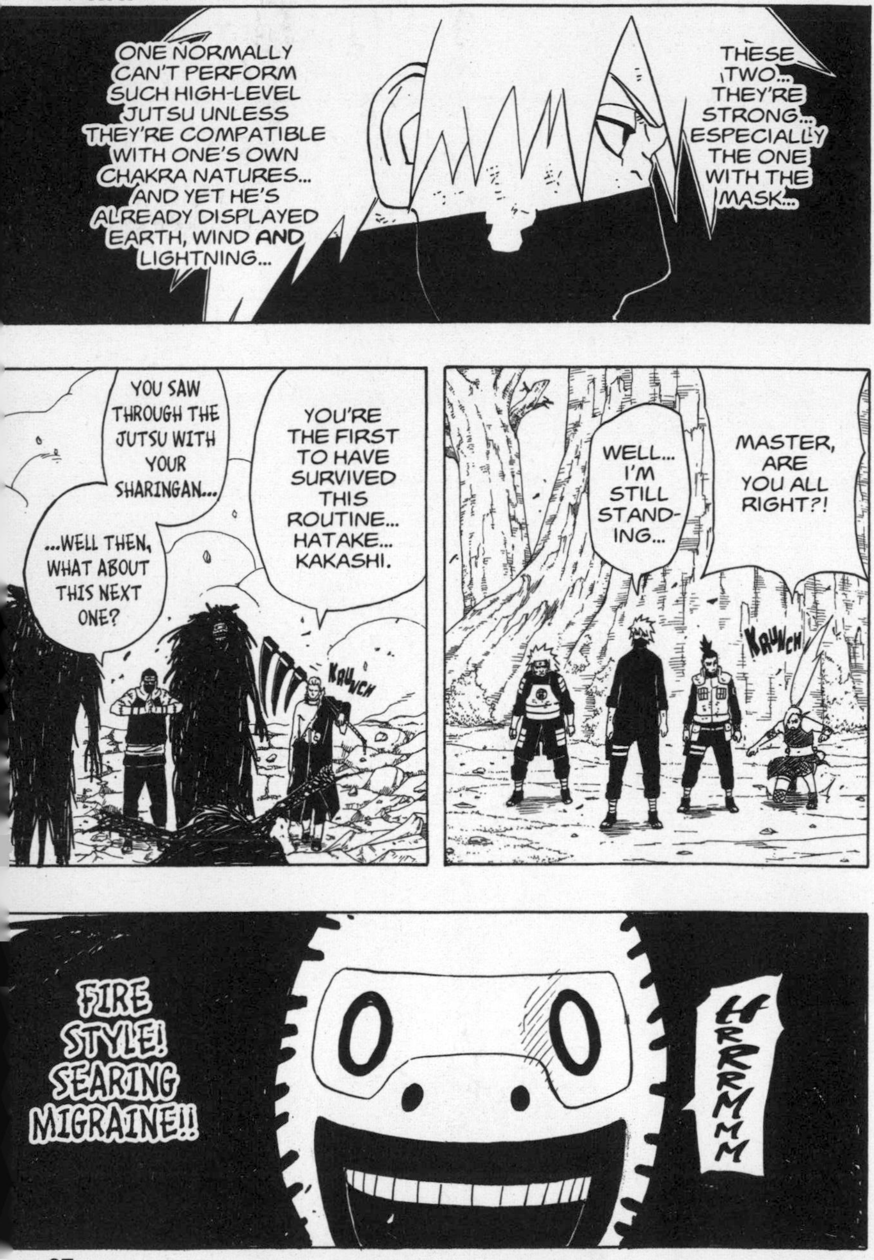
THESE TWO... THEY'RE STRONG... ESPECIALLY THE ONE WITH THE MASK...
ONE NORMALLY CAN'T PERFORM SUCH HIGH-LEVEL JUTSU UNLESS THEY'RE COMPATIBLE WITH ONE'S OWN CHAKRA NATURES... AND YET HE'S ALREADY DISPLAYED EARTH, WIND AND LIGHTNING...
MASTER, ARE YOU ALL RIGHT?!
WELL... I'M STILL STAND-ING...
KRUNCH
YOU'RE THE FIRST TO HAVE SURVIVED THIS ROUTINE... HATAKE... KAKASHI.
YOU SAW THROUGH THE JUTSU WITH YOUR SHARINGAN...
...WELL THEN, WHAT ABOUT THIS NEXT ONE?
KRUNCH
HRRRMMM
FIRE STYLE! SEARING MIGRAINE!!

NARUTO

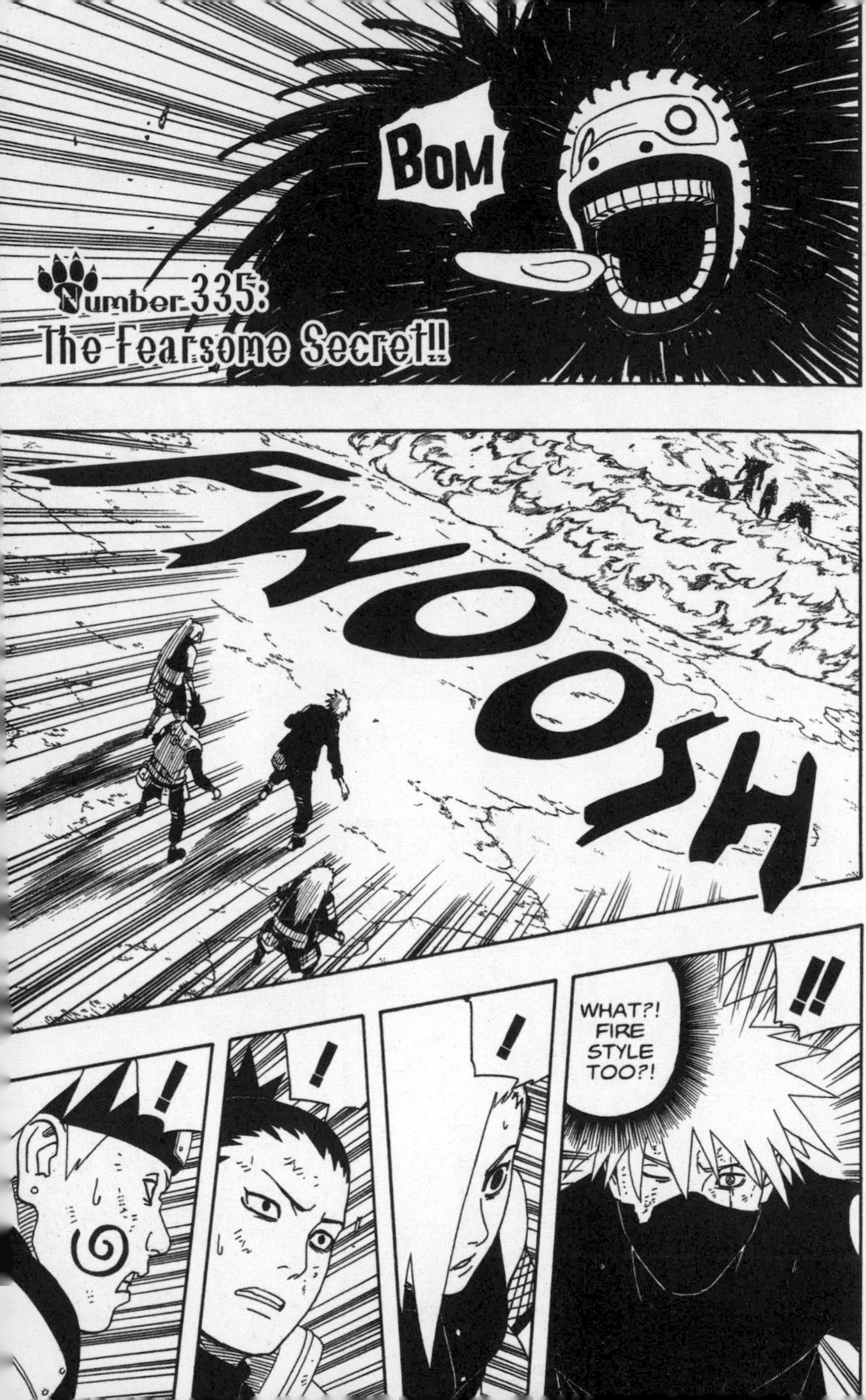
BOM
Number 335:
The Fearsome Secret!!
WHOOSH
!!
WHAT?! FIRE STYLE TOO?!
!
!
!

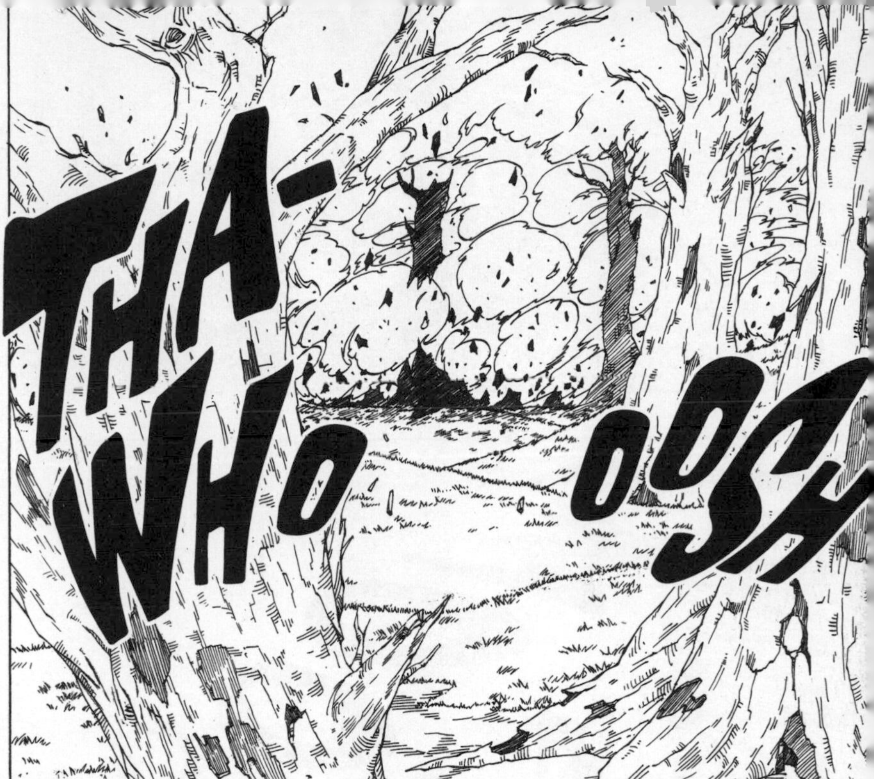
THA-WHOOOSH

Number 335: The Fearsome Secret!!

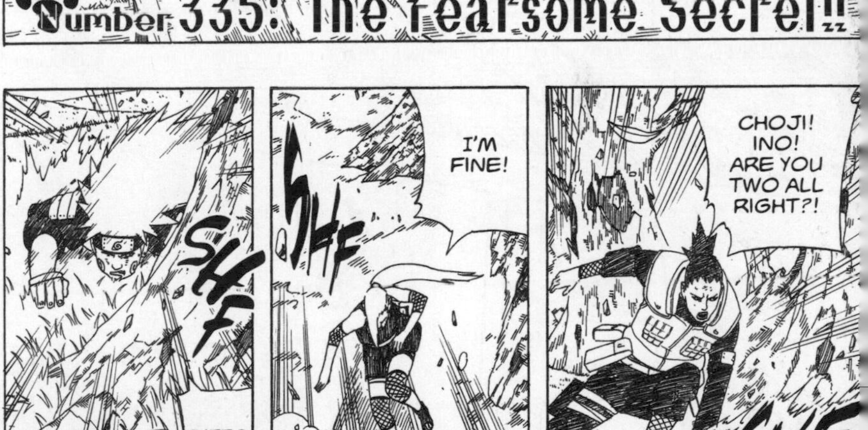
CHOJI! INO! ARE YOU TWO ALL RIGHT?!
SHF
I'M FINE!
SHF
SHF
DITTO!

READ THIS WAY

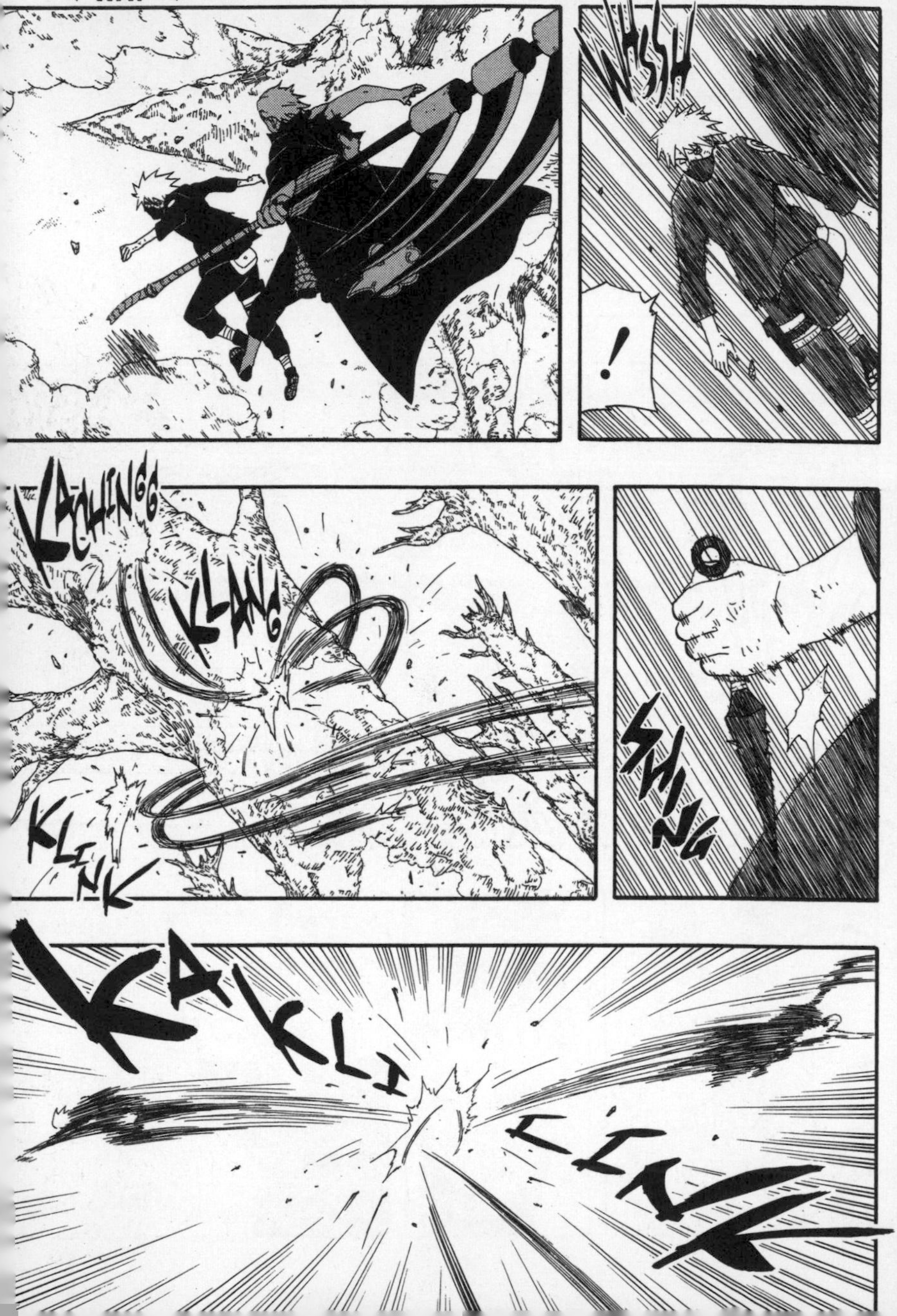
WHSSH
!
SHING
KACHINGG
KLANG
KLINK
KAKLICLINK

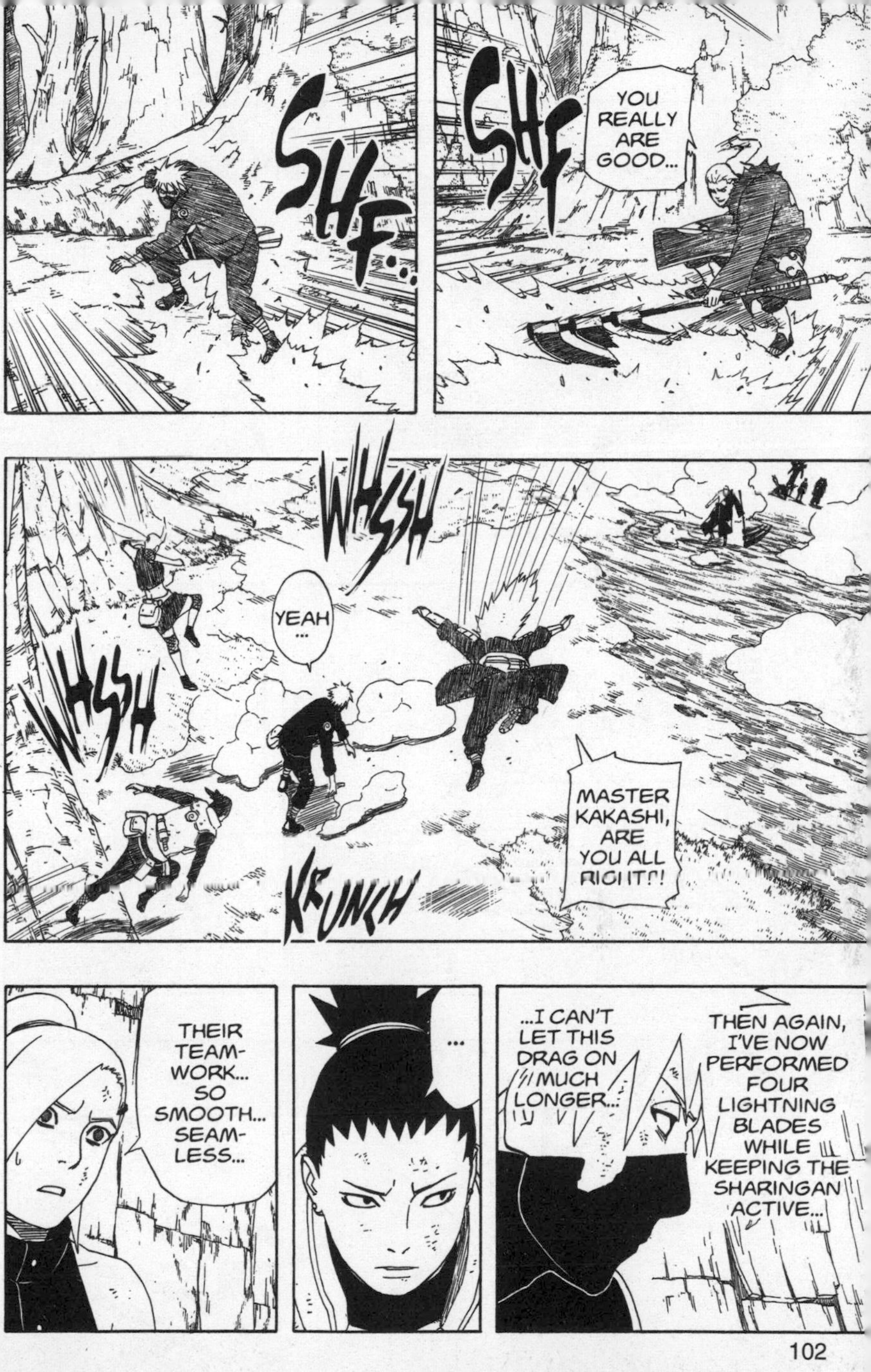
SHF
YOU REALLY ARE GOOD...
SHF...
WHSSH
YEAH...
MASTER KAKASHI, ARE YOU ALL RIGHT?!
WHSSH
KRUNCH
THEN AGAIN, I'VE NOW PERFORMED FOUR LIGHTNING BLADES WHILE KEEPING THE SHARINGAN ACTIVE...
...I CAN'T LET THIS DRAG ON MUCH LONGER...
...
THEIR TEAM-WORK... SO SMOOTH... SEAM-LESS...

READ THIS WAY

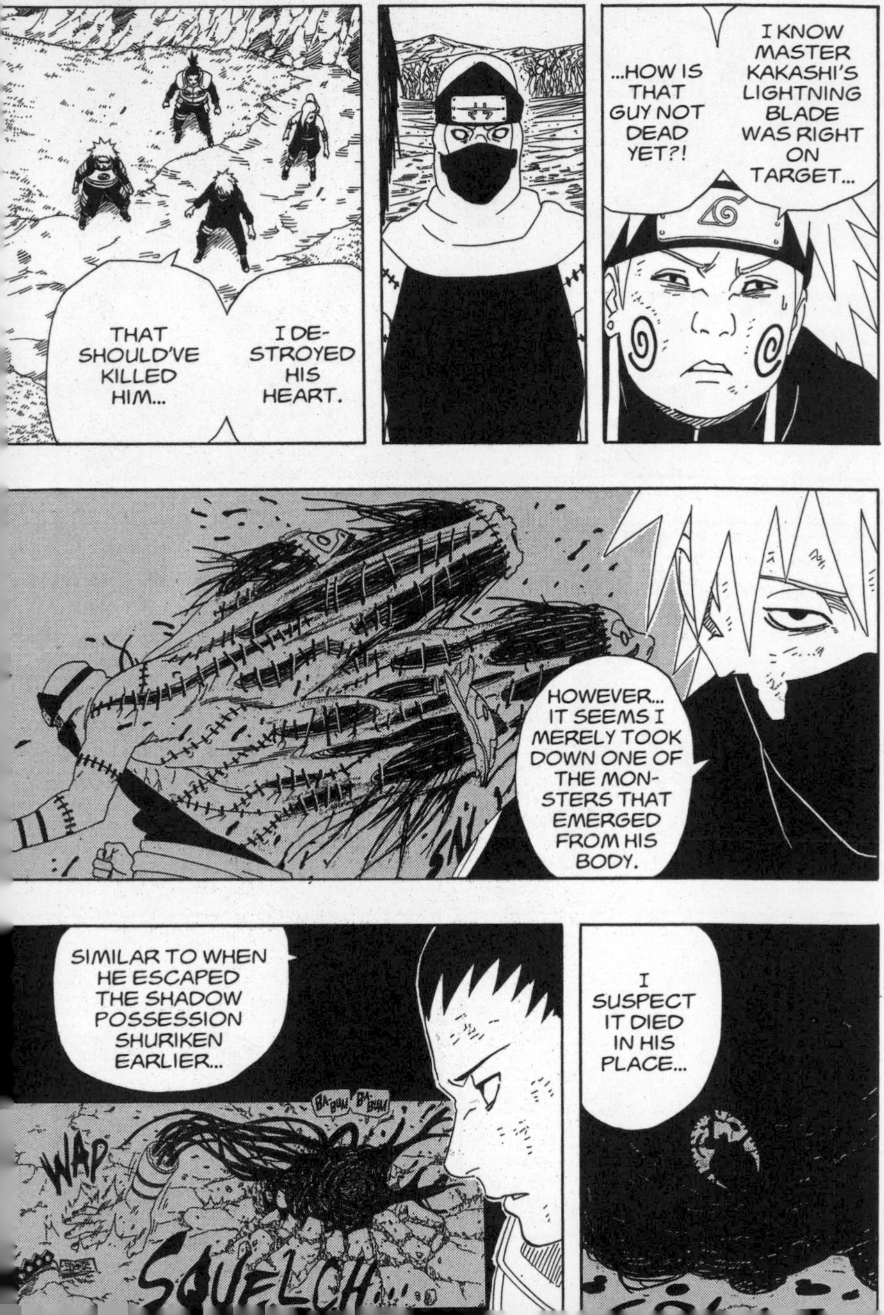
I KNOW MASTER KAKASHI'S LIGHTNING BLADE WAS RIGHT ON TARGET...
...HOW IS THAT GUY NOT DEAD YET?!
I DESTROYED HIS HEART.
THAT SHOULD'VE KILLED HIM...
HOWEVER... IT SEEMS I MERELY TOOK DOWN ONE OF THE MONSTERS THAT EMERGED FROM HIS BODY.
I SUSPECT IT DIED IN HIS PLACE...
SIMILAR TO WHEN HE ESCAPED THE SHADOW POSSESSION SHURIKEN EARLIER...
BA-BUM
BA-BUM
WAP
SQUELCH

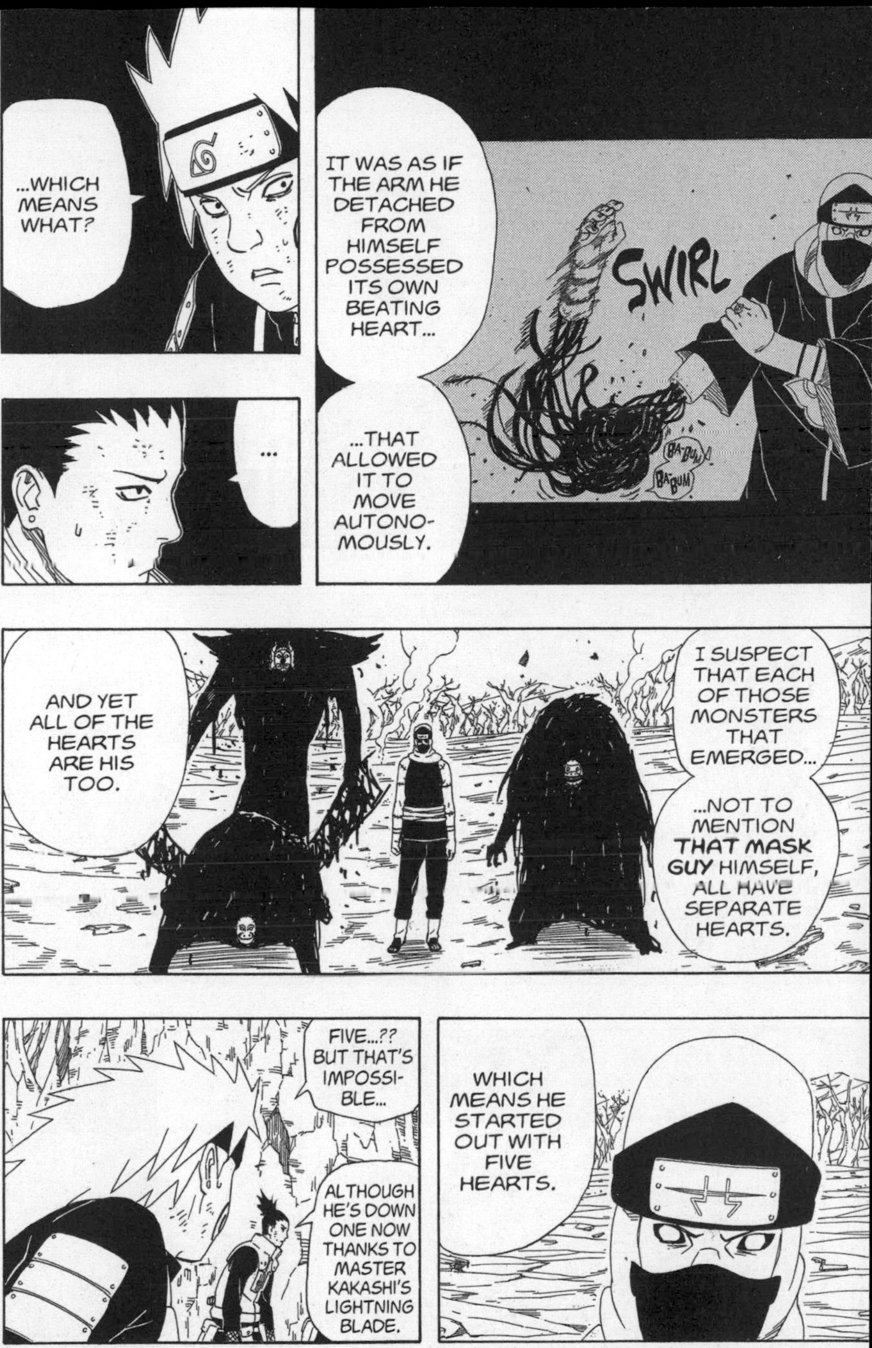
IT WAS AS IF THE ARM HE DETACHED FROM HIMSELF POSSESSED ITS OWN BEATING HEART...
...THAT ALLOWED IT TO MOVE AUTONOMOUSLY.
SWIRL
BA-DUM
BA-DUM
...WHICH MEANS WHAT?
...
I SUSPECT THAT EACH OF THOSE MONSTERS THAT EMERGED...
...NOT TO MENTION **THAT MASK GUY** HIMSELF, ALL HAVE SEPARATE HEARTS.
AND YET ALL OF THE HEARTS ARE HIS TOO.
WHICH MEANS HE STARTED OUT WITH FIVE HEARTS.
FIVE...?? BUT THAT'S IMPOSSIBLE...
ALTHOUGH HE'S DOWN ONE NOW THANKS TO MASTER KAKASHI'S LIGHTNING BLADE.

READ THIS WAY

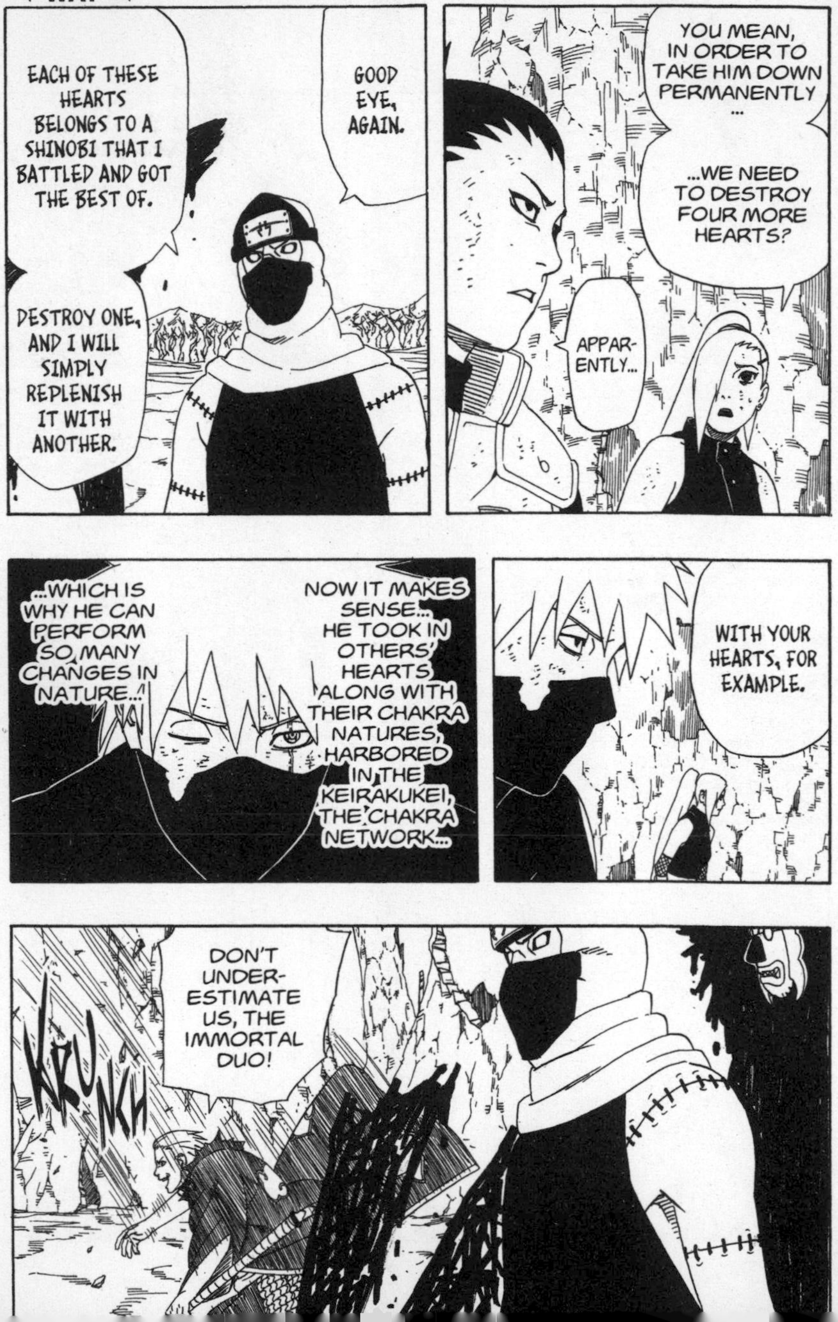
YOU MEAN, IN ORDER TO TAKE HIM DOWN PERMANENTLY...
...WE NEED TO DESTROY FOUR MORE HEARTS?
APPARENTLY...
GOOD EYE, AGAIN.
EACH OF THESE HEARTS BELONGS TO A SHINOBI THAT I BATTLED AND GOT THE BEST OF.
DESTROY ONE, AND I WILL SIMPLY REPLENISH IT WITH ANOTHER.
WITH YOUR HEARTS, FOR EXAMPLE.
NOW IT MAKES SENSE... HE TOOK IN OTHERS' HEARTS ALONG WITH THEIR CHAKRA NATURES, HARBORED IN THE KEIRAKUKEI, THE CHAKRA NETWORK...
...WHICH IS WHY HE CAN PERFORM SO MANY CHANGES IN NATURE...!
DON'T UNDER-ESTIMATE US, THE IMMORTAL DUO!
KRUNCH

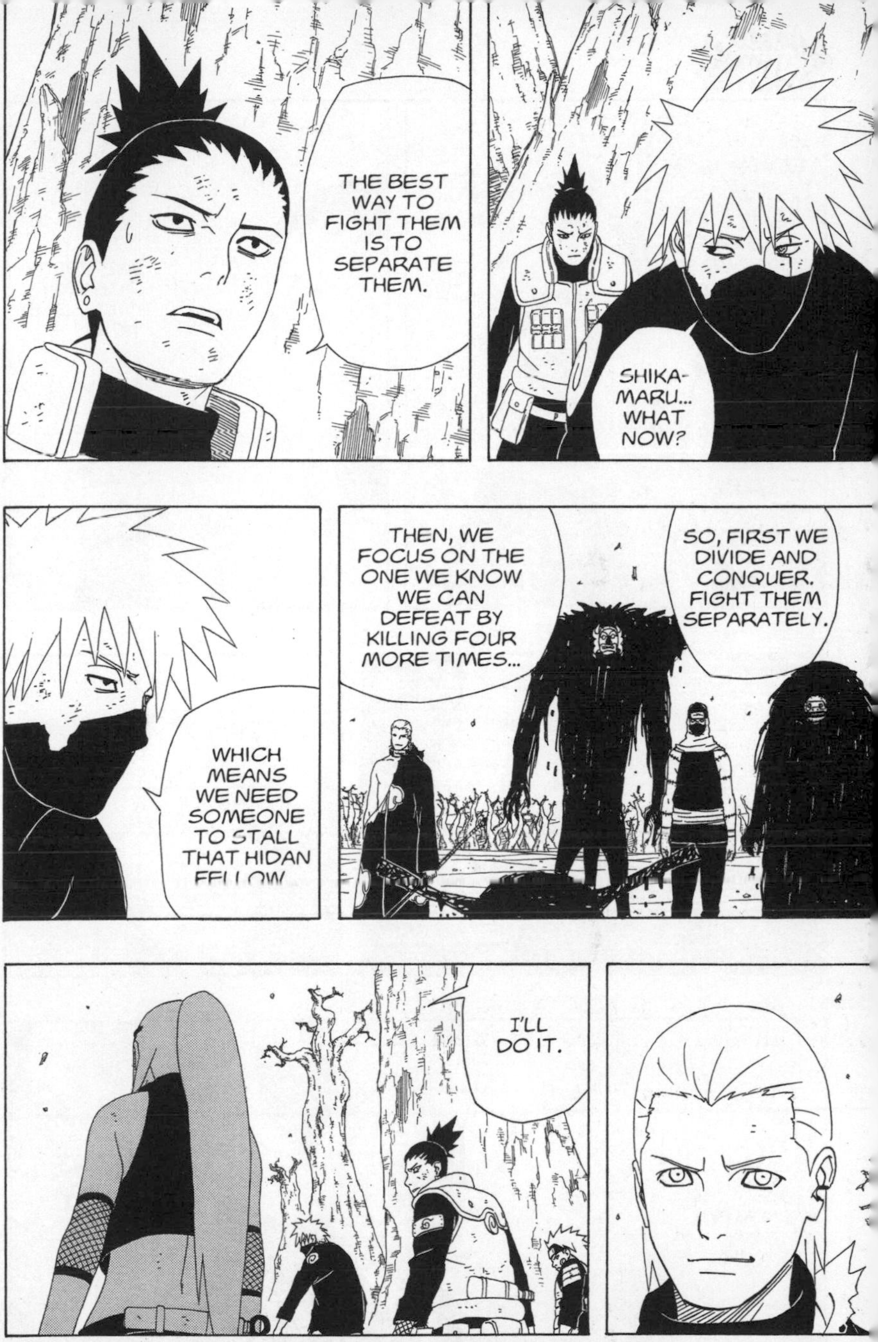
SHIKA-MARU... WHAT NOW?
THE BEST WAY TO FIGHT THEM IS TO SEPARATE THEM.
SO, FIRST WE DIVIDE AND CONQUER. FIGHT THEM SEPARATELY.
THEN, WE FOCUS ON THE ONE WE KNOW WE CAN DEFEAT BY KILLING FOUR MORE TIMES...
WHICH MEANS WE NEED SOMEONE TO STALL THAT HIDAN FELLOW.
I'LL DO IT.

READ THIS WAY

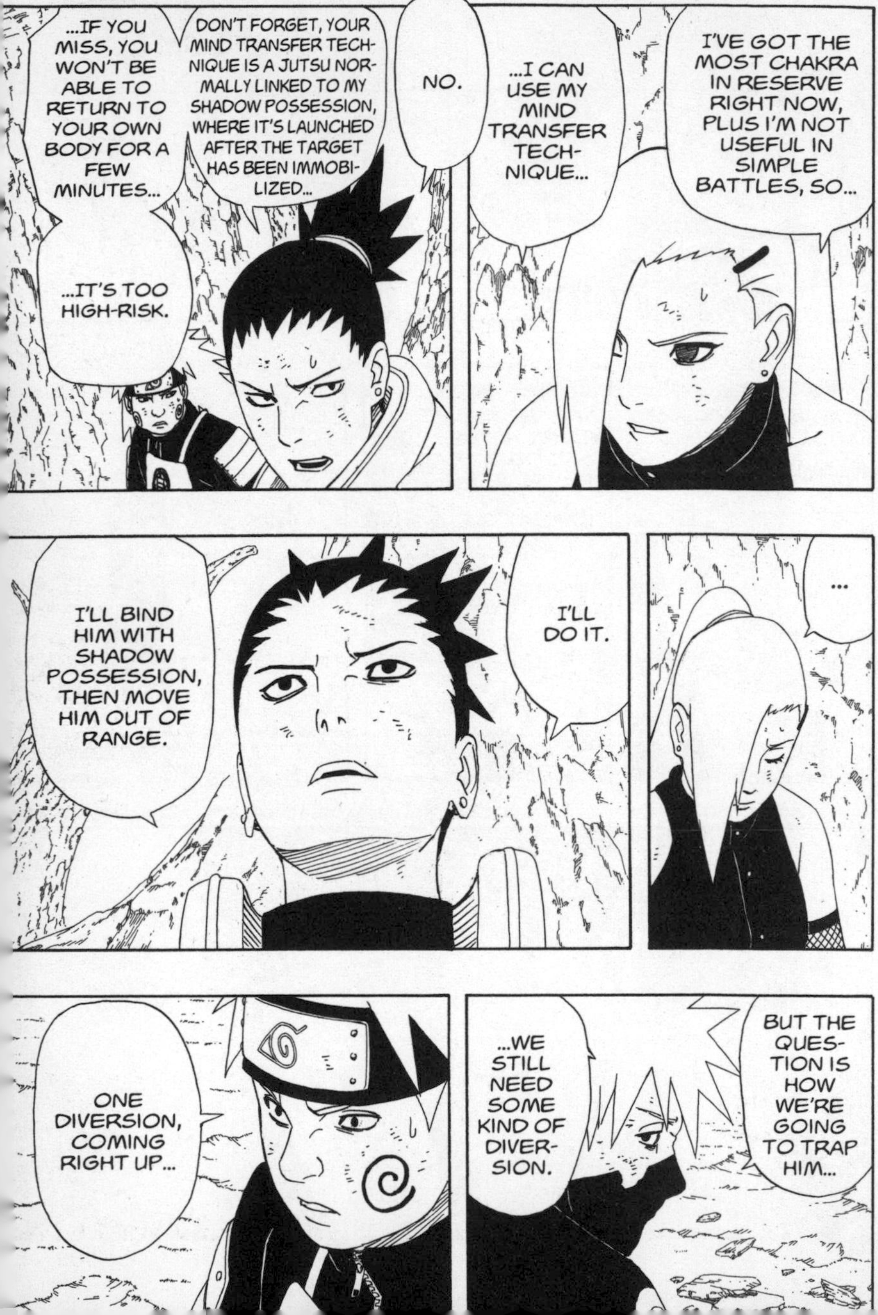
I'VE GOT THE MOST CHAKRA IN RESERVE RIGHT NOW, PLUS I'M NOT USEFUL IN SIMPLE BATTLES, SO...
...I CAN USE MY MIND TRANSFER TECHNIQUE...
NO.
DON'T FORGET, YOUR MIND TRANSFER TECHNIQUE IS A JUTSU NORMALLY LINKED TO MY SHADOW POSSESSION, WHERE IT'S LAUNCHED AFTER THE TARGET HAS BEEN IMMOBILIZED...
...IF YOU MISS, YOU WON'T BE ABLE TO RETURN TO YOUR OWN BODY FOR A FEW MINUTES...
...IT'S TOO HIGH-RISK.
...
I'LL DO IT.
I'LL BIND HIM WITH SHADOW POSSESSION, THEN MOVE HIM OUT OF RANGE.
BUT THE QUESTION IS HOW WE'RE GOING TO TRAP HIM...
...WE STILL NEED SOME KIND OF DIVERSION.
ONE DIVERSION, COMING RIGHT UP...

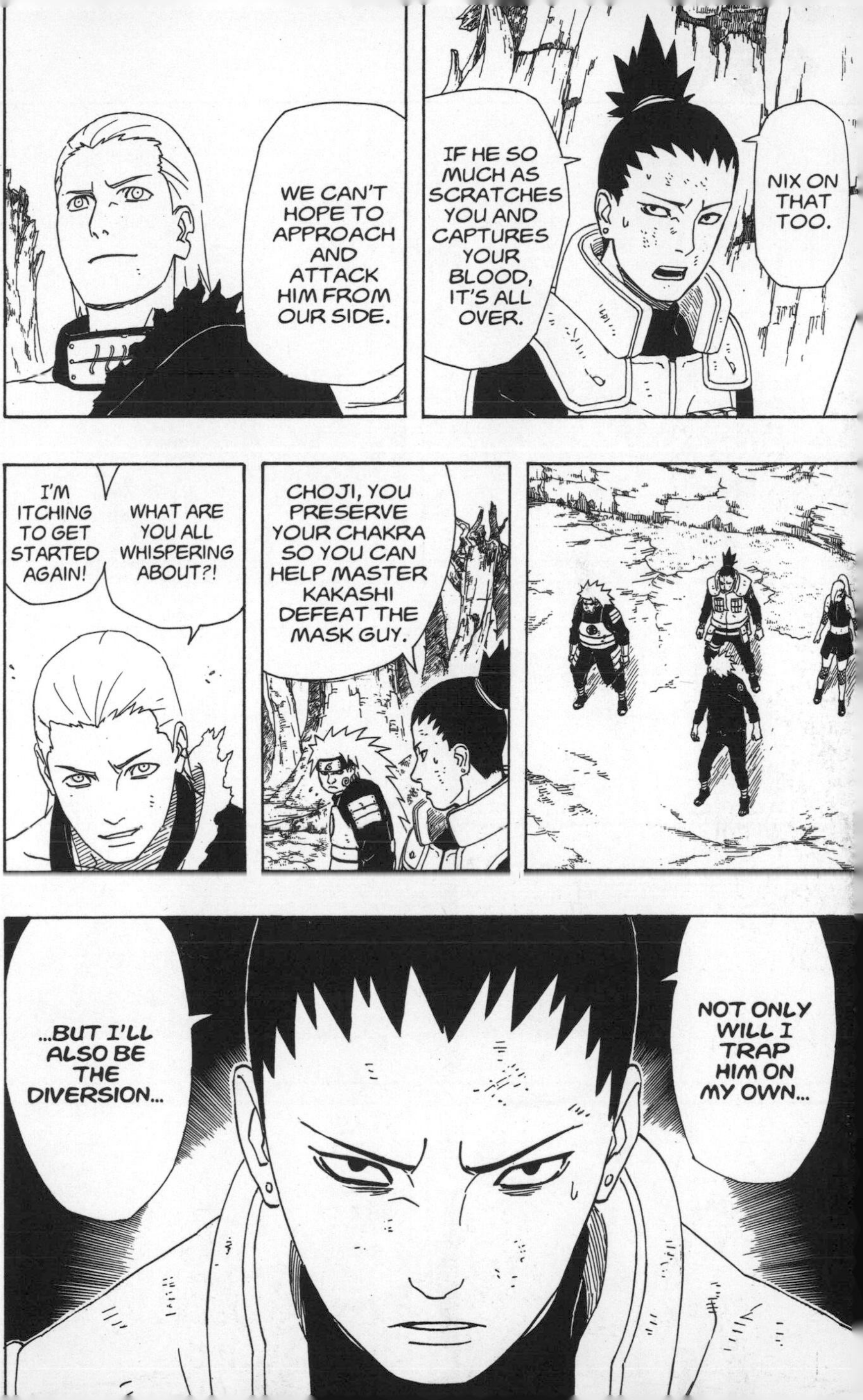
NIX ON THAT TOO.
IF HE SO MUCH AS SCRATCHES YOU AND CAPTURES YOUR BLOOD, IT'S ALL OVER.
WE CAN'T HOPE TO APPROACH AND ATTACK HIM FROM OUR SIDE.
CHOJI, YOU PRESERVE YOUR CHAKRA SO YOU CAN HELP MASTER KAKASHI DEFEAT THE MASK GUY.
WHAT ARE YOU ALL WHISPERING ABOUT?!
I'M ITCHING TO GET STARTED AGAIN!
NOT ONLY WILL I TRAP HIM ON MY OWN...
...BUT I'LL ALSO BE THE DIVERSION...

READ THIS WAY

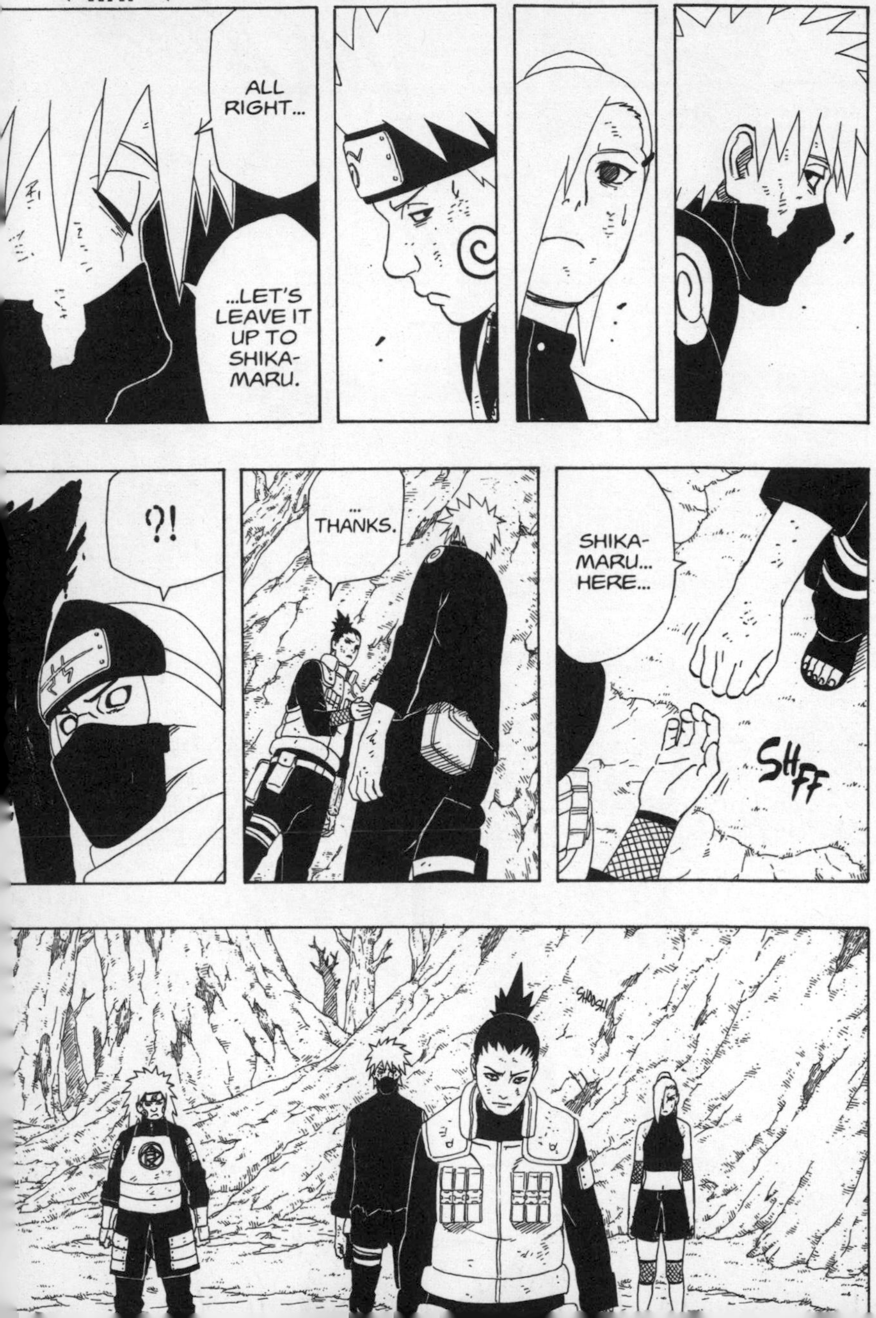
ALL RIGHT...
...LET'S LEAVE IT UP TO SHIKA-MARU.
SHIKA-MARU... HERE...
SHFF
...THANKS.
?!
SHOOSH

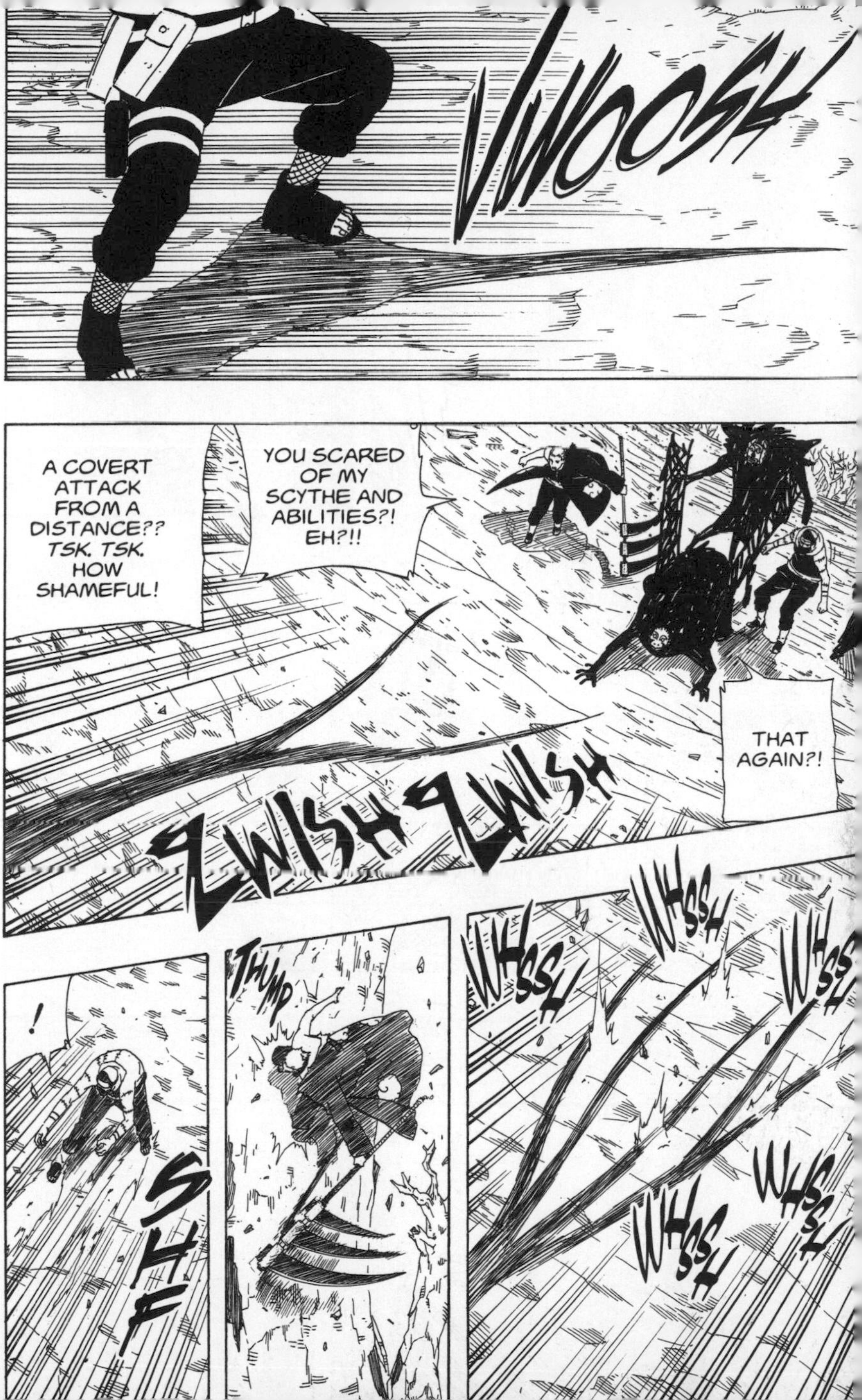
VWOOSH
YOU SCARED OF MY SCYTHE AND ABILITIES?! EH?!!
A COVERT ATTACK FROM A DISTANCE?? TSK. TSK. HOW SHAMEFUL!
THAT AGAIN?!
ZWISH ZWISH
WHSSH
WHSSH
WHSSH
WHSSH
WHSSH
THUMP
!
SHF

READ THIS WAY

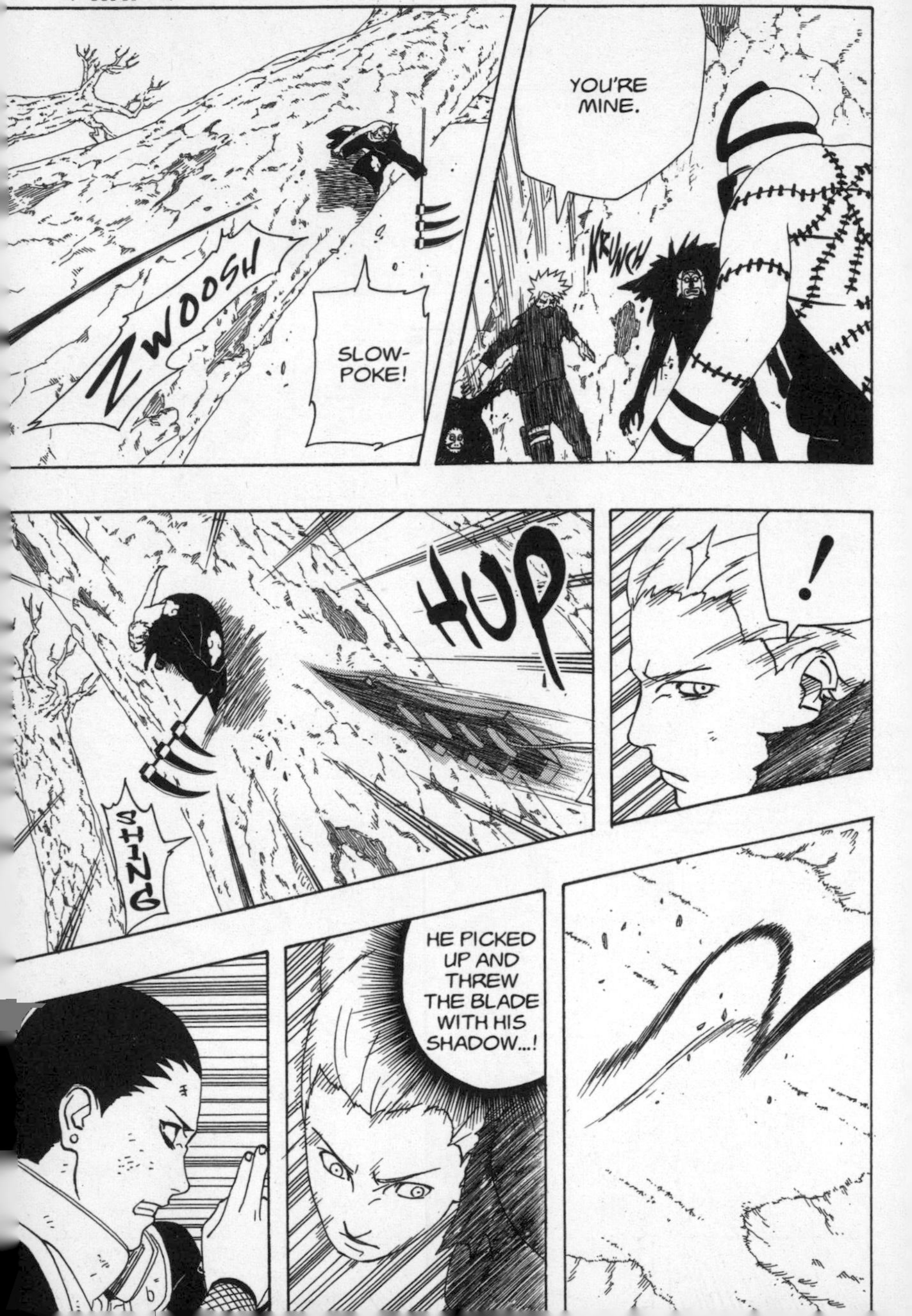
YOU'RE MINE.
KRUNCH
SLOW-POKE!
ZWOOSH
!
HUP
SHING
HE PICKED UP AND THREW THE BLADE WITH HIS SHADOW...!

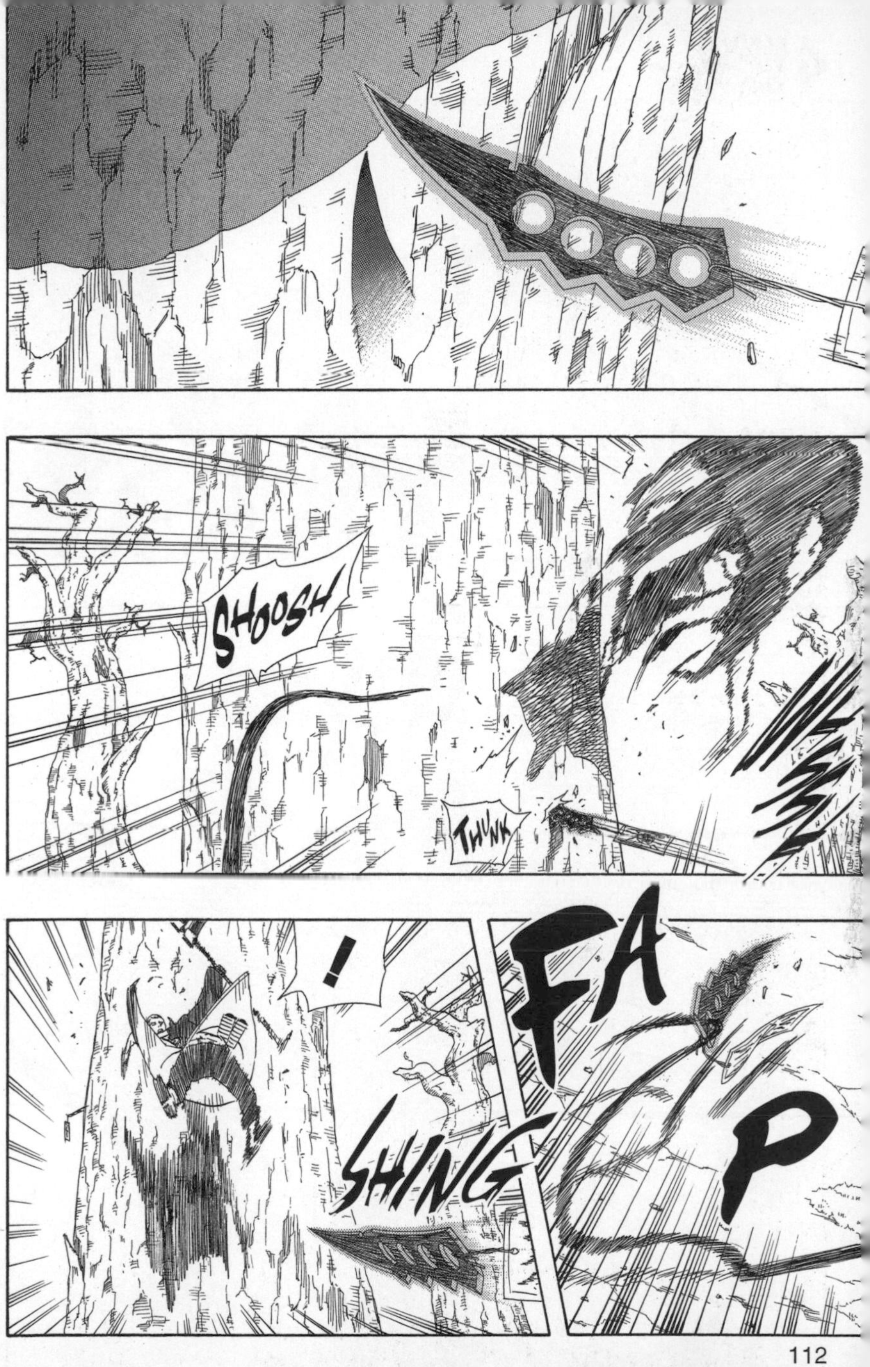
SHOOSH
THUNK
FA
P
!
SHING

READ THIS WAY

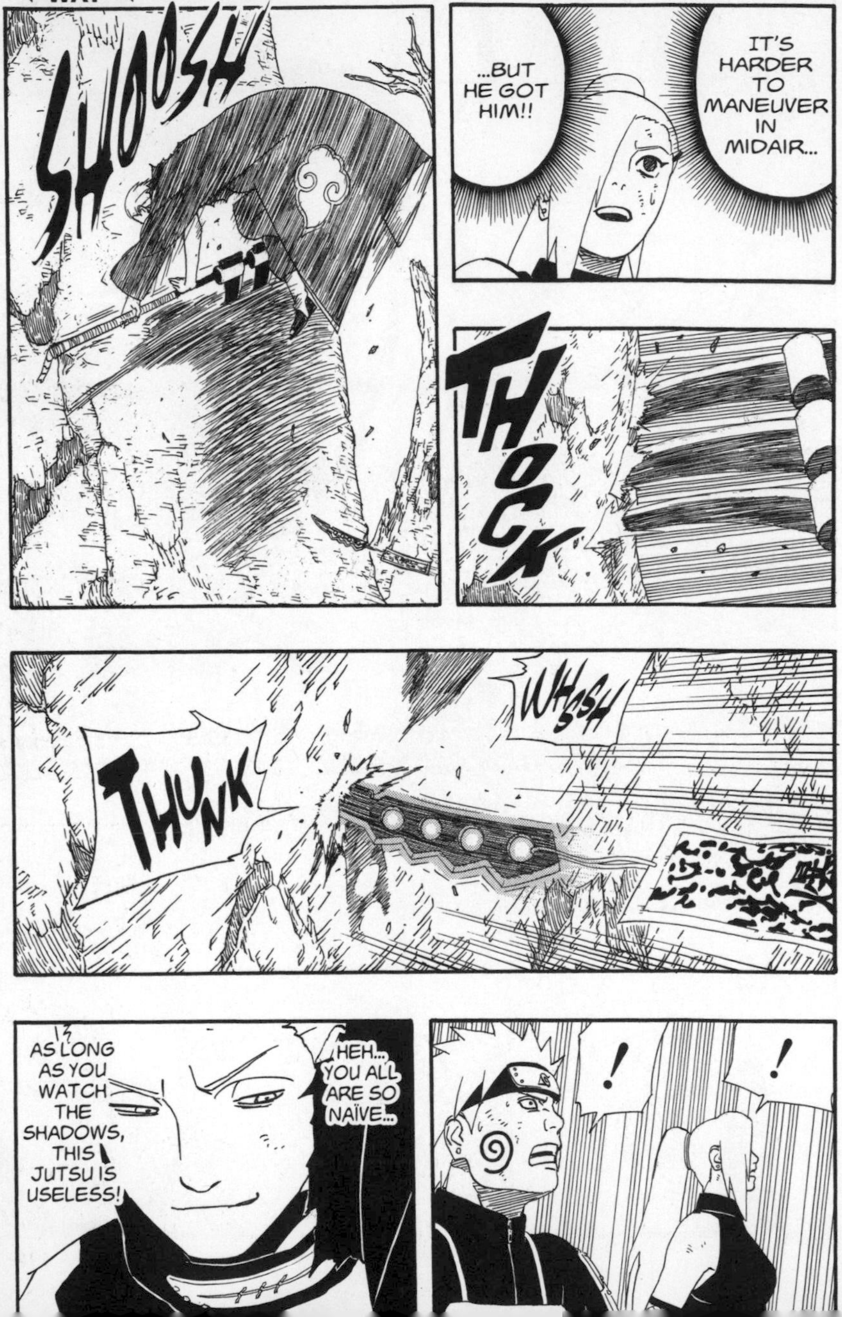
IT'S HARDER TO MANEUVER IN MIDAIR...
...BUT HE GOT HIM!!
THOCK
SHOOSH
WHSSH
THUNK
!
!
HEH... YOU ALL ARE SO NAÏVE...
AS LONG AS YOU WATCH THE SHADOWS, THIS JUTSU IS USELESS!

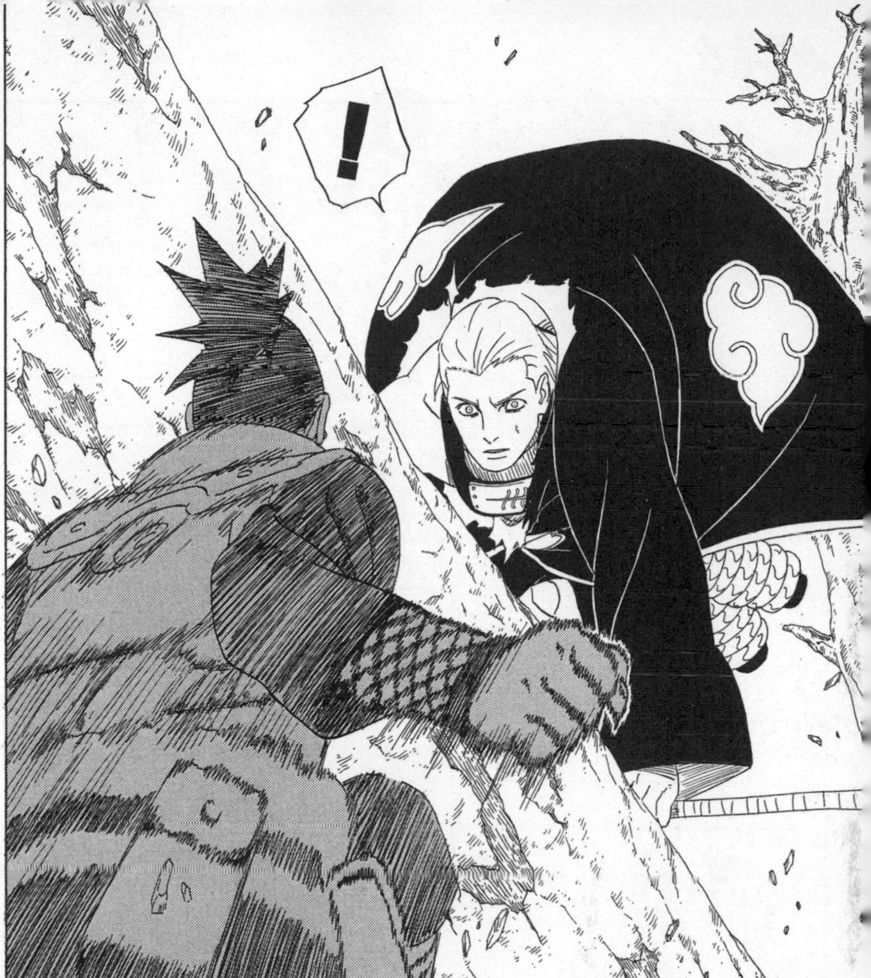
!

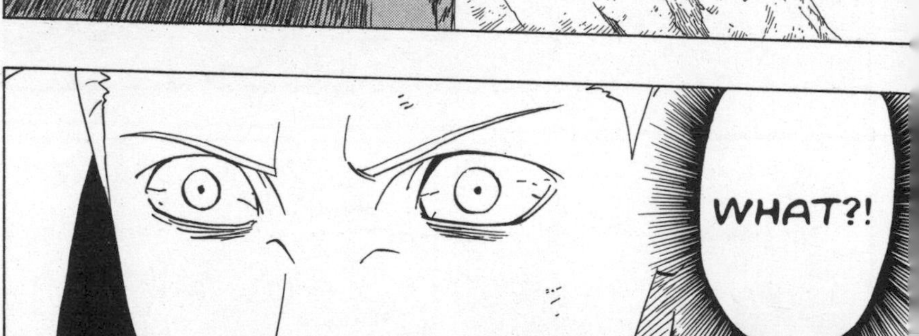
WHAT?!

READ THIS WAY

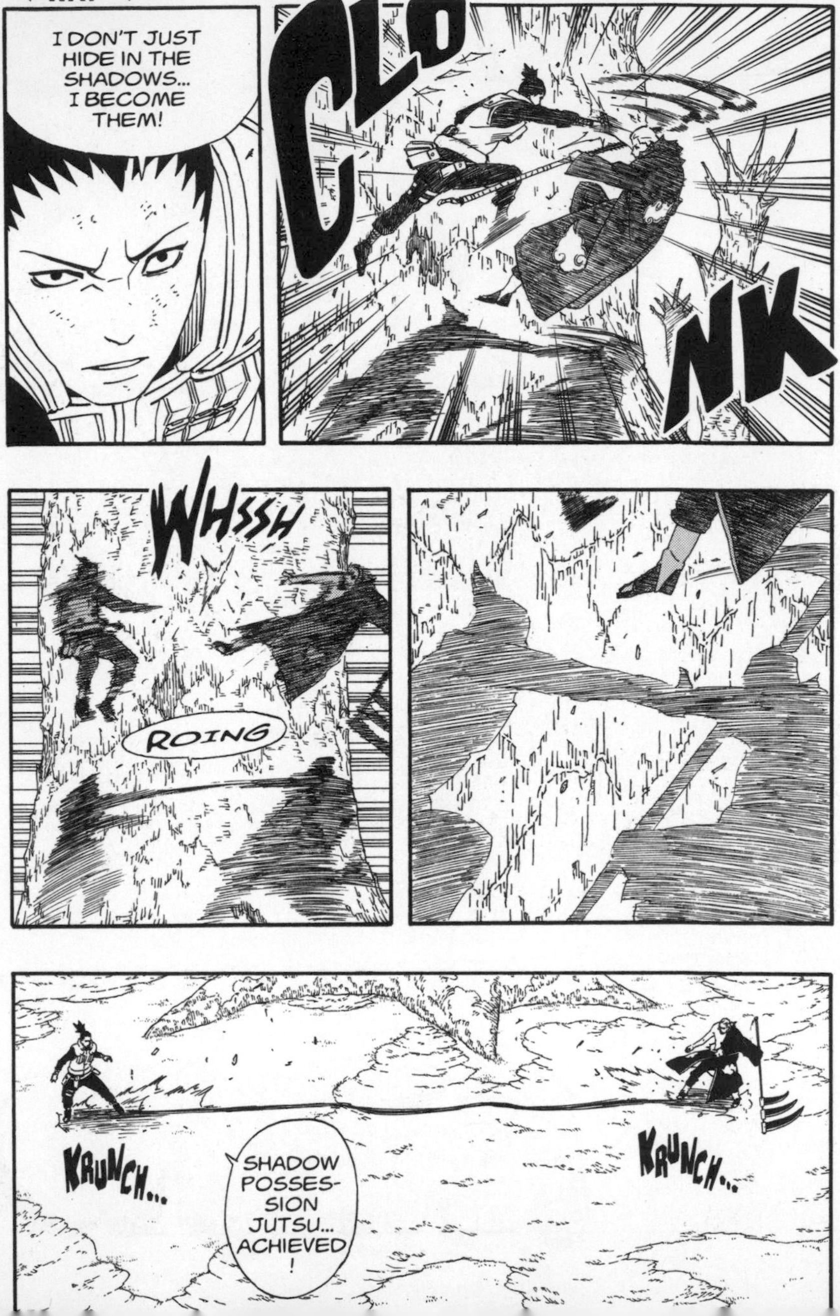
CLONK
I DON'T JUST HIDE IN THE SHADOWS... I BECOME THEM!
WHSSH
ROING
KRUNCH...
SHADOW POSSESSION JUTSU... ACHIEVED!
KRUNCH...

NARUTO

Number 336: Turnabout Dilemma...!!

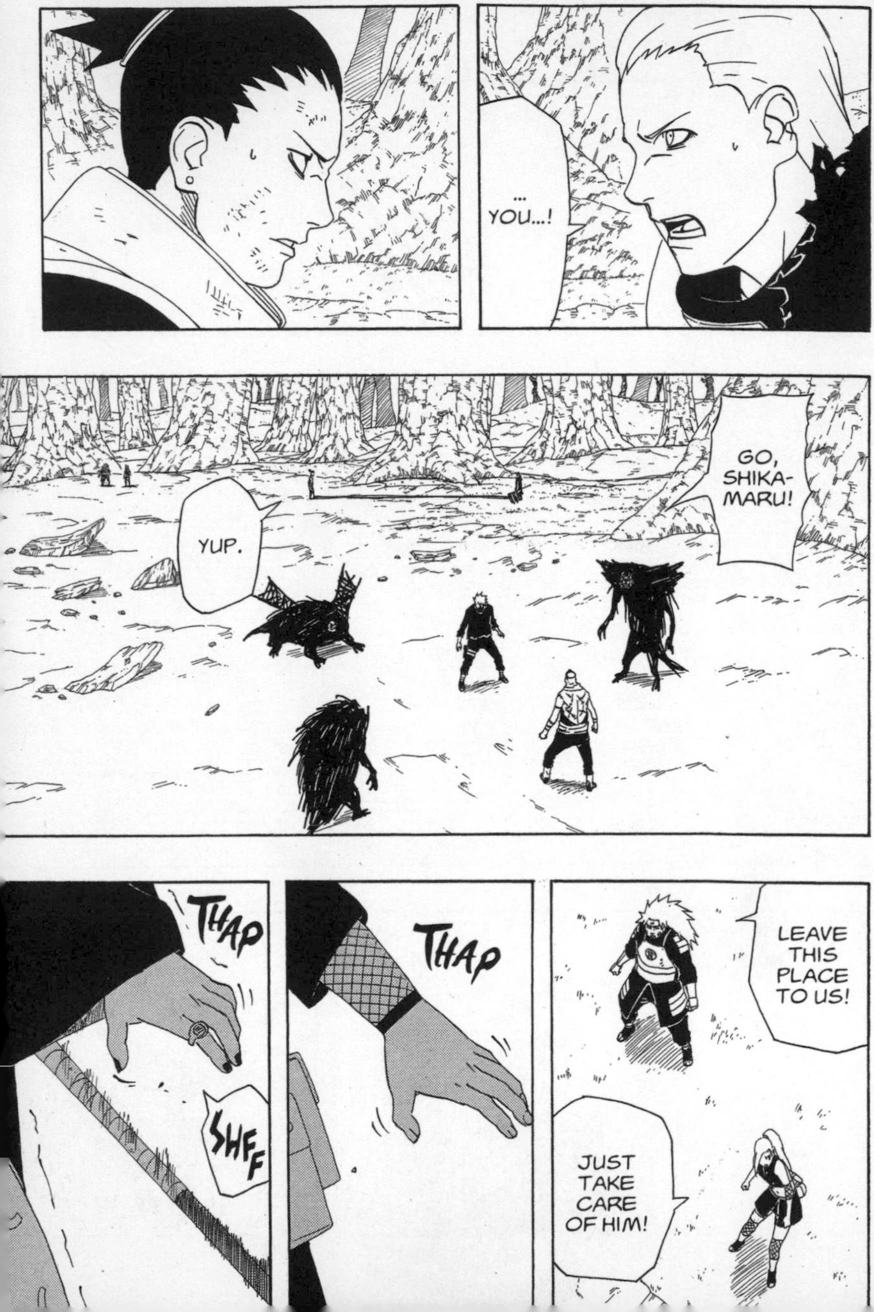
... YOU...!
GO, SHIKA-MARU!
YUP.
LEAVE THIS PLACE TO US!
JUST TAKE CARE OF HIM!
THAP
THAP
SHFF

Number 336: Turnabout Dilemma...!!

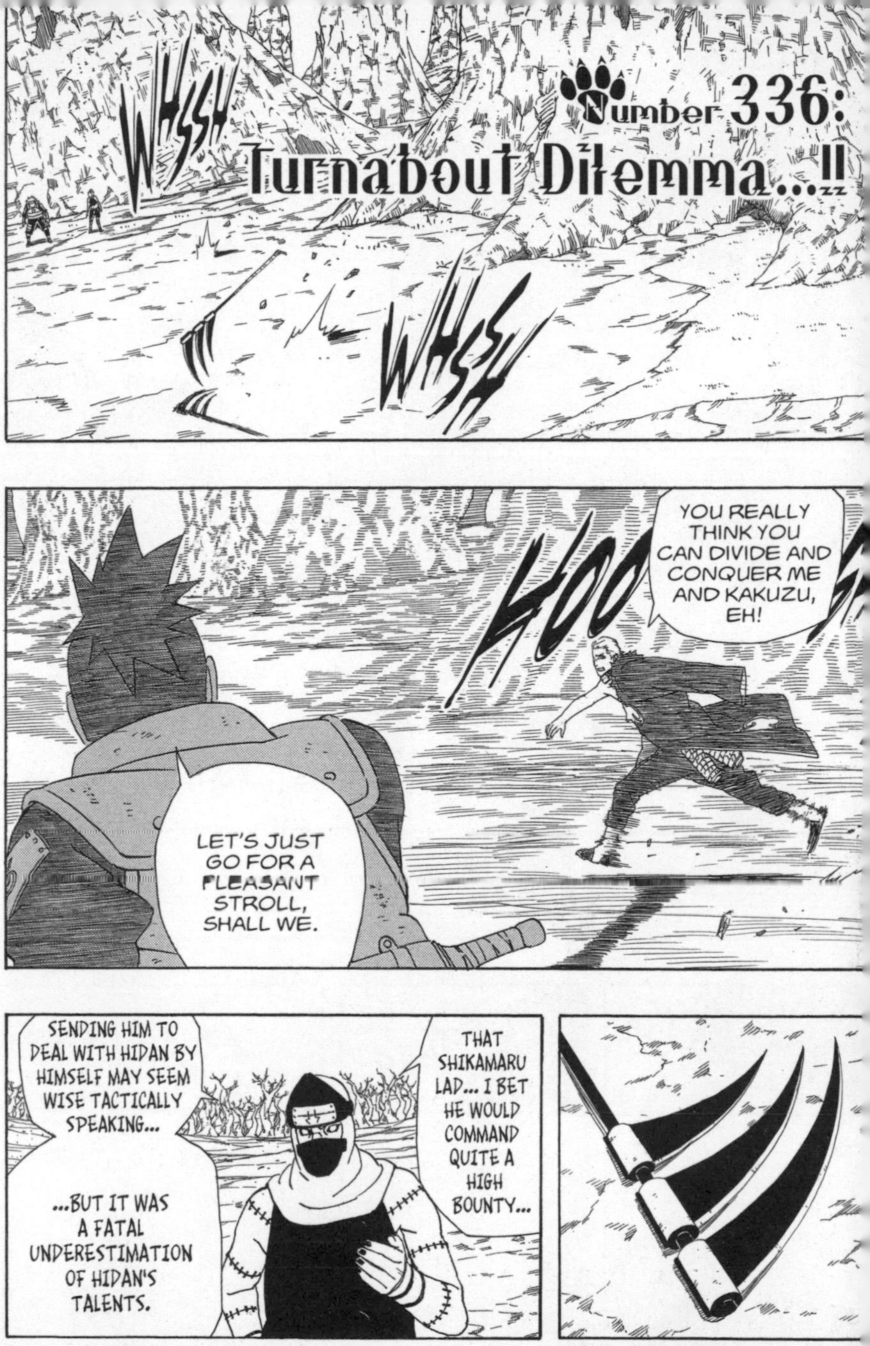
WHSSH
WHSSH
YOU REALLY THINK YOU CAN DIVIDE AND CONQUER ME AND KAKUZU, EH!
LET'S JUST GO FOR A PLEASANT STROLL, SHALL WE.
THAT SHIKAMARU LAD... I BET HE WOULD COMMAND QUITE A HIGH BOUNTY...
SENDING HIM TO DEAL WITH HIDAN BY HIMSELF MAY SEEM WISE TACTICALLY SPEAKING...
...BUT IT WAS A FATAL UNDERESTIMATION OF HIDAN'S TALENTS.

READ THIS WAY

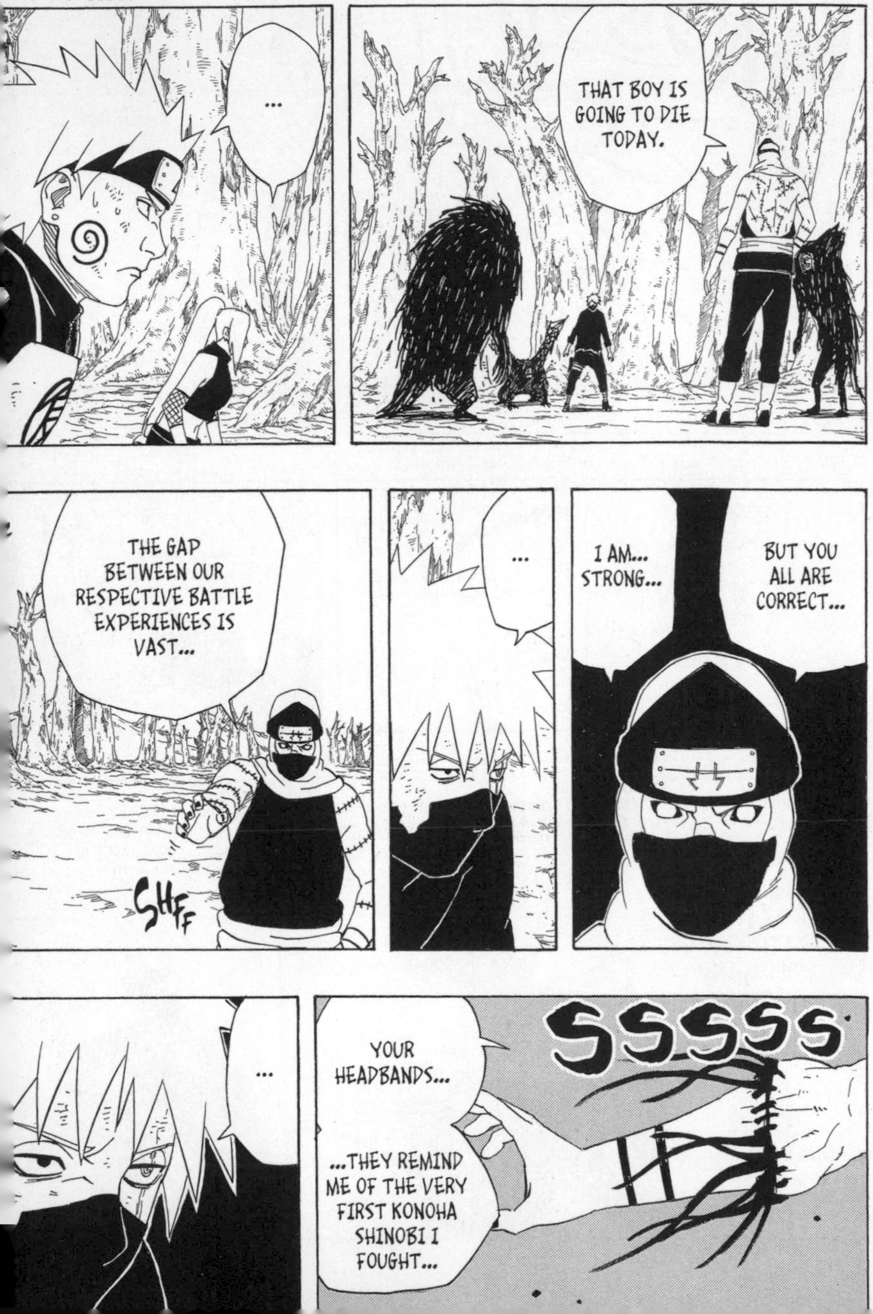
THAT BOY IS GOING TO DIE TODAY.
...
BUT YOU ALL ARE CORRECT...
I AM... STRONG...
...
THE GAP BETWEEN OUR RESPECTIVE BATTLE EXPERIENCES IS VAST...
SHFF
SSSSS
YOUR HEADBANDS...
...THEY REMIND ME OF THE VERY FIRST KONOHA SHINOBI I FOUGHT...
...

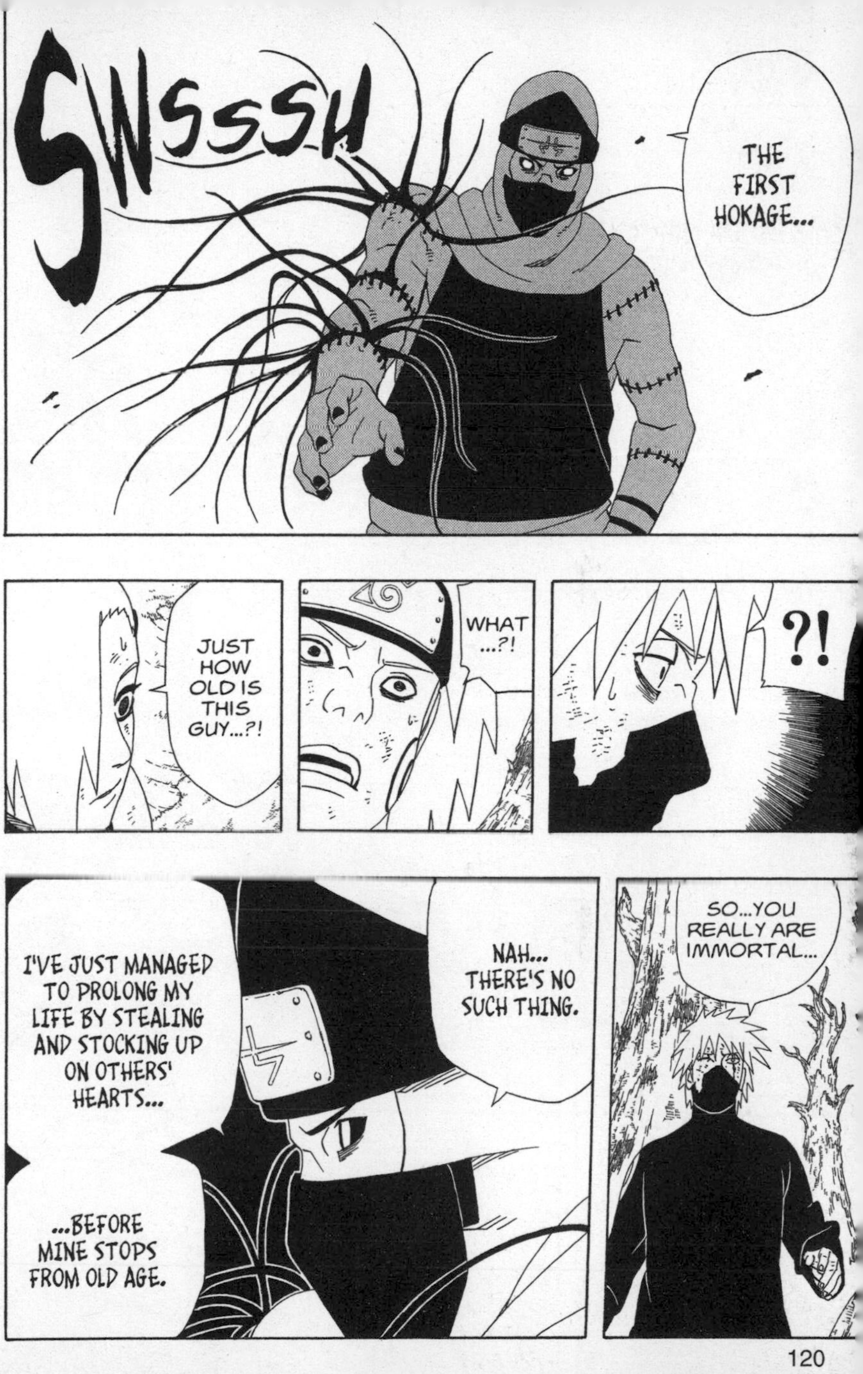
THE FIRST HOKAGE...
SWSSSH
?!
WHAT ...?!
JUST HOW OLD IS THIS GUY...?!
SO...YOU REALLY ARE IMMORTAL...
NAH... THERE'S NO SUCH THING.
I'VE JUST MANAGED TO PROLONG MY LIFE BY STEALING AND STOCKING UP ON OTHERS' HEARTS...
...BEFORE MINE STOPS FROM OLD AGE.

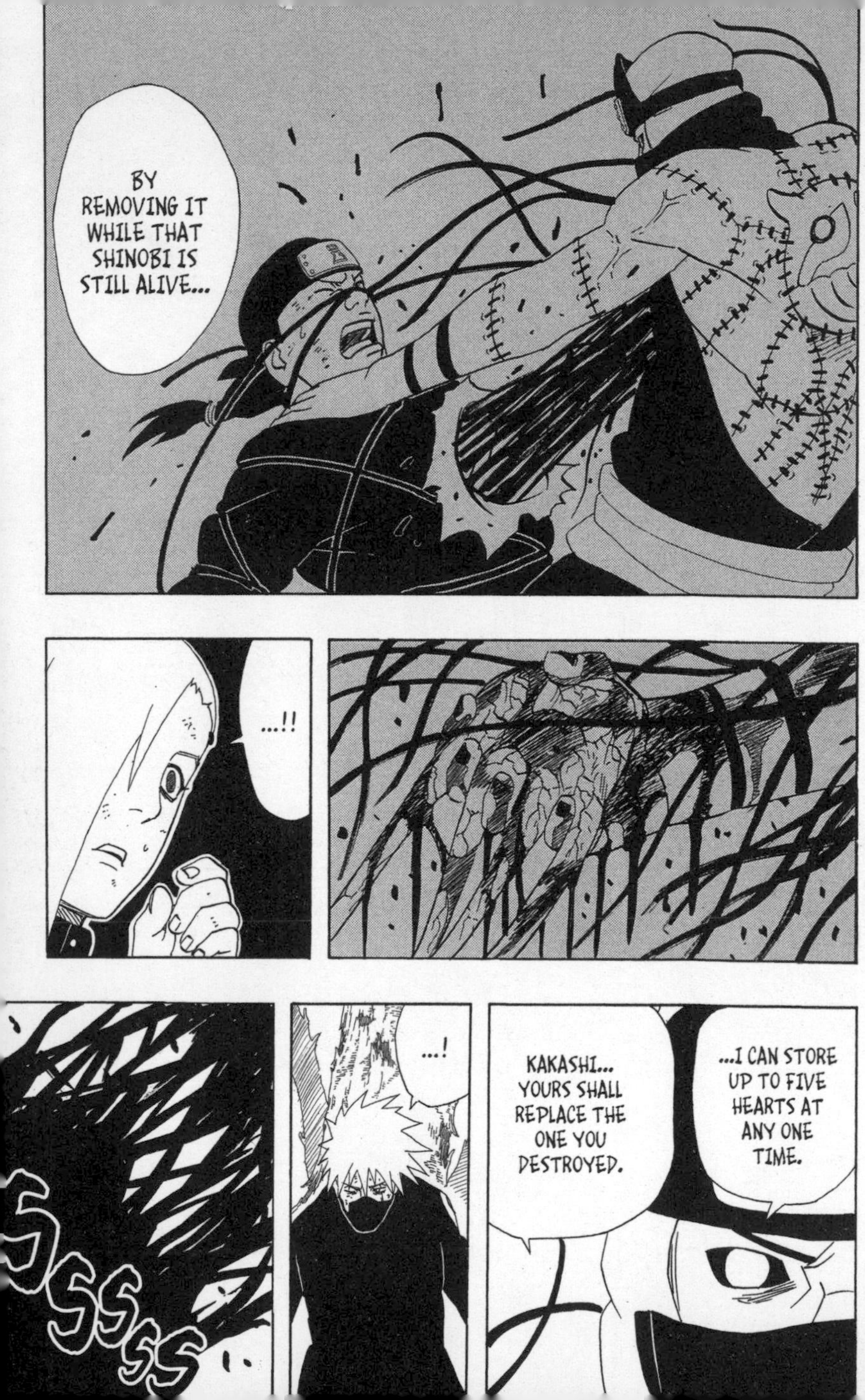
BY REMOVING IT WHILE THAT SHINOBI IS STILL ALIVE...
...!!
...I CAN STORE UP TO FIVE HEARTS AT ANY ONE TIME.
KAKASHI... YOURS SHALL REPLACE THE ONE YOU DESTROYED.
...!
SSSSSS

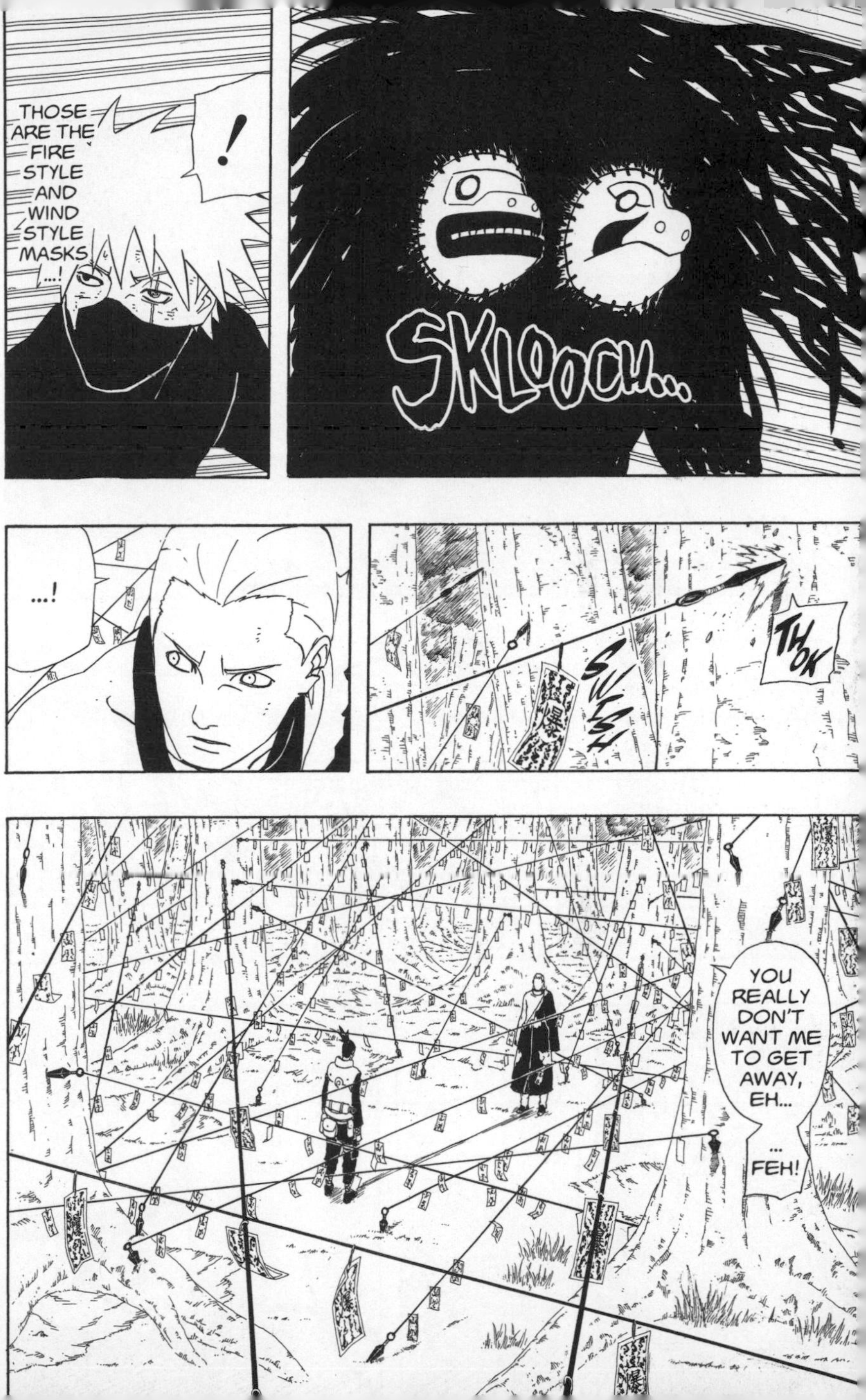
SKLOOCH...
!
THOSE ARE THE FIRE STYLE AND WIND STYLE MASKS ...!
SWISH
THOK
...!
YOU REALLY DON'T WANT ME TO GET AWAY, EH...
... FEH!

READ THIS WAY

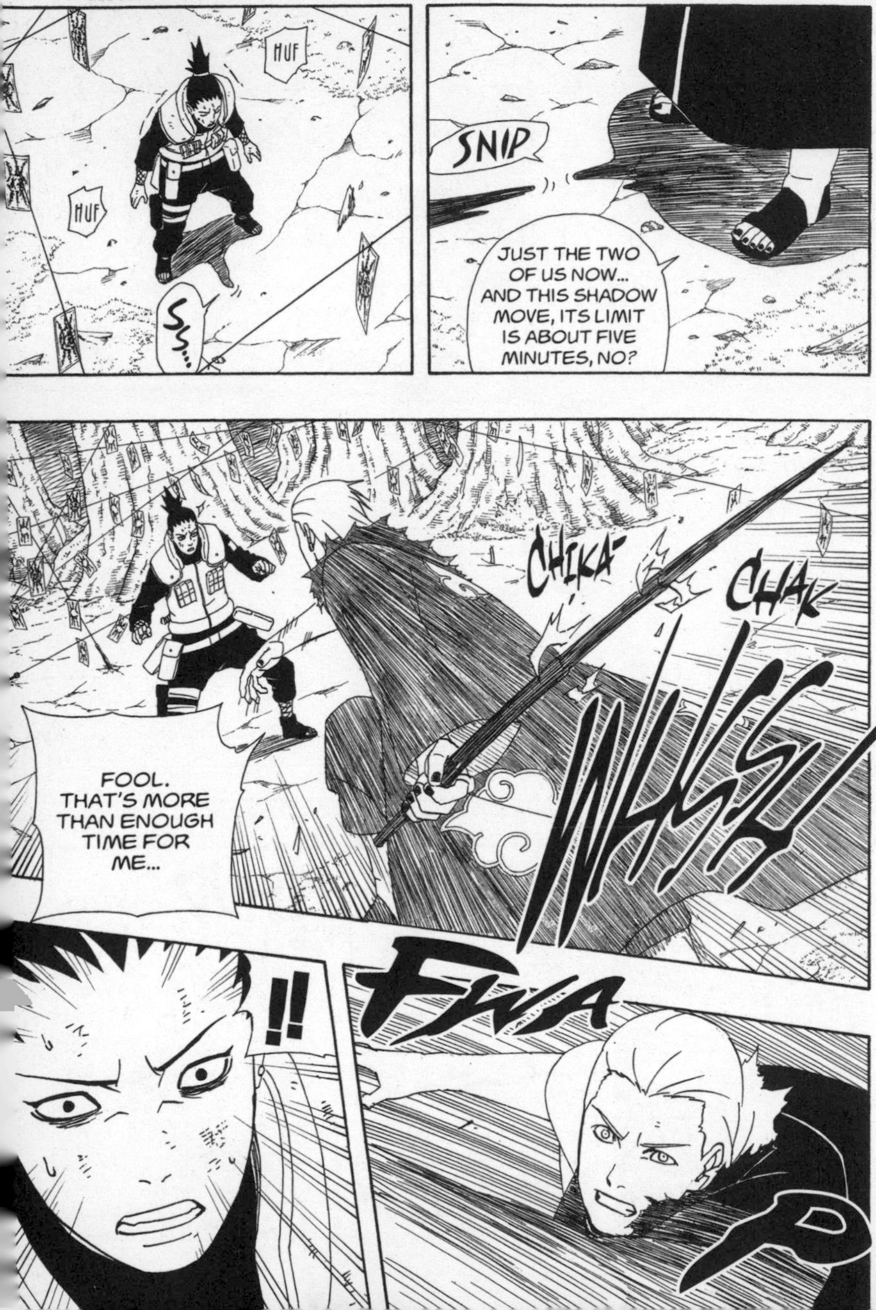
SNIP
JUST THE TWO OF US NOW... AND THIS SHADOW MOVE, ITS LIMIT IS ABOUT FIVE MINUTES, NO?
HUF
HUF
SS...
CHAK
CHIKA
WHSSH
FOOL. THAT'S MORE THAN ENOUGH TIME FOR ME...
FWA
!!

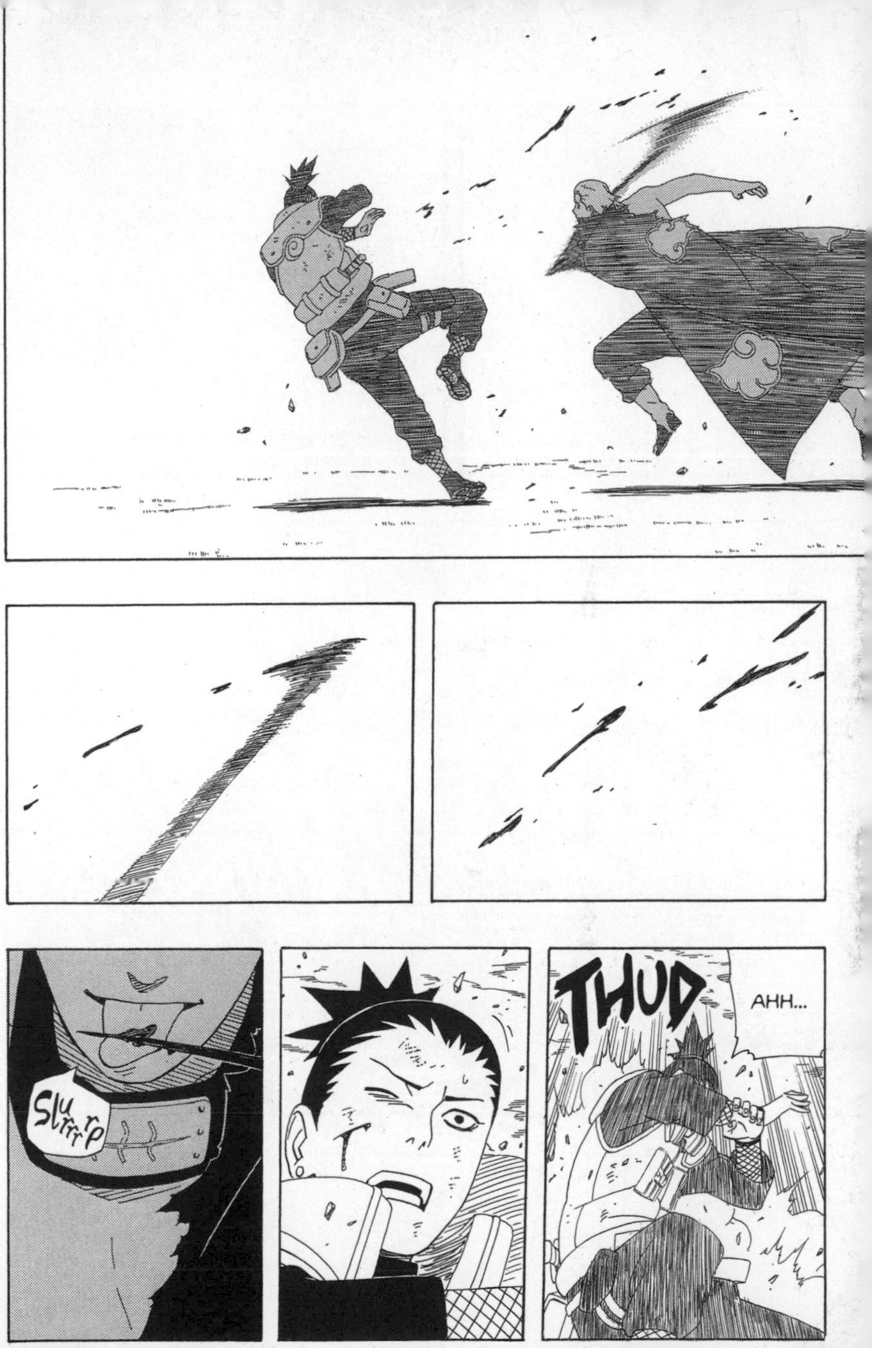
THUD
AHH...
Slurrrp

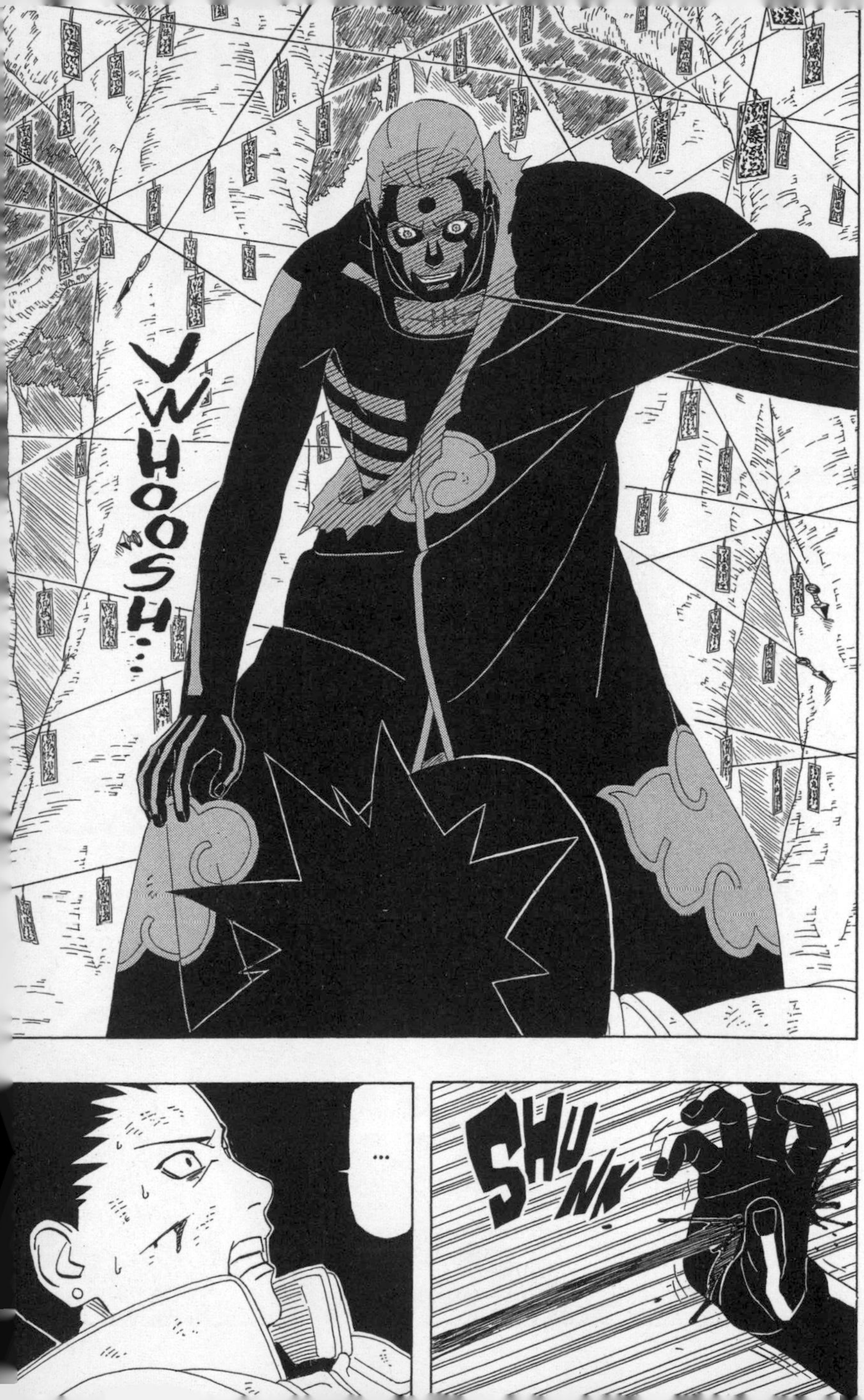
VWHOOOSH...
SHUNK
...

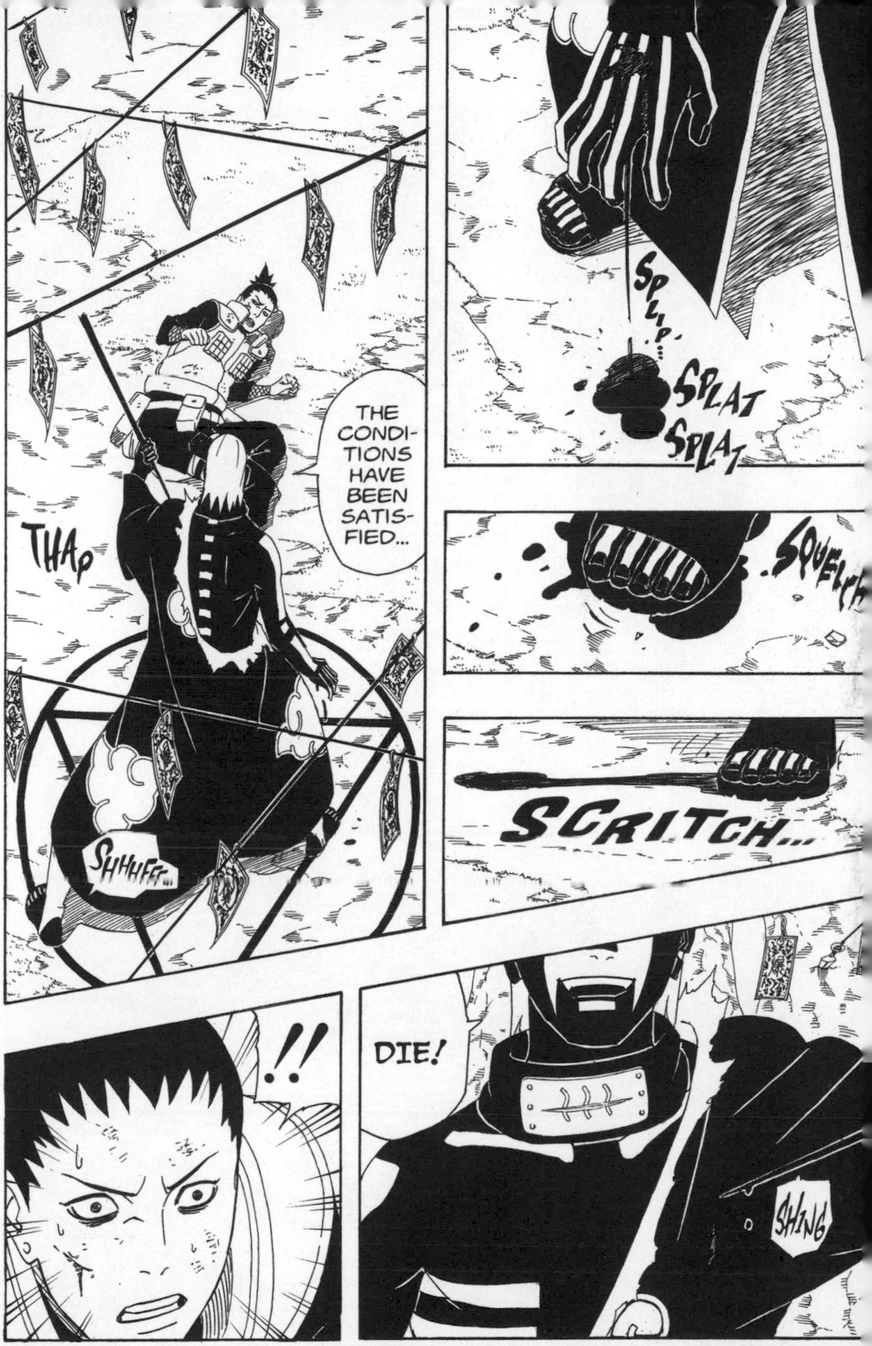
SPLIP...
SPLAT
SPLAT
SQUELCH
SCRITCH...
THE CONDITIONS HAVE BEEN SATISFIED...
THAP
SHHHFFF...
DIE!
SHING
!!

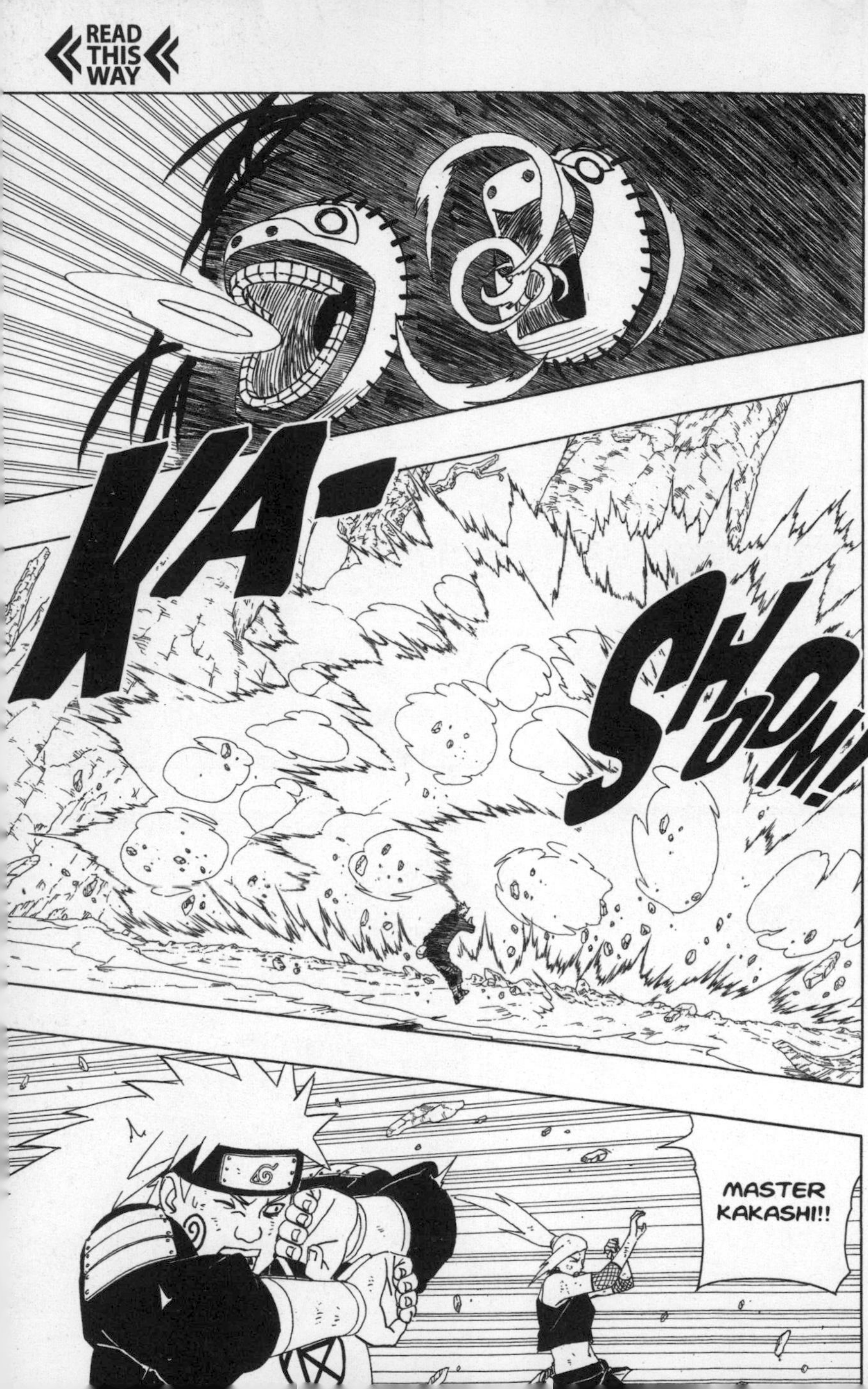
READ THIS WAY
KA-SHOOM!!
MASTER KAKASHI!!

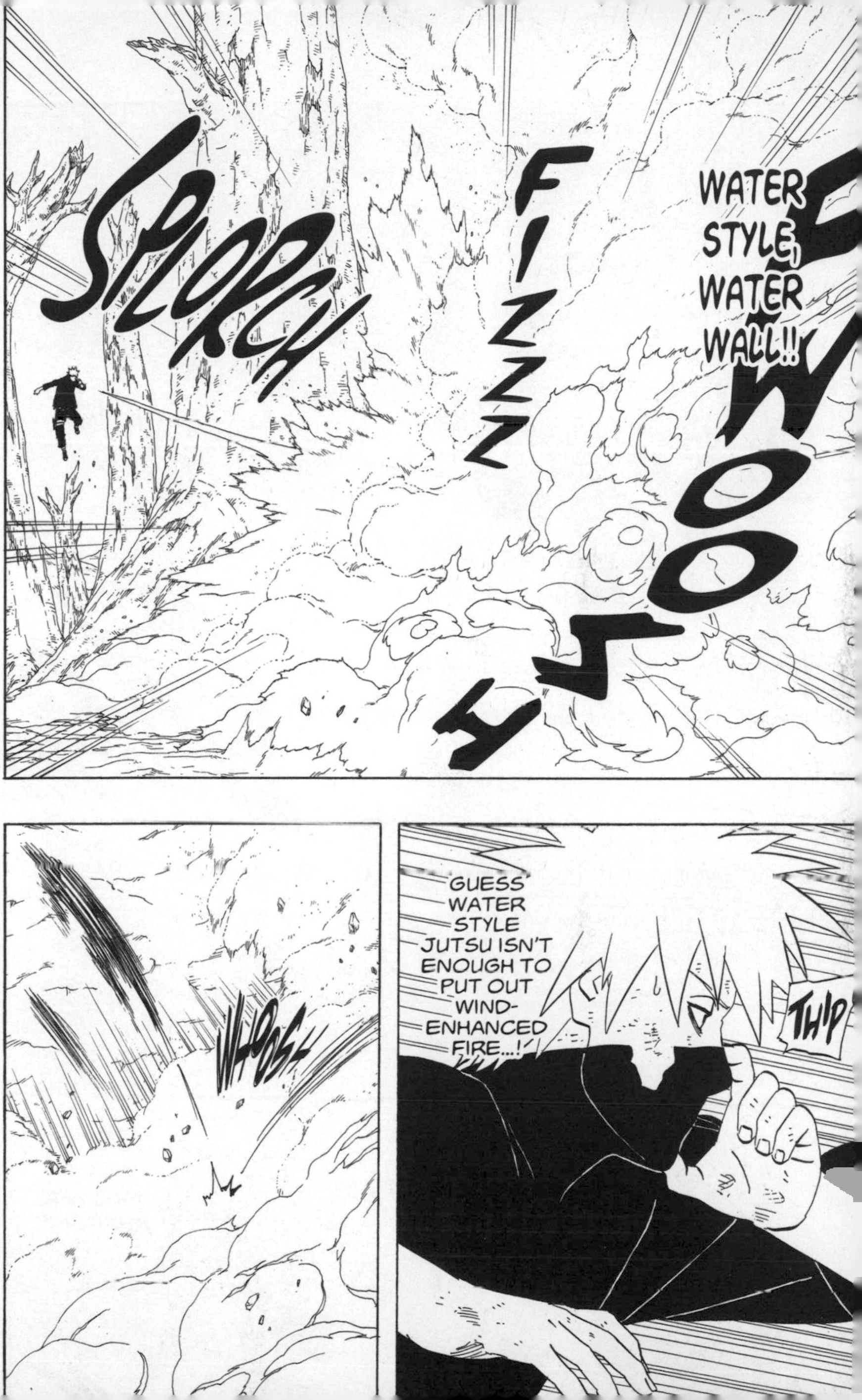
WATER STYLE, WATER WALL!!
WHOOSH
FIZZZZ
SPLORCH
GUESS WATER STYLE JUTSU ISN'T ENOUGH TO PUT OUT WIND-ENHANCED FIRE...!
THIP
WHOOSH

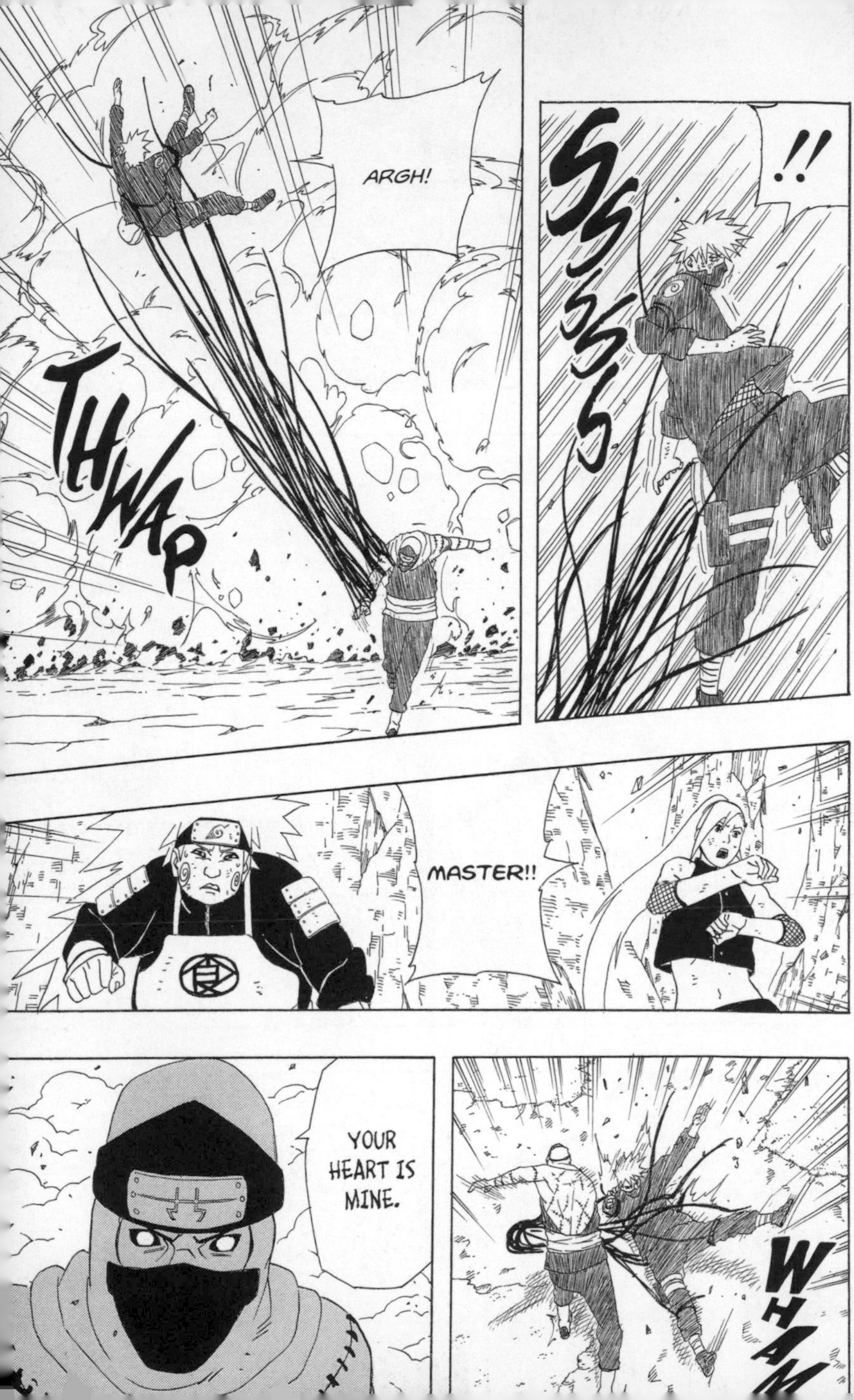
SSSSS
!!
ARGH!
THWAP
MASTER!!
WHAM
YOUR HEART IS MINE.

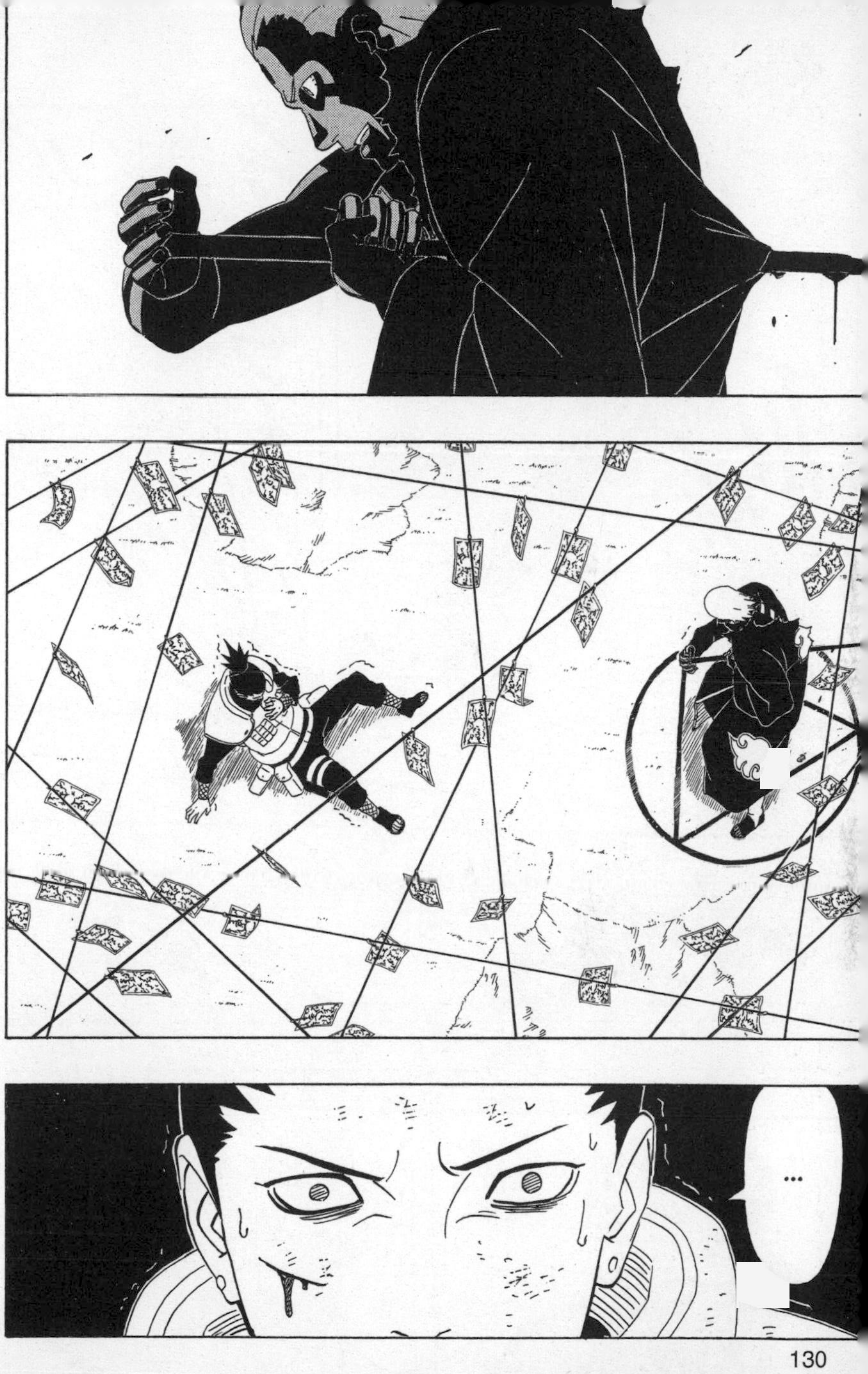
...

READ THIS WAY

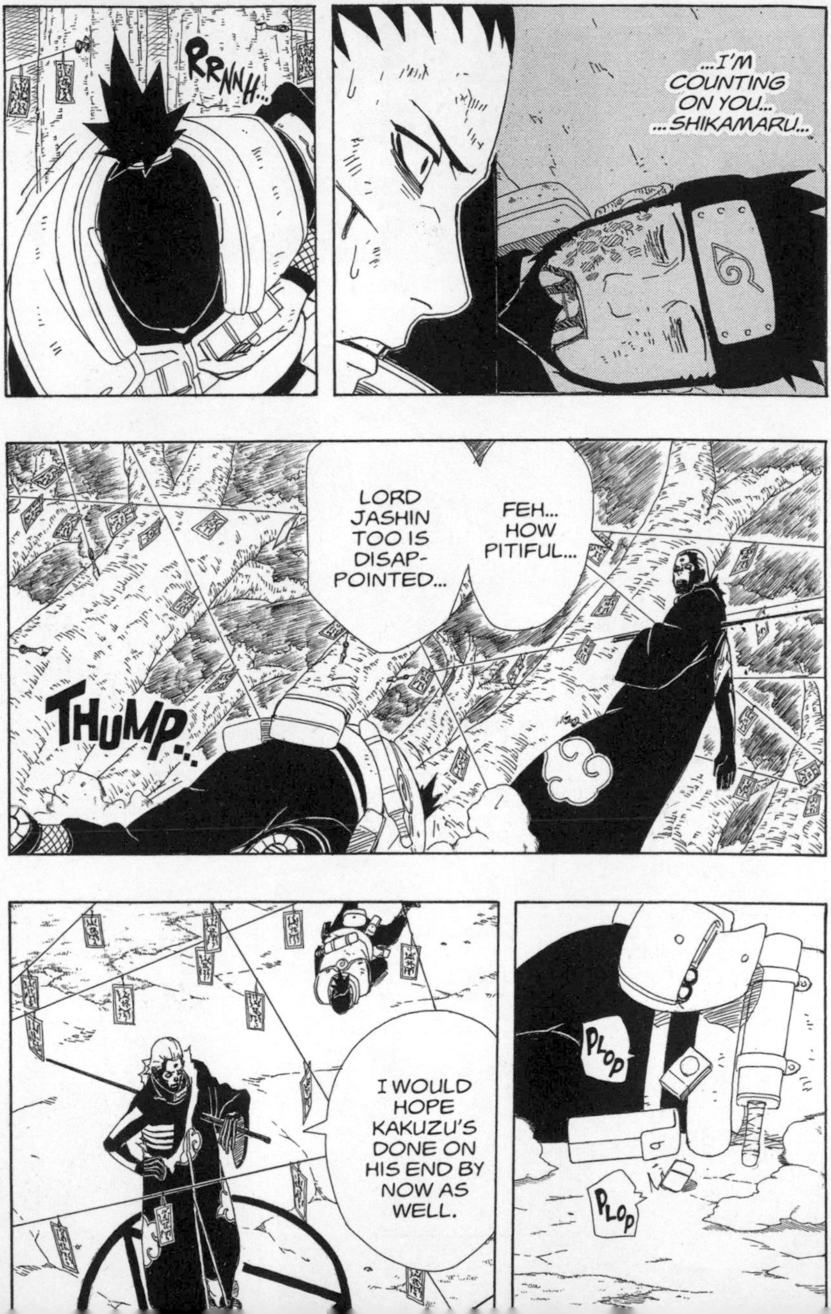
...I'M COUNTING ON YOU... ...SHIKAMARU...
RRNNH...
FEH... HOW PITIFUL...
LORD JASHIN TOO IS DISAP-POINTED...
THUMP...
PLOP
PLOP
I WOULD HOPE KAKUZU'S DONE ON HIS END BY NOW AS WELL.

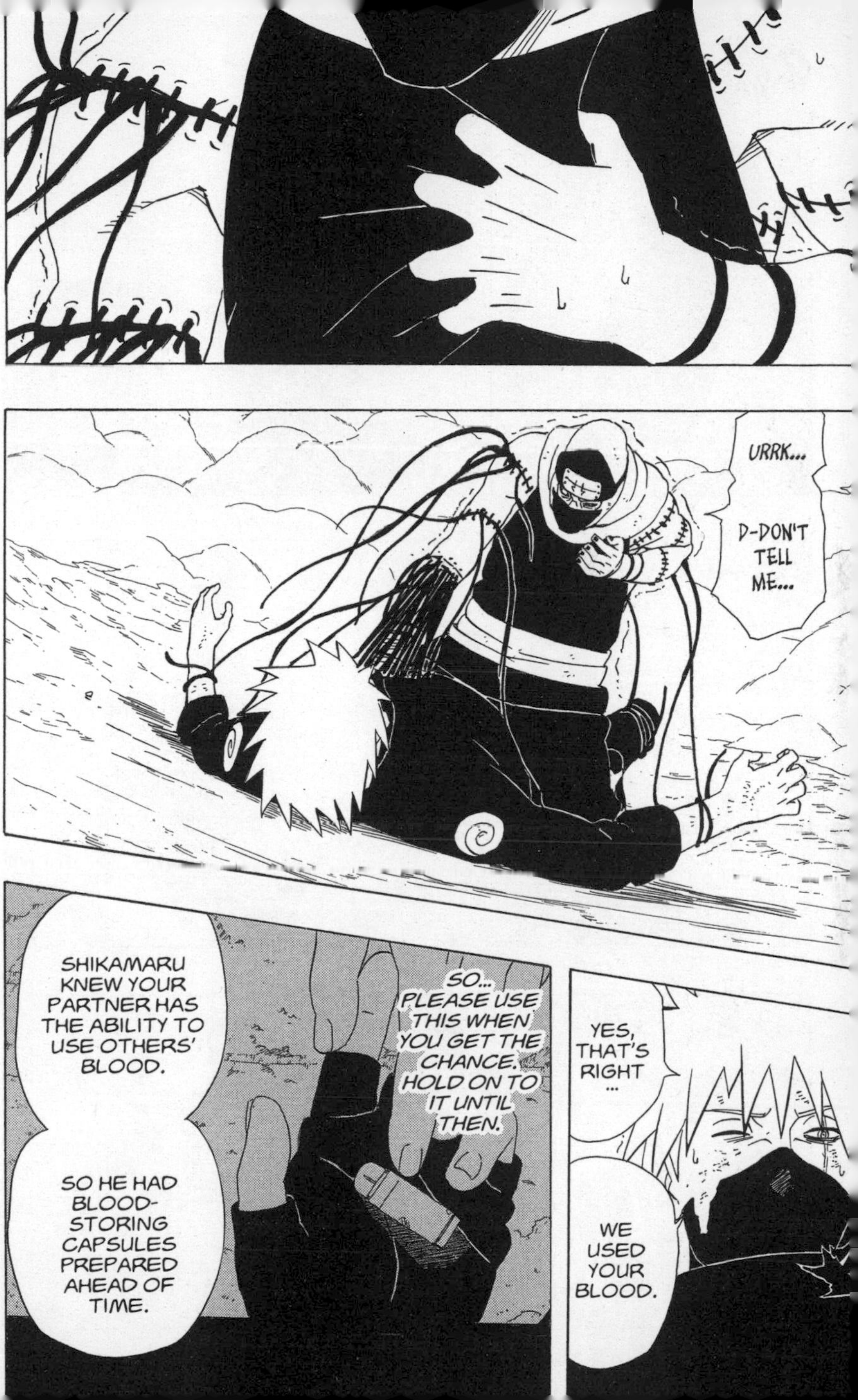
URRK...
D-DON'T TELL ME...
YES, THAT'S RIGHT ...
WE USED YOUR BLOOD.
SO... PLEASE USE THIS WHEN YOU GET THE CHANCE. HOLD ON TO IT UNTIL THEN.
SHIKAMARU KNEW YOUR PARTNER HAS THE ABILITY TO USE OTHERS' BLOOD.
SO HE HAD BLOOD-STORING CAPSULES PREPARED AHEAD OF TIME.

READ THIS WAY

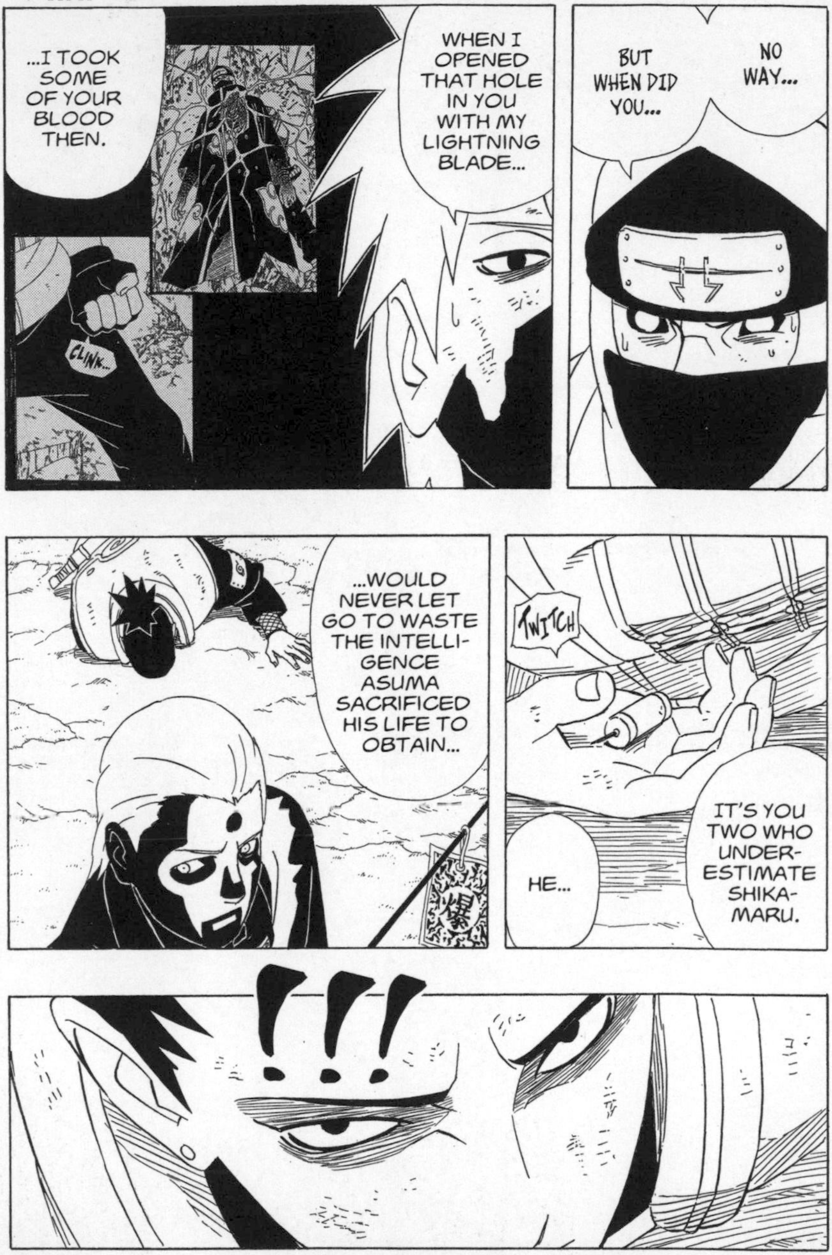
NO WAY...
BUT WHEN DID YOU...
WHEN I OPENED THAT HOLE IN YOU WITH MY LIGHTNING BLADE...
...I TOOK SOME OF YOUR BLOOD THEN.
CLINK...
TWITCH
IT'S YOU TWO WHO UNDER-ESTIMATE SHIKA-MARU.
HE...
...WOULD NEVER LET GO TO WASTE THE INTELLI-GENCE ASUMA SACRIFICED HIS LIFE TO OBTAIN...
!!!

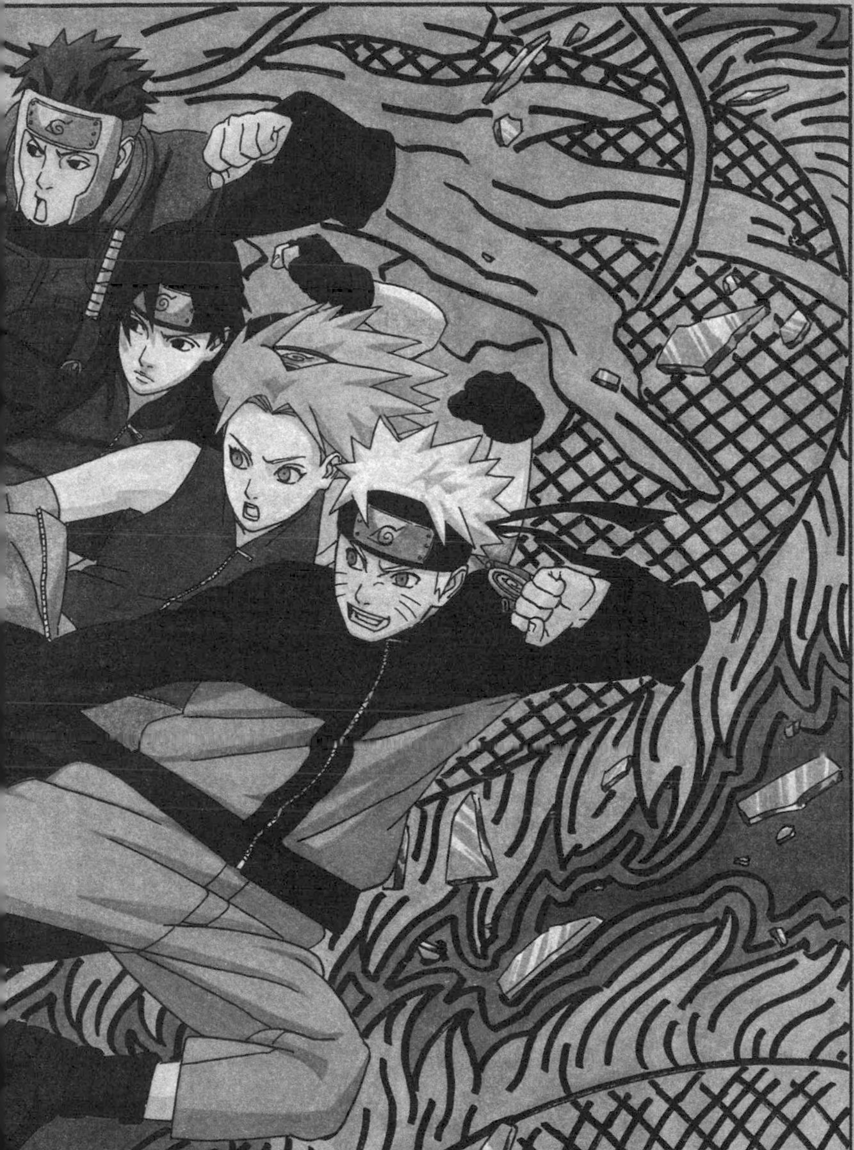

Number 337: Shikamaru's Genius!!

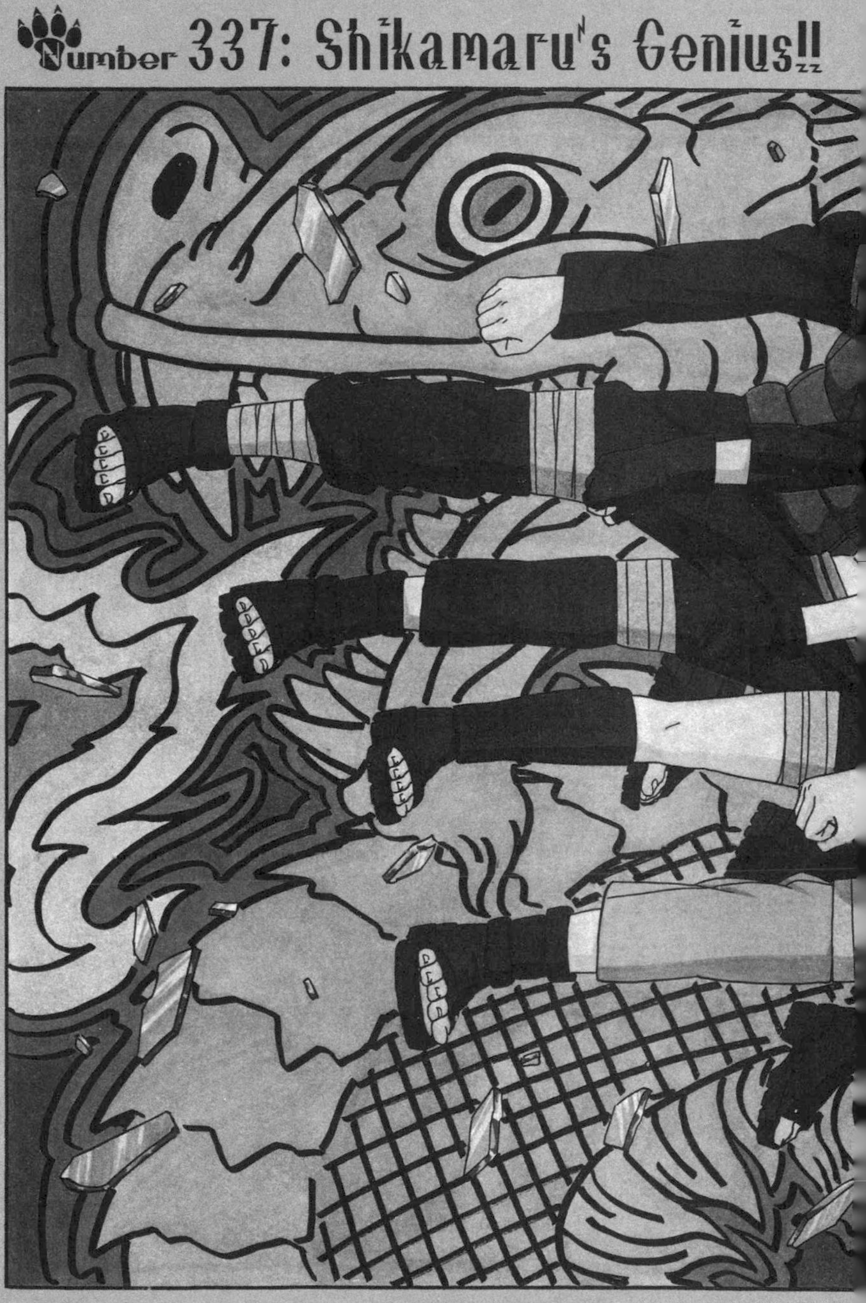

NARUTO

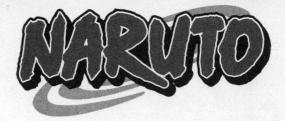

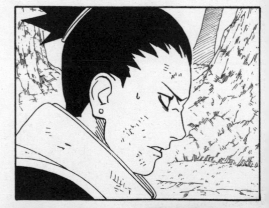

READ THIS WAY

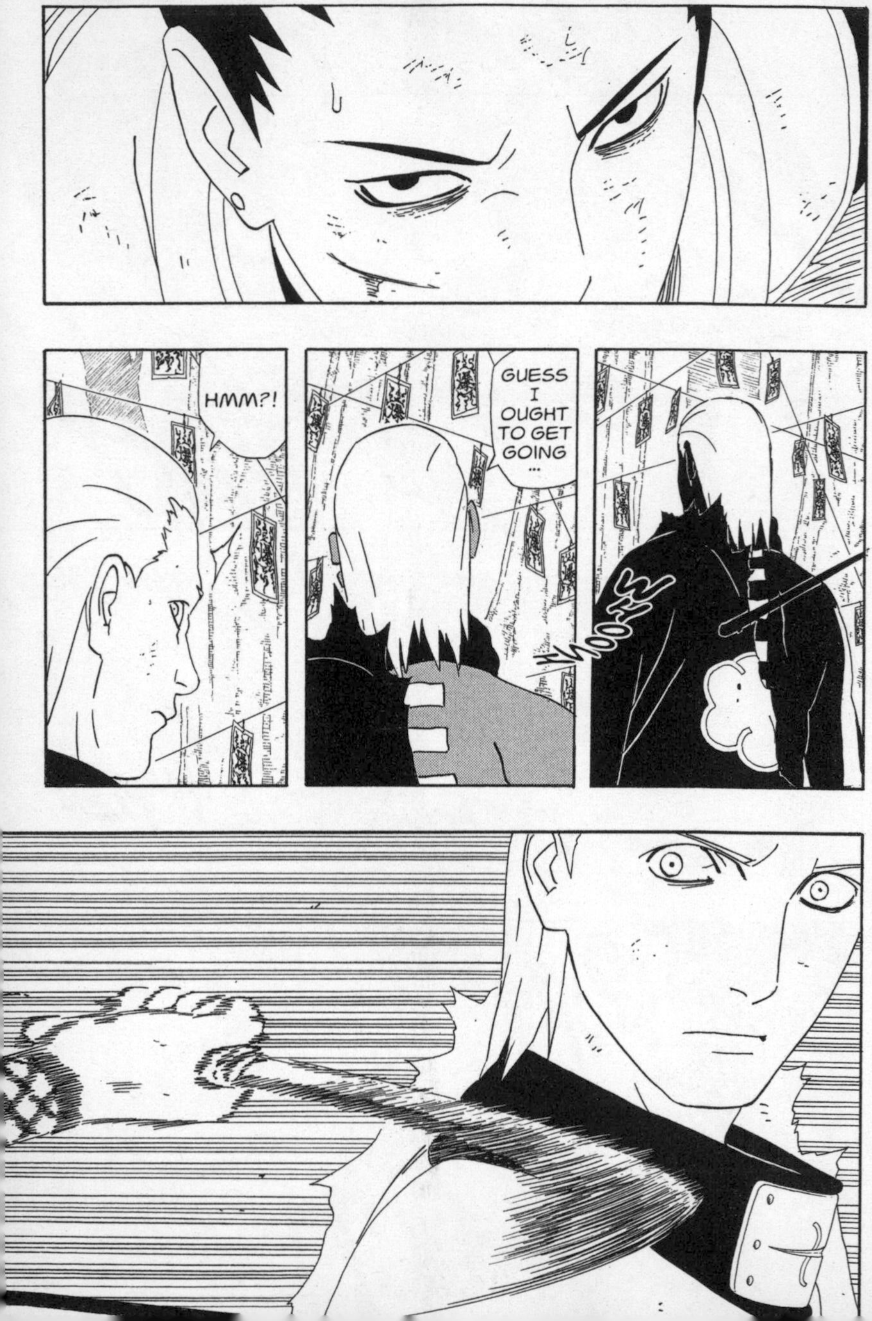
WHOOSH
GUESS I OUGHT TO GET GOING ...
HMM?!

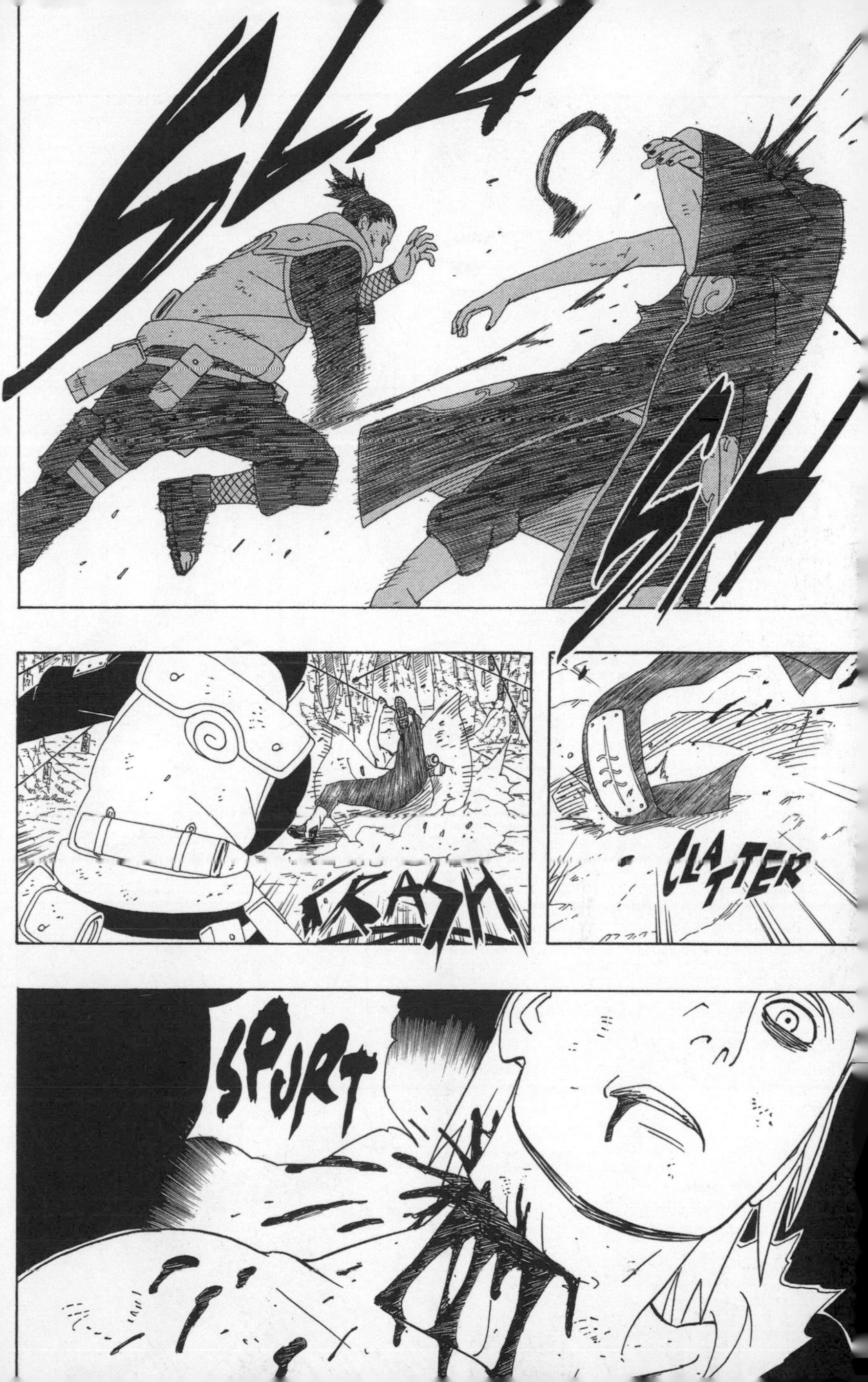
SLASH
CLATTER
CRASH
SPURT

READ THIS WAY

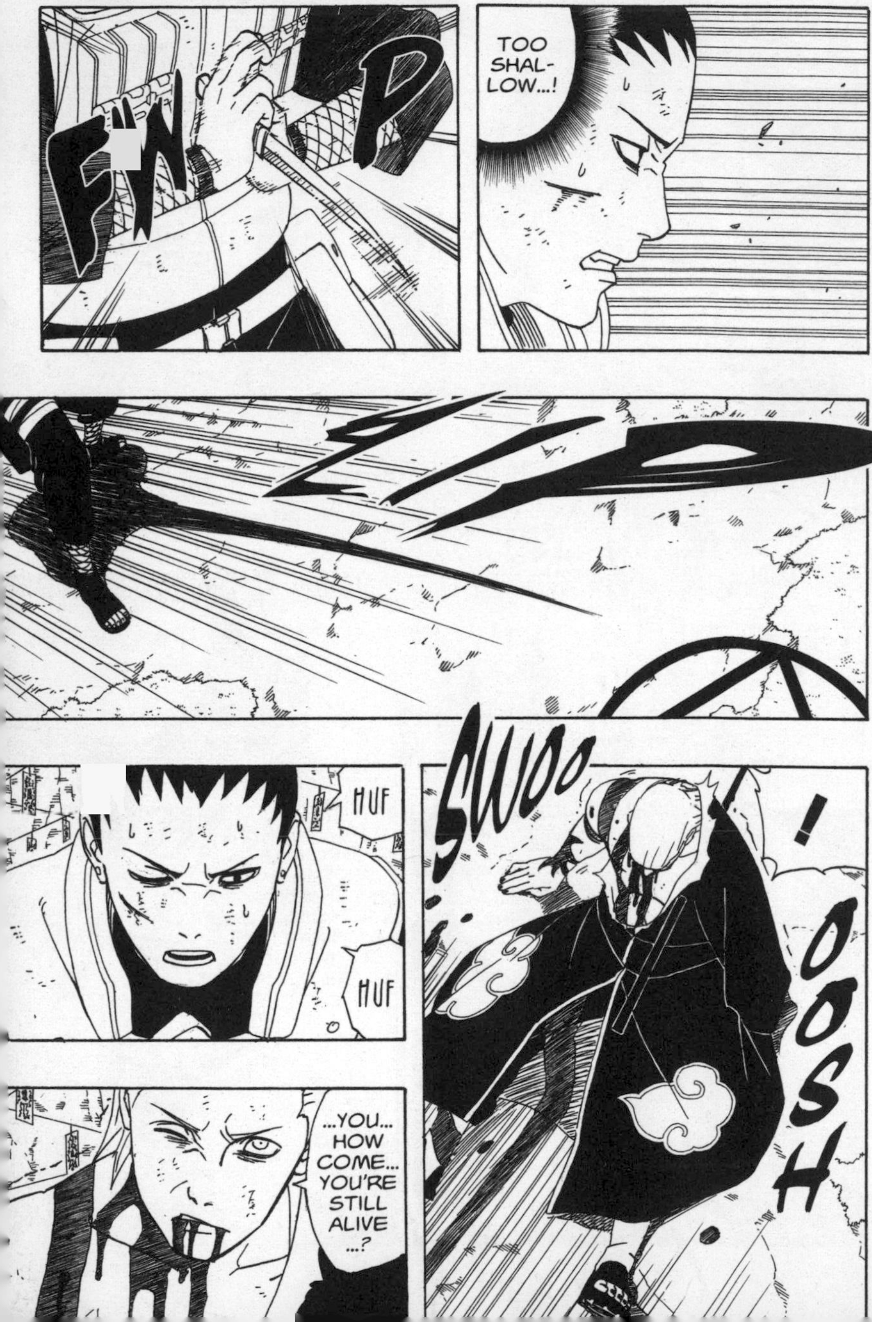

TOO SHAL- LOW...!
SWOO
OOSH
!
HUF
HUF
...YOU... HOW COME... YOU'RE STILL ALIVE ...?

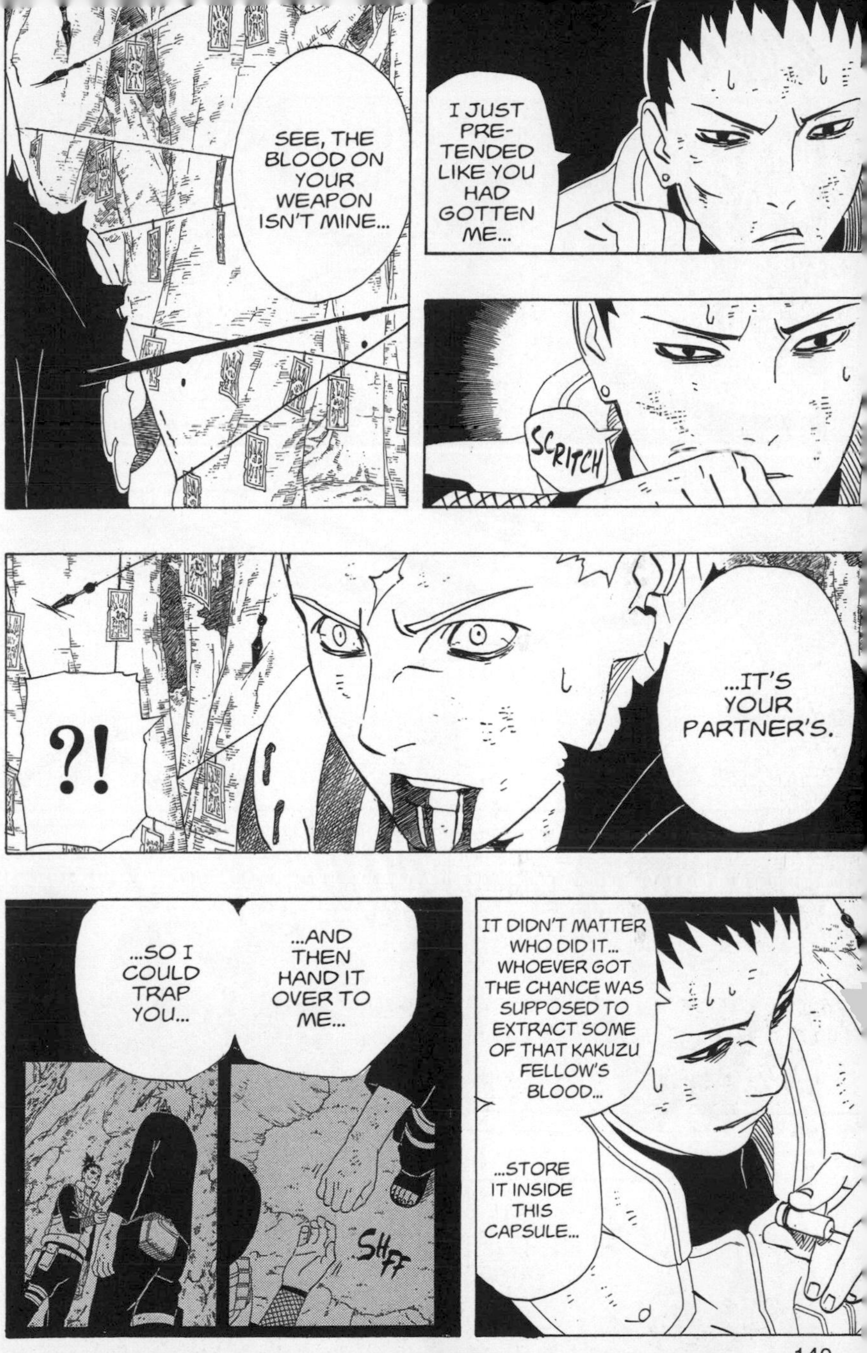
I JUST PRETENDED LIKE YOU HAD GOTTEN ME...
SCRITCH
SEE, THE BLOOD ON YOUR WEAPON ISN'T MINE...
...IT'S YOUR PARTNER'S.
?!
IT DIDN'T MATTER WHO DID IT... WHOEVER GOT THE CHANCE WAS SUPPOSED TO EXTRACT SOME OF THAT KAKUZU FELLOW'S BLOOD...
...STORE IT INSIDE THIS CAPSULE...
...AND THEN HAND IT OVER TO ME...
SHFF
...SO I COULD TRAP YOU...

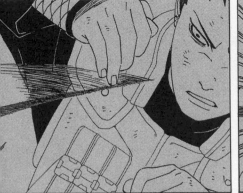

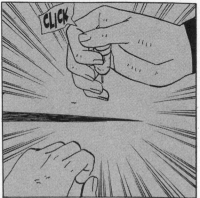

CLICK

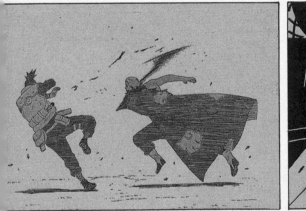

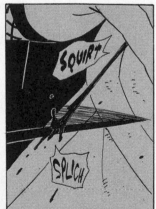

SQUIRT

SPLICH

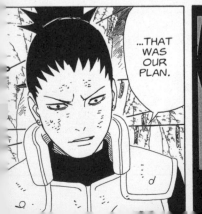

...THAT WAS OUR PLAN.

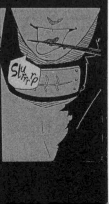

SLURRP

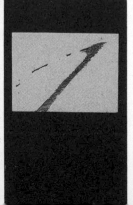

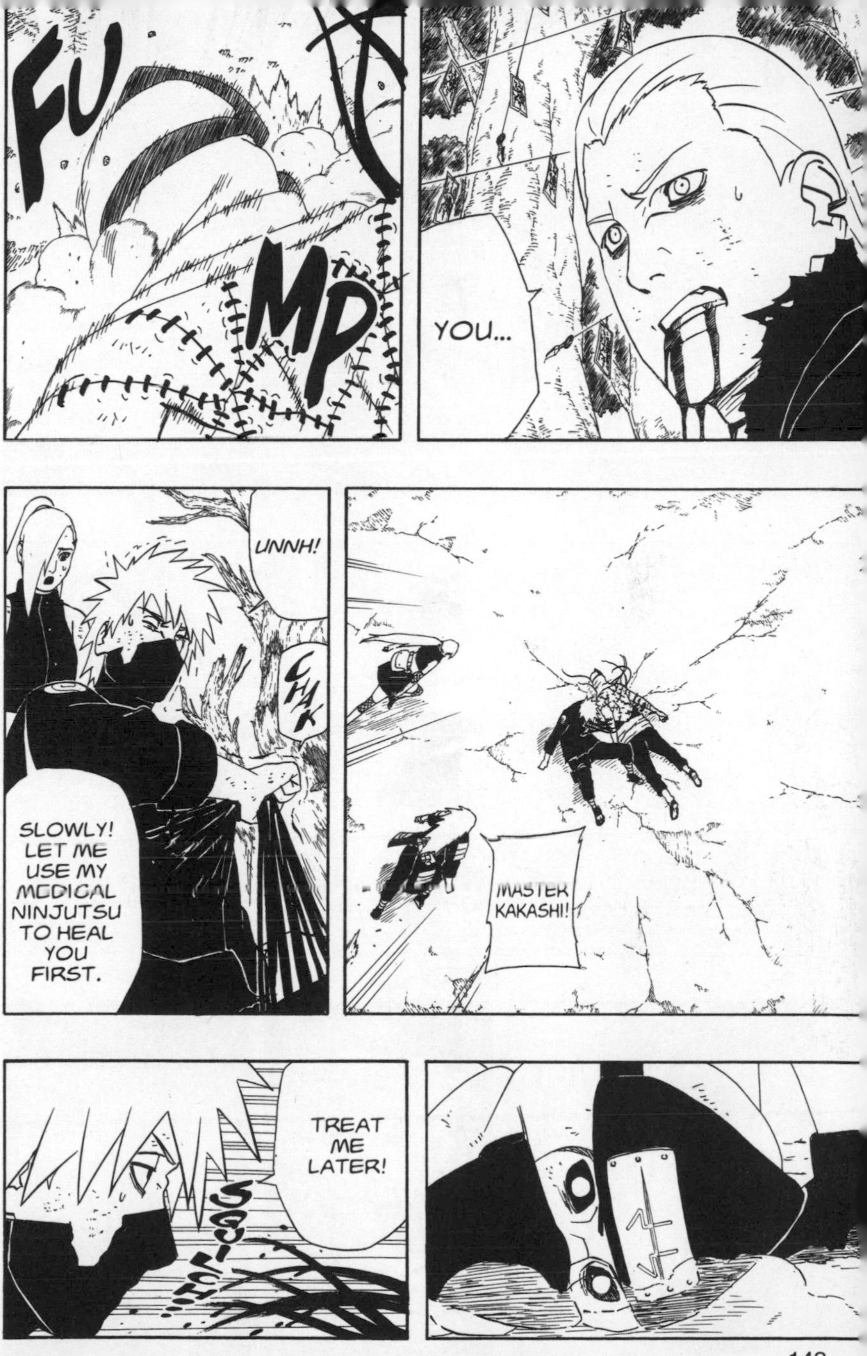
YOU...
FUMP
MASTER KAKASHI!
UNNH!
CHAK
SLOWLY! LET ME USE MY MEDICAL NINJUTSU TO HEAL YOU FIRST.
TREAT ME LATER!
SQUICH!!

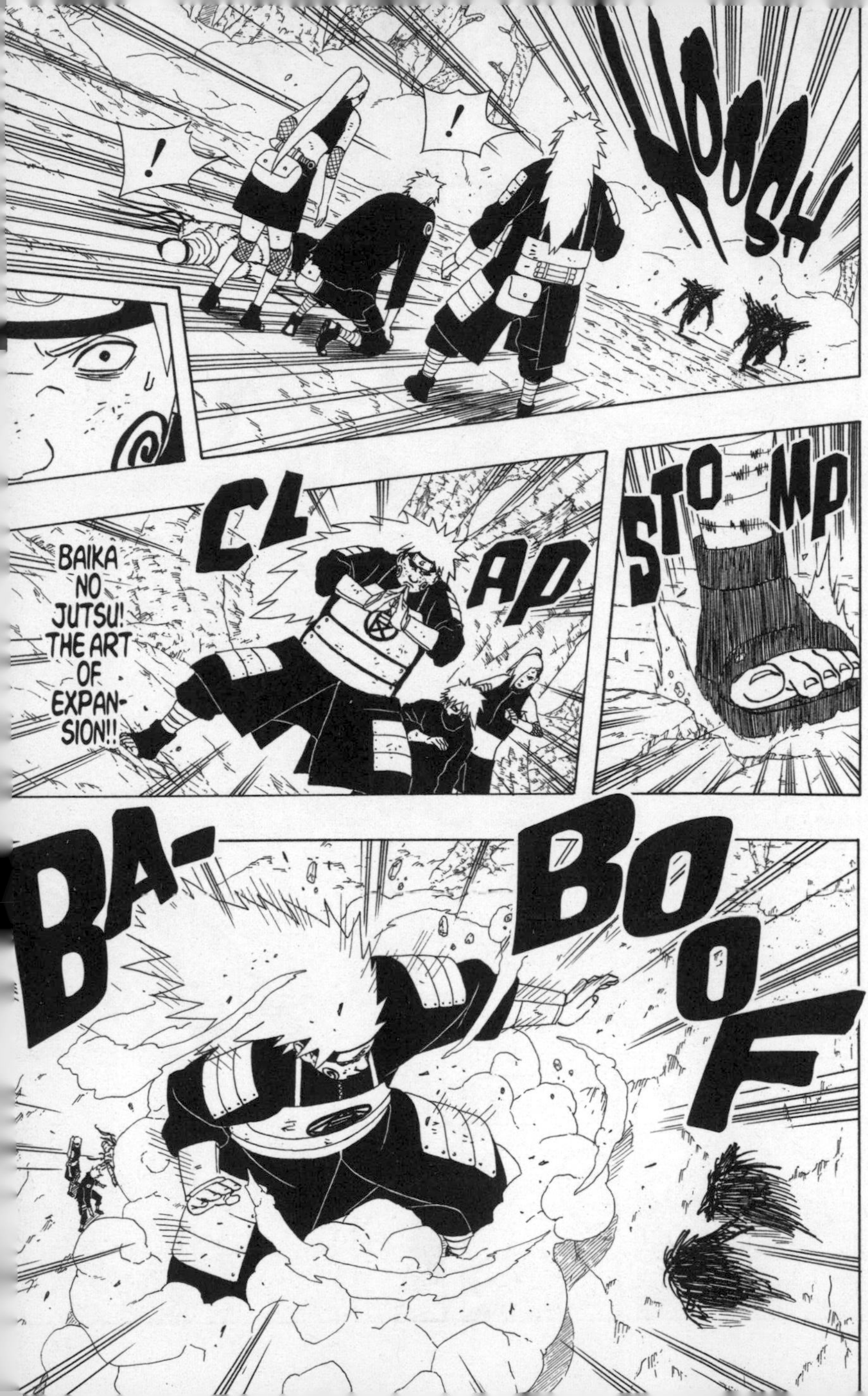
WOOSH
!
!
STOMP
CLAP
BAIKA NO JUTSU! THE ART OF EXPANSION!!
BA-BOOF

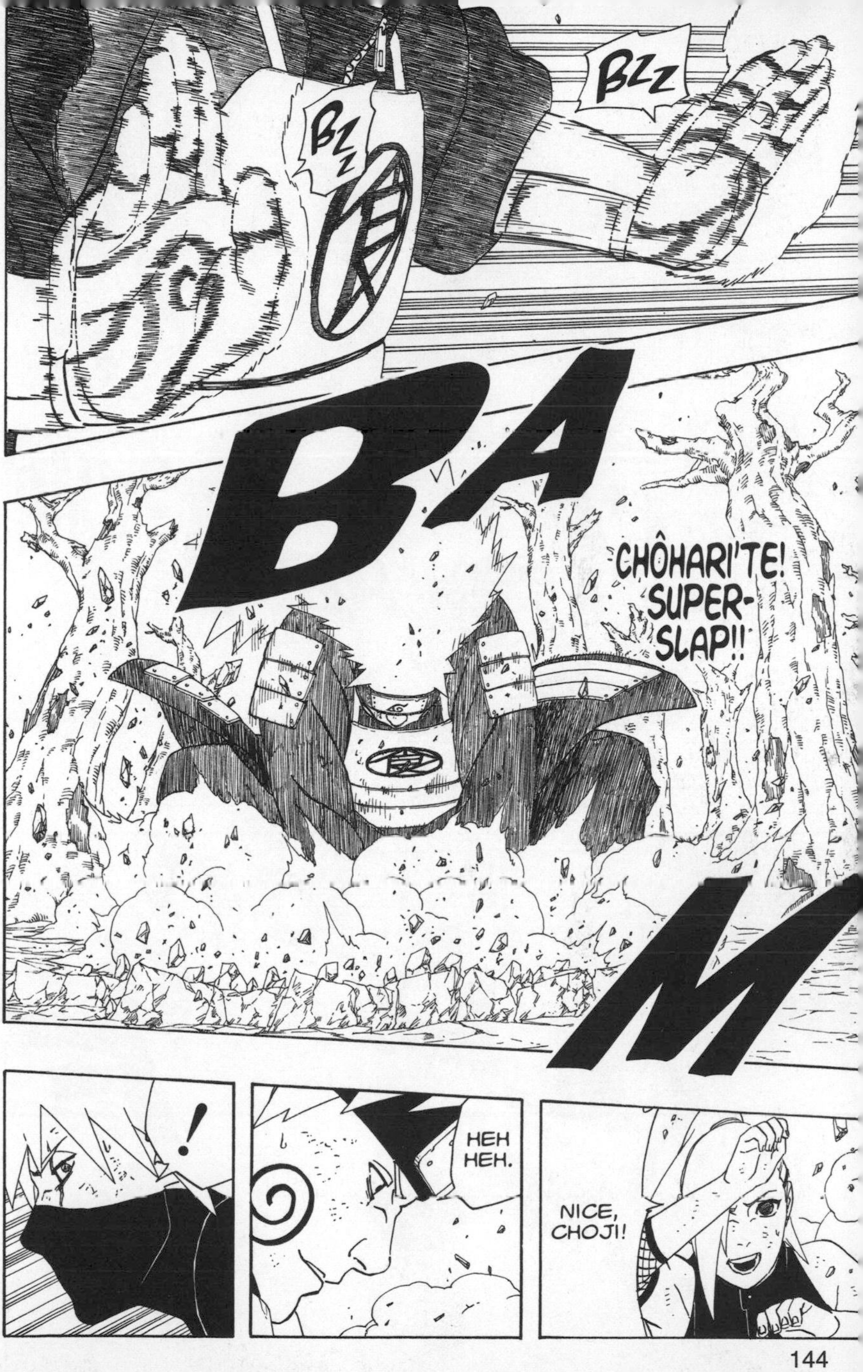
BZZ
BZZ
BAM
CHÔHARI'TE! SUPER-SLAP!!
NICE, CHOJI!
HEH HEH.
!

READ THIS WAY

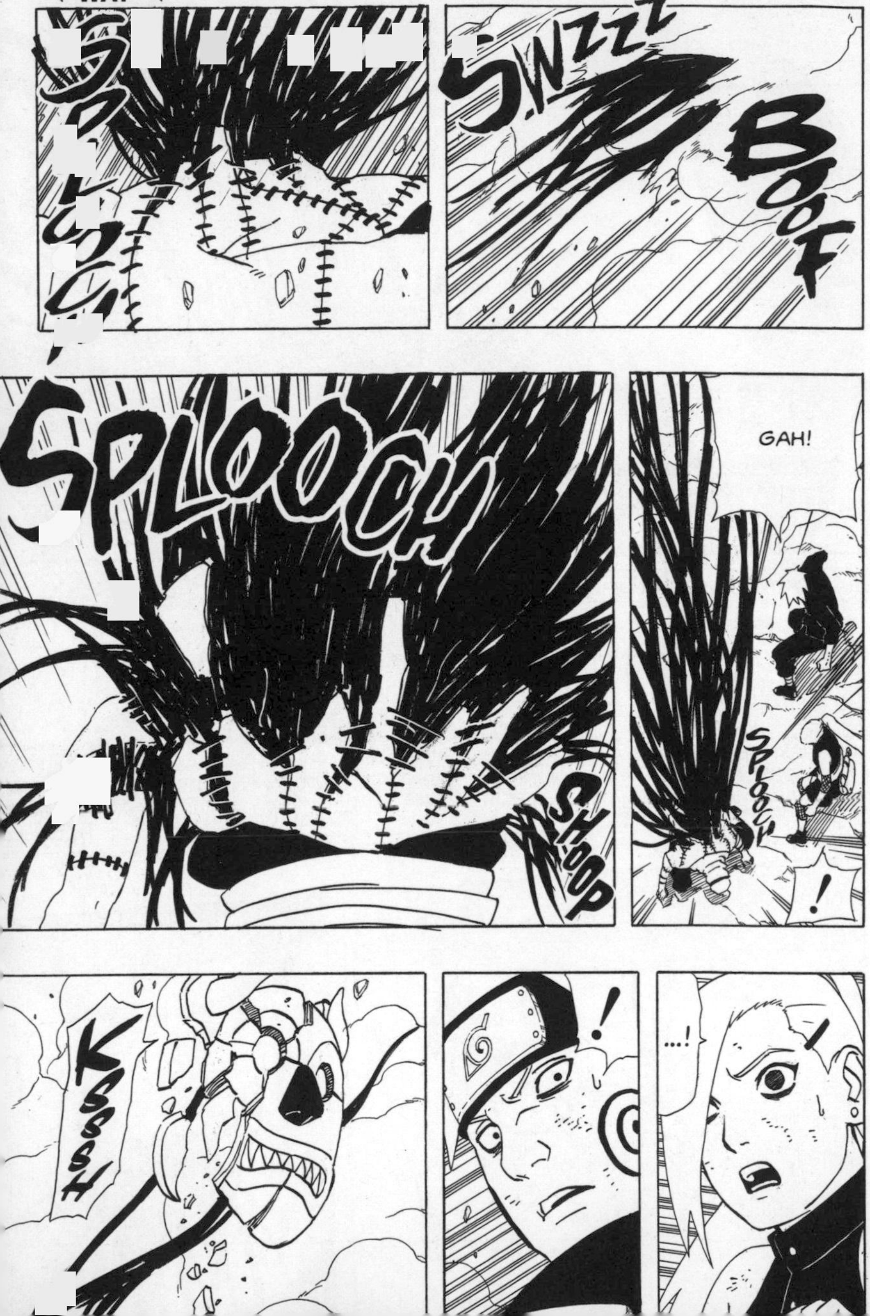
SWZZZ
BOOF
GAH!
SPLOOCH
!
SPLOOCH
SHOOP
....!
!
KSSSH

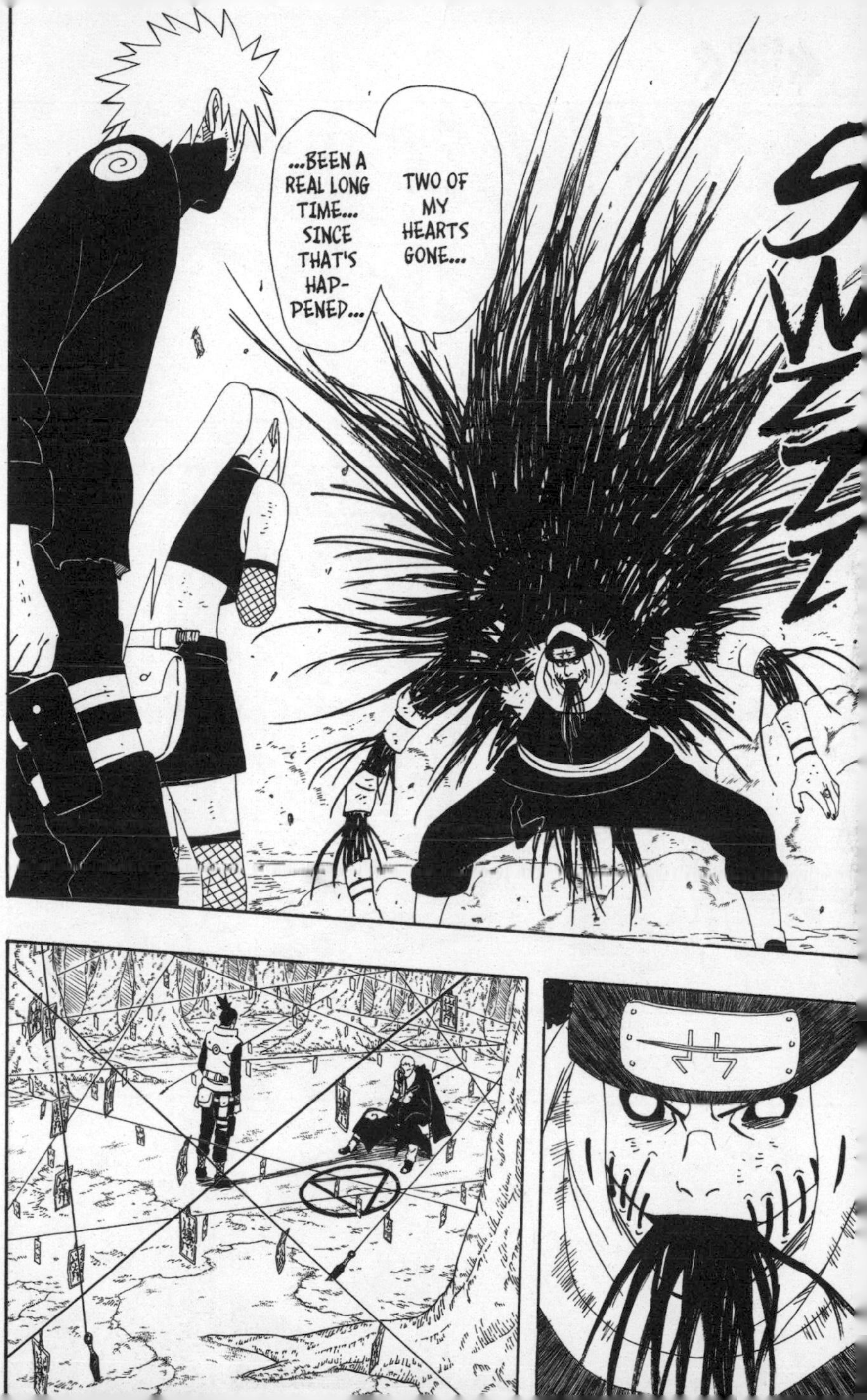
TWO OF MY HEARTS GONE...
...BEEN A REAL LONG TIME... SINCE THAT'S HAPPENED...
SWZZZ

READ THIS WAY

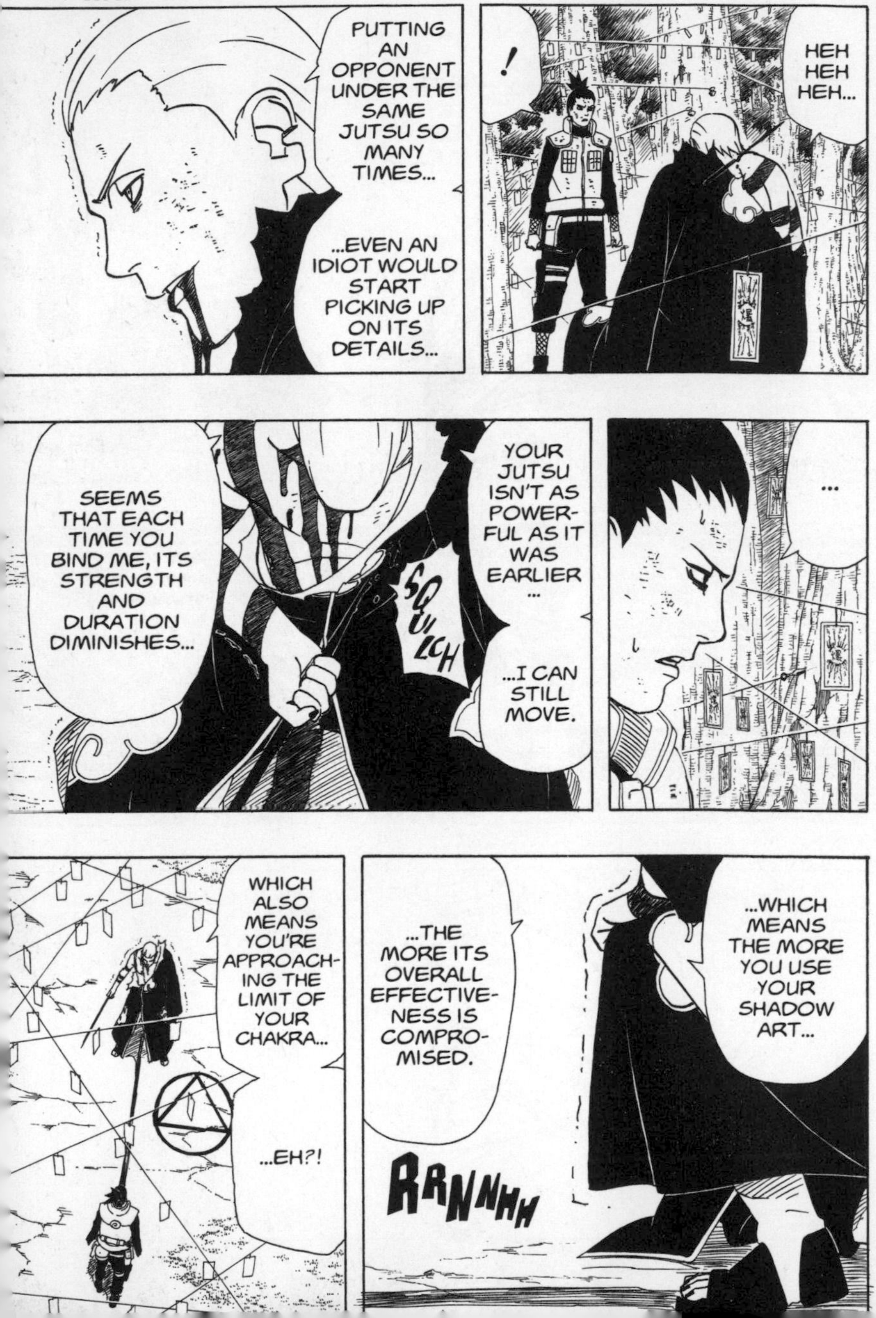
!
HEH HEH HEH...
PUTTING AN OPPONENT UNDER THE SAME JUTSU SO MANY TIMES...
...EVEN AN IDIOT WOULD START PICKING UP ON ITS DETAILS...
...
YOUR JUTSU ISN'T AS POWER-FUL AS IT WAS EARLIER ...
SQUELCH
...I CAN STILL MOVE.
SEEMS THAT EACH TIME YOU BIND ME, ITS STRENGTH AND DURATION DIMINISHES...
...WHICH MEANS THE MORE YOU USE YOUR SHADOW ART...
...THE MORE ITS OVERALL EFFECTIVE-NESS IS COMPRO-MISED.
RRNNHH
WHICH ALSO MEANS YOU'RE APPROACH-ING THE LIMIT OF YOUR CHAKRA...
...EH?!

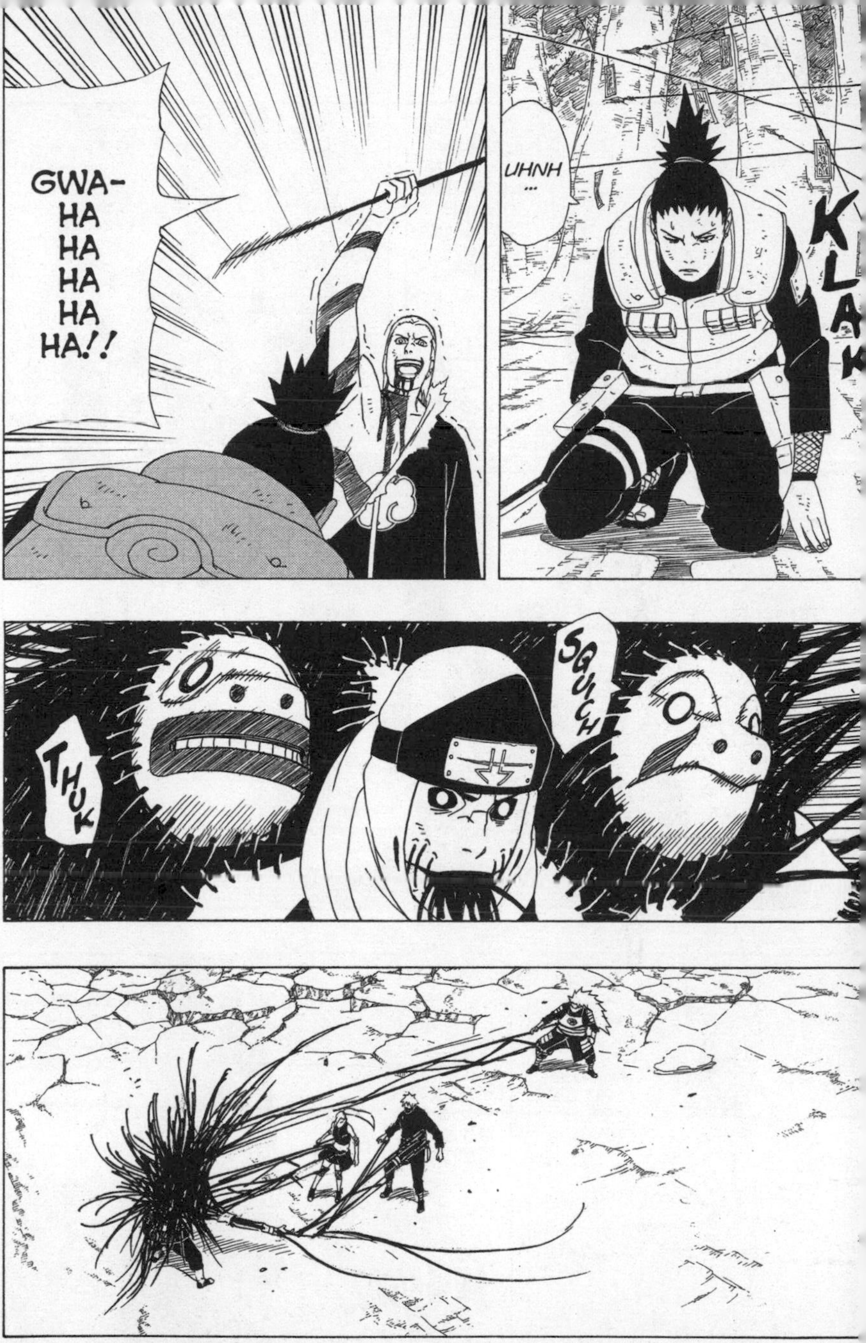
UHNH ...
KLAK
GWA-HA HA HA HA HA!!
SQUICH
THUK

READ THIS WAY

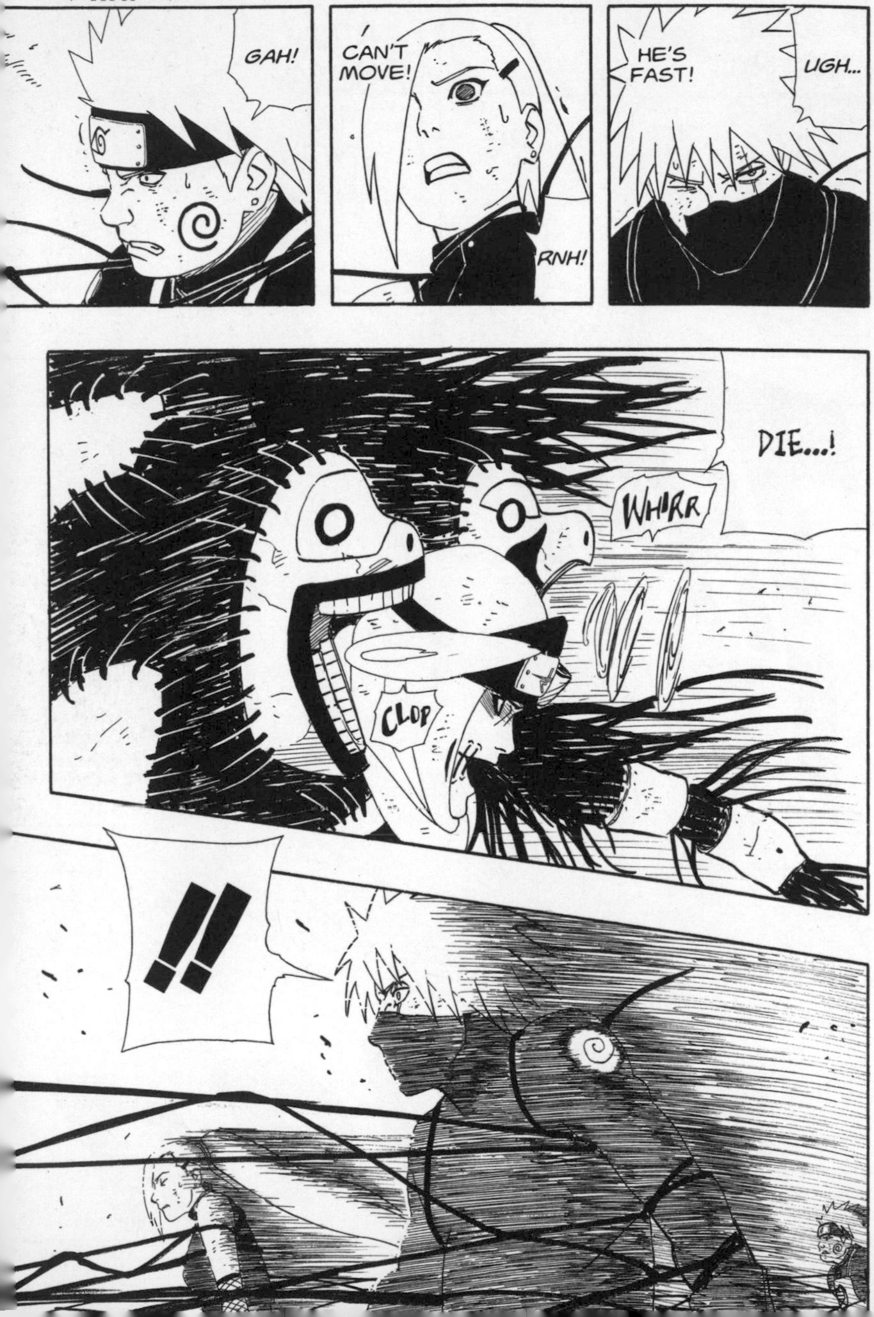
UGH...
HE'S FAST!
I CAN'T MOVE!
RNH!
GAH!
DIE...!
WHIRR
CLOP
!!

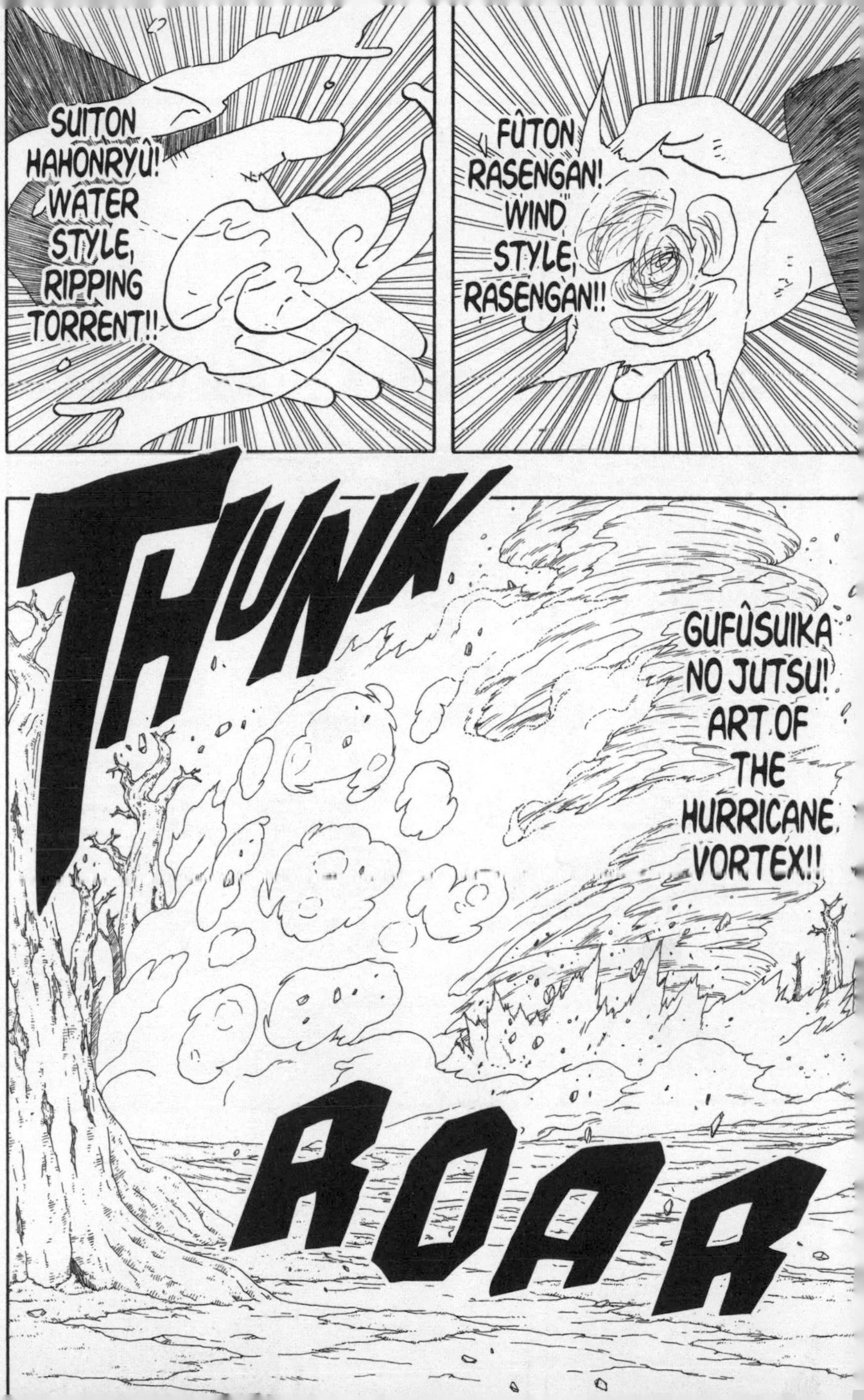
FÛTON RASENGAN! WIND STYLE, RASENGAN!!
SUITON HAHONRYÛ! WATER STYLE, RIPPING TORRENT!!
GUFÛSUIKA NO JUTSU! ART OF THE HURRICANE VORTEX!!
THUNK
ROAR

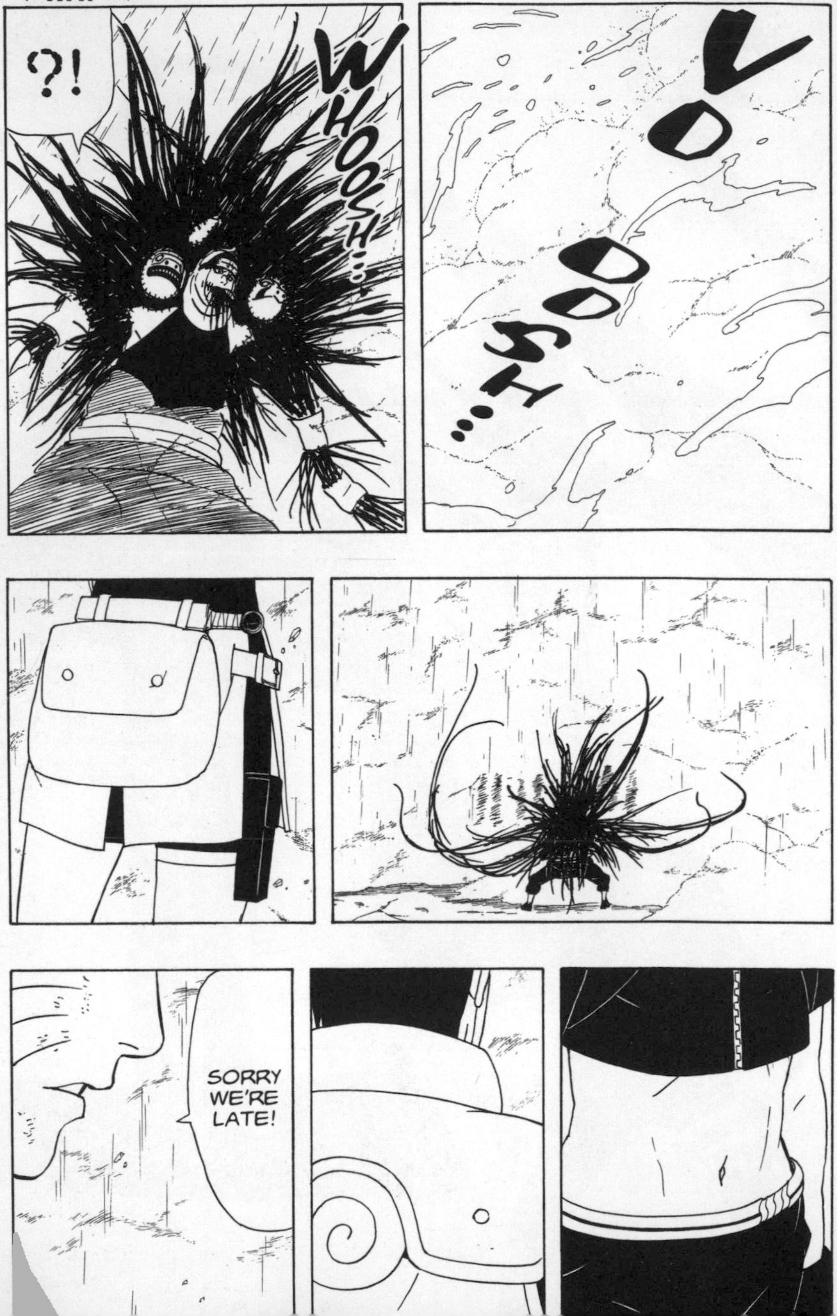
VOOOSH...
WHOOOSH...
?!
SORRY WE'RE LATE!

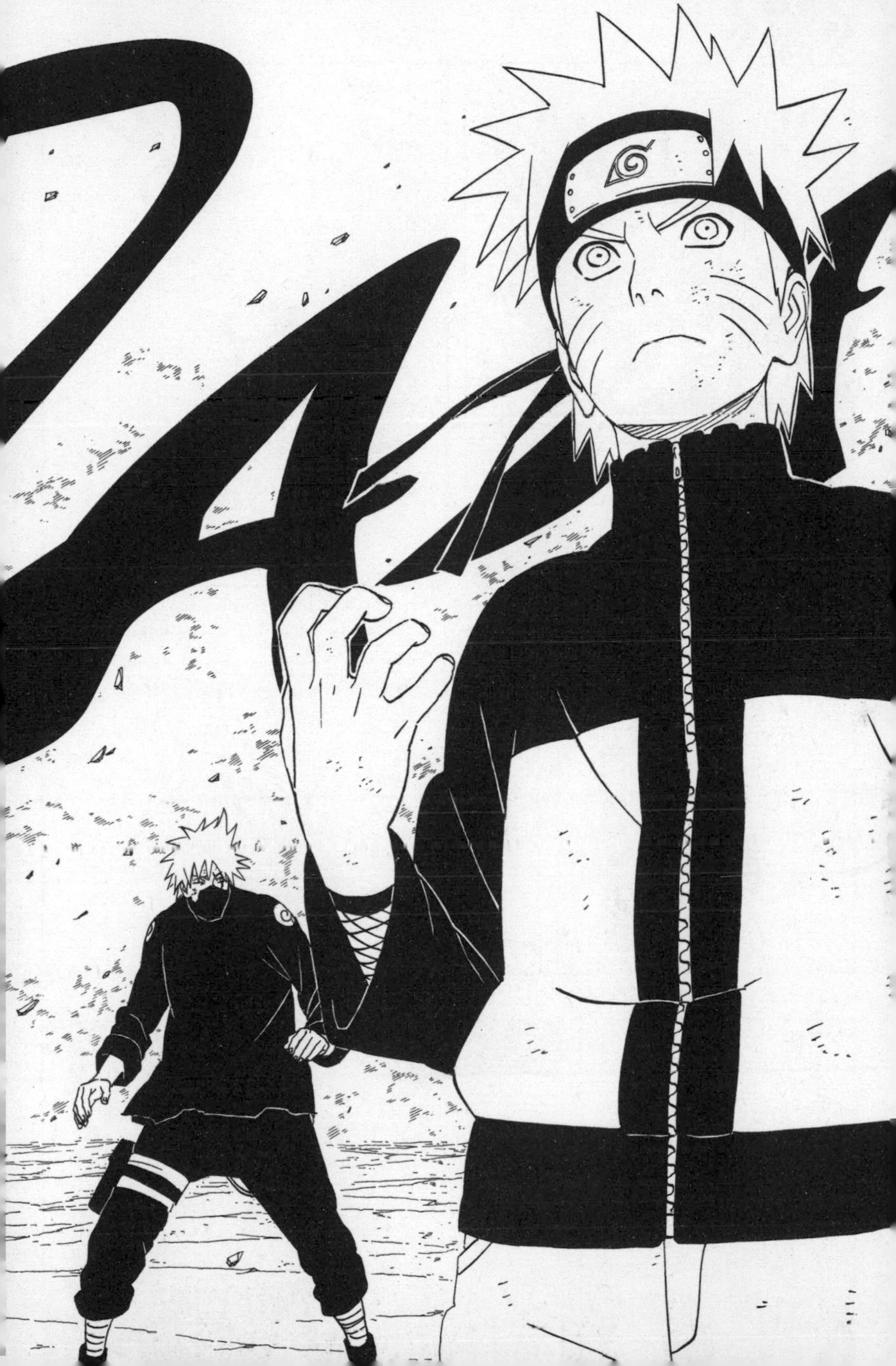

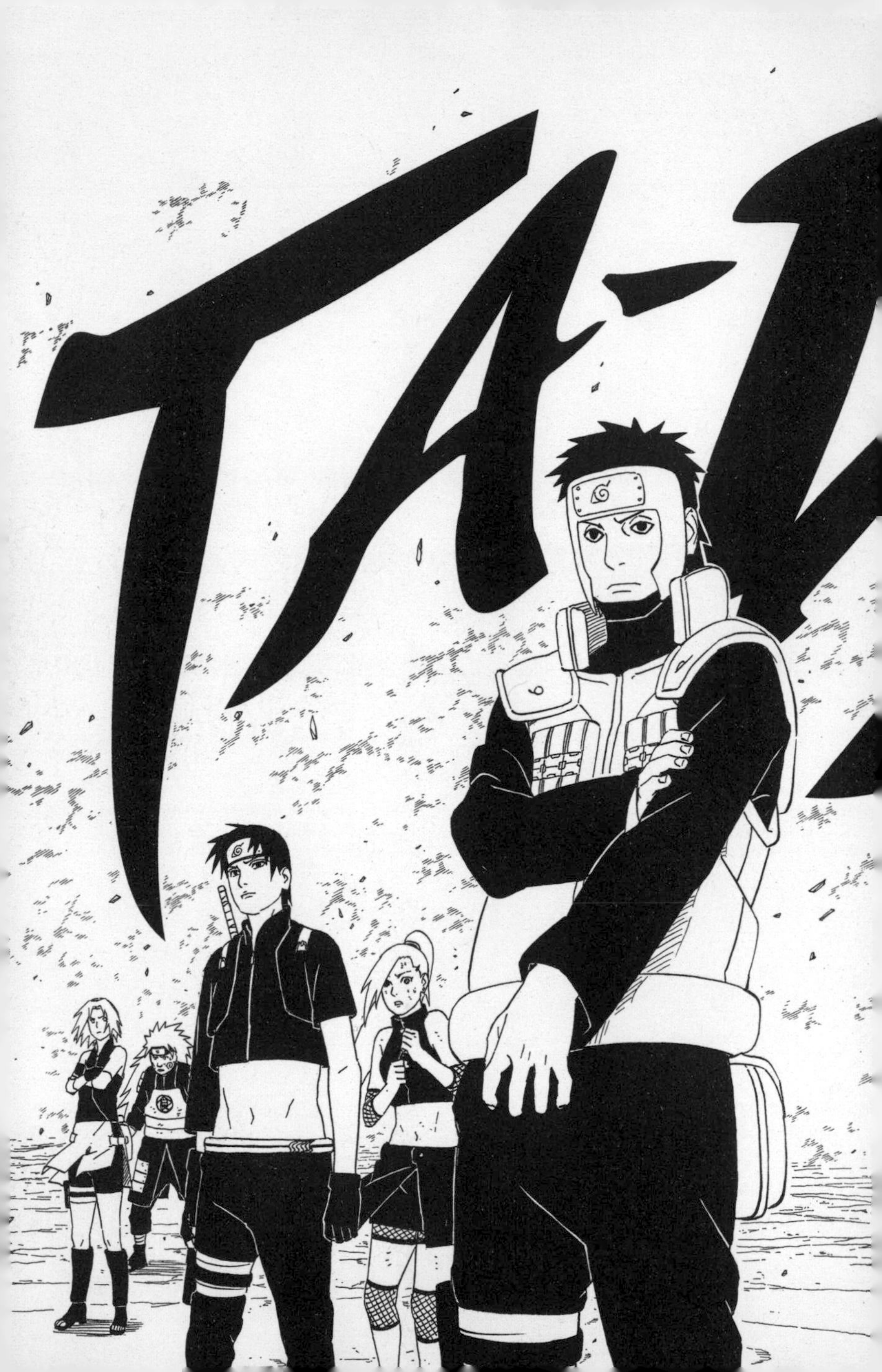
TA-

NARUTO

Number 338: Payback...

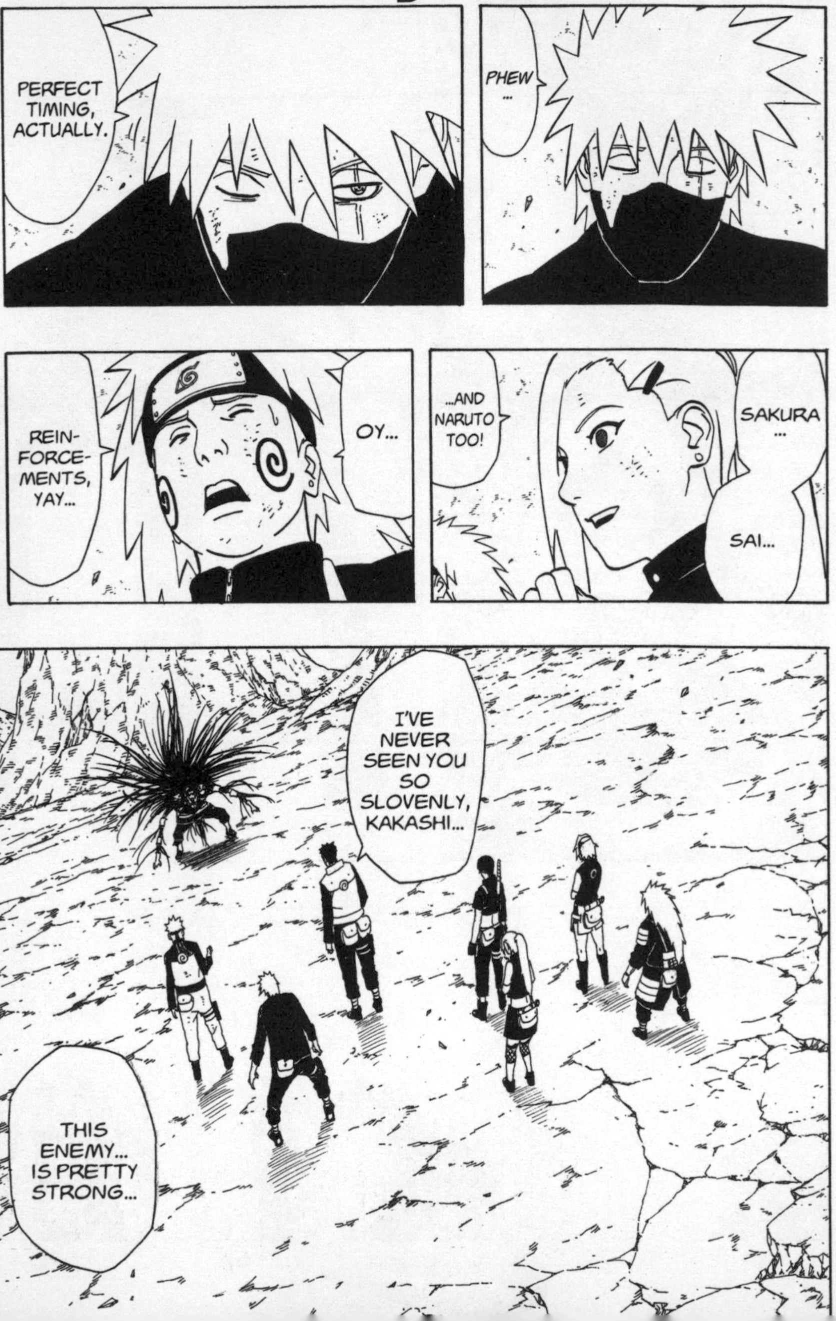
PHEW ...
PERFECT TIMING, ACTUALLY.
SAKURA ...
SAI...
...AND NARUTO TOO!
OY...
REIN-FORCE-MENTS, YAY...
I'VE NEVER SEEN YOU SO SLOVENLY, KAKASHI...
THIS ENEMY... IS PRETTY STRONG...

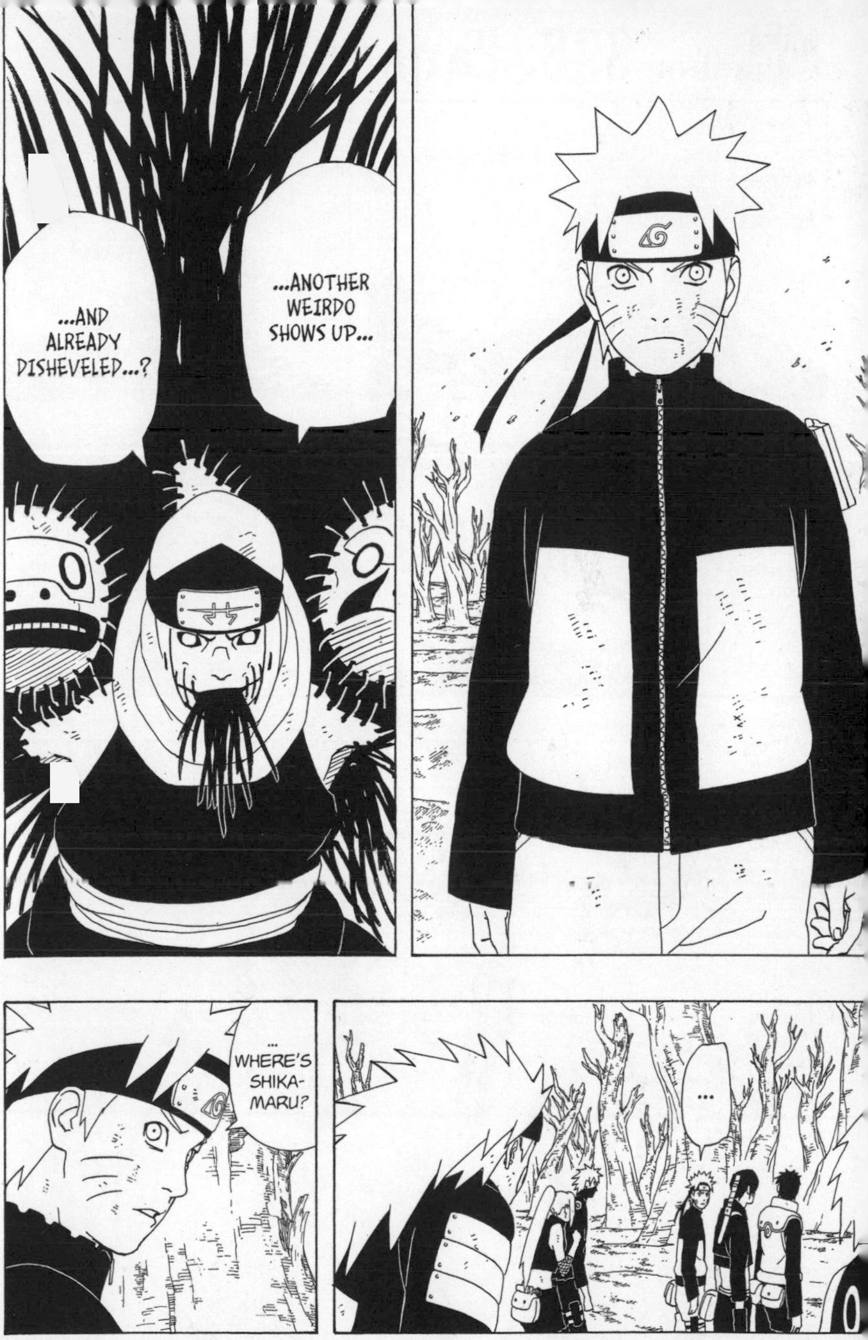
...ANOTHER WEIRDO SHOWS UP...
...AND ALREADY DISHEVELED...?
...
... WHERE'S SHIKA-MARU?

READ THIS WAY

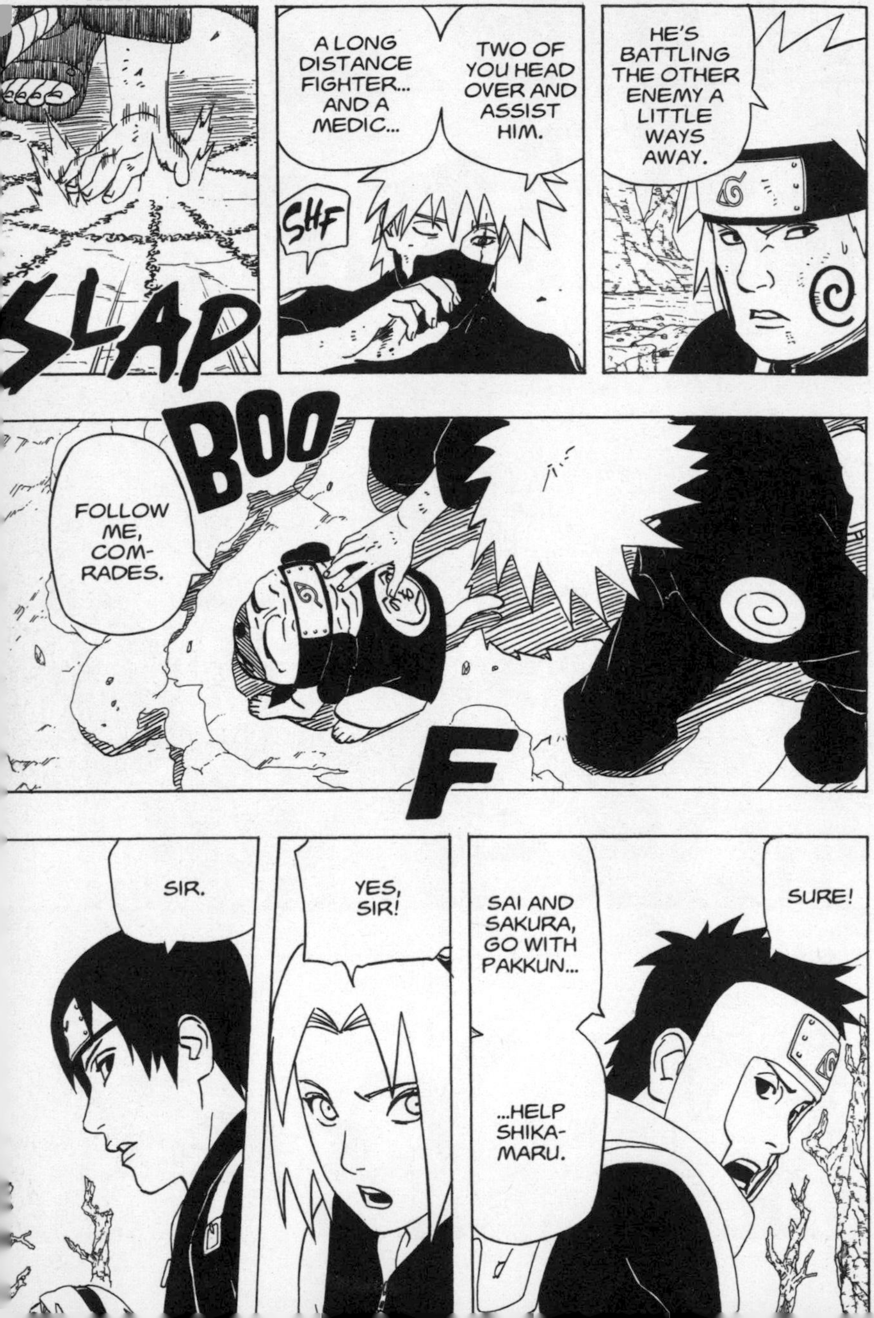
HE'S BATTLING THE OTHER ENEMY A LITTLE WAYS AWAY.
TWO OF YOU HEAD OVER AND ASSIST HIM.
A LONG DISTANCE FIGHTER... AND A MEDIC...
SHF
SLAP
BOOF
FOLLOW ME, COM-RADES.
SURE!
SAI AND SAKURA, GO WITH PAKKUN...
...HELP SHIKA-MARU.
YES, SIR!
SIR.

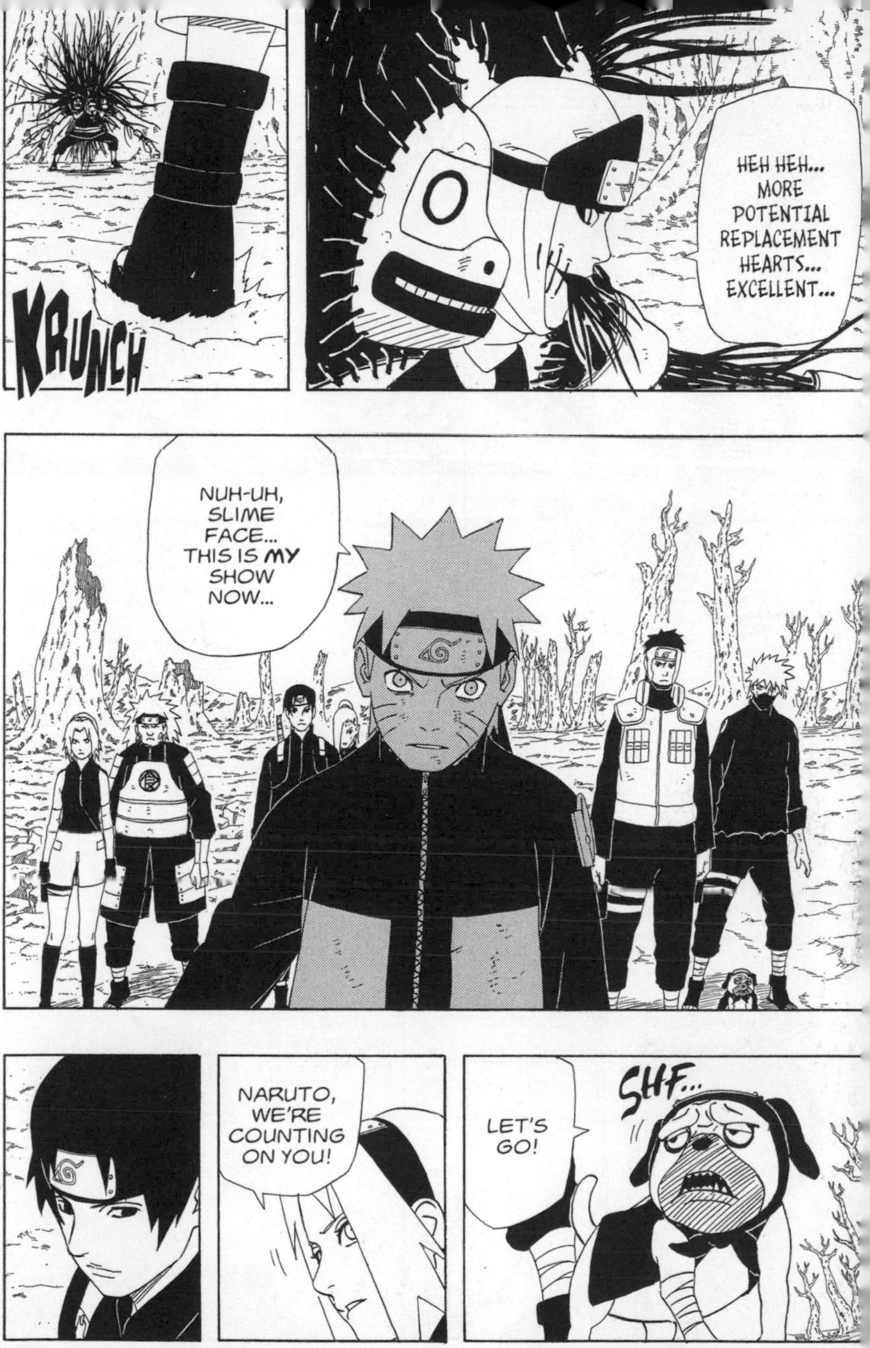
HEH HEH... MORE POTENTIAL REPLACEMENT HEARTS... EXCELLENT...
KRUNCH
NUH-UH, SLIME FACE... THIS IS MY SHOW NOW...
SHF...
LET'S GO!
NARUTO, WE'RE COUNTING ON YOU!

READ THIS WAY

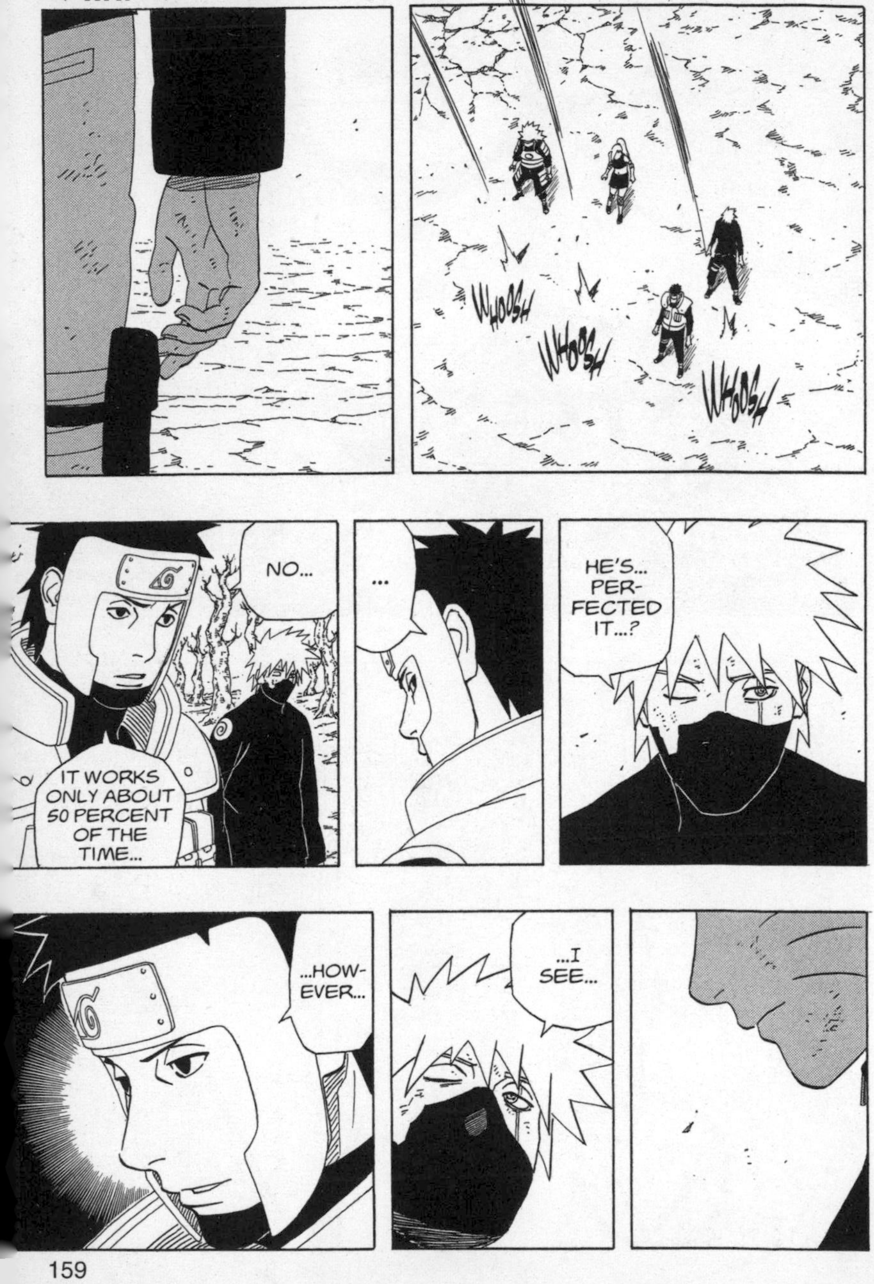
WHOOSH
WHOOSH
WHOOSH
HE'S... PER-FECTED IT...?
...
NO...
IT WORKS ONLY ABOUT 50 PERCENT OF THE TIME...
...I SEE...
...HOW-EVER...

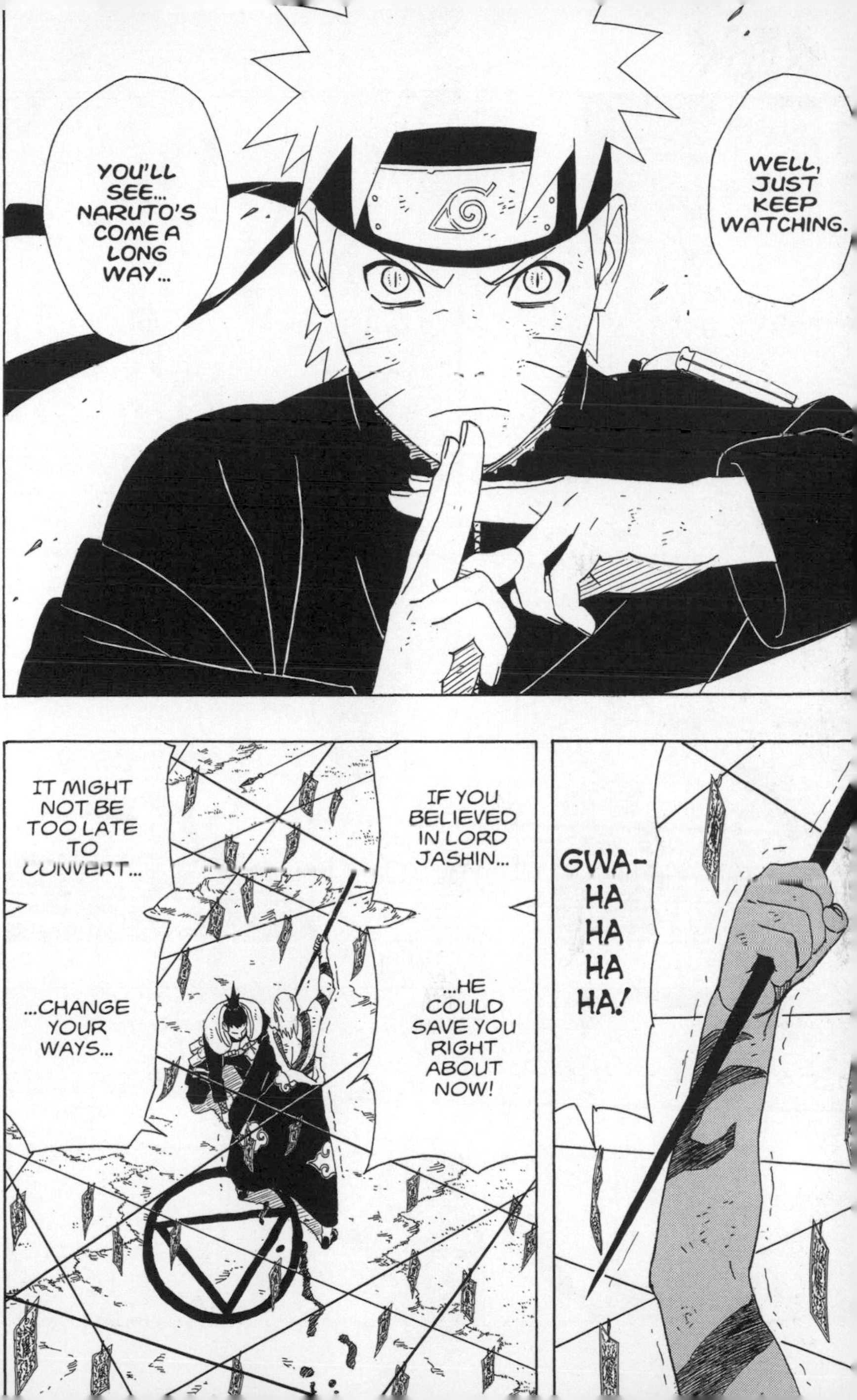
WELL, JUST KEEP WATCHING.
YOU'LL SEE... NARUTO'S COME A LONG WAY...
GWA-HA HA HA HA!
IF YOU BELIEVED IN LORD JASHIN...
IT MIGHT NOT BE TOO LATE TO CONVERT...
...HE COULD SAVE YOU RIGHT ABOUT NOW!
...CHANGE YOUR WAYS...

READ THIS WAY

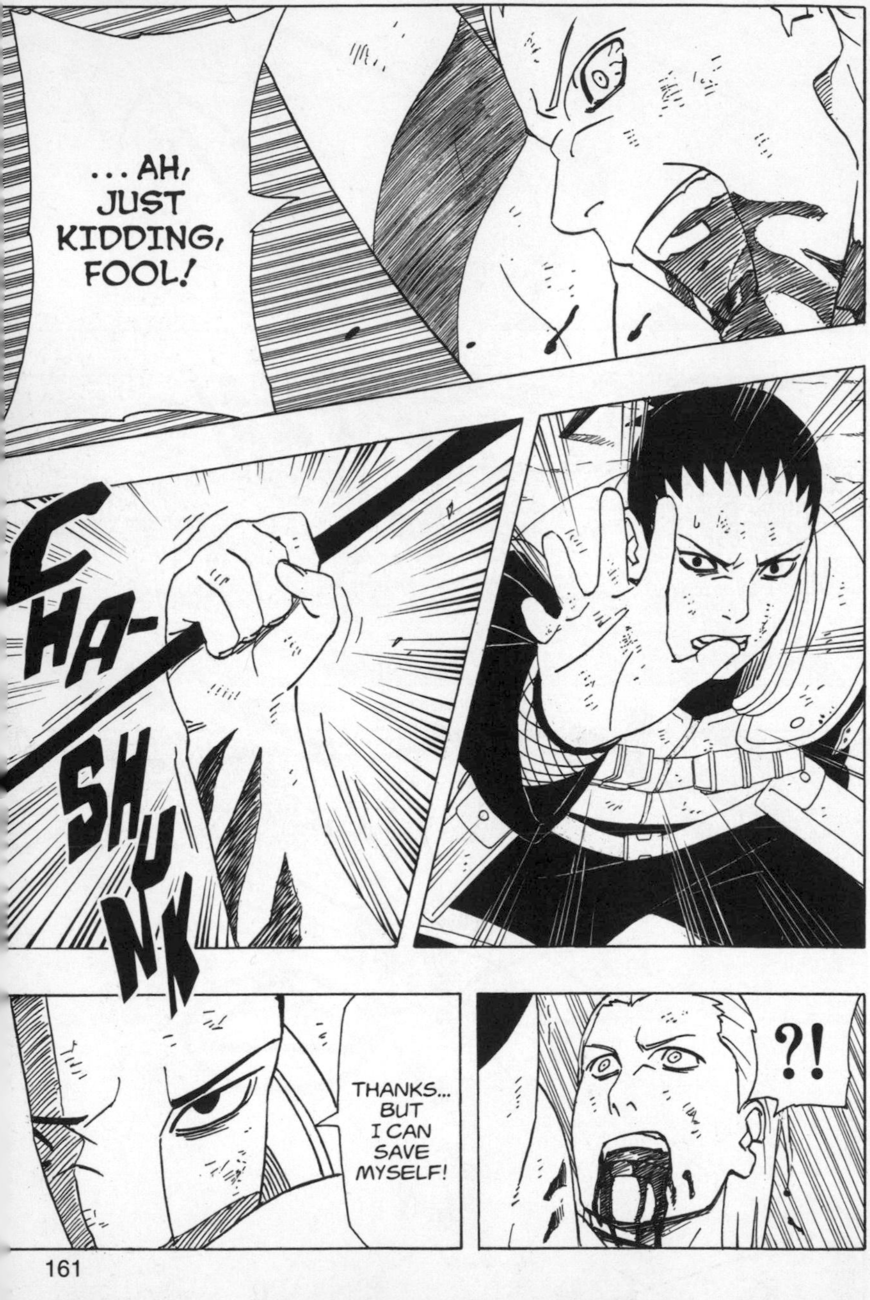
...AH, JUST KIDDING, FOOL!
CHA-SHUNK
?!
THANKS... BUT I CAN SAVE MYSELF!

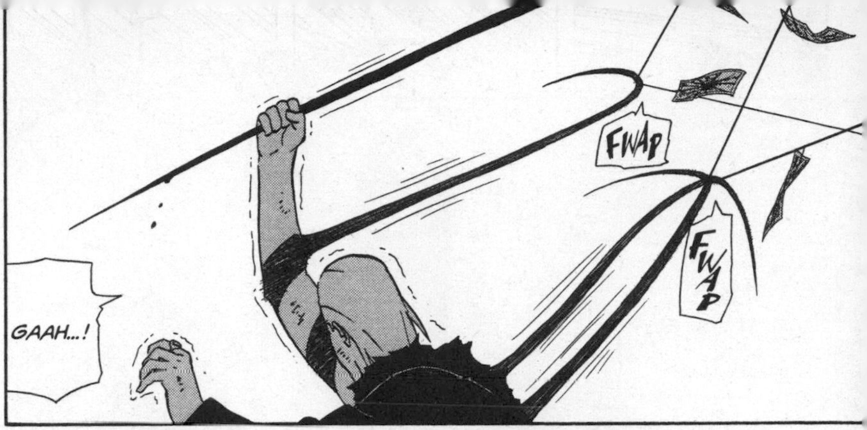
FWAP
FWAP
GAAH...!
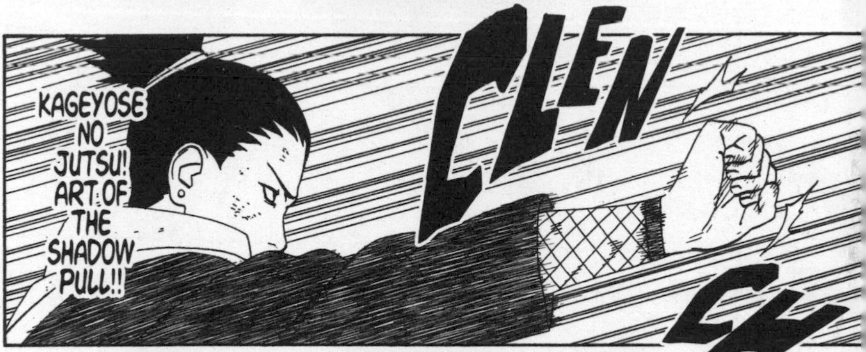
CLEN
CH
KAGEYOSE NO JUTSU! ART OF THE SHADOW PULL!!
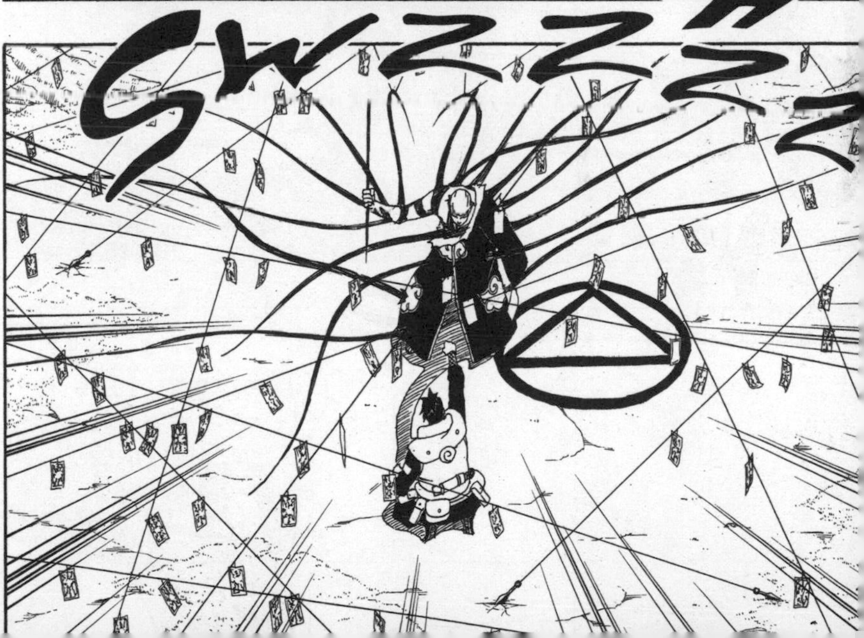
SWZZZZ

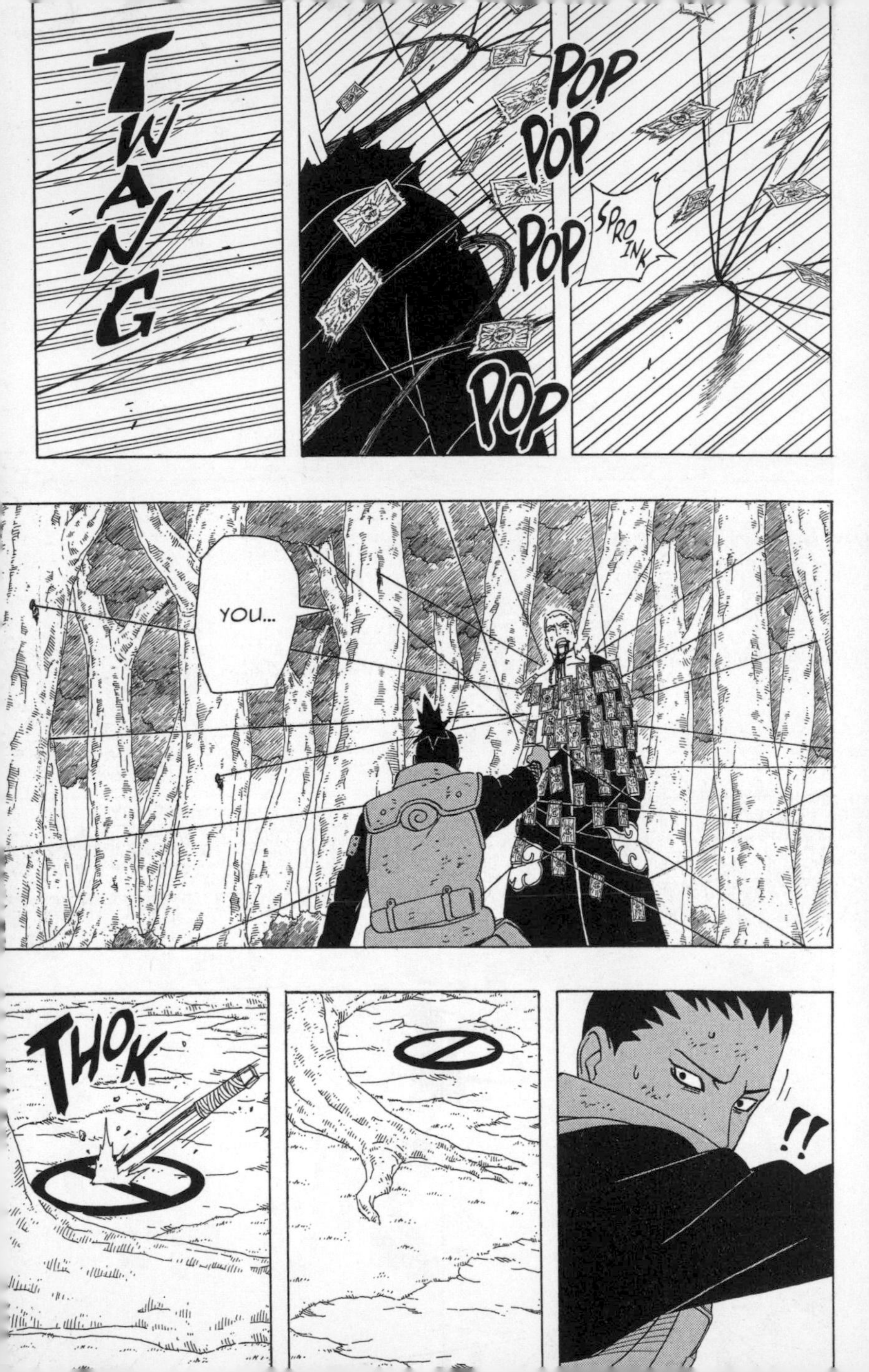
SPROINK
POP POP POP POP
TWANG
YOU...
!!
THOK

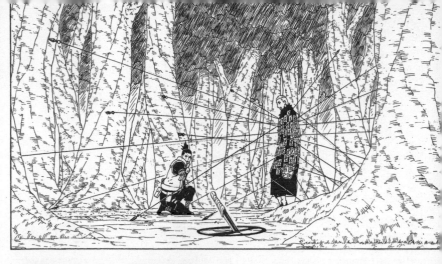

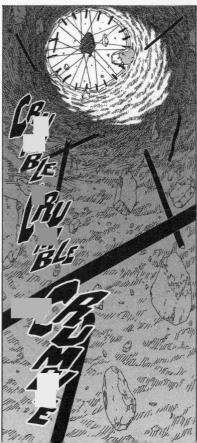

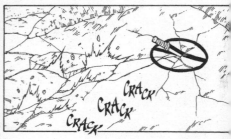

CRACK
CRACK
CRACK

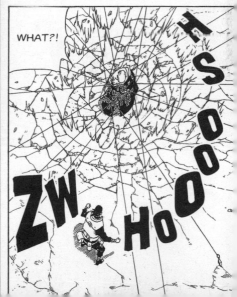

WHAT?!

ZW HOOOO HSOO

READ THIS WAY

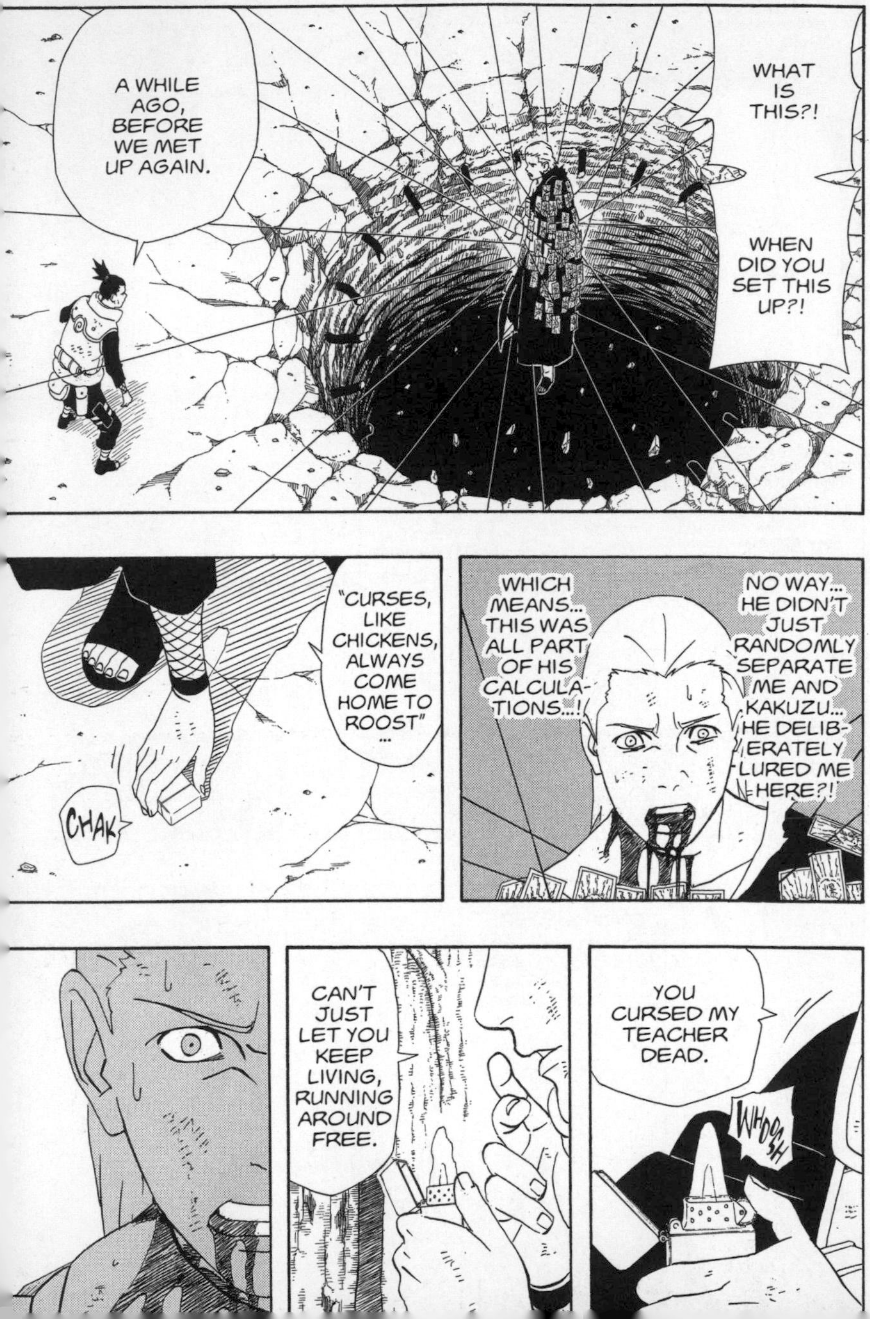
WHAT IS THIS?!
WHEN DID YOU SET THIS UP?!
A WHILE AGO, BEFORE WE MET UP AGAIN.
NO WAY... HE DIDN'T JUST RANDOMLY SEPARATE ME AND KAKUZU... HE DELIBERATELY LURED ME HERE?!
WHICH MEANS... THIS WAS ALL PART OF HIS CALCULATIONS...!
"CURSES, LIKE CHICKENS, ALWAYS COME HOME TO ROOST"...
CHAK
YOU CURSED MY TEACHER DEAD.
WHOOSH
CAN'T JUST LET YOU KEEP LIVING, RUNNING AROUND FREE.

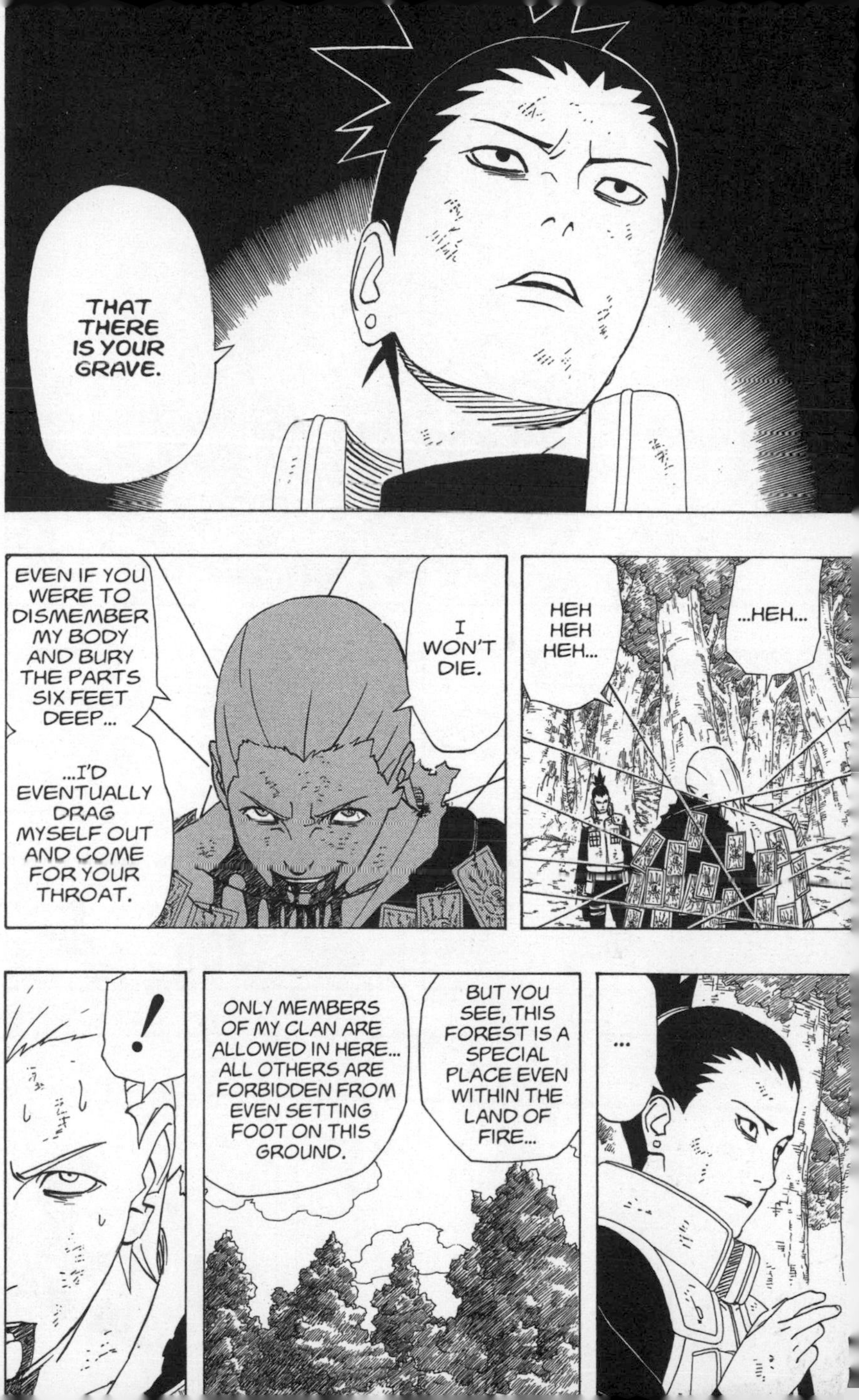
THAT THERE IS YOUR GRAVE.
...HEH...
HEH HEH HEH...
I WON'T DIE.
EVEN IF YOU WERE TO DISMEMBER MY BODY AND BURY THE PARTS SIX FEET DEEP...
...I'D EVENTUALLY DRAG MYSELF OUT AND COME FOR YOUR THROAT.
...
BUT YOU SEE, THIS FOREST IS A SPECIAL PLACE EVEN WITHIN THE LAND OF FIRE...
ONLY MEMBERS OF MY CLAN ARE ALLOWED IN HERE... ALL OTHERS ARE FORBIDDEN FROM EVEN SETTING FOOT ON THIS GROUND.
!

READ THIS WAY

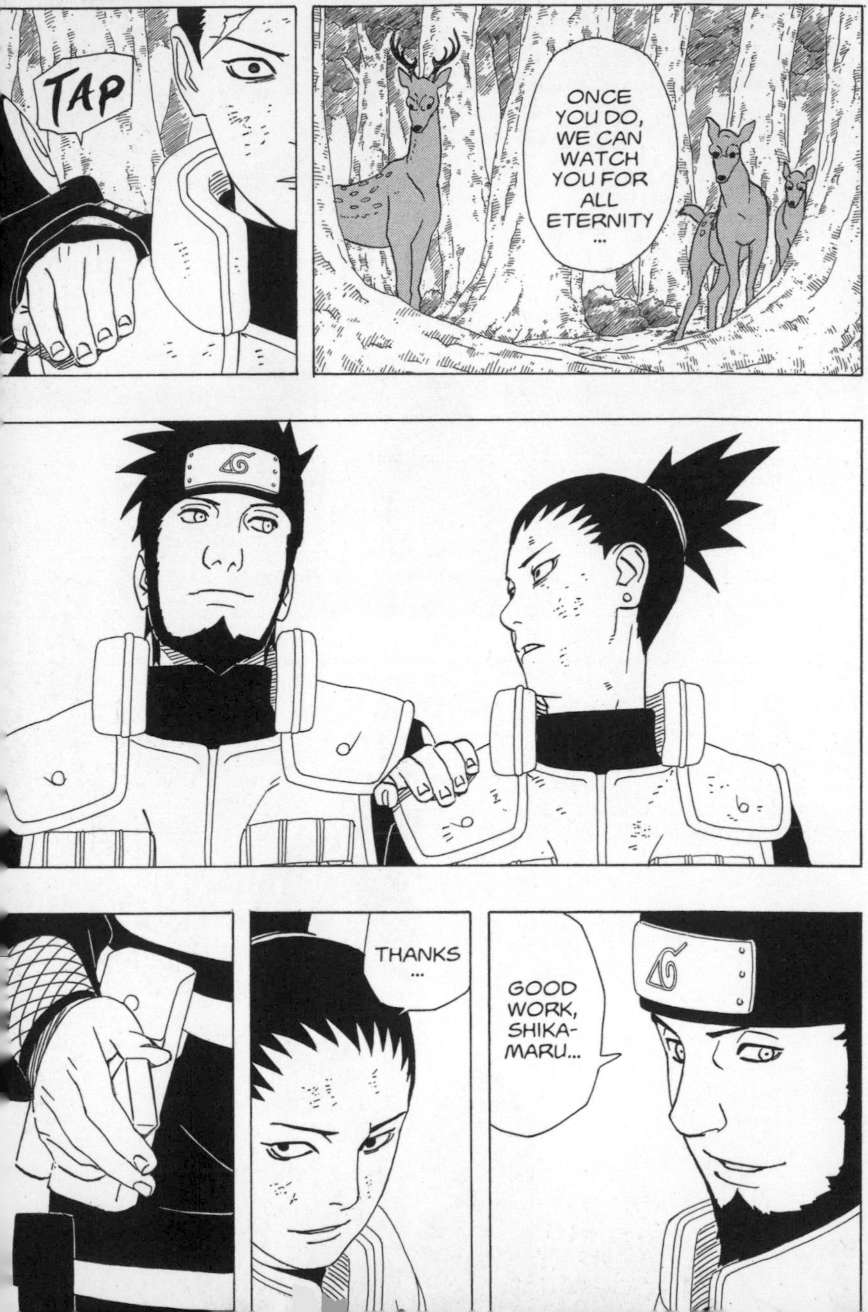

ONCE YOU DO, WE CAN WATCH YOU FOR ALL ETERNITY ...
TAP
GOOD WORK, SHIKA-MARU...
THANKS ...

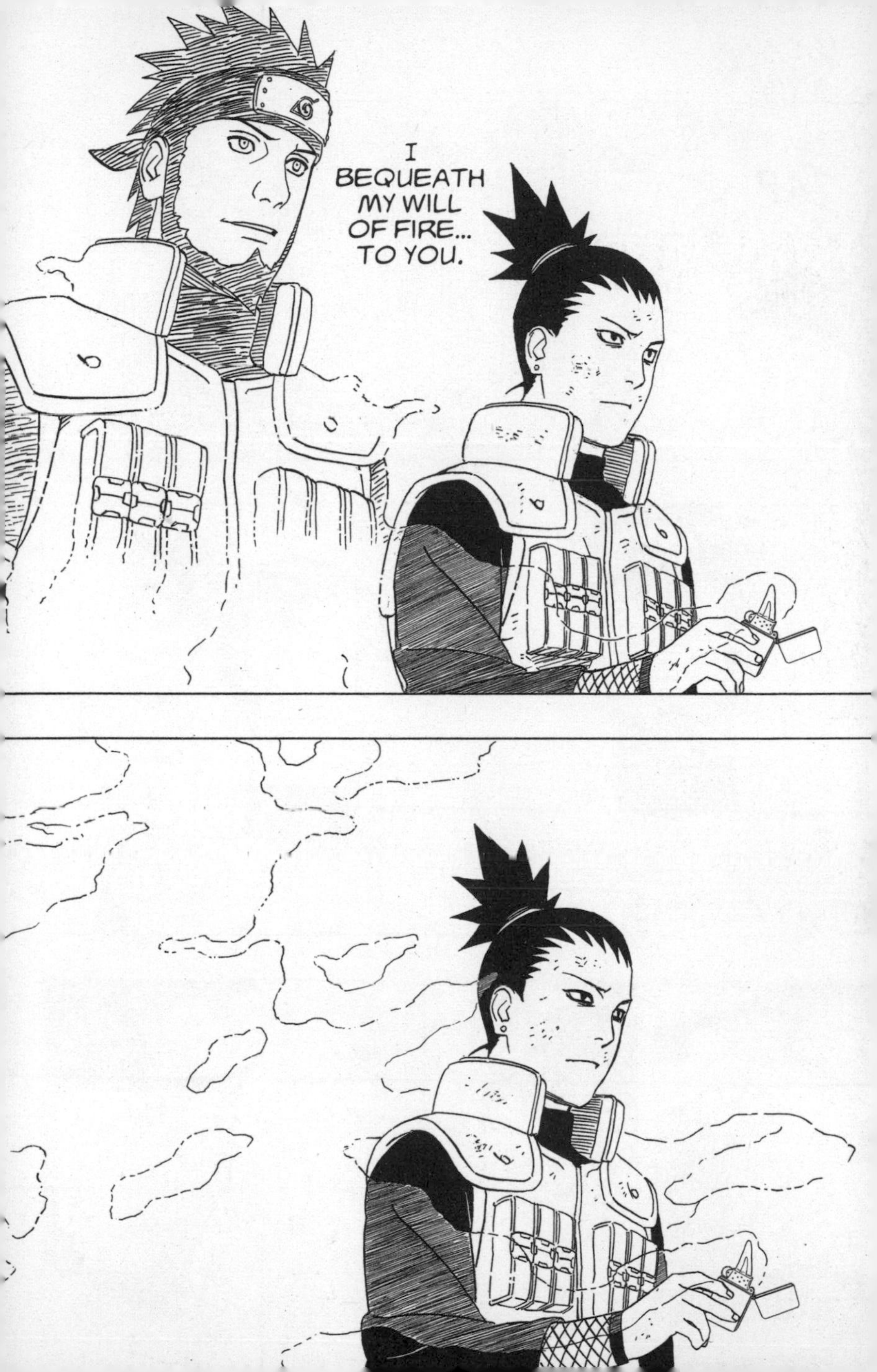
I BEQUEATH MY WILL OF FIRE... TO YOU.

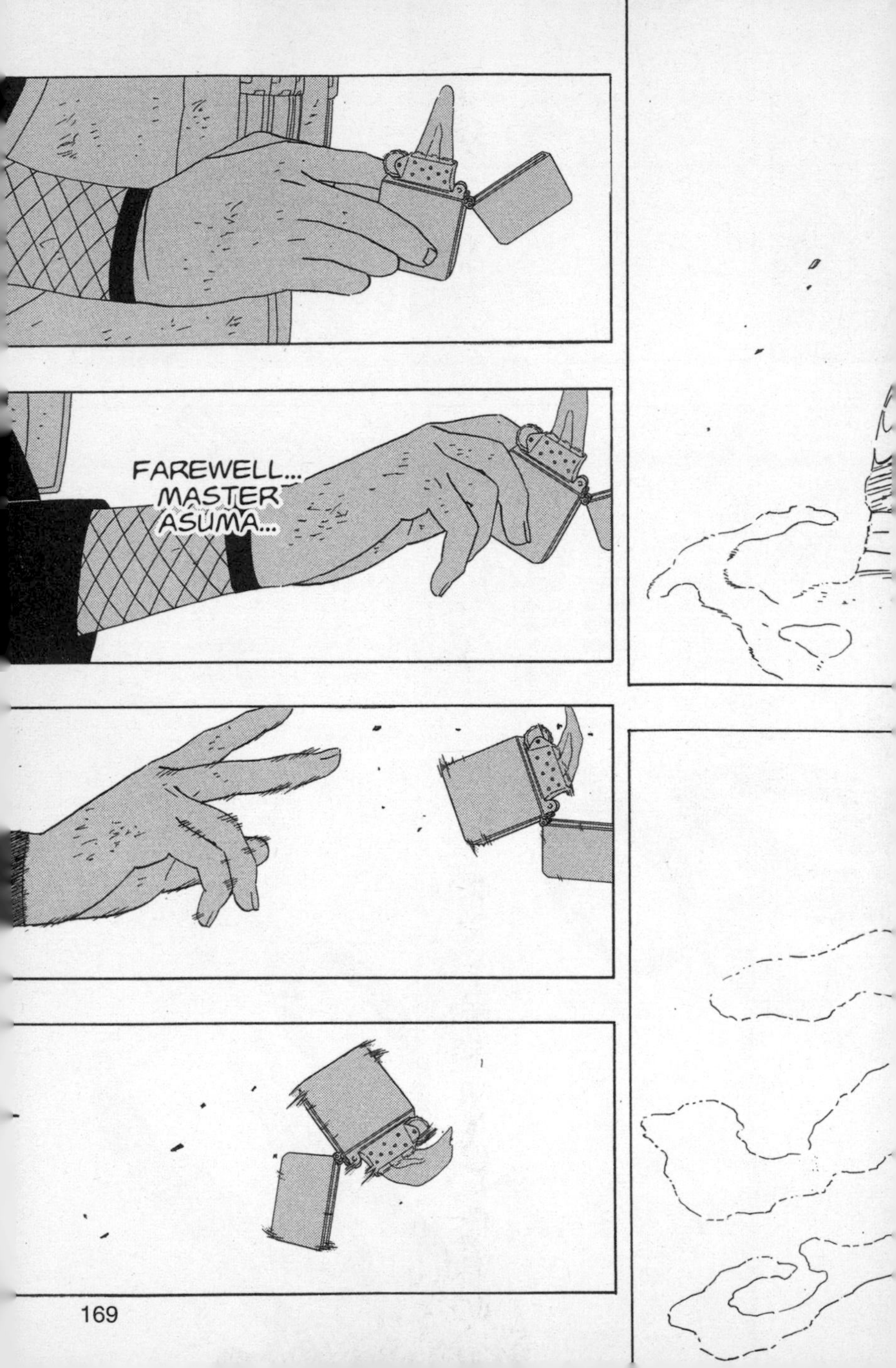
FAREWELL... MASTER ASUMA...

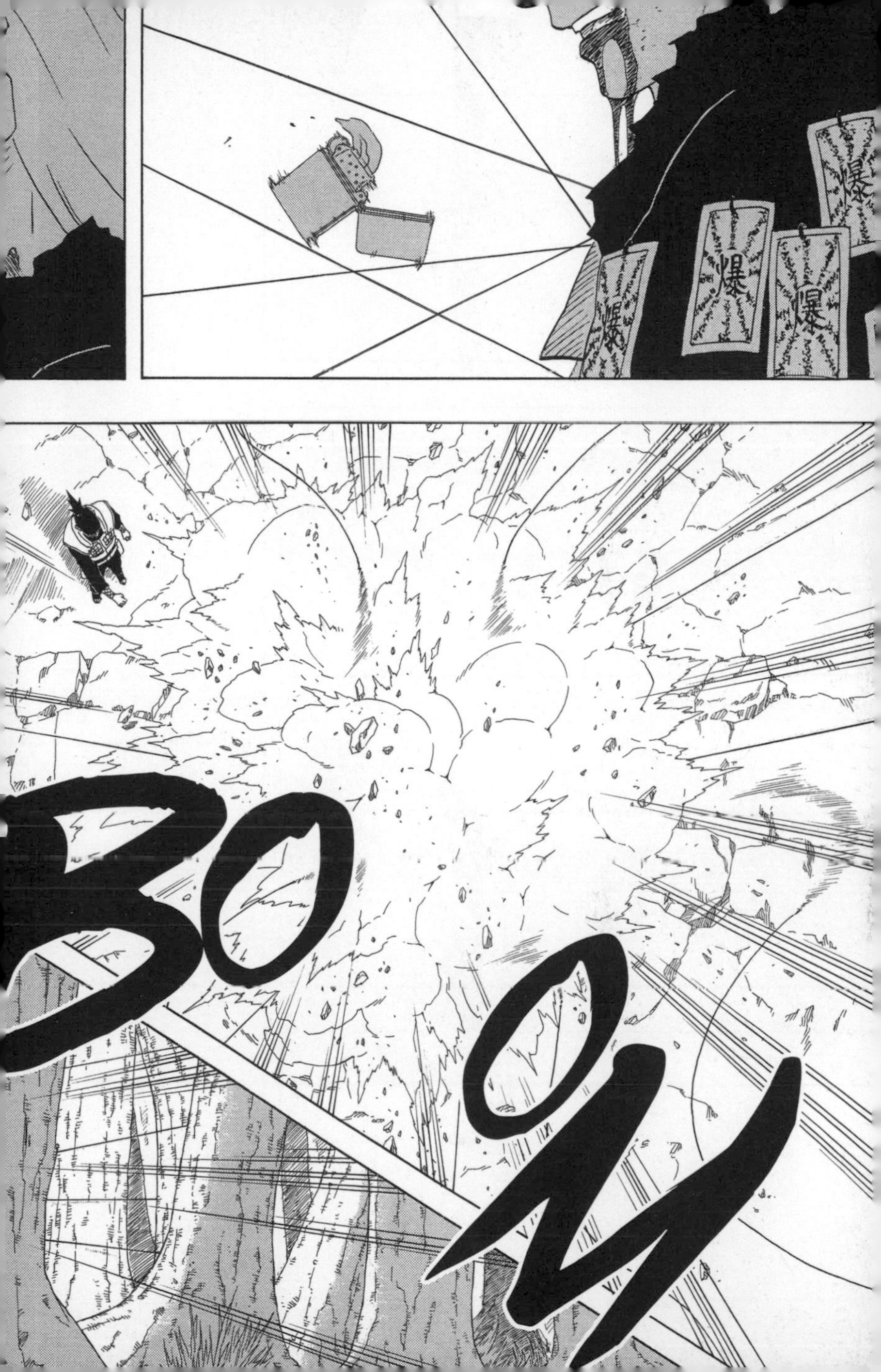
爆
爆
爆
爆
BOOM

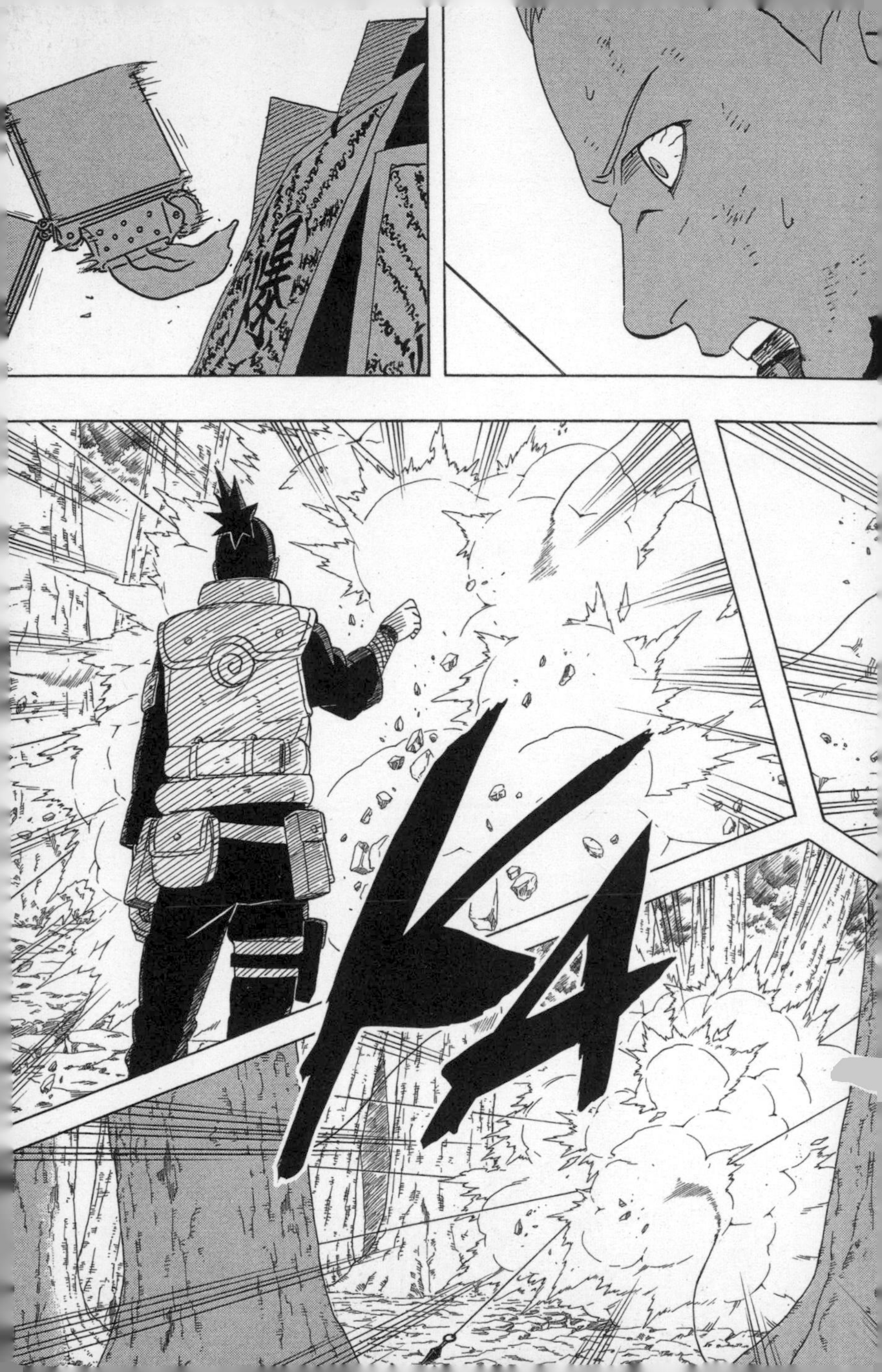
KA

NARUTO

Number 339: The New Jutsu...!!

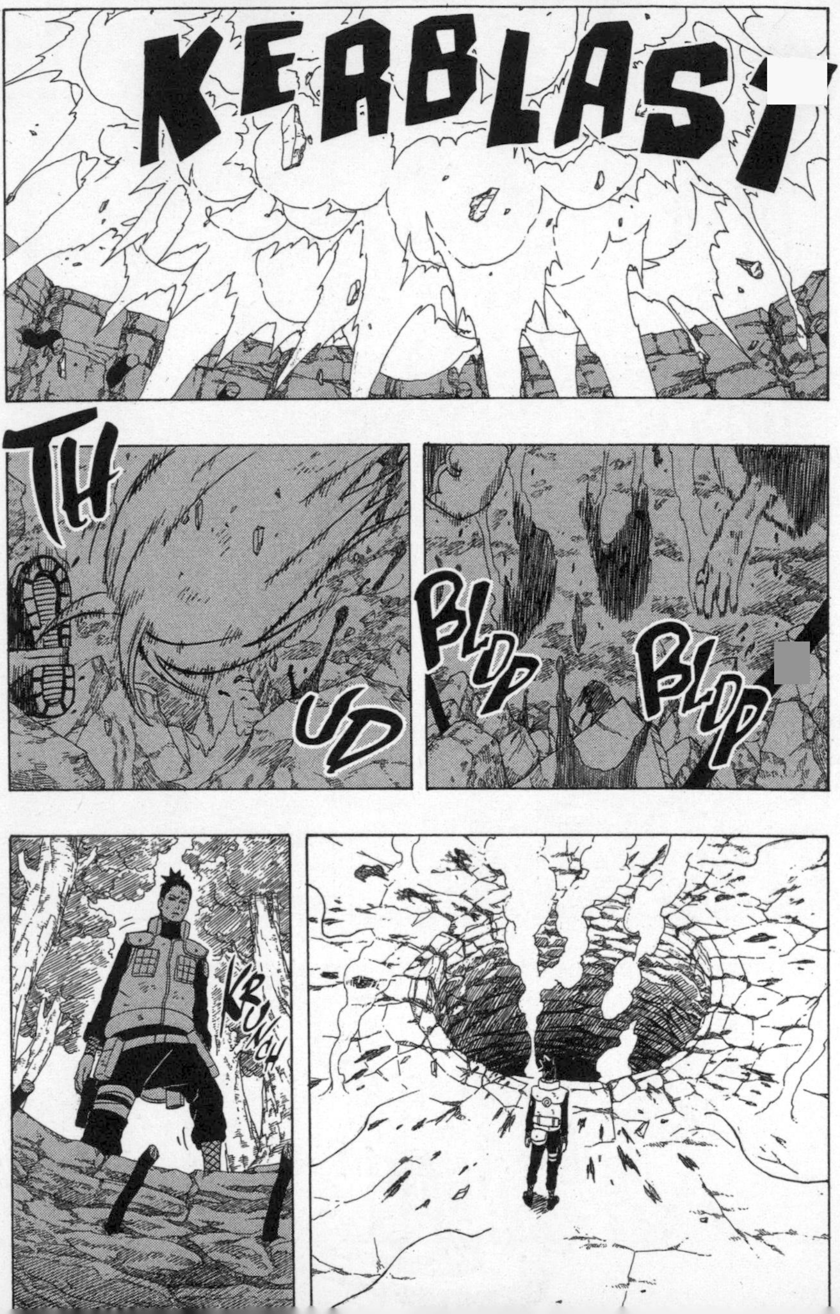
KERBLAST
BLDD
BLDD
THUD
KRUNCH

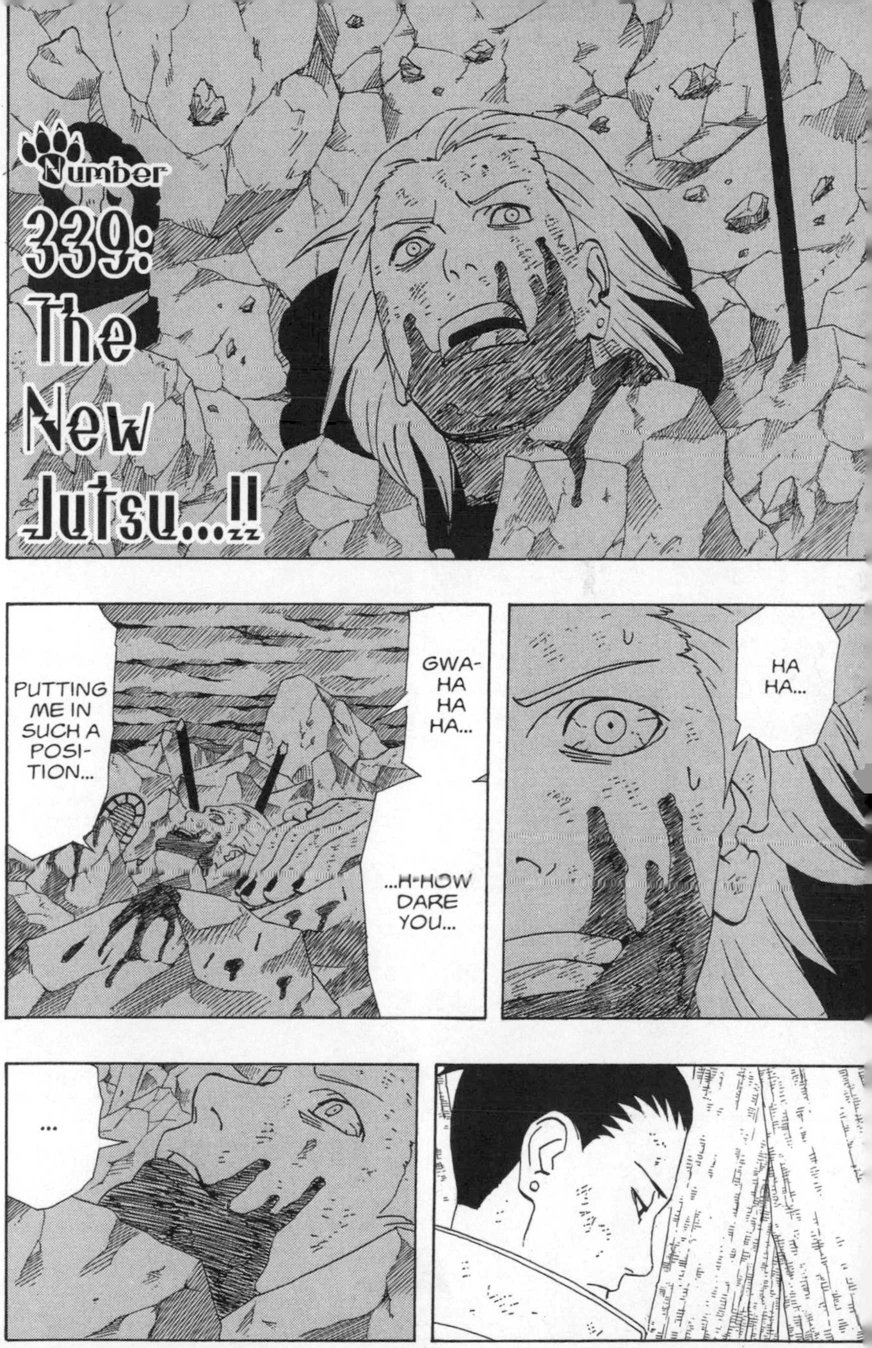
Number 339: The New Jutsu...!!
HA HA...
GWA-HA HA HA...
...H-HOW DARE YOU...
PUTTING ME IN SUCH A POSITION...
...

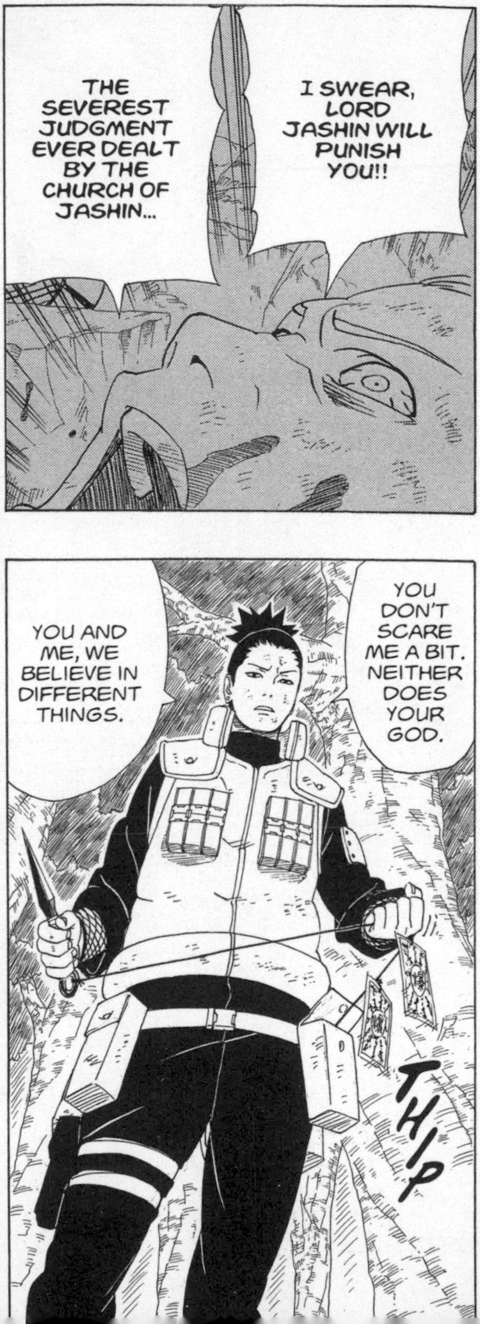
I SWEAR, LORD JASHIN WILL PUNISH YOU!!
THE SEVEREST JUDGMENT EVER DEALT BY THE CHURCH OF JASHIN...
YOU DON'T SCARE ME A BIT. NEITHER DOES YOUR GOD.
YOU AND ME, WE BELIEVE IN DIFFERENT THINGS.
THIP
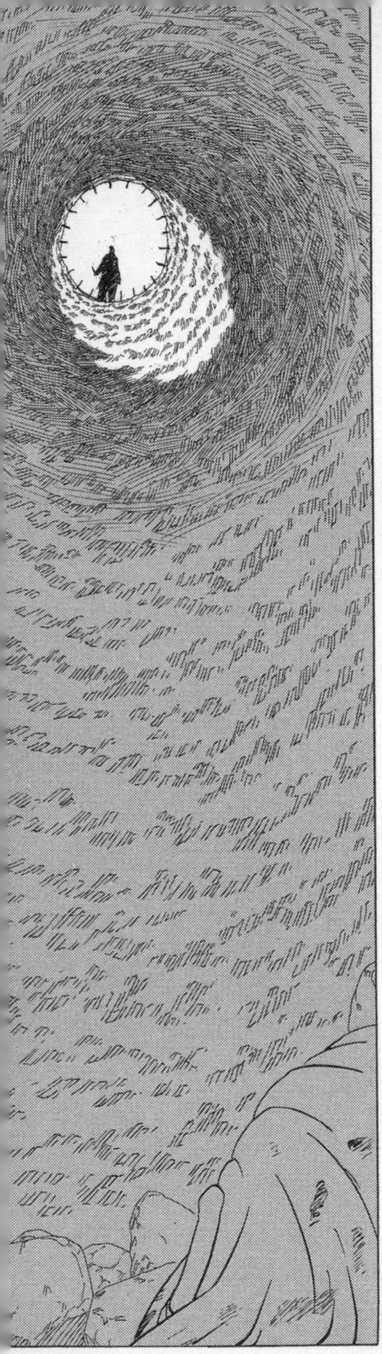

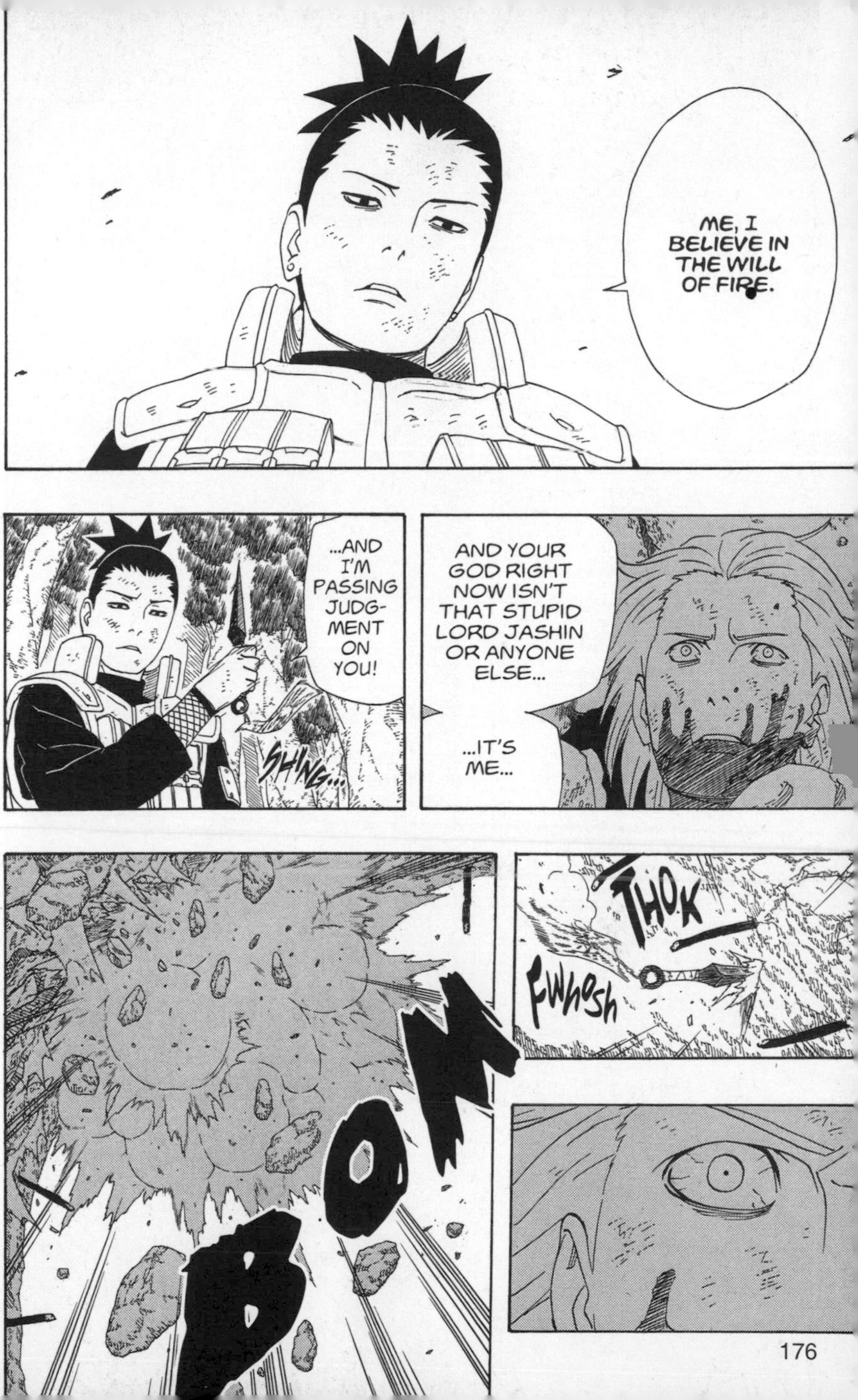
ME, I BELIEVE IN THE WILL OF FIRE.
AND YOUR GOD RIGHT NOW ISN'T THAT STUPID LORD JASHIN OR ANYONE ELSE...
...IT'S ME...
...AND I'M PASSING JUDG-MENT ON YOU!
SHING...
THOK
FWHOSH
BOOM

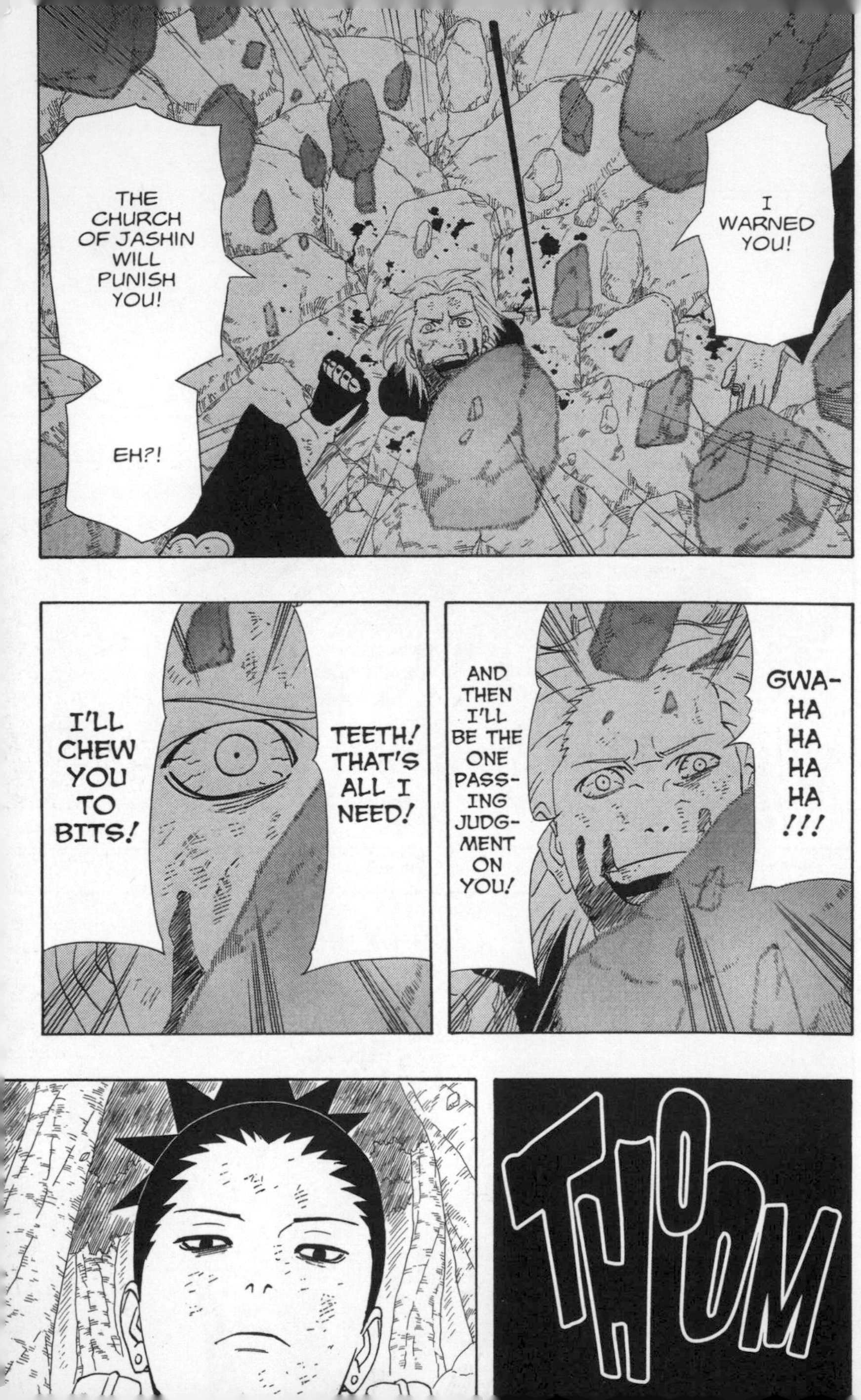
I WARNED YOU!
THE CHURCH OF JASHIN WILL PUNISH YOU!
EH?!
GWA-HA HA HA HA!!!
AND THEN I'LL BE THE ONE PASSING JUDGMENT ON YOU!
TEETH! THAT'S ALL I NEED!
I'LL CHEW YOU TO BITS!
THOOM

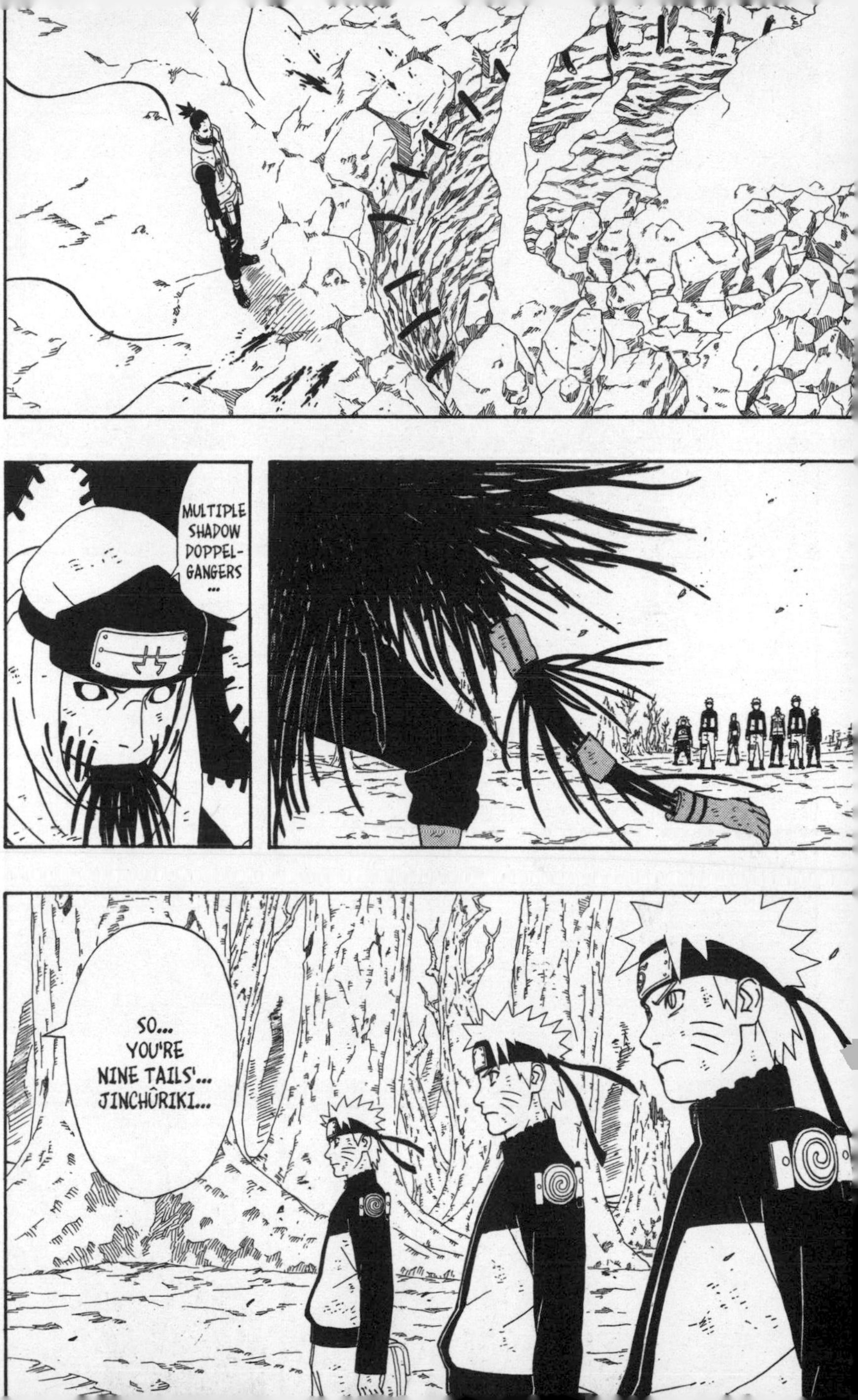
MULTIPLE SHADOW DOPPEL-GANGERS...
SO... YOU'RE NINE TAILS'... JINCHÛRIKI...

READ THIS WAY

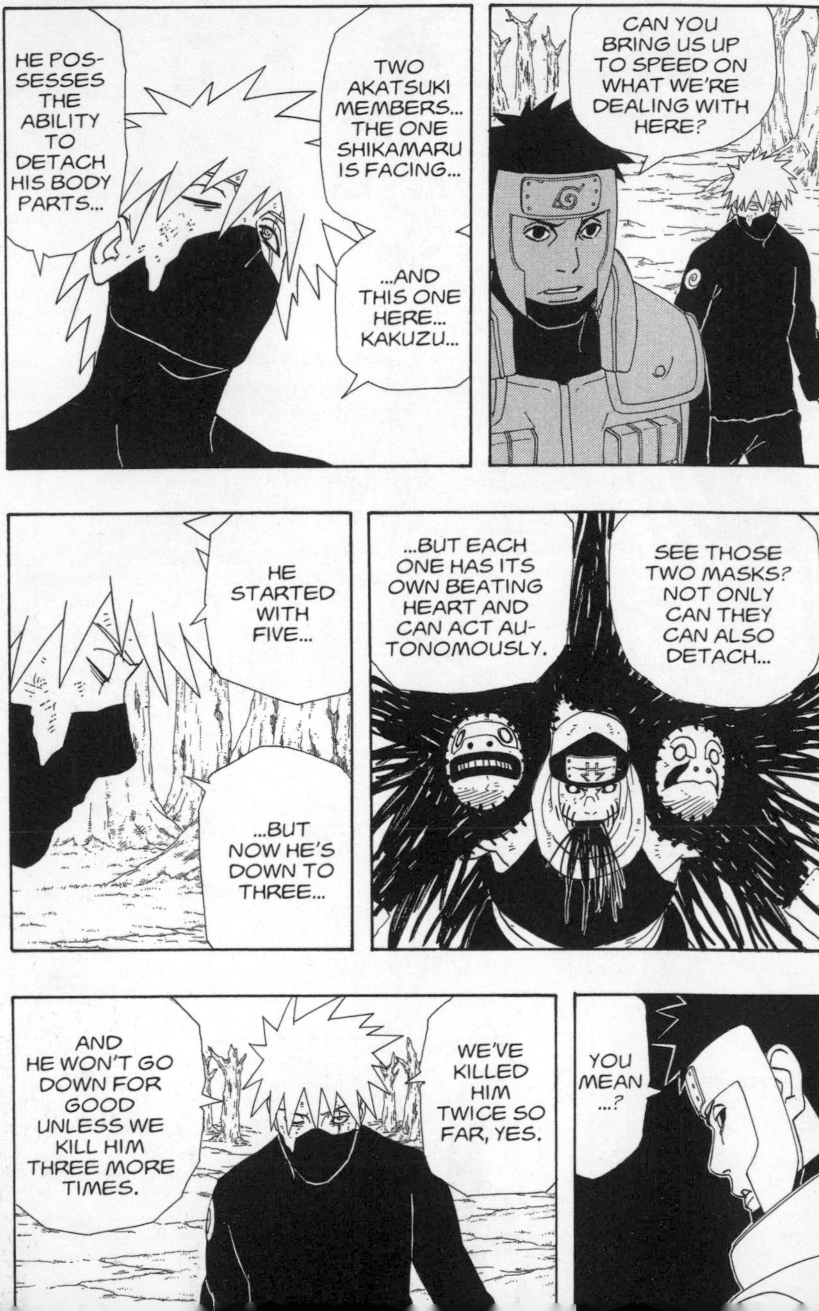
CAN YOU BRING US UP TO SPEED ON WHAT WE'RE DEALING WITH HERE?
TWO AKATSUKI MEMBERS... THE ONE SHIKAMARU IS FACING...
...AND THIS ONE HERE... KAKUZU...
HE POSSESSES THE ABILITY TO DETACH HIS BODY PARTS...
SEE THOSE TWO MASKS? NOT ONLY CAN THEY CAN ALSO DETACH...
...BUT EACH ONE HAS ITS OWN BEATING HEART AND CAN ACT AUTONOMOUSLY.
HE STARTED WITH FIVE...
...BUT NOW HE'S DOWN TO THREE...
YOU MEAN ...?
WE'VE KILLED HIM TWICE SO FAR, YES.
AND HE WON'T GO DOWN FOR GOOD UNLESS WE KILL HIM THREE MORE TIMES.

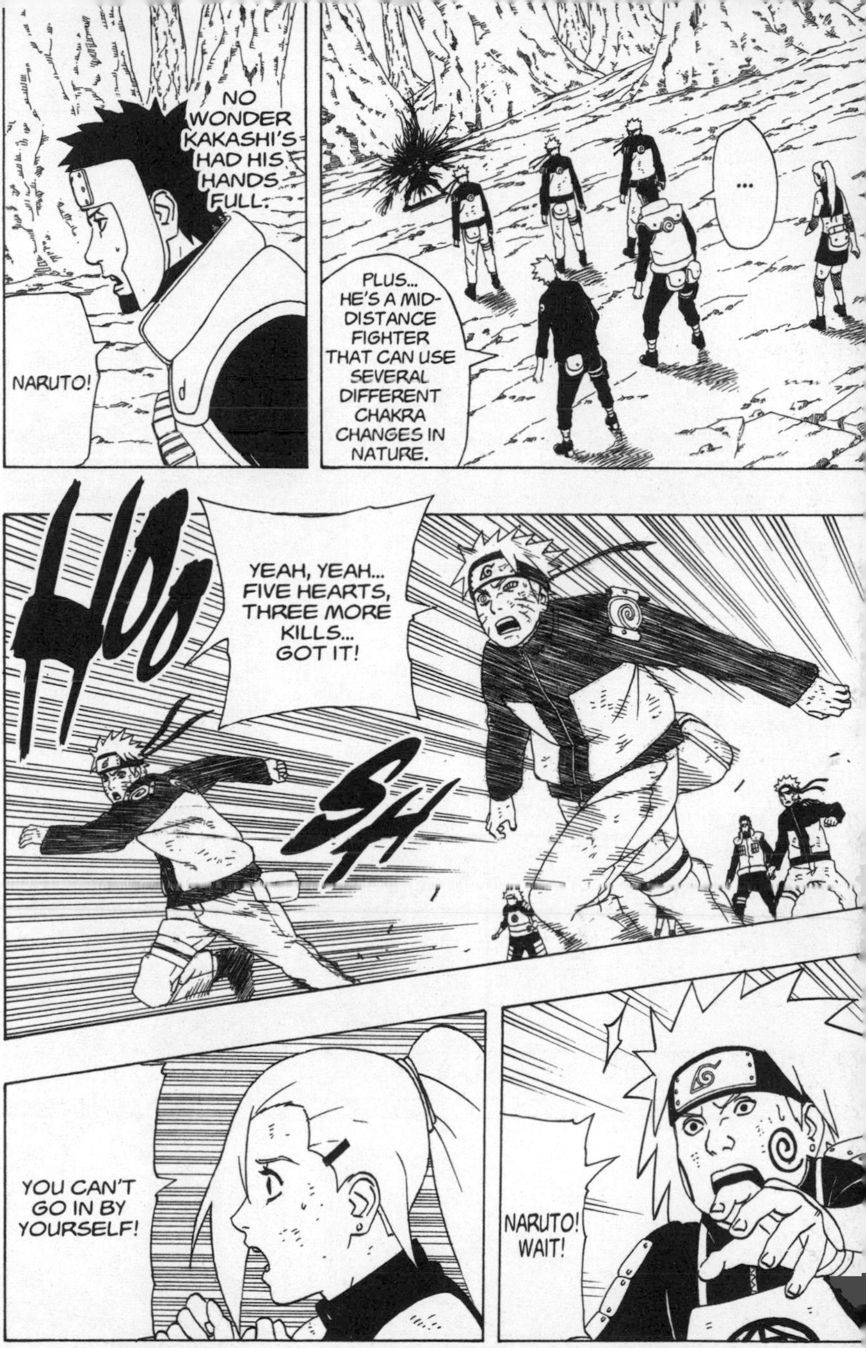
...
PLUS... HE'S A MID-DISTANCE FIGHTER THAT CAN USE SEVERAL DIFFERENT CHAKRA CHANGES IN NATURE.
NO WONDER KAKASHI'S HAD HIS HANDS FULL.
NARUTO!
YEAH, YEAH... FIVE HEARTS, THREE MORE KILLS... GOT IT!
HOO
SH
NARUTO! WAIT!
YOU CAN'T GO IN BY YOURSELF!

READ THIS WAY

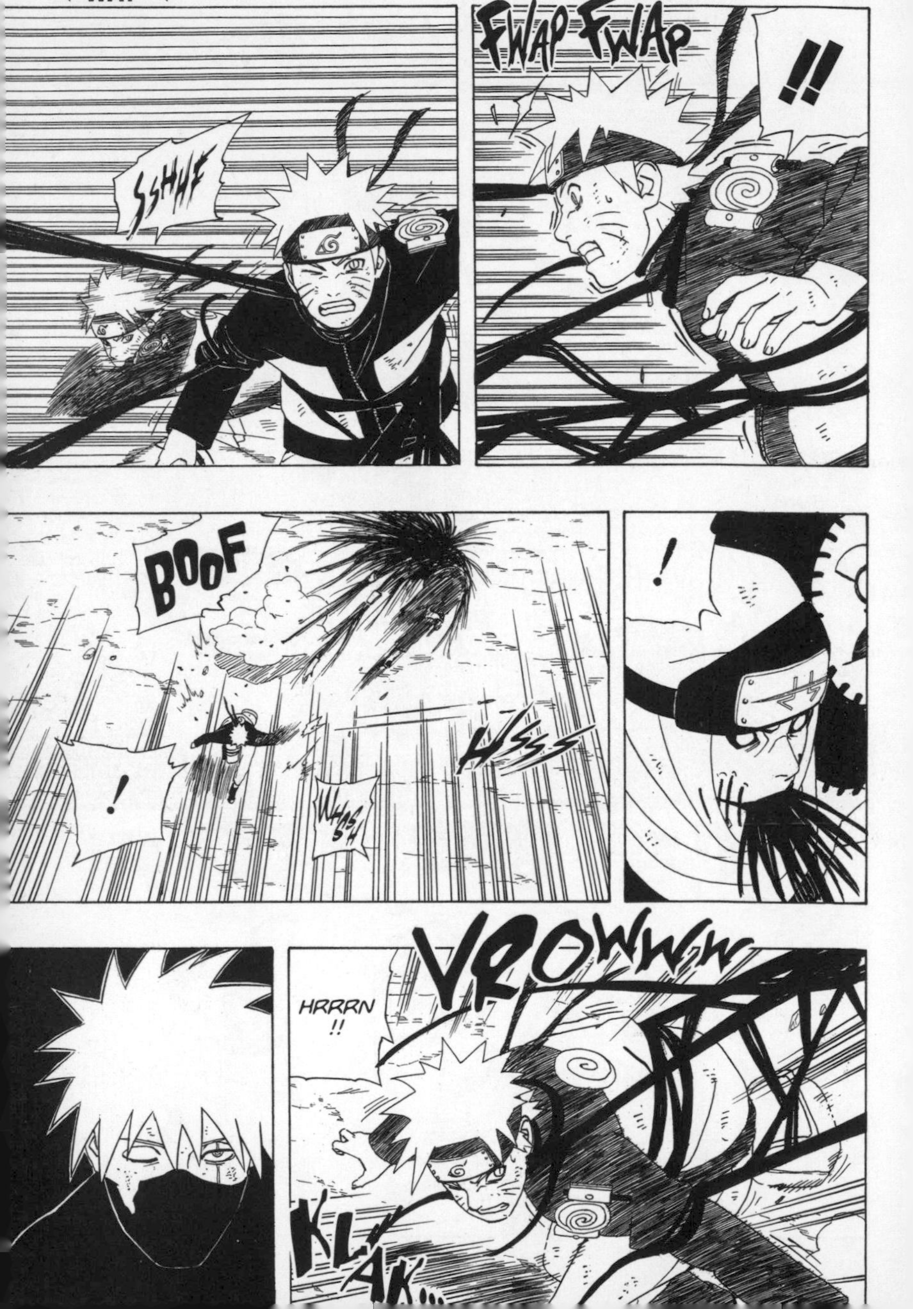
FWAP FWAP
!!
SSHHF
!
BOOF
!
HISSS
WHASSH
VROWWW
HRRRN !!
KLAK...

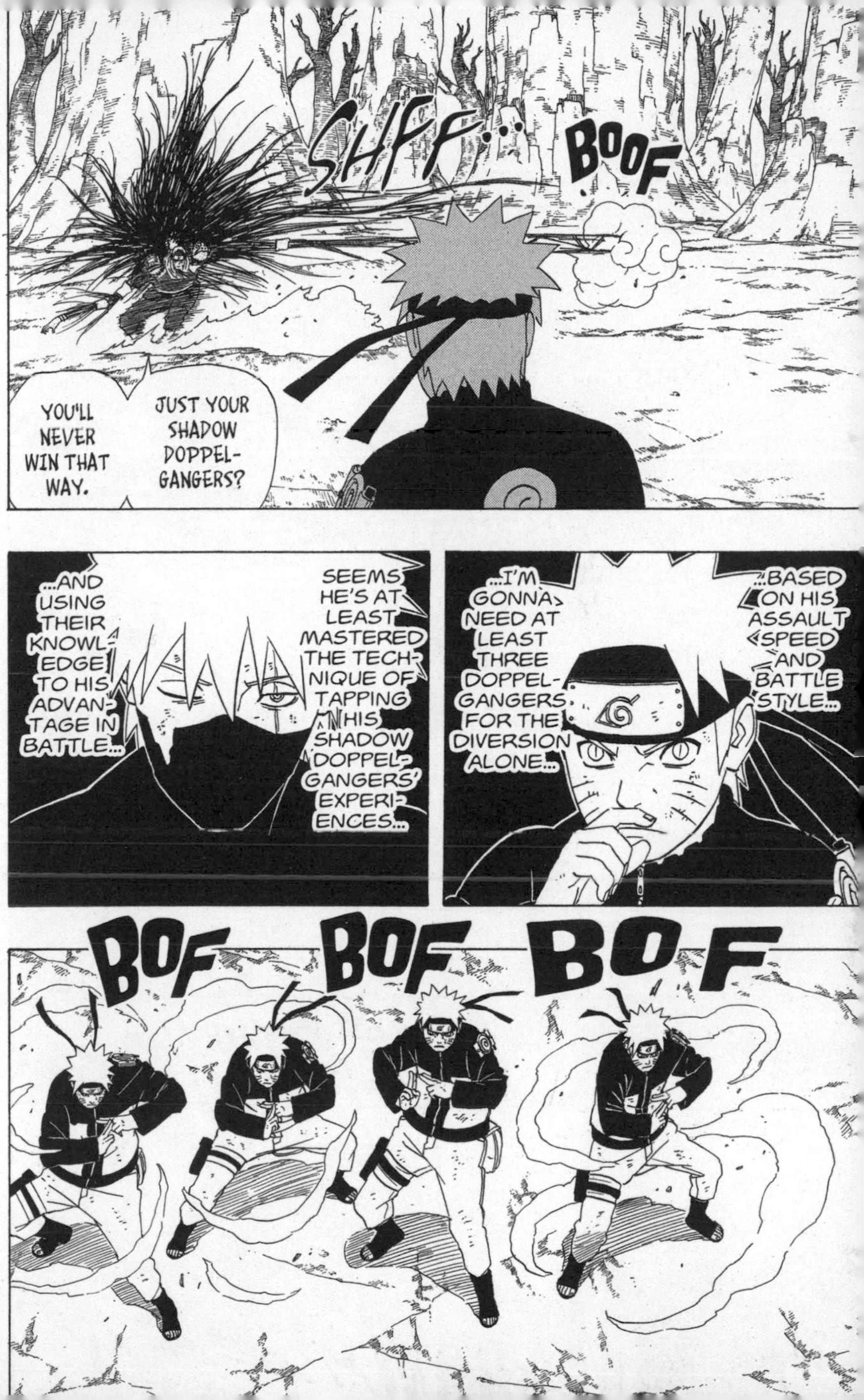
BOOF
SHFF...
JUST YOUR SHADOW DOPPEL-GANGERS?
YOU'LL NEVER WIN THAT WAY.
...BASED ON HIS ASSAULT SPEED AND BATTLE STYLE...
...I'M GONNA NEED AT LEAST THREE DOPPEL-GANGERS FOR THE DIVERSION ALONE...
SEEMS HE'S AT LEAST MASTERED THE TECH-NIQUE OF TAPPING HIS SHADOW DOPPEL-GANGERS' EXPERI-ENCES...
...AND USING THEIR KNOWL-EDGE TO HIS ADVAN-TAGE IN BATTLE...
BOF
BOF
BOF

READ THIS WAY

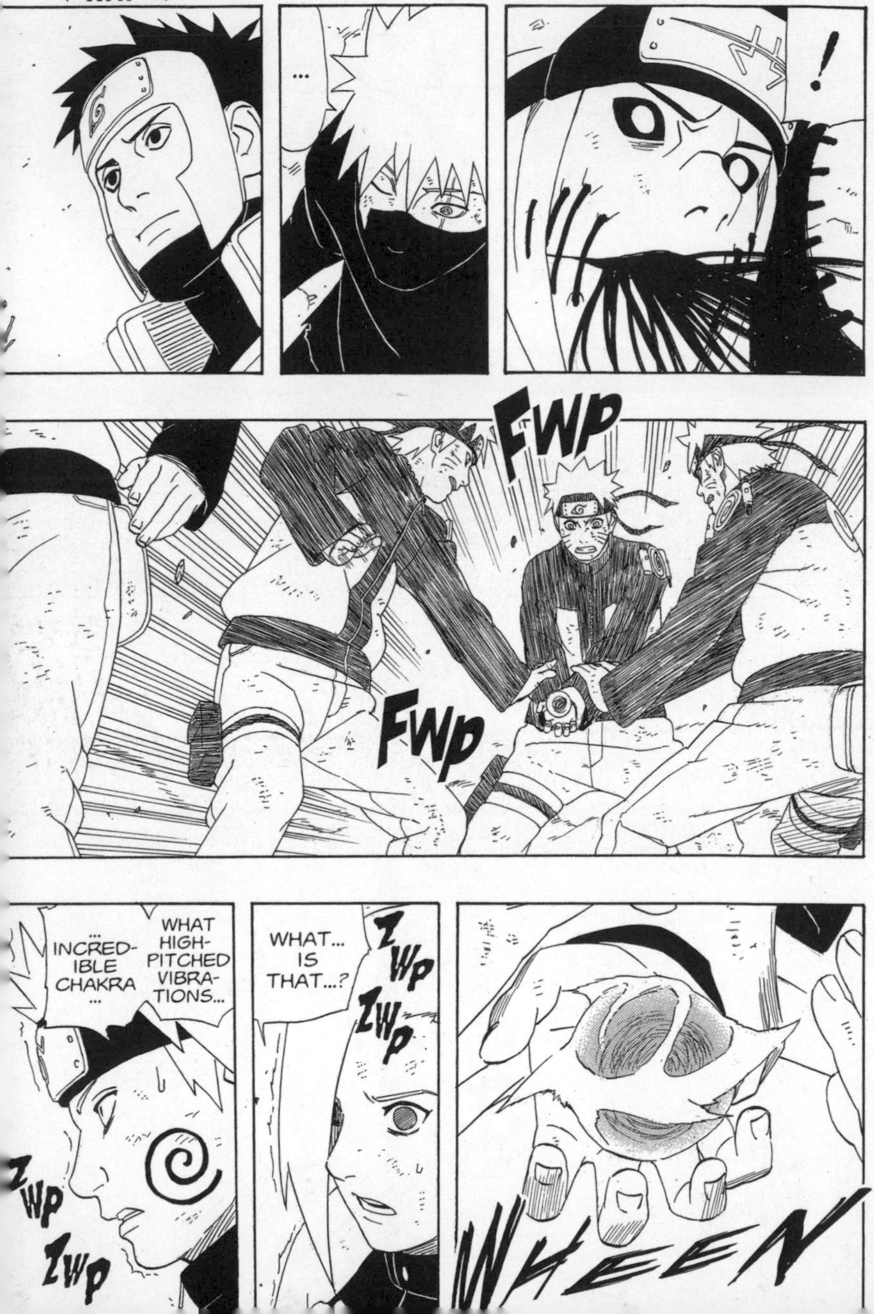
!
...
FWP
FWP
WHEEN
WHAT... IS THAT...?
ZWP
ZWP
WHAT HIGH-PITCHED VIBRATIONS...
... INCRED-IBLE CHAKRA ...
ZWP
ZWP
ZWP

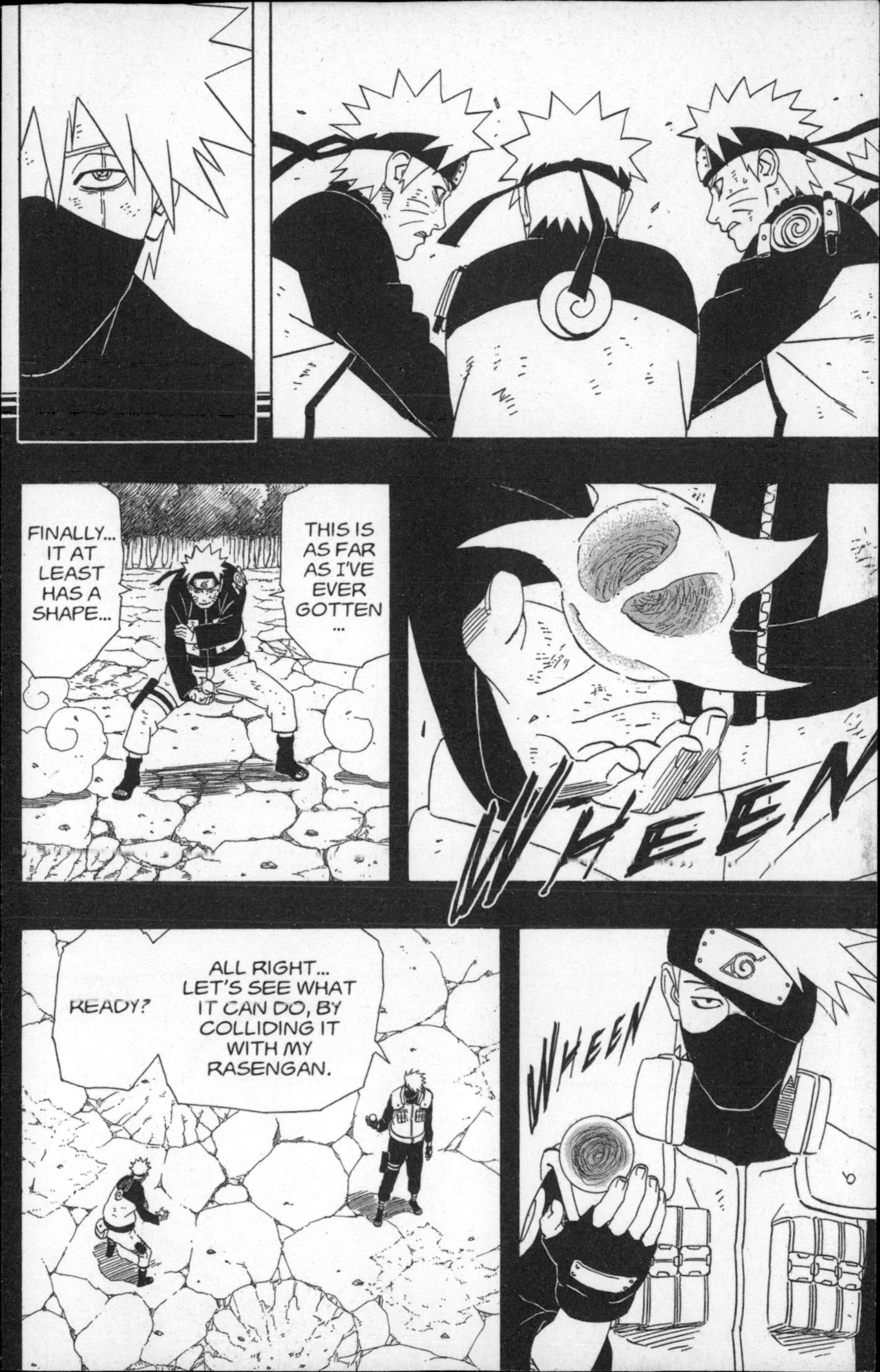
WHEEN
THIS IS AS FAR AS I'VE EVER GOTTEN ...
FINALLY... IT AT LEAST HAS A SHAPE...
WHEEN
ALL RIGHT... LET'S SEE WHAT IT CAN DO, BY COLLIDING IT WITH MY RASENGAN.
READY?

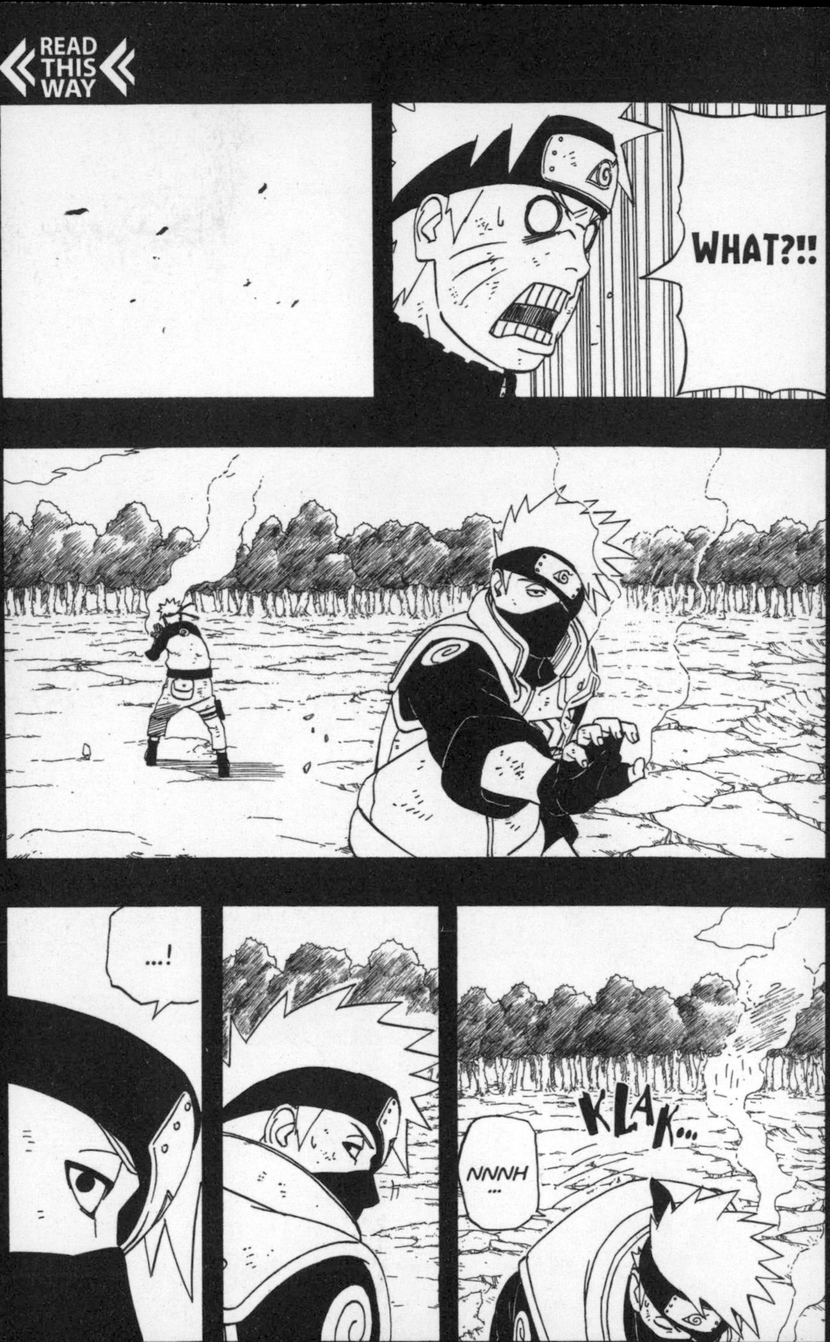
READ THIS WAY
WHAT?!!
...!
KLAK...
NNNH ...

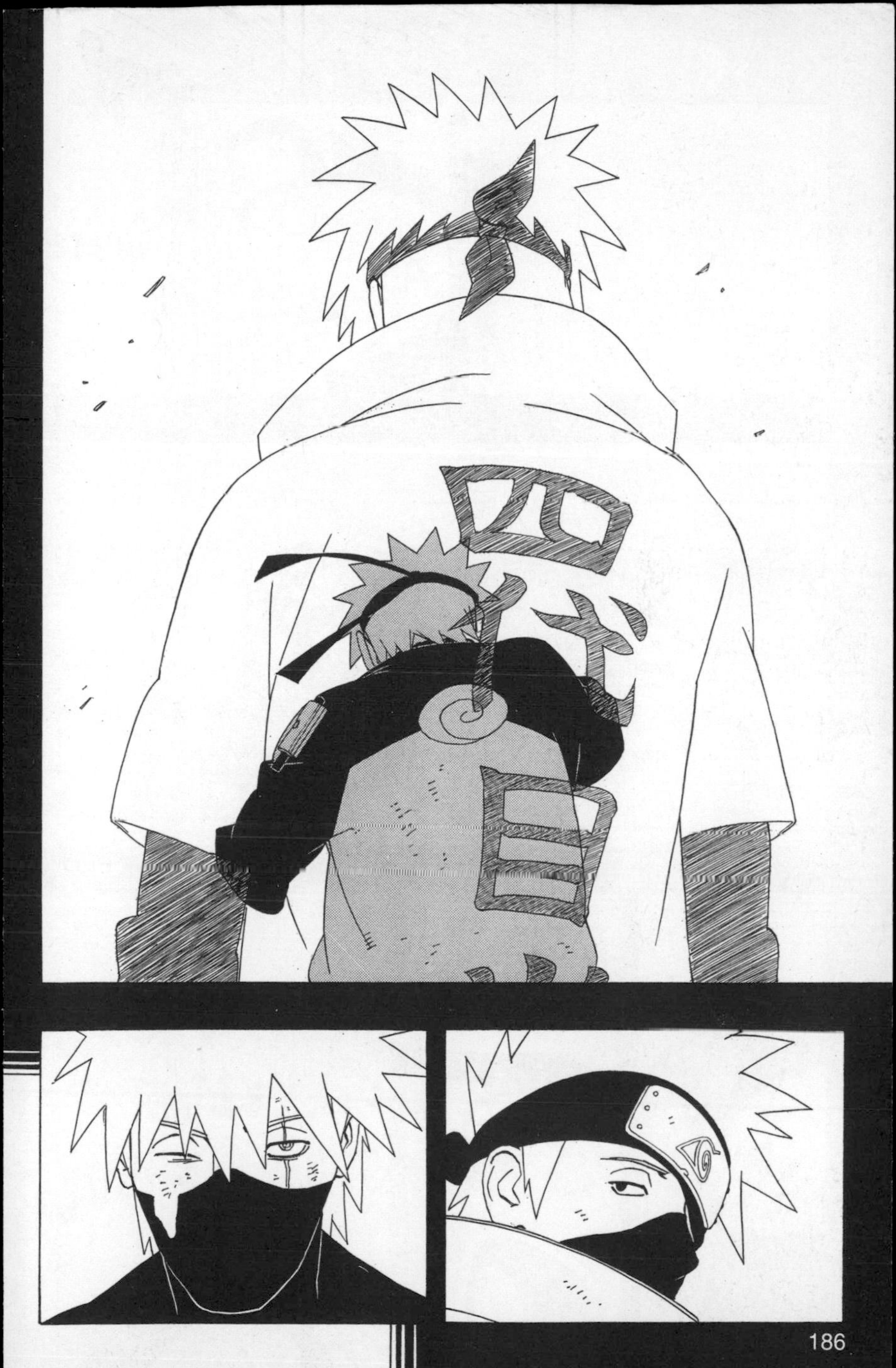
四代目

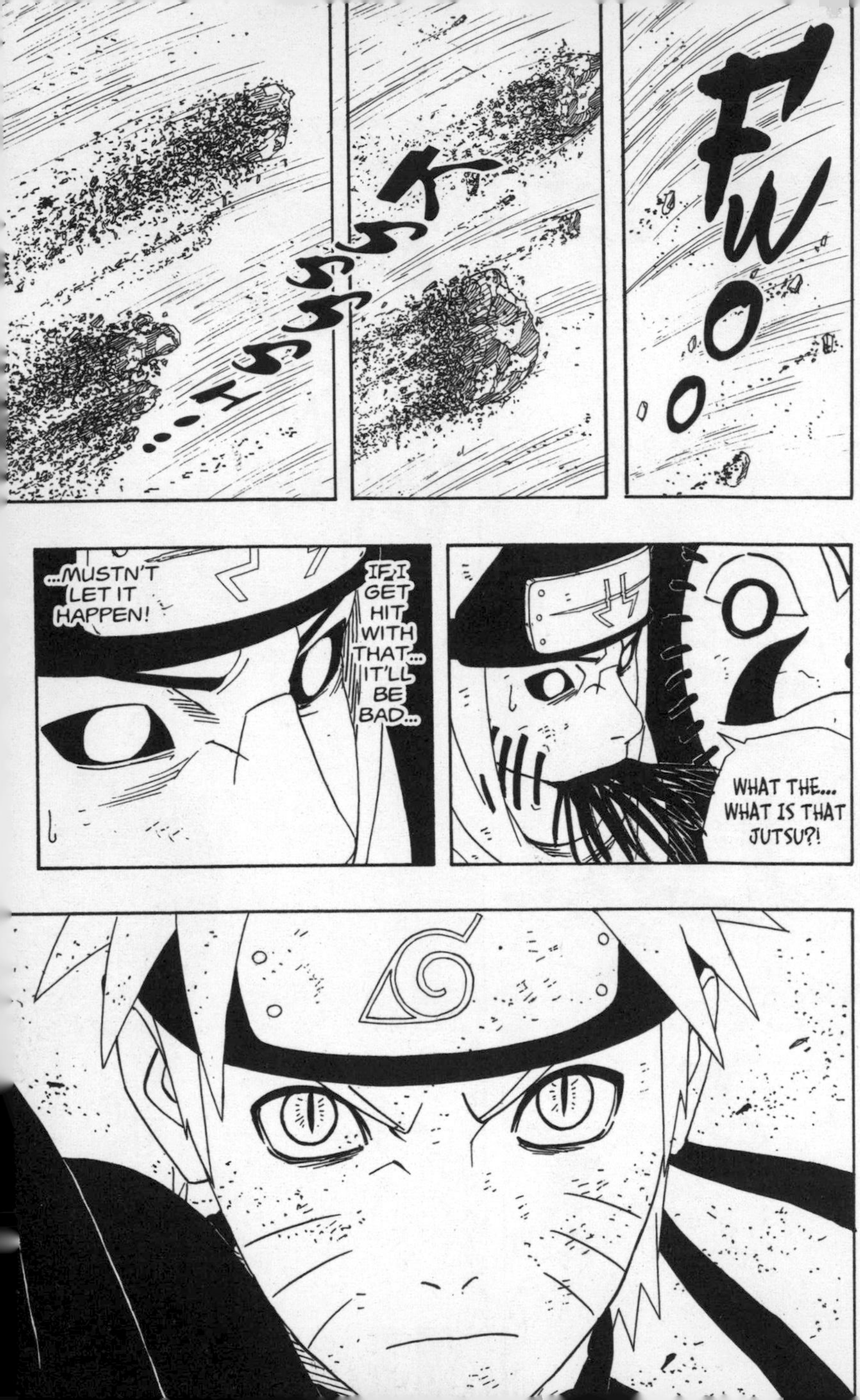
FWOO
KSSSSH...
WHAT THE... WHAT IS THAT JUTSU?!
IF I GET HIT WITH THAT... IT'LL BE BAD...
...MUSTN'T LET IT HAPPEN!

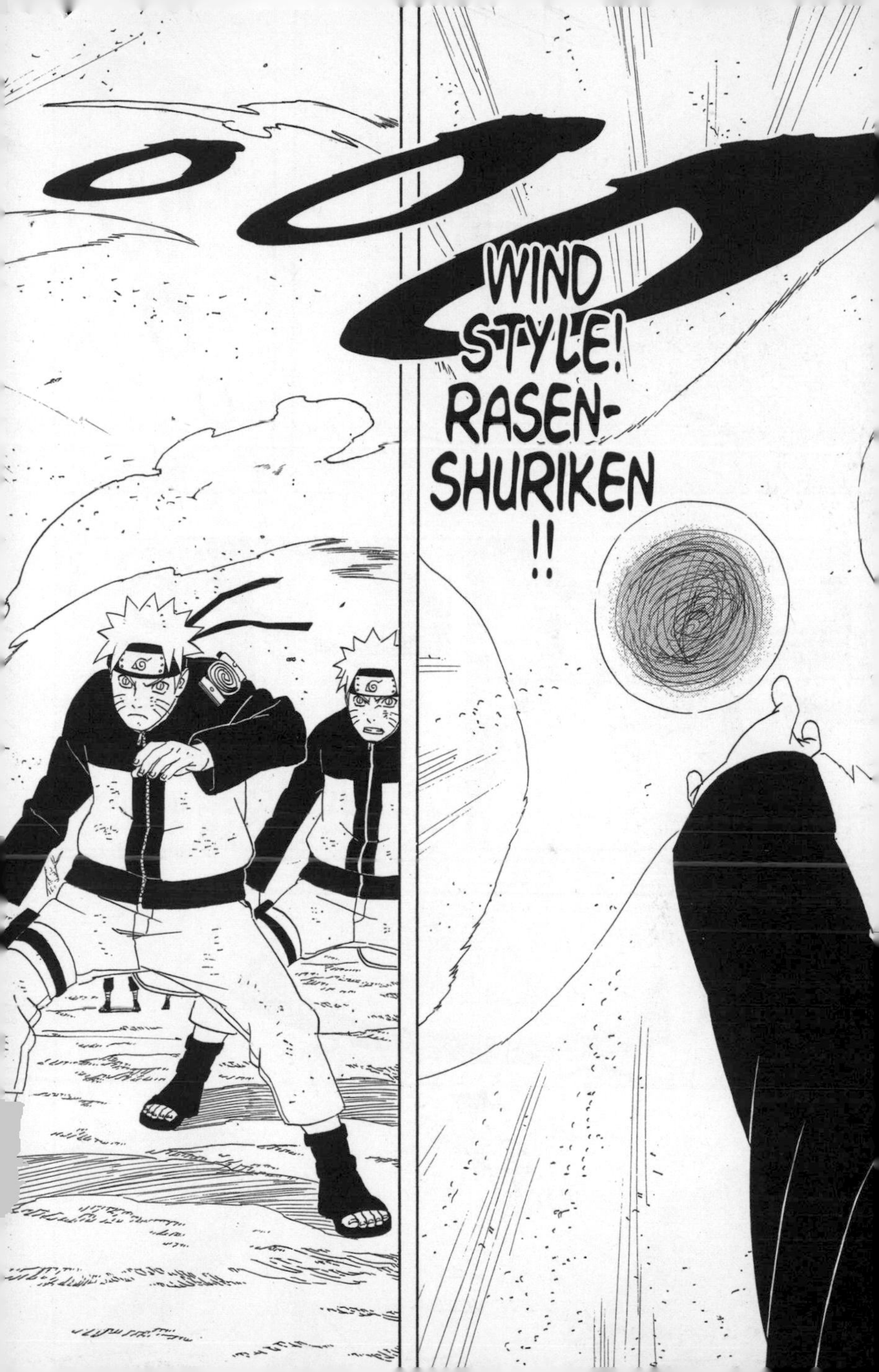
WIND STYLE! RASEN-SHURIKEN!!

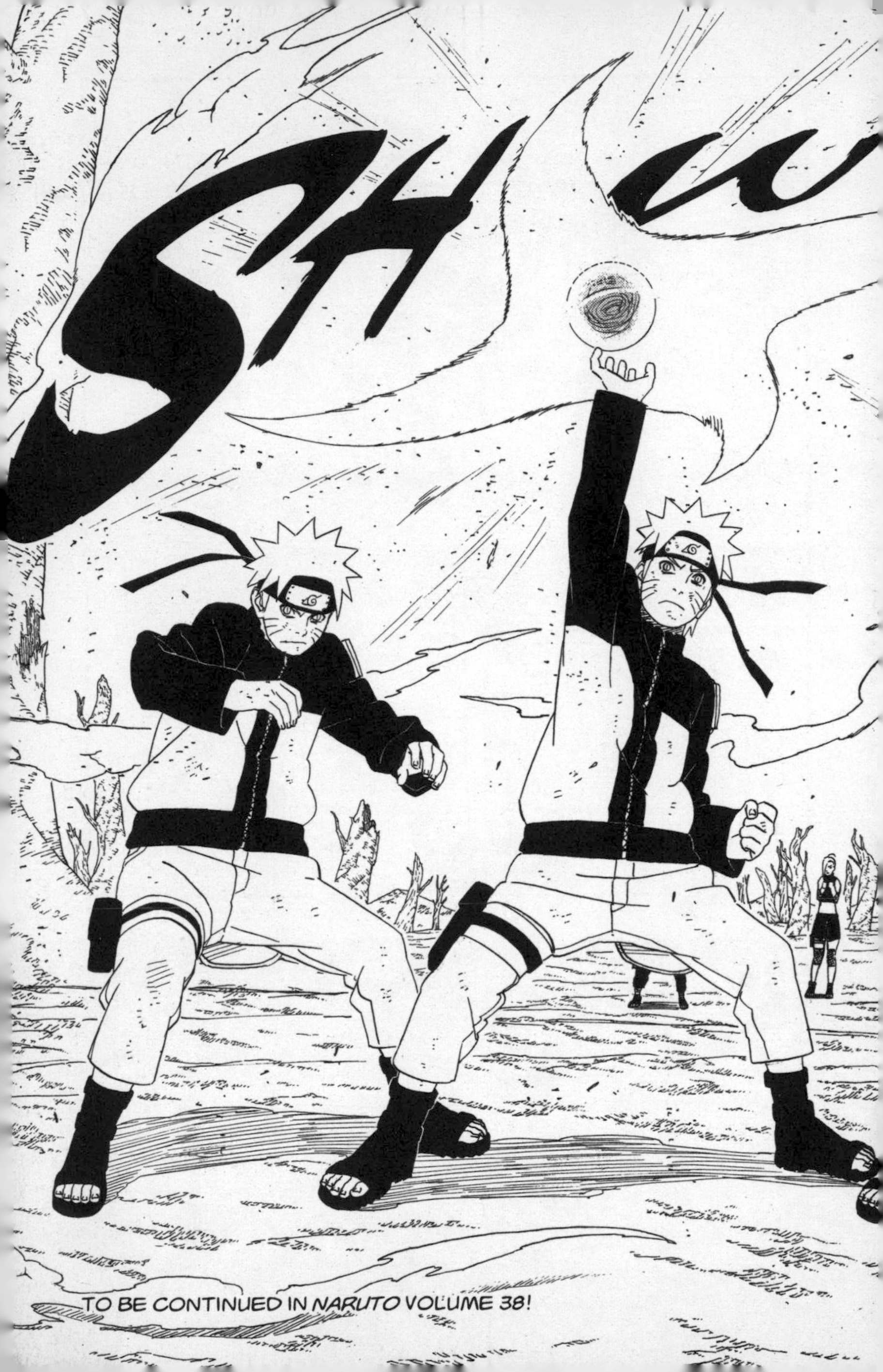
TO BE CONTINUED IN *NARUTO* VOLUME 38!

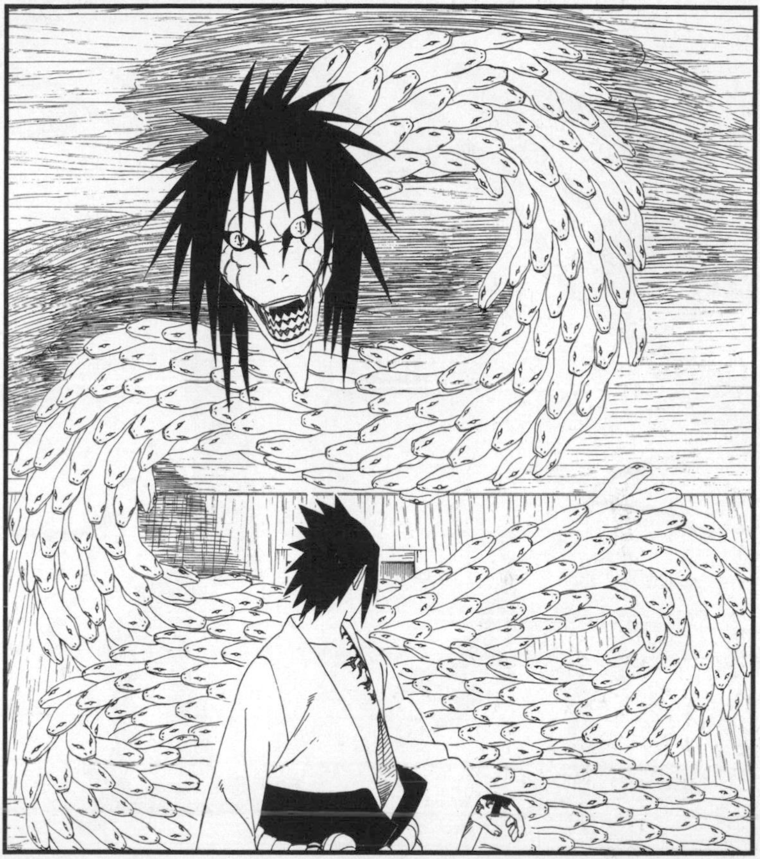

IN THE NEXT VOLUME...

PRACTICE MAKES PERFECT

Naruto finds that his new jutsu is harder to handle than he thought. Meanwhile, Sasuke seems to be falling even more under Orochimaru's spell. Despite all Naruto's efforts, he may have finally lost his best friend forever. But Naruto will use all his skills as a ninja to keep that from happening!

AVAILABLE NOW!

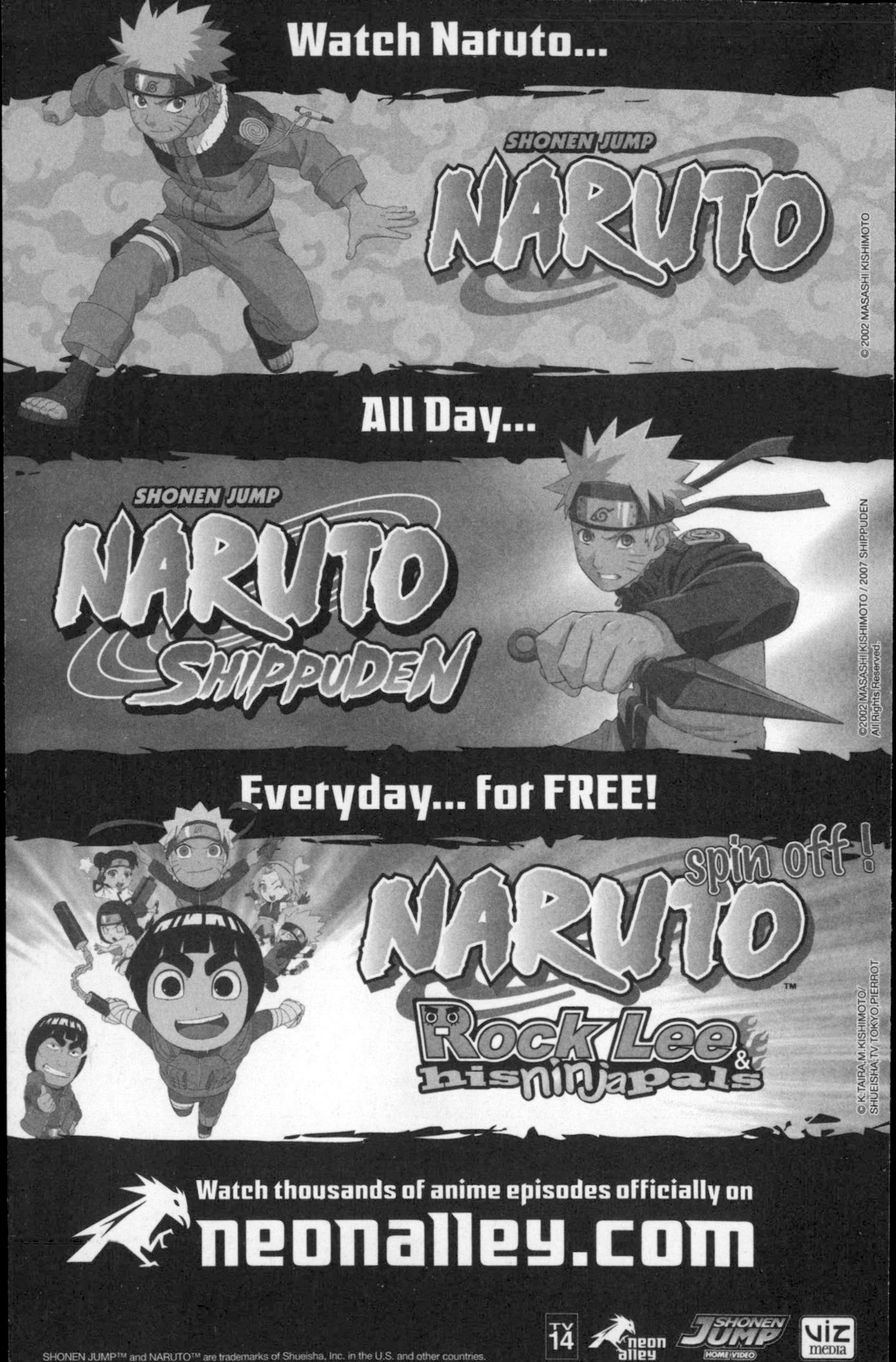
Watch Naruto...
SHONEN JUMP
NARUTO
© 2002 MASASHI KISHIMOTO
All Day...
SHONEN JUMP
NARUTO
SHIPPUDEN
©2002 MASASHI KISHIMOTO / 2007 SHIPPUDEN All Rights Reserved.
Everyday... for FREE!
spin off!
NARUTO™
Rock Lee & his ninja pals
© K.TAIRA,M.KISHIMOTO/ SHUEISHA,TV TOKYO,PIERROT
Watch thousands of anime episodes officially on
neonalley.com
TV 14
neon alley
SHONEN JUMP HOME VIDEO
viz media
SHONEN JUMP™ and NARUTO™ are trademarks of Shueisha, Inc. in the U.S. and other countries.

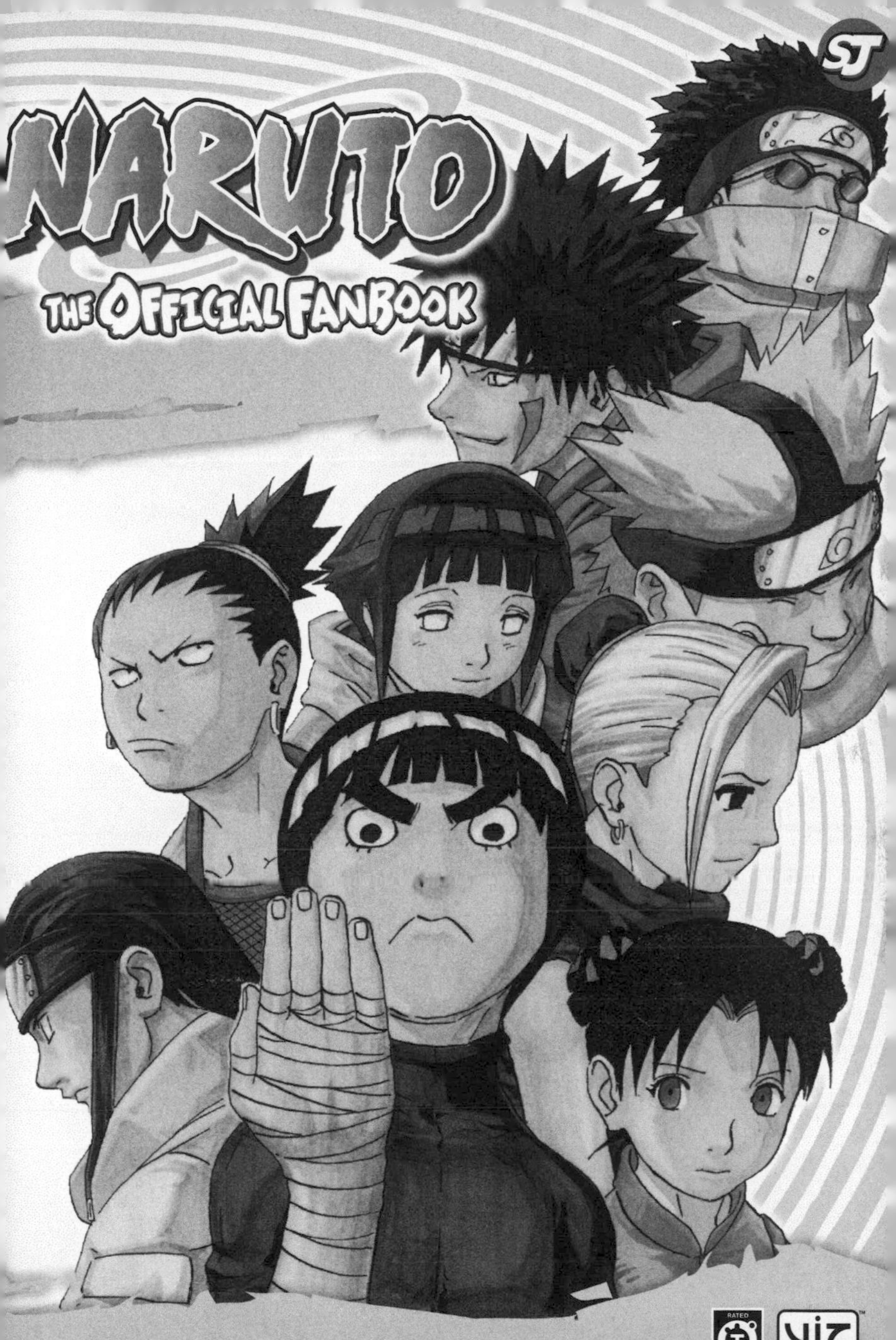
SJ
NARUTO
THE OFFICIAL FANBOOK

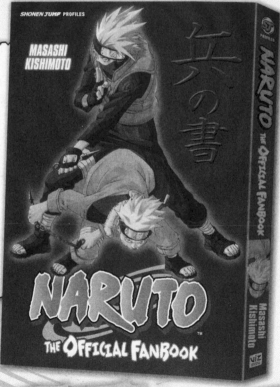
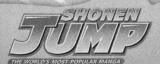

ARE YOU A NARUTO EXPERT?

THIS BOOK HAS ALL YOU NEED TO KNOW TO BECOME ONE!

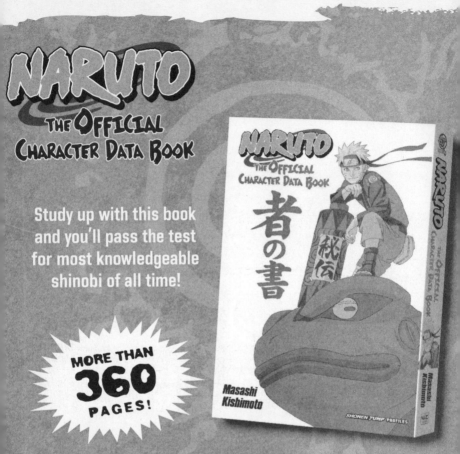

Study up with this book and you'll pass the test for most knowledgeable shinobi of all time!

MORE THAN
360
PAGES!

Covers 43 volumes of the Naruto series!

www.shonenjump.viz.com

www.viz.com

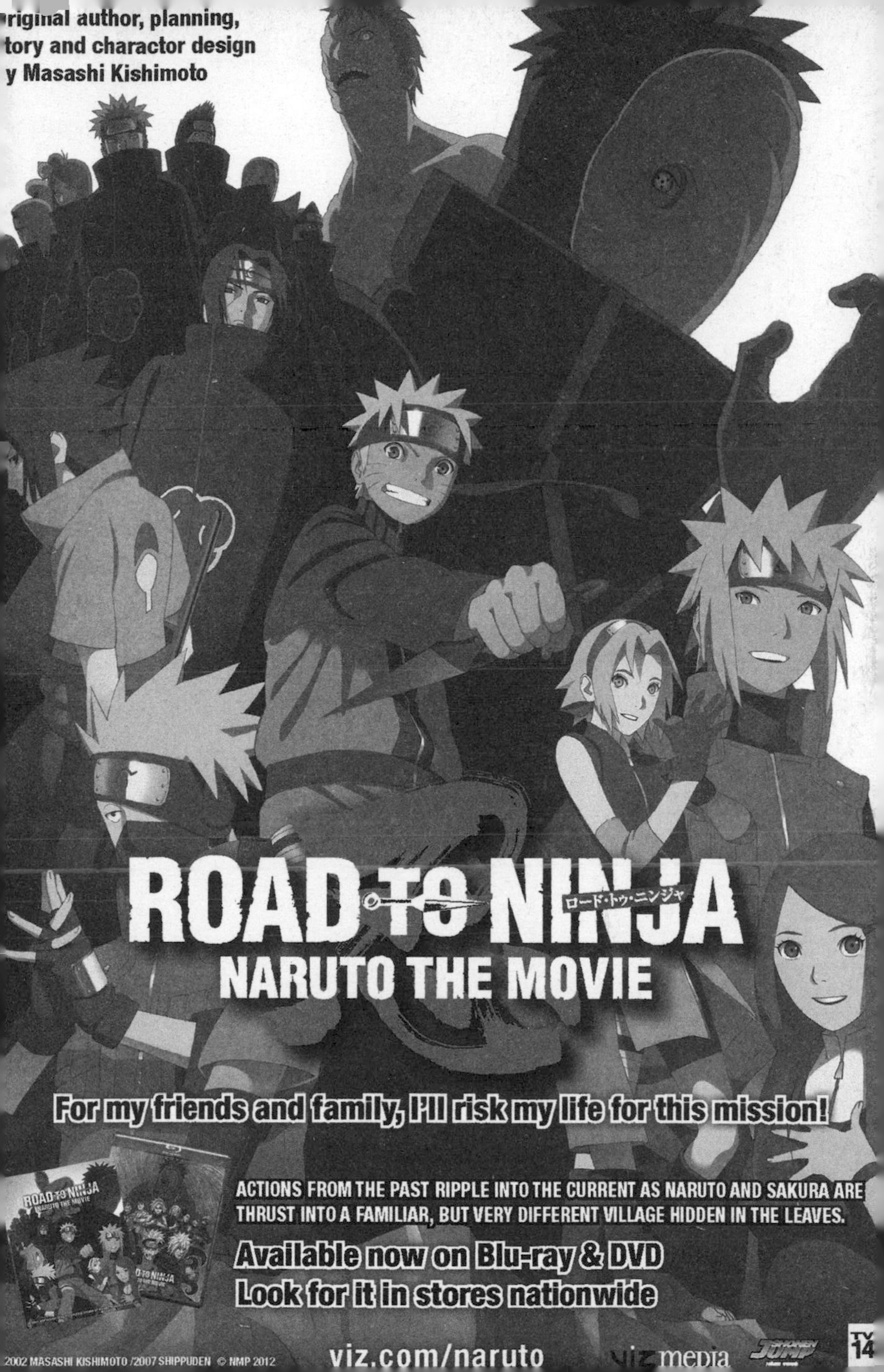

riginal author, planning,
tory and charactor design
y Masashi Kishimoto
ROAD TO NINJA
ロード・トゥ・ニンジャ
NARUTO THE MOVIE
For my friends and family, I'll risk my life for this mission!
ROAD TO NINJA
NARUTO THE MOVIE
ACTIONS FROM THE PAST RIPPLE INTO THE CURRENT AS NARUTO AND SAKURA ARE THRUST INTO A FAMILIAR, BUT VERY DIFFERENT VILLAGE HIDDEN IN THE LEAVES.
Available now on Blu-ray & DVD
Look for it in stores nationwide
2002 MASASHI KISHIMOTO /2007 SHIPPUDEN © NMP 2012
viz.com/naruto
viz media
JUMP
TV 14

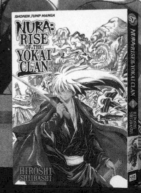

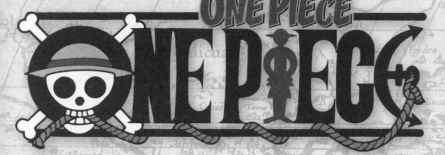
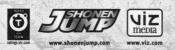

A PREMIUM BOX SET OF THE FIRST TWO STORY ARCS OF ONE PIECE!

A PIRATE'S TREASURE FOR ANY MANGA FAN!

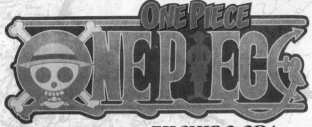

STORY AND ART BY EIICHIRO ODA

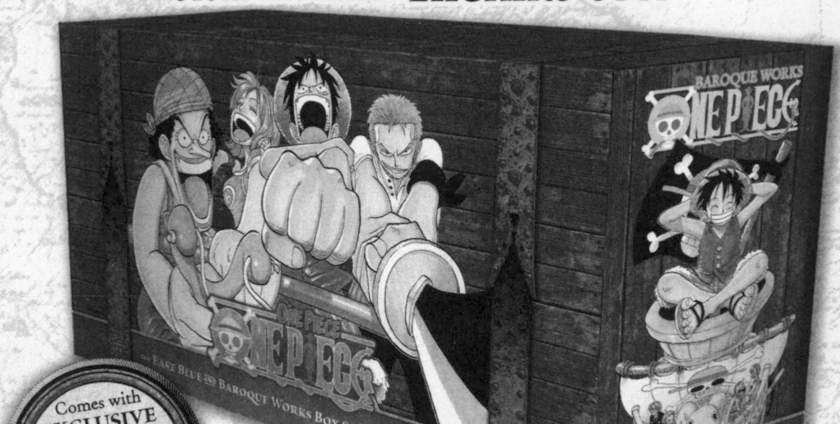

Comes with EXCLUSIVE POSTER and the ROMANCE DAWN mini-comic!

As a child, Monkey D. Luffy dreamed of becoming King of the Pirates. But his life changed when he accidentally gained the power to stretch like rubber...at the cost of never being able to swim again! Years later, Luffy sets off in search of the "One Piece," said to be the greatest treasure in the world...

This box set includes VOLUMES 1-23, which comprise the EAST BLUE and BAROQUE WORKS story arcs.

EXCLUSIVE PREMIUMS and GREAT SAVINGS over buying the individual volumes!

WWW.SHONENJUMP.COM

ONE PIECE © 1997 by Eiichiro Oda/SHUEISHA Inc.

RATED FOR TEEN
ratings.viz.com

www.viz.com

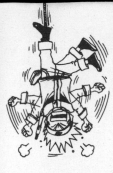

You're Reading in the Wrong Direction!!

Whoops! Guess what? You're starting at the wrong end of the comic!

...It's true! In keeping with the original Japanese format, **Naruto** is meant to be read from right to left, starting in the upper-right corner.

Unlike English, which is read from left to right, Japanese is read from right to left, meaning that action, sound effects and word-balloon order are completely reversed... something which can make readers unfamiliar with Japanese feel pretty backwards themselves. For this reason, manga or Japanese comics published in the U.S. in English have sometimes been published "flopped"—that is, printed in exact reverse order, as though seen from the other side of a mirror.

By flopping pages, U.S. publishers can avoid confusing readers, but the compromise is not without its downside. For one thing, a character in a flopped manga series who once wore in the original Japanese version a T-shirt emblazoned with "M A Y" (as in "the merry month of") now wears one which reads "Y A M"! Additionally, many manga creators in Japan are themselves unhappy with the process, as some feel the mirror-imaging of their art alters their original intentions.

We are proud to bring you Masashi Kishimoto's **Naruto** in the original unflopped format. For now, though, turn to the other side of the book and let the ninjutsu begin...!

—Editor

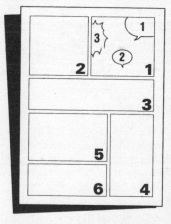